**HISTORICAL DICTIONARIES
OF WAR, REVOLUTION, AND CIVIL UNREST
Edited by Jon Woronoff**

1. *Afghan Wars, Revolutions, and Insurgencies,* by Ludwig W. Adamec. 1996.
2. *United States–Mexican War,* by Edward H. Moseley and Paul C. Clark, Jr. 1997.
3. *World War I,* by Ian V. Hogg. 1998.
4. *United States Navy,* by James M. Morris and Patricia M. Kearns. 1998.
5. *United States Marine Corps,* by Harry A. Gailey. 1998.
6. *Wars of the French Revolution,* by Steven T. Ross. 1998.
7. *American Revolution,* by Terry M. Mays. 1998.

Historical Dictionary of the Wars of the French Revolution

Steven T. Ross

Historical Dictionaries of War, Revolution, and Civil Unrest, No. 6

The Scarecrow Press, Inc.
Lanham, Md., & London
1998

SCARECROW PRESS, INC.

Published in the United States of America
by Scarecrow Press, Inc.
4720 Boston Way
Lanham, Maryland 20706

British Library Cataloguing in Publication Information Available

Library of Congress Cataloging-in-Publication Data

Ross, Steven T.
    Historical dictionary of the wars of the French Revolution /
    Steven T. Ross.
        p.   cm. — (Historical dictionaries of wars, revolutions, and
    civil unrest ; no. 6)
    Includes bibliographical references.
    ISBN 0-8108-3409-X (alk. paper)
    1. France—History—Revolution, 1789-1799—Dictionaries.
        2. France—History—Revolution, 1789-1799—Chronology.
    I. Title.
    II. Series.
    DC147.R7   1998
    944.04—dc21   97–32905
                                                                     CIP

ISBN 0-8108-3409-X (cloth : alk. paper)

♾ ™The paper used in this publication meets the minimum requirements
of American National Standard for Information Sciences—Permanence
of Paper for Printed Library Materials, ANSI Z39.48-1984.
Manufactured in the United States of America.

Contents

Maps

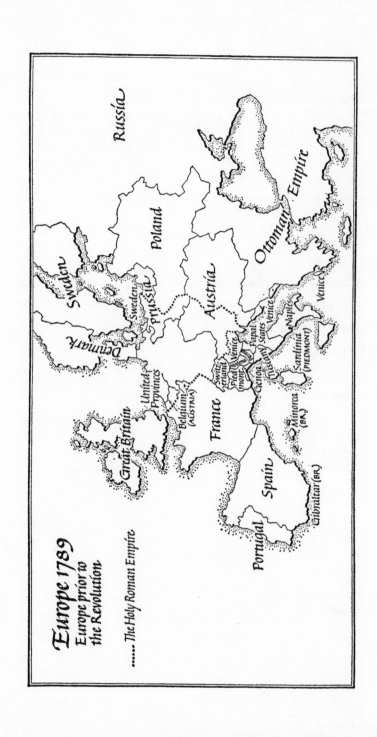

Europe 1789
Europe prior to
the Revolution

..... The Holy Roman Empire

Russia

Sweden

Poland

Ottoman Empire

Denmark

Sweden

Prussia

Austria

Venice

United Provinces

Great Britain

Belgium (AUSTRIA)

France

Switzerland

Piedmont

Modena

Venice

Papal (Vatican) States

Venice

Naples

Genoa

Tuscany

Sardinia (PIEDMONT)

Spain

Minorca (BR.)

Portugal

Gibraltar (BR.)

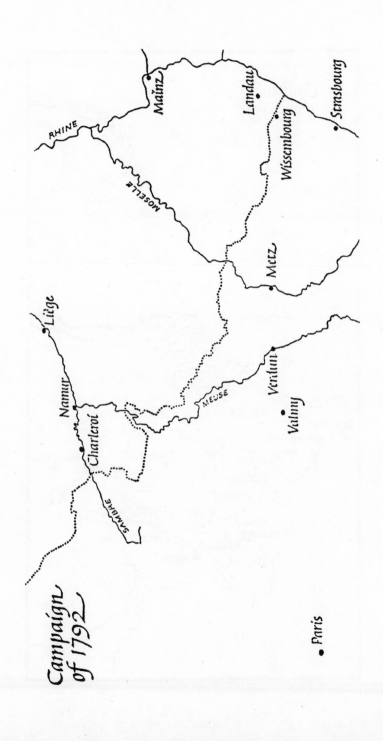

Campaign of 1792

Campaigns
of 1793-1794

Ostend
Dunkirk
Hondschoote
Bruges
Antwerp
Ypres
Courtrai
SCHELDT
Brussels
Maastricht
Neerwinden
Tourcoing
Lille
Tournai
Liège
Condé
Jemappes
Fleurus
Namur
Valenciennes
Mons
MEUSE
Maubeuge
Charleroi
Cambrai
Wattignies
SAMBRE

THE VENDÉE 1793–1799

Rennes

Brittany

Savenay

Loire River

Quiberon

Nantes

Cholet

Saumur

Vendée

La Rochelle

Zurich
Berne
Lucerne
Innsbruck
St.Gotthard Pass
St. Bernard Pass
ADIGE
Trent
Campo Fornio
Aosta
Milan
Brescia
Rivoli
Verona
TICINO
Lodi
Padua
Turin
Pavia
Castiglione
Arcole
Venice
Alessandria
Marengo
Mantua
Cremona
PO
Cherasco
Alba Novi
Piacenza
Reggio
Ferrara
Ceva
Parma
Modena
Bologna
Genoa
Leghorn
Florence
Ancona

Corsica

Rome

Naples

Sardinia

Italy and
Switzerland
1796-1801

Sicily

Ireland
1796-1798

Ulster

Killala Bay

Dublin•

Wicklow•

County
Wexford

New Ross •   •Wexford

Bantry Bay

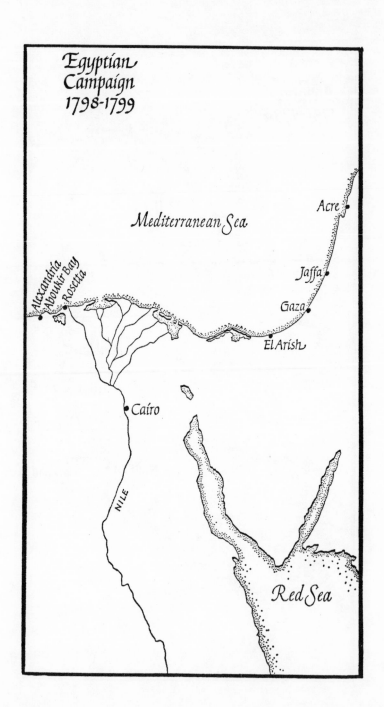

Egyptian
Campaign
1798-1799

Mediterranean Sea

Acre

Alexandria
Aboukir Bay
Rosetta

Jaffa

Gaza

El Arish

Cairo

NILE

Red Sea

India
1797–1799

Mahratta Confederacy

Bengal

Calcutta

Bombay

Hyderabad

Mysore

Seringapatam

Carnatic

Madras

Ceylon

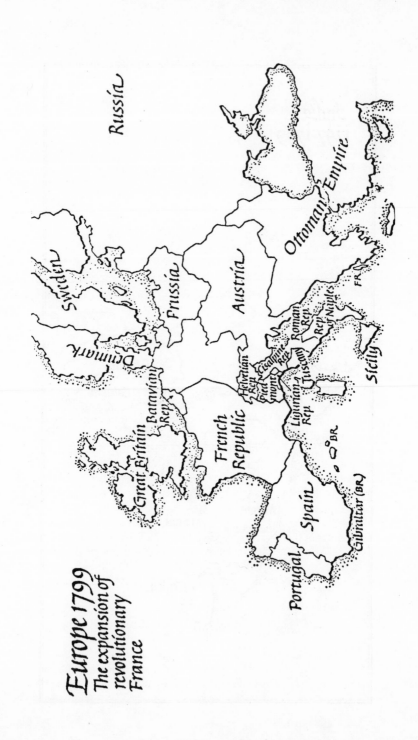

Europe 1799
The expansion of
revolutionary
France

Russia

Sweden

Denmark

Prussia

Austria

Ottoman Empire

Great Britain

Batavian Rep.

French Republic

Helvetian Rep.
Piedmont
Cisalpine Rep.
Ligurian Rep.
Tuscany
Roman Rep.
Rep. of Naples

FR.

Sicily

Spain

Portugal

Gibraltar (BR.)

BR.

Editor's Foreword

Extremely few events in human history have wrought such broad and deep changes as the French Revolution. However, because our lives were more directly affected by the political, social, and cultural changes, we are often less aware of one sector where the impact was truly revolutionary, namely military affairs. Warfare would never be the same again, at least not for the sides that learned the lessons . . . and won the wars. The officers and soldiers of the French Republic were obviously among the first to learn, willy-nilly, in an attempt to survive against the daunting odds. But some of their opponents, although less noticeably at first, were also changing their tactics, strategy, and weaponry. That changes did occur is generally known; just what they were and how they came about can do with retelling.

This addition to the new series of Historical Dictionaries of War, Revolution, and Civil Unrest does several things. Most visibly, it describes significant persons, places and events, battles and encounters on land and sea, victories and defeats. It presents not only the stars like Kléber, Masséna, and Scherer, or Suvorov and Lord Nelson, and the superstar Napoleon Bonaparte, but a vast cast of characters who determined the outcome in their own ways. It also evaluates the crucial ones, not in today's terms but within the actual historical context. Finally, it examines how warfare was changing. As the bibliography clearly shows, much has been written about these wars, and there are excellent works to consult for further reading. But this *Historical Dictionary of the Wars of the French Revolution* should remain a handy companion for further reading with its chronology, historical survey, and especially the many specific entries.

This sort of book could best be written by a historian, but one with a particular interest in military matters. The author, Steven T. Ross, fits the bill. After teaching at several universities, he moved to the Naval War College in 1973, where he is presently in the Strategy Department. He has an abiding interest in the wars of the French Revolution and Napoleon as a military leader, having lectured and written many papers and articles on various aspects of the Revolutionary Wars. He has also authored several books, two of which are particularly relevant here: *The French Revolution: Conflict or Continuity?* and *Quest for Victory: French Military Strategy 1792–1799.* This historical dictionary sums up one of the most eventful periods of military history in yet another way.

Jon Woronoff
Series Editor

Chronology of Significant Military and Diplomatic Events 1792–1802

1792   France declares war on Austria; Prussia joins Austria; start of the War of the First Coalition 1792–1797 (20 April).

"La Marseillaise" written (25) April.

Brunswick Manifesto (25 July).

Louis XVI overthrown and imprisoned (10 August).

Battle of Valmy. French halt Prussian advance on Paris (20 September).

National Convention meets for first time (20 September).

National Convention proclaims France to be a republic (22 September).

Battle of Jemappes. French victory opens Belgium to invasion (6 November).

First Propaganda Decree (19 November).

Second Propaganda Decree (15 December).

1793   Louis XVI executed (21 January).

France declares war on Britain and Holland (1 February).

Levée of 300,000 men (24 February).

France declares war on Spain (7 March).

Revolt in the Vendée begins (10–16 March).

Battle of Neerwinden. French defeat exposes Belgium to reconquest (18 March).

Dumouriez defects (5 April).

Committee of Public Safety established by the National Convention (6 April).

Antwerp Conference. Allies meet to divide the anticipated spoils of a French defeat (8 April).

Battle of Samur. Major Vendean victory (9 June).

Battle of Perpignan. French halt Spanish offensive (17 July).

Mainz surrenders to Coalition forces after a siege that began in March (24 July).

Levée en masse (23 August).

Toulon surrenders to the British (27 August).

Battle of Hondschoote. French relieve Dunkirk and halt Allies in Flanders (6–8 September).

General Maximum Law (29 September).

Lyon retaken by the Republic (9 October).

Battle of Wissembourg. French defeated but retreat in good order in Alsace (13–14 October).

Battle of Wattignies. French relieve Maubeuge Halt Allied offensive on the Sambre (15–17 October).

Battle of Cholet. Republican troops inflict major defeat on Vendeans (17 October).

Toulon recaptured (19 December).

1794   Battle of Mouscron. French defeat an Austrian force attempting to relieve Menin (29 April).

Battle of Tourcoing. French defeat Allied offensive that tried to recapture Menin and Courtrai (17–18 May).

Battle of Tournai. Allies defeat French efforts to take Tournai (22 May).

Battle of the First of June. British navy defeats French navy but gain fleet reaches Brest (29 May–1 June).

Battle of Fleurs. French victory near Charleroi Belgium again open to French invasion (26 June).

Robespierre and close associates arrested and executed by Convention (27–28 July).

Siege of Warsaw. Prussians and Russians besiege and take Warsaw (July–November).

Battle of Black Mountain. French defeat Spanish opening the way to Barcelona (17–20 November).

1795   Armistice in the Vendée (17 February).

Treaty of Basel. Prussia leaves the First Coalition (5 April).

Battle of Irurzun. French defeat Spanish army and advance on Bilabo (6 July).

Quiberon Bay. Émigré forces defeated (21 July).

Treaty of Basel. Spain leaves the First Coalition (22 July).

Battle of Handschusheim. Austrians defeat French near Heidelberg (24 September).

Siege of Mainz. French fail to take Mainz (September–November).

Battle of Manheim. Austrians defeat French (18 October).

Convention gives way to Directory (26 October).

Battle of Loano. French victory forces Austrians to retreat to Genoa (23 November).

1796   Battle of Montenotte. Bonaparte defeats an Austro-Piedmontese force (12 April).

Battle of Dego. French defeat Austrian force and resume pursuit of Piedmontese (14–15 April).

Battle of Ceva. Bonaparte drives enemy from fortified position (16–17 April).

Battle of Mondovi. Bonaparte defeats a Piedmontese force (21 April).

Cherasco Armistice. Piedmont leaves the First Coalition (28 April).

Battle of Lodi. Bonaparte defeats an Austrian force, crosses the Adda River (10 May).

Battle of Borghetto. Bonaparte defeats Austrians, drives them behind the Mincio River (30 May).

Battle of Altenkirchen. Austrians driven back to Lahn River (3 June).

Battle of Castiglione. Bonaparte repulses Austrian force attempting to relieve Mantua (5 August).

Battle of Lonato. Bonaparte defeats another Austrian force trying to relieve Mantua (5–6 August).

Battle of Neresheim. French drive Austrians back to Germany (11 August).

Battle of Neumarck. Austrians force one of two French armies in Germany to retreat (21 August).

Battle of Amberg. Austrians continue to drive French back toward the Rhine (24 August).

Battle of Wurzburg. Austrian victory. French forced to continue to retreat (3 September).

Battle of Roveredo. The French defeat another Austrian effort to reach Mantua (4 September).

Battle of Bassano. Bonaparte defeats a major effort by the Austrians to relieve Mantua. Some Austrians reach the city but are besieged along with the original garrison (8 September).

Battle of Biberach. French rearguard in south Germany temporarily halts Austrian advance (20 October).

Battle of Caldiero. Austrian victory in advance to relieve Mantua (12 November).

Battle of Arcola. French defeat Austrians. Mantua remains under siege (15–17 November).

Bantry Bay Expedition. French force reaches coast of Ireland but does not land (15 December [date of departure]).

1797   Battle of Rivoli. Bonaparte defeats last effort to relieve Mantua (14 January).

Mantua garrison surrenders to the French (2 February).

Battle of Imola. French defeat Papal army (3 February).

Battle of Cape Saint Vincent. British navy defeats Spanish fleet (14 February).

Treaty of Tolentino. Papacy leaves the war (19 February).

Battle of Neuwied. French victory in Germany followed by vigorous pursuit (18 April).

Leoben Armistice. Austria leaves the First Coalition (18 April).

Battle of Diersheim. French victory in Germany (21 April).

Battle of Camperdown. British navy defeats a Dutch fleet (11 October).

Peace of Campo Formio. Austria signs peace treaty with France (17 October).

1798 French expedition leaves for Egypt (19 May).

Battle of Vinegar Hill. British crush Irish rebels (21 June).

French land in Egypt (1 July).

Storming of Alexandria. French take Alexandria (2 July).

Battle of Pyramids. Bonaparte crushes Mameluke army (21 July).

Battle of the Nile. Nelson destroys Bonaparte's fleet (1 August).

Jourdan Conscription Law (5 September).

Naples invades Roman Republic (23 November).

French defeat Neopolitan army (3 and 5 December).

French take over Piedmont (11 December).

1799 French take Gaetta (11 January).

French secure control of Naples (January 14).

El Arish falls to Bonaparte after a brief siege (8–19 February).

French storm Jaffa (3–7 March).

War of the Second Coalition (1799–1802) begins (13 March).

Battle of Stockach. French in south Germany defeated by Austrians (25 March).

Battle of Pastrengo. French defeated by Austrians in Italy (26–27 March).

Battle of Verona. Austrians defeat French forcing them back from the Adige (5 April).

Battle of Mount Tabor. Bonaparte defeats Turkish army (16 April).

Battle of Cassano. Coalition forces defeat French (26 April).

Fall of Milan. Coalition forces take Milan (28 April).

Seringapatam falls to the British (4 May).

Bonaparte abandons siege of Acre (18 March–20 May).

Battle of Lurichberg. French repulse Austrian attack and then abandon Lurich for shorter stronger position (3–4 June).

Battle of Trebbia. Coalition forces defeat the French forcing them back to Genoa (17–18 June).

Battle of Pech David. French defeat Royalist forces near Toulouse (7–8 August).

Battle of Novi. French counteroffensive near Genoa defeated (15 August).

Battle of Montrijeau. French defeat Royalists forcing them to scatter into small bands around Toulouse (20 August).

Anglo-Russian force lands in Holland (August 27).

Battle of Bergen. French defeat Allied effort to advance in Holland (19 September).

Battle of Zurich. French crush Coalition force and retake Zurich (25–26 September).

Battle of Egmont. French foil Anglo-Russian effort to advance into Holland (2 October).

Battle of Kastrikum. French halt a second Allied effort to advance south into Holland (6 October).

Napoleon returns from Egypt (9 October).

Convention of Alkmaar. Allied army agrees to leave Holland (18 October).

Brumaire Coup, Sieyès, Ducos, and Bonaparte seize power (9–10 November).

Formation of Provisional Consulate (1 November).

Constitution of Consulate (15 December).

1800 Austrians begin siege of Genoa (5 April).

Battle of Stockach. French enter south Germany and defeat Austrians (3 May).

Battle of Möskirch. French victory over Austrians in Germany (5 May).

Battle of Erback. French throw back Austrian attack (16 May).

Having crossed the Alps, Napoleon enters Milan (2 June).

Genoa falls to Austrians (4 June).

Battle of Marengo. Napoleon defeats Austrians (14 June).

Battle of Hochstadt. French attack and defeat Austrians who abandon Munich (19 June).

Battle of Hohenlinden. French victory in Germany (3 December).

Austria agrees to armistice (25 December).

1801 Peace of Luneville. Austria leaves war of the Second Coalition (8 February).

British land in Egypt (8 March).

Night battle of Aboukir. French fail to drive British out of Egypt (18 March).

Naval Battle of Copenhagen. Nelson defeats Danish navy (2 April).

French in Egypt surrender to British (30 August).

1802 Treaty of Amiens. Britain and France end hostilities. Europe at peace for first time since 1792 (25 March).

Bonaparte becomes Consul for life (2 August).

Introduction

In May 1789, when delegates gathered at Versailles, virtually everybody in France was a monarchist. In January 1793 France was a republic, and the new government tried and executed the deposed king. The startling transformation of French political and social life was accompanied not only by rapid change but also by considerable domestic violence. The situation was further complicated by the advent of foreign war.

When superimposed upon an already volatile situation, the war exacerbated existing problems and created new ones never before faced by a modern nation. The war led directly to the overthrow of the monarchy and efforts of the new Republic to mobilize resources for battle produced massive counterrevolutionary responses as well as strife within Republican ranks.

Survival, however, required Republican leaders to create a nation in arms sustained by a centrally directed economy. Moreover, the Republic had to undertake military measures unheard of outside of the writing of a few theorists. French leaders had to create massive new armies and, since most Royalist officers refused to fight for the Republic, create a new officer corps based on loyalty and talent rather than status. Republican leaders had to organize the new troops and devise a tactical system for their employment. A mass citizen army required hitherto unheard of tactics in order to cope with the professional Old Regime armies deployed by the Republic's enemies.

Between 1792 and 1802 the First French Republic fought two great power coalitions and defeated both of them. Simultaneously, Republican forces defeated internal counterrevolutionary armed movements. From the battle of Valmy in 1792 to the Battles of Marengo and Hohenlinden in 1800, warfare was almost uninterrupted. From the plains of Germany to northern Italy and from the high seas to Syria, French land and sea forces were in constant action. They did not win every battle, but republican methods of organization and tactics were effective especially in the hands of a growing number of talented generals, including Napoleon Bonaparte.

Having unleashed such vast military power, various republican governments had difficulty controlling the new military leaders. Consequently, a general finally seized power just as France emerged victorious against the Second Coalition. Nevertheless, the Republic had established a new style and method of warfare. Old Regime warfare was ultimately doomed and warfare was forever changed.

Old Regime Warfare

During the eighteenth century, rulers and statesmen were constantly at war. The great powers waged numerous conflicts for limited political objectives, including the seizure of a province or a colonial possession. Countries also embarked on unlimited wars designed to overthrow an enemy or reduce the power of a major state to the status of minor principality. France and her Allies tried to dismember the Hapsburg domains in the 1740s. During the Seven Years' War Austria, Russia, and France attempted to destroy Prussia as a major power, and the three Eastern Powers executed three partitions of Poland, thus eliminating that state from the map of Europe.

In their perpetual search for power, monarchs did not hesitate to intervene in the internal affairs of other states. Both Spain and France supported the efforts of Stuart pretenders to overthrow the Hanovarian dynasty in Great Britain. The French and Spanish Bourbons assisted American rebels in their struggle against British rule. Prussia aided Belgian revolutionaries against the Hapsburgs, and Russia supported a Polish magnate faction that opposed the king and his reform-minded clique.

The quest for power was relentless. No belief in the virtues of balance, order, and moderation restrained ambitious statesmen. No principles of law, religion, or morality held aggressive rulers in check. Maria Theresa was reputed to have been horrified at the First Partition of Poland, since Catholic Austria was taking land from Catholic Poland, yet one monarch noted that the more she wept the more she took. Great powers regarded weaker states as legitimate prey and were equally content to turn on each other if a favorable opportunity arose. There was no lack of greed or dearth of ambition within the ranks of Old Regime politicians. In fact, the only check upon the greed of one power was the countergreed of others. Since each power looked upon the others as actual or potential rivals, no state was willing to allow another to increase its strength. Consequently, if a ruler sought new conquests, other powers would either resist or demand a share of the spoils.

The general equality of armed might prevailing among the great powers made it difficult for a state, acting unilaterally, to make extensive conquests. The major Continental powers—France, Austria, Prussia, and Russia—possessed armies numbering anywhere from 130,000 to 350,000 men. Officers came from the aristocracy, while the rank and file were drawn from society's lower orders—conscripted serfs, the unemployed, and even vagabonds and criminals. Governments in the west occasionally conscripted peasants but generally preferred to obtain their long-service soldiers from the marginal elements of society. Armies also made extensive use of mercenaries. The French army, for example, contained Swiss, Italian, Irish, and German formations, and the Prussian army was often over 50 percent non-Prussian. Great Britain depended upon an excellent navy plus a small standing army that could be expanded by hiring regiments from German princes. Mutual animosity and rough military parity made it almost impossible for a single power to impose its will on the others, and consequently, most aggressive enterprises fell short of complete success.

In the Austrian War of the Succession, for example, Britain supported Austria against France, Bavaria and Prussia, and the Hapsburg state emerged intact save for the loss of Silesia, which (though serious) was far from crippling. During the Seven Years War Britain aided Prussia, and the Hohenzollern monarchy preserved its territorial integrity while Great Britain scored significant colonial victories against France and Spain. To redress their losses, France and Spain helped the Americans win their independence from England.

The advent of the revolution in France did not change the nature and objectives of diplomacy. Security and expansion remained the fundamental goals of statesmen, including the leaders of Revolutionary France. French leaders in the 1790s employed diplomacy, armed force, and subversion in a manner similar to that of their Old Regime counterparts. The French did, however, devise new military methods of recruiting, organization, and tactics that gave the nation hitherto unimagined power, thereby enabling France to resist and defeat two great power coalitions and emerge as Europe's single strongest state.

France at War

Ironically, France went to war in April 1792 because politicians—including the king, a variety of political factions, ranging from Royalist to Republican, and a number of ambitious generals—sought to use a foreign war as a means of gaining power at home. The king hoped that foreign bayonets would destroy the revolution and the Constitution of 1791 and restore his power, while the Brissotins believed that a victory would gain popular approval and solidify their power in Paris. France was, however, not prepared for hostilities. There was no coherent strategy or clearly stated political objectives, the nation had no Allies, and the army volunteer units were unready for battle.

At Valmy the steadiness of volunteer battalions and the expertise of French gunners managed to halt the half-hearted invasion of the Prussian army. Louis XVI had been deposed by crowds convinced that he was in league with foreign powers, a National Convention had been elected, and two days after Valmy the Convention proclaimed France to be a republic. Enthusiastic volunteers plus old regular units then launched a series of offensives that overwhelmed enemy forces and enabled the Republic to overrun Belgium and the Rhineland.

The Nation in Arms

The tide of victory soon turned. Austria and Prussia reinforced their armies in the west, and new powers including Great Britain, the Dutch Republic, Spain, Portugal, the Italian princes, and the states of the German Empire joined the war against France in 1793. The Coalition armies drove the French from their initial conquests and invaded the Republic at the same time counterrevolution erupted in the Vendée, Brittany, Normandy, Lyon, Marseilles, and Toulon. The Convention was internally divided, and the Parisian *sans culottes* were ready to strike at the national government unless the Convention undertook a successful war effort and guaranteed stable prices for basic necessities. Thus, by the spring of 1793, the Republic appeared to be on the brink of military defeat and internal anarchy.

French leaders, however, understood that to avoid catastrophe and probable partition they had to take immediate and drastic action. The Convention therefore, created the Committee of Public Safety to act as an emergency executive authority to direct the war effort. The Committee undertook a mobilization of the Republic's human and economic resources by introducing universal conscription and controls over the economy in order to equip and supply the growing armies. The Committee's efforts were generally successful. By the end of 1793 there were, including the old line army, earlier volunteers from 1792, and new conscripts, nearly 650,000 men under arms. By 1794 there were over 800,000 active troops.

The Committee also found officers to lead the expanded troops. Loyalty and talent replaced birth and purchase as the basis of promotion. Together the officers and the Committee devised a tactical system that combined the discipline of the line army with the élan of the volunteers and conscripts. The tactical system emerged over many months but ultimately provided French combat formations with flexible effective tactics that combined fire, shock, and skirmishing techniques.

The Committee of Public Safety also had to devise a strategy to fulfill the Republic's political objectives and employ the army effectively. Essentially, the Republic's goals were survival, recognition by other powers of the Republic's legitimacy, and a victorious peace — the precise details of which varied significantly from faction to faction and even from individual to individual.

Wars of the Republic

In 1793 French leaders called for attacks at virtually all points of the compass simply to halt the advance of the Coalition armies and defeat internal insurrections. By year's end the Republic had succeeded. Allied advances were halted and counterrevolutionary movements were either destroyed or drastically reduced in strength. The nation had fended off the danger of imminent destruction and gained the time to devise a coherent approach to the war.

In devising strategy for the 1794 campaign, the French government took into account the policies of their major enemies and the existing military situation. The Committee realized that Britain and Austria were the Republic's most determined foes and would agree to peace only in the wake of military defeat. Prussia, on the other hand, was at odds with Austria over the final partition of Poland and was a reluctant belligerent in the west. Furthermore, British and Austrian armies were located in French Flanders and in the northeastern departments, whereas the Prussian forces were further east and posed no immediate threat to Paris. The French, therefore, decided to mount major offensives against coalition forces from Flanders to the Sambre while standing on the strategic defensive against the Prussians.

The 1794 campaign, characterized by constant French attacks designed to wear down and ultimately break the British, Dutch, and Austrian armies along the Franco-Belgian frontier, was militarily successful. Republican armies defeated the coalition armies, overran Belgium, and, in the winter of 1795, successfully invaded the Dutch Republic. The British army was forced to leave the Continent; the Austrians fell back into Germany; and in the summer of 1795, despite a failure to defeat the Austrians in Germany, Prussia and Spain left the war and signed peace treaties with the Republic. Spain even became a French ally in 1796 and declared war on Britain.

Austria and England, however, remained at war with the Republic. Consequently, the post-Thermidorian Convention and the Directory had to devise new strategies to force Vienna and London to sue for peace. In 1796 France struck at Austria by launching campaigns in Germany and Italy. The German campaign called for two armies to advance east towards Vienna. The Italian campaign was to distract Austrian attention from operations in Germany. In Germany, however, the armies failed to support each other, and the Austrians defeated them in detail. The Italian campaign on the other hand was, under Bonaparte's leadership, spectacularly successful. The Directory also tried to strike at Britain by invading Ireland, but bad weather dispersed the expedition.

In 1797 Bonaparte continued his successful operations in Italy, while armies operating in Germany were also victorious. In the spring the

Austrians asked for an armistice and peace talks, and concluded a formal peace with the Republic in October. Bereft of Continental allies, Britain undertook negotiations with France. The talks failed. Britain remained at war with the Republic, which had nevertheless destroyed the First Coalition.

In 1798 French leaders sought to force Britain to conclude a peace before Austria and other powers resumed hostilities. The government concluded that a direct invasion of the British Isles was too risky given the strength of the Royal Navy. The Directory, therefore, decided upon a less direct approach of striking at British holdings in India rejecting the strategy of striking again at Ireland, where an insurrection was on the verge of exploding. The government appointed Bonaparte to lead an invasion of Egypt in order to establish a forward base for additional operations. From Egypt, Bonaparte was to send troops to India to cooperate with Mysore in a campaign against British holdings on the subcontinent. The loss of British India would, Paris hoped, be so devastating to Britain's economy that London would leave the war.

While the Irish rebellion was drowned in blood, the invasion of Egypt was quite successful; but the British sent a fleet into the Mediterranean that virtually annihilated the French fleet, thereby isolating Bonaparte's army. Furthermore, the French invasion of Egypt and the British riposte unleashed a chain of events that led to the formation of a Second Coalition. Russia, antagonized by the French intrusion into the Middle East where St. Petersburg had ambitions of its own, decided upon war with France. Austria also decided to renew hostilities, and by the first months of 1799 England, Russia, and Austria were ready to begin military operations.

As renewed war loomed on the Continent, events in Egypt, Syria, and India followed their own related course. Bonaparte decided to attempt to reach India by land and marched into Syria at the beginning of 1799. He was, however, unable to take the fortress of Acre and had to retreat to Egypt. He crushed a Turkish counter-offensive but realized that additional major operations were beyond his capabilities and in the fall left his army and returned to France. In India the British struck at Mysore and destroyed the hostile dynasty, thus securing their hold on the subcontinent.

For France, the opening campaigns of the War of the Second Coalition were little short of disastrous. In Germany, Switzerland, Italy, and Holland the Republic's armies suffered defeat after defeat. In the fall, however, France, taking advantage of divisions within the Allied ranks, launched a successful counterblow in Switzerland and soon after forced an Anglo-Russian army in Holland to capitulate. At this juncture Bonaparte, having returned from Egypt, seized control of the government, but the Coalition had already been broken.

In 1800 Bonaparte, like his predecessors, launched a dual campaign in Italy and Germany. Commanding personally in Italy, Bonaparte turned a near defeat into a victory at Marengo. Austria, nevertheless, fought on until defeated in Germany and then sued for peace. Austria left the war in 1801, and Britain, again isolated, came to terms in 1802. France had thus achieved the national goals of survival, recognition, and a victorious peace although the Republic had perished in the process.

The political and economic changes wrought by the French Revolution enabled the Republic to mobilize the nation and wage a people's war. France without Allies fought and defeated two major coalitions. Waging a popular war, however, produced problems rarely encountered by nonrevolutionary states.

Civil–military relations, where military men challenged the authority of the government, had not been a serious issue during the Old Regime but became critically important in Republican France. Ambitious generals often tried to impose their own plans on the civil power and occasionally attempted to overthrow the regime. Lafayette and Dumouriez tried to march on Paris; Bonaparte dictated peace terms to Austria in 1797, ignoring the Directory's policy; Championnet on his own invaded Naples; and in 1799 Bonaparte seized power by force of arms.

Public opinion also became an important factor in French strategic decision making. Old Regime rulers had been able to send their armies to war and conclude treaties without reference to popular wishes. In England, parliamentary opinion did have an impact on foreign policy, but parliamentary politics involved a rather narrow elite. In Republican France, however, governments did have to consider public reactions to the great issues of war and peace. The public could and did manifest its opinions on the great affairs of state either by direct popular insurrection or via the electoral process. Public opinion thus became a major element in government.

During the wars of the First French Republic, political and diplomatic methods and objectives were remarkably similar to the goals and objectives of Old Regime states. What changed dramatically was the means available to French statesmen, means that enabled the Republic to survive, expand the national frontiers, and defeat the combined might of the rest of Europe.

Two contemporary commentators, Goethe and Clausewitz, recognized that the Revolution had introduced fundamental changes in the way states made war. An enormous gulf had opened between the cabinet wars of the Old Regime and the people's wars of the French Revolution.

On the evening of 20 September 1792, Johann Wolfgang von Goethe, who had accompanied the Prussian army during the invasion of France, was discussing the French victory at the Battle of Valmy. Goethe informed the Prussian officers that a new era had dawned.

Carl von Clausewitz, in reflecting on the impact of the Revolutionary and Napoleonic wars, also understood that a fundamental change had taken place. He described Old Regime warfare as a game of kings and princes noting that

> War thus became solely the concern of the government to the extent that governments parted company with their peoples and behaved as if they were themselves the state. Their means of waging war came to consist of the money in their coffers and of such idle vagabonds as they could lay their hands on either at home or abroad.[1]

Warfare was ineffective, not because the rulers of Europe were peacefully inclined, but rather because commanders leading fragile armies were reluctant to risk battle. Clausewitz noted that before the Revolution

> The plan for a given campaign was to take an enemy fortress or prevent the capture of one's own. No battle was ever sought, or fought, unless it were indispensable for that purpose. Anyone who fought a battle that was not strictly necessary, simply out of an innate desire for victory, was considered reckless. A campaign was usually spent on a siege, or two at the most. Winter quarters were assumed to be necessary for everyone. The poor condition of one side did not constitute an advantage to the other, and contact almost ceased between both. Winter quarters set strict limits to the operations of a campaign.[2]

The results of war were limited not by design but by circumstance. Rough military equality among the great powers and the limitations of Old Regime armies set finite limits on the results of warfare. The French Revolution, by transforming the subject into a citizen, in turn changed the face of war by making possible a people's war. Clausewitz understood the fundamental transformation of war noting that

> In 1793 a force appeared that beggared all imagination. Suddenly war again became the business of the people—a people of thirty million all of whom considered themselves to be citizens. The people became a participant in the war; instead of governments and armies as heretofore, the full weight of the nation was thrown into the balance. The resources and efforts now available for use surpassed all conventional limits; nothing now impeded the vigor with which war could be waged, and consequently the opponents of France faced the utmost peril.[3]

Despite some hyperbole and oversimplification, both Goethe and Clausewitz understood that if the political ends of warfare remained fairly constant, the means had changed dramatically.

Notes

1. Carl von Clausewitz, *On War,* edited by Michael Howard and Peter Paret (Princeton: Princeton University Press, 1988), p. 589.
2. *On War*, p. 591.
3. *On War*, pp. 591–92.

The Dictionary

-A-

AAR RIVER, BATTLE OF THE (16–17 AUGUST 1799). During the second week of August 1799 Masséna's Army of Helvetia carried out a series of successful local counterattacks and retook the St. Gothard Pass. The Austrians responded by attacking French positions along the Aar River. On the night of 16 August the Austrians tried to throw a bridge across the Aar, but it was not long enough. The next morning two Helvetian companies supported by French field guns prevented the Austrian engineers from completing the bridge.

ABERCROMBY, SIR RALPH, GENERAL (1734–1801). Abercromby was born in Scotland and studied at Edinburgh and Leipzig. He purchased a coronetcy in the army and fought in Hanover during the Seven Years' War. He became a lieutenant colonel in 1773 and served in Parliament between 1774 and 1780. Returning to the army in 1793, Abercromby fought in Belgium and northern France and commanded the rear guard during the British retreat from Holland in 1794–95. He then served in the West Indies, Ireland, and the Anglo-Russian invasion of Holland in 1799. Given command of British forces in the Mediterranean, he captured Minorca in 1800 and commanded the Anglo-Turkish amphibious landing at Aboukir Bay in Egypt on 8 March 1801. Severely wounded during a French attack on the night of 21 March Abercromby died of his wounds on 28 March.

ABOUKIR, BATTLE OF (25 JULY 1799). Following his failure to take Acre and his return to Cairo, Bonaparte (q.v.) learned that a Turkish army of 15,000 men had landed at Aboukir Bay. The Turks, with only 7,000 men fit for action, had captured Aboukir Castle and prepared defense lines to seal off the isthmus on which the castle was located. Bonaparte, with 11,000 men, moved to Aboukir, and even though his army was not fully concentrated, attacked the Turkish positions on 25 July. The Turkish army quickly collapsed. The French cut down 2,000

11

at the water's edge and even more drowned trying to reach their ships. The remaining Turks took shelter in the castle where they held out until 2 August. The French victory secured Bonaparte's control of Egypt at least for the moment. French isolation, however, meant that Egypt was in fact a trap for the Army of the Orient. On 23 August Bonaparte put to sea to return to France, abandoning his troops to their fate.

ABOUKIR, NIGHT BATTLE OF (22 MARCH 1801). On 8 March 1801, 18,000 British troops landed on Aboukir Bay and advanced along the narrow isthmus leading to Alexandria. After a sharp skirmish with the French, the British retired to a strong defensive position about five miles from the city. General Menou (q.v.) brought up 10,000 reinforcements from Cairo and launched a night attack on the British positions. In confused and vicious fighting, the French were finally repulsed. The French lost about 3,000 men and the British 1,370. Perhaps the most famous event of the battle took place when the British 28th Foot, heavily engaged to their front, found their flank turned and rear threatened. The colonel ordered the rear rank to turn about and engage the new threat, and the troops fought back to back. The British victory guaranteed that the invasion force would not be driven into the sea.

ACRE. See Saint Jean D'Acre, Siege of

ADDINGTON, HENRY (1757–1844). A childhood friend of William Pitt (q.v.), Addington entered Parliament in 1783, becoming speaker in 1789, a post he held for 11 years. In 1801 the king asked him to form a government, and he entered upon negotiations with France which led to the Peace of Amiens (q.v.) in 1802.

AIX LA CHAPELLE, BATTLE OF (3 MARCH 1793). General Miranda (q.v.) commanded the right flank of Dumouriez's army in the invasion of Holland. His force met an Austrian army under the Duke of Saxe-Coburg (q.v.). The ill-trained French, many of them new recruits, broke and fled in disorder, losing 3,500 killed and wounded and 1,500 prisoners. Saxe-Coburg thus checked the French efforts to invade the Dutch Republic.

ALESSANDRIA, BATTLE OF (20 JUNE 1799). Moreau (q.v.) was enroute to join Macdonald (q.v.) on the Trebbia. His force of 14,000 men initially drove back the Austrians who were besieging Alessandria. The Austrians, with 20,000 men, suffered 3,000 casualties. Suvorov (q.v.), however, had defeated Macdonald the previous day at the Trebbia River, and upon hearing the news, Moreau retreated. Had Moreau moved more rapidly, he might have joined Macdonald before the Trebbia engagements.

ALESSANDRIA, CONVENTION OF (15 JUNE 1800). After the Battle of Marengo (q.v.), General Melas (q.v.) sued for an armistice. He agreed to withdraw his forces behind the Tiano River and not to resume hostilities until an offer of peace terms was considered by Vienna.

ALEXANDRIA, STORMING OF (2 JULY 1798). After landing in Egypt, Bonaparte (q.v.) sent 5,000 men to seize Alexandria. At a cost of some 300 casualties the French took the city.

ALGECIRAS, BATTLE OF (6 JULY 1800). On 13 June 1800, a French squadron of three ships of the line carrying 1,600 troops sailed from Toulon in order to join a Franco-Spanish squadron. The combined force was to reinforce the Army of the Orient in Egypt. The Toulon squadron, learning that Cadiz was blockaded, sailed to Algeciras where Admiral Saumarez (q.v.) attacked on 6 July. Supported by Spanish shore batteries, the French avoided defeat and inflicted severe losses on the British. On 8 July several Spanish ships reinforced the French squadron. On 12 July the French and Spanish set sail to Cadiz. The British attacked, destroying several Spanish ships of the line. Although the combined fleet did reach Cadiz, their losses were so severe that efforts to relieve Egypt were abandoned.

ALKMAAR, CONVENTION OF (18 OCTOBER 1799). Unable to break out of the Helder Peninsula and faced with worsening weather, which would make resupply impossible, the Duke of York (q.v.) opened negotiations with General Brune (q.v.). The Convention of Alkmaar called for the Anglo-Russian force to leave the Batavian Republic by the end of November. The Allies also agreed to return captured guns and soldiers. Brune might have captured the Allied force, but the French and Batavian governments were happy enough to rid themselves of the invaders without additional costly battles.

ALTENKIRCHEN, BATTLE OF (3 JUNE 1796). Having crossed the Rhine and driven back Austrian advanced posts, Jourdan's troops attacked the Austrians at Altenkirchen. Lefebvre's division, with cavalry commanded by Richepanse (q.v.), led the attack. The Austrians lost over 1,500 men and retreated to the Lahn River.

ALVINTIZI, JOSEF, BARON, GENERAL (1735–1810). An experienced Hapsburg commander, Alvintizi fought against the Turks and later the French during the Seven Years' War. He served in the Low Countries in 1793 and defeated the French at Neerwinden (q.v.) in March 1793. He was sent to Italy in 1799 and was defeated by Bonaparte at Arcola and Rivoli. Alvintizi subsequently became a field marshal and governor of Hungary.

AMALGAMATION (1793–1794). In early 1793 the Republic had in effect two different armies, the old regular units and the new volunteers and conscripts. The armies had different uniforms, methods of recruitment, pay, and discipline. The National (q.v.) Convention wanted to create a single force to improve efficiency, standardize the size of units, and create half-brigades to enhance tactical proficiency. The government wanted to create a single republican force by placing two volunteer battalions and a regular battalion into half-brigades. In theory, the volunteers would convey revolutionary spirit to the regulars, who would in turn teach the volunteers the profession of arms. Consequently, a decree of 21 February 1793 nationalized the army. Volunteers and line troops would, henceforth, have the same uniforms, equipment, pay, and discipline. Leaders would be chosen the same way. The pressures of war and domestic political turmoil delayed the application of the decree, although it was applied sporadically by some generals throughout 1793.

On 10 January 1794, instructions were given to begin the amalgamation process throughout the army. The process involved incorporating new conscripts, the creation of half-brigades, and even the mixing of regular conscripts and volunteers at the company level. Despite some problems, the government was successful in its efforts to create a national army, which in turn was a means of unifying the French people.

AMBERG, BATTLE OF (24 AUGUST 1796). Archduke Charles (q.v.), with 61,000 men, attacked Jourdan's army of 45,000 at Amberg. Using his advantage of interior lines, the archduke left a small force to delay Moreau (q.v.) and threw the full weight of his army against Jourdan (q.v.). In sustained fighting each side lost about 2,000 men. The French had to continue to retreat towards the Rhine. The failure of the Rhine and Moselle Army to the south to advance rapidly had enabled the Austrians to concentrate over 60,000 men against Jourdan's force.

AMBOINA, CAPTURE OF (16–18 FEBRUARY 1796). In February 1796, the British occupied Amboina, the capital of the Dutch Spice Islands (Moluccas Islands) with no opposition. At the Peace of Amiens (1802) (q.v.), Amboina was returned to the Dutch along with other possessions in the East Indies. The British retook Amboina in 1810 and returned it again in 1814.

AMIENS, PEACE OF (25 MARCH 1802). By 1801 Britain was virtually isolated: the Second Coalition (q.v.) had collapsed and Vienna had sued for peace. The League of Armed Neutrality (q.v.) had halted British trade in Baltic grain, and the successful British attack on Copenhagen, notwithstanding, demonstrated the extent of Britain's isolation. Success in Egypt did, however, give the British confidence to open negotiations in September.

A preliminary peace was signed on 1 October 1801, and a final treaty on 15 March 1802. The terms were very favorable to France, which gained British recognition of the Republic including the Rhineland, Belgium, and Piedmont. The British also recognized the Batavian Republic. Britain also agreed to return the Cape, Egypt, Malta, Tobago, Martinique, Demerara, Berbice, and Curaçao, retaining only Ceylon and Trinidad. France agreed to return the Papal States and Naples and offered vague promises of compensation for the rulers of Piedmont and Holland. The treaty achieved the essential goals of the Republic but lasted barely a year. Bonaparte's aggressive policies virtually forced Great Britain to resume hostilities. Amiens was literally the only pause in the Revolutionary and Napoleonic wars.

ANDRÉOSSY, ANTOINE FRANÇ (1761–1828). Of noble origin, he entered the artillery in 1781 and saw service in Holland in 1787. He supported the Revolution and in 1796 commanded the bridging train of the Army of Italy. Andréossy fought at Arcola (q.v.) and before Mantua (q.v.). He was promoted general of brigade in 1797 and in 1798–99 saw service in Egypt and Syria. Andréossy earned a reputation as a master of improvisation. He returned to France with Bonaparte (q.v.). After 1802 he served the Empire and in 1814 accepted the Restoration, holding a number of high administrative posts under the Bourbons.

ANNEXATIONS 1792–1799. During the Revolutionary Wars France made a number of annexations including Savoy, Avignon, Belgium, the Rhineland, part of southern Holland, and Piedmont. The annexations were the results of success in war. French annexations were, however, little different from annexations made during the Old Regime and territorial gains made by conservative powers during the Revolutionary period.

Between 1792 and 1795 Prussia, Russia, and Austria made annexations at the expense of Poland, destroying Polish independence in the process. Austria annexed Venice and had made plans to seize Bavaria and parts of northern France. The search for new provinces was in fact universal. The French annexation of Belgium was actually no different from the British seizure of Ceylon or successful Russian efforts to take territory from Sweden and the Ottoman Empire. The fact that France was a republican regime instead of a monarchy is beside the point. All states sought to expand their territory and population. In this France was no different. What was new was the dramatic increase in French military capabilities, which enabled the Republic to pursue traditional methods of statecraft with greater success.

ANTWERP CONFERENCE (APRIL 8, 1793). While their armies advanced, representatives of the Coalition (q.v.) powers met at Antwerp to divide the anticipated spoils. Saxe-Coburg (q.v.) suggested trying to undermine French resistance by promising to refrain from taking any French territory. The powers rejected this approach. The British laid claim to several French colonies, and Austria put forth a plan to exchange Belgium for Bavaria. The British wanted the Hapsburgs to retain Belgium, since Austria posed no naval problems for Britain and suggested that Vienna retain Belgium and add to the province several French fortress cities. The Austrians, to keep British support in order to balance the entente between Prussia and Russia, agreed to keep Belgium and expand the Belgian border south to the Somme River. The Austrians also reserved the right to grab additional French territory. Thugut (q.v.), the Austrian foreign minister, began to contemplate taking Lorraine and exchanging it for Bavaria.

The Antwerp Conference revealed that the Allies were overly optimistic about the prospects for victory. The Conference also revealed that Coalition war aims were less ideological and more focused on the traditional goals of expansionism.

ARCOLA, BATTLE OF (15–17 NOVEMBER 1796). Advancing in several columns, a 58,000-man Austrian army commanded by General Josef Alvintizi (q.v.) attempted to relieve the garrison of Mantua (q.v.). Bonaparte (q.v.) moved to cut Alvintizi's communications, and on 14 November Generals Augereau (q.v.) and Masséna (q.v.) crossed the Adige and on the 15th attacked the Austrians at Arcola, but three assaults on a bridge over the Adige were defeated. The French finally seized Arcola but withdrew in the evening. Two more days of fighting elapsed before the French gained control of Arcola and its bridge. The Austrians lost 7,000 men in the fighting. The French suffered 4,500 casualties, but the Austrians were forced to retreat. Napoleon reoccupied Verona, and the Hapsburg garrison of Mantua remained under French blockade.

ARKLOW, BATTLE OF (9 JUNE 1798). Irish rebels attempted to advance on Dublin. The garrison of Arklow, however, defeated the Irish force of over 20,000. The Irish were ill-armed lacking muskets and artillery and had little chance against an entrenched, well-armed foe.

ARMED NEUTRALITY, LEAGUE OF (1800–1801). Russia, Prussia, Denmark, and Sweden formed a league of armed neutrality designed to counter British methods of search and seizure at sea. Organized by Russia, the League asserted the rights of neutral commerce in time of war. The League's conditions included: the right of neutrals to sail from port to port of a belligerent in wartime; goods, except contraband, belonging to a belligerent were, on neutral ships free goods. Blockades had to be effective to be legal—to seize a neutral ship, the blockaders had to prove clearly that the ship was clearly trying to run a blockade, and a simple declaration by an officer commanding neutral warships convoying merchant ships that vessels in the convoy contained no contraband sufficed to prevent the merchantmen from being stopped and searched.

The British countered the League by sending a fleet to Danish waters. In retaliation, Danish and Prussian troops occupied Hanover and Bremen and blocked the Weser and Ems Rivers. In early April the British attacked Copenhagen, but it was the murder of Tsar Paul (q.v.) that finally destroyed the League.

ARTILLERY. Often called the ultimate argument of kings, artillery played a crucial battlefield role during the Revolutionary wars. Napoleon himself began his military career as an artilleryman. At the start of the Revolution, the Royal Artillery was probably the best in Europe due to the work of J. B. Gribeauval between 1764 and 1789. Despite much opposition from conservative elements, Gribeauval succeeded in reducing the number of field gun calibers to 3-, 12-, 8- and 4-pounders plus a 6-pound howitzer. (In artillery terminology, guns were described by the weight of shot, which also determined the gun's caliber.) Guns and carriages were supplied with interchangeable parts, prepackaged rounds, sights, and elevating screws. Gunners were organized into seven regiments, each with a depot and training school. In 1789 the Royal Artillery contained 11,000 men plus nearly 10,000 militia men and 2,106 colonial gunners equipped with 1,300 field and 8,500 fortress guns.

A standard 12-pounder cannon had a caliber of 121 mm. The barrel was 7 feet, 7 inches long and weighed 2,172 pounds. The carriage weighed 2,192 pounds. Guns were drawn by between four and six horses and had crews ranging from fifteen for the larger pieces to eight for smaller ones. Cannon fired round shot, bagged grapeshot, and canister shot. Howitzers used explosive shells. A twelve-pounder cannon had a direct fire range of up to 1,000 meters, an 8-pounder 900 meters, and a 4-pounder 850 meters. In some cases, ricochet fire with solid shot could increase a cannon's range. Heavier guns could fire one round per minute while a 4-pounder could fire two shots per minute.

A number of pre-Revolutionary artillerists argued that the main mission of field artillery should be to support the infantry by firing on the enemy foot soldiers. Counter-battery fire should be undertaken only in cases of dire necessity. Many artillery officers, like their counterparts in other branches, left their posts out of opposition to the Revolution, but the artillery arm suffered less than the infantry or cavalry from emigration. Thus, in 1792, the artillery was well-prepared to play a leading role, and its power was enhanced by the introduction of horse batteries, where gunners rode along with the field pieces.

During the battles between 1792 and 1799, artillery played a significant role. French divisions and half-brigades contained their own artillery, and in 1795 the divisions and armies of the Republic contained 1,250 field guns, while another 1,350 lighter cannon were posted to the half-brigades. Guns were usually organized into batteries of eight pieces and subdivided into pairs. A perennial problem for the artillery was that the army hired horses and drivers from private contractors. In July 1793, for example, four firms supplied 142,000 horses. Occasionally, civilian drivers refused to move into dangerous positions and at times fled in droves, as happened after Neerwinden (q.v.). It was not until 1800 that field gun drivers were permanently militarized. French field artillery, because of pre-Revolutionary reforms and an innovative officer corps, thus became an integral part of the Republic's combined arms formations and played a crucial battlefield role.

ARTILLERY AMMUNITION. The artillery of European armies employed a variety of munitions including:

Bar-shot: a solid metal bar surrounded by musket balls enclosed in a metal container.

Canister: a tin container filled with musket balls.

Case-shot: almost identical to canister.

Grapeshot: a cloth bag filled with musket balls like canister and case-shot; the balls scattered when fired.

Langridge: pieces of iron packed like case shot and often used at sea to destroy sails and rigging.

Roundshot: a round solid ball of metal; its weight varied according to a gun's caliber.

Shrapnel: invented by a British officer, Henry Shrapnel (1761–1842), it consisted of a hollow sphere packed with powder and musket balls. It exploded in the air by means of a fuse. The French did not use shrapnel.

ARTOIS, CHARLES-PHILIPPE COMTE DE (1757–1863). A younger brother of Louis XVI (q.v.), Artois distinguished himself before the Revolution by his dissolute lifestyle and large debts. Prior to 1789, he became the leader of a court faction that sought to block significant institutional reform. His irresponsible conduct, decadence, and opposition to reform helped undermine the institution of monarchy.

After the fall of the Bastille, Artois left France, going first to Brussels and then Turin, where he began to agitate for other European rulers to destroy the Revolution and restore absolute power to Louis XVI. Artois then joined his brother at Coblenz where Royalists had set up a shadow government. Artois became the leader of those émigrés (q.v.) who called for the complete destruction of the Revolution. Artois accompanied the émigré army that joined the invasion of France in 1792 and retreated with Coalition (q.v.) forces after Valmy.

By 1795 Artois and his mistress were living in near-poverty in Germany. The English in 1795 promoted a plan for a royalist landing in Brittany, spearheaded by émigrés led by Artois, but the Quiberon disaster took place while Artois was still in Germany. In September a second expedition with Artois in tow sailed for France but returned without placing forces ashore. Artois returned to England, living first in Edinburgh and then London. He continued to promote conspiracies but returned to France only in 1814 in the wake of Allied armies. He became King Charles X in 1824, but his reactionary policies led to his overthrow in 1830. It might well be said of Artois that he typified the cliché that the Bourbons forgot nothing and learned nothing.

ASSIGNATS. A form of paper money issued initially as debt instruments redeemable in crown and church lands to liquidate the national debt. The assignats ultimately became legal tender but by 1793 had lost much of their value. To finance the war effort the government imposed price and wage controls, and assignats had to be accepted at par value. The government measures temporarily stabilized the assignat's value, protected the government's purchasing power, and enabled the Republic to pay for the war. Once controls were lifted, the assignat's value plummeted. They were eventually demonetized, and by 1797 France had returned to a monetary system based on metallic currency.

AUGEREAU, PIERRE-FRANÇOIS-CHARLES, GENERAL (1757–1816). Born in Paris, Augereau was the son of a mason and sometime servant. He enlisted in the Royal Army in 1774 and became a sergeant. He then served in the Russian army and the Prussian army, from which he deserted. Augereau supported the Revolution and reentered the French army via the National Guard. By 1794 he was a major-general. He served under Bonaparte (q.v.) during the Italian campaign of 1796–1797, emerging as one of Bonaparte's best tactical commanders. He later became a marshal of the Empire, serving Napoleon in Spain, Russia, and Germany. Though not a great strategist, Augereau was a vigorous and able tactical commander.

-B-

BAGRATION, PETER, GENERAL (1765–1812). Bagration came from a noble Georgian family and entered the Russian army in 1782. He served in the Caucasus and Poland. In 1799 he served in the Italian and Swiss campaigns. In Italy he captured Brescia, and in Switzerland during Suvorov's (q.v.) escape, Bagration, on 1 October 1799, forced the French position at Näfels. In the bloodiest action of the War of the Second Coalition (q.v.), Bagration lost 31 percent of his force, but opened the way for the Russians to continue their retreat. He later participated in the major campaigns in Germany and Russia and died as a result of a wound suffered at Borodino in 1812.

BALANCE OF POWER. The concept of the balance of power in the 18th century received much lip service but little or no observance. Many argued that the European great powers united to defeat states with hegemonic ambitions and came to a tacit understanding that there existed rules of conduct in international relations. Alliance systems would balance each other so that no state or coalition would attain hegemony, and if a great power made territorial gains, other powers would obtain equivalent compensation. The powers did wage wars, but conflicts were limited in aims and not total in effort. Rational rulers avoided ideological wars and wars of hegemony in the interest of the European system as a whole.

Political philosophers, scholars, and statesmen all spoke about the European balance of power as if it were real and worth sustaining. Nothing could be further from the reality of diplomacy and war. Long before 1789, powers were greedy and rapacious, and in fact the only check upon the greed of one power was the counter-greed of others. States did fight wars of limited objectives but also waged conflicts whose aims were far from limited. Russia broke the power of the Swedish Empire in the Great Northern War. In the War of the Austrian Succession a French-led Coalition sought to reduce the Hapsburg Empire to the status of a minor power, and in the Seven Years' War an Austrian crafted alliance sought the destruction of Prussia as a major power.

Nor did the powers hesitate to interfere in the internal affairs of a rival. Elizabethan England supported Dutch rebels against Spain. Spain intervened in the French Wars of Religion. France supported rebellions in Ireland and Scotland and intervened directly against Britain in the American Revolution. Prussia dealt with Hungarian rebels against Austria.

The Revolution wrought no change in the conduct of states. The coalition in 1793 intended to wrest provinces from France. Austria took Venice in exchange for Belgium in 1797. When France annexed Belgium in 1795, French leaders noted that one motive was to obtain compensation for Austrian gains in Poland, a state that was in fact obliterated by the eastern powers. France did support revolutions abroad, not a new technique. There was an element of ideological fervor in French policy, but the primary motives were diplomatic and strategic. The First French Republic sought a victorious peace but never sought Continental hegemony. Ironically, perhaps, French policy, despite dramatic internal changes, was remarkably consistent with the common practices of the Old Regime.

BALLOONS. Before the Revolution Frenchmen had been experimenting with hot air balloons. The Committee of Public Safety (q.v.) established a research center in a Parisian suburb to develop advanced weaponry, and scientists produced an observation balloon. In 1793 the garrisons of Valenciennes and Condé had employed small balloons to send messages. The effort failed since the balloons drifted into the Austrian lines. Nevertheless, the Committee on 2 April 1794 created the army's first balloon company.

The balloon was made of silk. It was about twelve yards in diameter and was filled with hydrogen gas. It was first used at the Battle of Fleurs (q.v.), where the crew sent messages to the ground forces concerning the Austrian movements. The observations were not particularly accurate since the crew lacked experience in observation from above, and smoke often obscured the battlefield.

After the battle, the Committee formed a second balloon company with twenty balloons. Napoleon used balloon observation in Italy and Egypt. Balloons were, however, difficult to transport. The gas generating machine was particularly cumbersome, and it took nearly two days to inflate a balloon. After coming to power in France, Napoleon disbanded the balloon companies.

BANTRY BAY, LANDING AT (DECEMBER 1796). In late 1796 the Directory (q.v.) instructed General Hoche (q.v.) to lead a 20,000-man expedition to Ireland (q.v.). His mission was to rouse the Irish populace and drive the British from the island. The French then intended to use Ireland as a bargaining chip in negotiations with London, trading Ireland back to Britain in return for British recognition of French Continental conquests. Embarking at Brest, the expedition evaded the British blockade and sailed to the Irish coast, where storms dispersed the fleet and prevented a landing.

BARD, FORT, SIEGE OF (21 MAY–5 JUNE 1800). Held by a small Austrian garrison, Fort Bard blocked the passage of Bonaparte's army into Italy. French infantry and cavalry were able to work around the fort, but the artillery and trains were unable to pass. The French did get a few field guns past the fortress, but most of the artillery and the supply trains had to wait until the garrison surrendered in June.

BASEL, TREATY OF (5 APRIL 1795). Prussia in 1792 had been a half-hearted member of the First Coalition (q.v.). Berlin had agreed to fight only after obtaining a promise of subsidies and territorial compensation at the expense of Poland. After Valmy (q.v.), Berlin threatened to leave the coalition unless Vienna allowed Prussia immediate compensation in Poland. Prussia and Russia grabbed parts of Poland in 1793. Excluded, Austria was furious and opened negotiations with Russia for a third partition that would deny Prussia any additional gains. Prussia then became anxious to free its hands in the west in order to concentrate its attentions and forces on the Polish question. Moreover, by late 1794 it was obvious that the Coalition was unable to crush the Republic, and in the winter of 1794 France and Prussia opened secret talks in Basel and concluded a treaty in April 1795.

By the terms of the Treaty, France agreed to remove its armies from the right bank of the Rhine while Prussia agreed that France could hold the Rhineland until the conclusion of a final peace treaty, which would decide the Rhineland's ultimate fate. Prussia also agreed to support French claims to the region in return for compensation elsewhere. Prussia agreed to remain neutral in the war between France and the Coalition and to guarantee the neutrality of all Germany north of the Main River. The French had thus split the Coalition and gained recognition as a legitimate government from one of Europe's great powers.

BASEL, TREATY OF (22 JULY 1795). Defeated on the Continent, Spain had also grown fearful of the growth of British power in the Caribbean, and opened peace talks with France. Madrid initially called for the creation of a kingdom for Louis XVII south of the Loire River. The French countered this bizarre proposal by demanding extensive colonial concessions and advancing to the Ebro River. Anxious to reduce the number of its enemies, Paris then modified its demands. In return for recognition and peace, France agreed to remove its troops from Spain and retained only the Spanish portion of Saint Domingue. Spain left the war and France gained recognition from another European power.

BASSANO, BATTLE OF (8 SEPTEMBER 1796). In a second attempt to relieve Mantua (q.v.), General Würmser (q.v.) with 20,000 men marched down the Brenta Valley in order to break into the Po Valley from the east, threaten Bonaparte's lines of communication, and relieve Mantua. Bonaparte, having occupied Trent on 5 September, learned of the offensive and set off in pursuit with 22,000 troops, leaving a small force to hold the Adige Valley. The Austrians turned to fight the pursuing French at Bassano. The French put the Austrians to flight on 8 September. Some 3,000 escaped to Trieste, while 12,000 under Würmser's personal command forced their way into Mantua, where Bonaparte quickly reestablished a siege. At Bassano the Austrians lost 4,000 prisoners. The French suffered minimal casualties and neutralized a major Hapsburg army.

BATAVIAN REPUBLIC. After conquest by French forces in 1795, the French created a "sister" republic in the United Provinces. The Batavian regime in fact enjoyed substantial local support. In 1799 the Coalition powers expected that the Dutch people would rise and support the Anglo-Russian invasion in the name of the deposed stadtholder. Nothing of the sort happened. There was no popular anti-French or anti-Batavian rising, and several Batavian divisions resisted Allied forces in the Helder Campaign.

BATTALION. In the French Republican army, a line battalion consisted of nine companies of about 150 men each. There were eight fusilier companies and a company of grenadiers. In practice, battalions in the field had about 100 men in each company. Light infantry battalions used the same tactics as line battalions. They were smaller, having only six companies, and in theory were supposed to move faster than line formations.

BEAUHARNAIS, ALEXANDRE, GENERAL (1760–1794). Born in Martinique, Beauharnais was a son of the island's governor. He entered the army and fought in the American Revolutionary War. In 1792 he joined the Army of the Rhine and ultimately became its commander. He failed to relieve Mainz and was recalled to Paris. Beauharnais was arrested for his failure, tried, and executed. Beauharnais's real claim to fame was his marriage in 1779 to Josephine, who later became Napoleon's first wife.

BEAULIEU, JOHANN PETER, GENERAL (1725–1819). Born in Brabant (now part of Belgium), he fought in the Austrian army during the Seven Years' War. In 1792 he won a victory at Valenciennes and in 1794 triumphed at Arlon. He was given command in Italy in 1796, but was defeated by Bonaparte (q.v.) who pushed his forces out of Po Valley into the Tyrol.

BEAUMONT-EN CAMBRESIS, BATTLE OF (26 APRIL 1794). General Pichegru (q.v.), as part of a general advance, moved to raise the Allied siege of Landrecis. A French column advancing from Cambrai and another moving from Ligny scored initial success. The Allies then counterattacked with 19 cavalry squadrons of British and Austrian troopers. Taking the French unawares, the Allies struck the

French before they could deploy. The French fled in disorder, losing over 3,200 men. Allied losses were about 500. Beaumont was one of the most successful cavalry actions of the war.

BELGIUM. Belgium consisted of several provinces officially known as the Austrian Netherlands. French troops first occupied Belgium in 1792 after the battles of Valmy (q.v.) and Jemappes (q.v.). Many Belgians hoped for independence, and General Dumouriez (q.v.) planned to become the ruler of a new Belgian state. To restrict the activities of Dumouriez and to find money to finance the war effort, France first insisted that Belgium be treated as a conquered region and in March 1793 annexed the area.

Allied counter-offensives in the same month drove the French out of Belgium, but in 1794 after the Battle of Fleurs (q.v.), the Republic conquered Belgium for a second time. The Committee of Public Safety (q.v.) was divided over what to do about Belgium. Carnot (q.v.) and Robespierre (q.v.) wanted limited annexations to strengthen the security of the Republic's northern frontier. Others wanted to repeat the annexation of 1793. Still others advocated the return of Belgium to Austria in return for peace. In September 1795 the Convention—presuming that Austria would never accept the Republic other than by force of arms, desiring more defensible frontiers, and seeking to off-balance the gains made by Austria, Prussia, and Russia in the partitions of Poland—voted to annex Belgium once again.

BELLIARD, AUGUSTE-DANIEL, GENERAL (1769–1832). Entering the army via the National Guard, Belliard served in a series of staff posts before becoming a general of brigade in 1796. He commanded a division in Egypt and in 1801 surrendered Cairo the British.

BERGEN, BATTLE OF (19 SEPTEMBER 1799). The Anglo-Russian expedition had landed in Holland, taking part of the Helder Peninsula with relative ease. The overall Coalition (q.v.) strategy called for the Anglo-Russian army to advance south through Holland and into Belgium. To break out of the peninsula, the Allies launched a major attack. The British took Hoorn, but at Bergen the Russians met ferocious resistance and were faced to retreat with heavy losses. The Russian defeat exposed the British, who also had to fall back.

BERNADOTTE, JEAN-BAPTIST JULES, GENERAL (1763–1844). The son of a lawyer, Bernadotte enlisted in the Royal Army in 1780, and by 1788 he was a sergeant major. The Revolution, which opened opportunities to non-nobles, enabled him to become an officer in the regular army in 1791. A Republican, who even had the phrase "death to tyrants" tattooed on his arm, he served in the armies of the Rhine, North, and Sambre-Meuse, rising to the rank of general of division by 1794.

In 1796 Bernadotte served with Bonaparte (q.v.) in Italy, and in 1798 the government appointed him ambassador to the Hapsburg Empire. During the War of the Second Coalition (q.v.) he led a division in the Army of Mainz and married Désirée Clary, an ex-girlfriend of Napoleon. From July to September 1799 he served as the war minister, and as a Jacobin Republican, refused to support the coup of November 1799. He did, however, serve Napoleon, becoming a marshal in 1804 and a prince in 1805. Bernadotte fought at Ulm, Austerlitz, Jena, and Wagram, where he mishandled his corps and was dismissed by Napoleon.

In 1810 the Swedish States General chose him to be the crown prince, since the reigning monarch was childless. The Swedes hoped that a French ruler would offer them some protection from Napoleonic aggression. In 1813, however, Bernadotte switched sides and joined the Coalition against Napoleon, perhaps hoping to become the new ruler of France with Russian support. The scheme failed, and in 1818 he became Charles XIV of Sweden. Regarded by many as a traitor, his career indeed was a strange odyssey from Jacobin to royalist.

BERTHIER LOUIS-ALEXANDRE, GENERAL (1753–1815). Known primarily as Napoleon's chief of staff, Berthier was also an experienced soldier. The son of an engineer officer, he joined the army in 1766, serving as both an infantry and cavalry officer. In 1781 he served in America as Rochambeau's (q.v.) chief of staff. In 1789 Berthier helped organize the Versailles National Guard and held staff posts under Rochambeau and Lafayette. He became a general of brigade in 1795 while serving in the Army of the Alps and general of division in the same year.

In 1796 Berthier joined the Army of Italy as Bonaparte's chief of staff, the start of an association that would last until 1814. In December 1797, while Bonaparte (q.v.) was in Paris, Berthier commanded the Army of Italy, occupying Rome in 1798. Berthier accompanied Bonaparte to Egypt and served in the Marengo (q.v.) campaign, where he was wounded. After 1800, he continued to serve as Napoleon's chief of staff, becoming a marshal in 1804 and a prince in 1806. In 1814 he accepted the Restoration and refused to join Napoleon during the Hundred Days. Overcome by remorse, he died from a fall from a window in Bamberg on 1 June 1815 — a possible suicide.

BESSIÈRES, JEAN-BAPTISTE, GENERAL (1768–1813). The son of a surgeon, Bessières entered the National Guard as a captain. On 10 August 1792, as a member of Louis XVI's Constitutional Guard, he defended the Tuileries against the Parisian populace. He left Paris to serve as a common soldier in the Army of the Pyrenees and was recommissioned in 1793. Bessières next served in the Army of Italy and the Army of the Orient. He supported Bonaparte's coup in 1799 and became a marshal in 1804. He served in Germany, Spain, and Russia and was killed during the German campaign of 1813. Bessières was an expert cavalry commander who could also lead combined arms units.

BIBERACH, BATTLE OF (2 OCTOBER 1796). The defeat of the Sambre-Meuse army in turn forced Moreau's army to retreat from Bavaria. Since pursuing Austrian forces were in separate columns, Moreau (q.v.) decided to turn and attack to gain time to allow a number of isolated French divisions to pull back to the west. The French attack led by Saint-Cyr (q.v.) and Desaix (q.v.) was successful. The Austrians lost over 5,000 men and their pursuit was delayed. Moreau continued his retreat to the Rhine. On 26 October after several additional rearguard actions, the French crossed to the left bank of the Rhine.

BIRON, ARMAND-LOUIS DE GONTAUT, DUC DE (1747–1794). Biron's father was a general and his uncle a marshal. Known until 1788 as the duc de Lauzon, Biron lived a dissolute life but was a competent officer. In 1780 he accompanied Rochambeau (q.v.) to North America and upon his return was promoted to major general. In 1791 he was appointed to serve with Rochambeau on the northern frontier. After a diplomatic mission to London, Biron returned to the army, and after the outbreak of war in April 1792, he invaded Belgium. On 30 April his troops, advancing on Mons, panicked and fled back to France. There followed a series of commands including the Army of the Rhine, the Army of Italy, and the Army of the Coast of LaRochelle. He enjoyed little success in any of his commands and complained constantly about the inefficiency of the army administration. He was arrested in July 1793, more for his social origins than for any military failures, and was executed in January 1794.

BLACK MOUNTAIN, BATTLE OF (17 AND 20 NOVEMBER 1794). In the eastern Pyrenees, the Spanish in the fall of 1794 took up a strong defensive position near Black Mountain. The Spanish had 46,000 men and 250 guns located in 97 redoubts. In preliminary attacks, Dugommier's Army of the Eastern Pyrenees made some progress, but Dugommier (q.v.) died in action, and Pérignon (q.v.), his replacement, halted to reorganize his forces. Attacking on 20 November, a French division led by Augereau (q.v.) stormed the main redoubt. The Spanish line collapsed, and the Spanish fled, losing more than 8,000 men. The way to Barcelona was open, and the Spanish soon asked for terms.

BON, LOUIS ANDRÉ, GENERAL (1758–1799). From 1776 to 1784 Bon served as a private soldier in the Royal Army. In 1792 he was elected lieutenant colonel in a National Guard battalion and served in the Army of the Alps and at the Siege of Toulon (q.v.). By 1797 Bon was a division commander. In 1798 he accompanied Bonaparte (q.v.) to Egypt and fought with distinction at Alexandria (q.v.), the Pyramids (q.v.), and El Arish (q.v.). Bon was mortally wounded during an attempt to storm Acre.

BONAPARTE, NAPOLEON (1769–1821). Napoleon Bonaparte was born at Ajaco, Corsica, on 15 August 1769. He was the second son of Carlo Bonaparte and Letiza (born Ramolino). His father was a lawyer with minor aristocratic credentials who died in 1785. Since Corsica had passed to French rule the year before Bonaparte's birth, his parents sent him and his brother Joseph to learn French at a preparatory school at Autun, to replace the Corsican dialect spoken at home. After Autun, Napoleon attended the Royal Military School at Brienne, where sons of poor aristocrats were given military training and education. At Brienne he was noted for his forceful temperament, Corsican patriotism, and an aptitude for science and mathematics. In 1784 Napoleon transferred to the military school in Paris and in 1785 was commissioned into the La Fère Artillery Regiment.

He then served in a number of garrison posts. Under the direction of his regimental commander, Jean Pierre du Teil (q.v.), Napoleon received expert instruction. The Baron's younger brother was an advocate of mobile artillery tactics that provided in battle direct support to the infantry. The Baron had his cadets experiment with his brother's new tactical concepts. Thus, by 1789, Napoleon had received an excellent military education including instruction in the most advanced artillery techniques.

Napoleon initially supported the Revolution but remained a Corsican patriot until a political feud with Paoli (q.v.), the leader of the Corsican nationalists, forced him and his family to leave the island and settle in southern France, where Napoleon sided with the Jacobins (q.v.) against both the Royalists and their rivals within the Republican camp. Still an obscure artillery captain, Napoleon joined forces with troops sent to recapture Toulon (q.v.) and Marseilles. Both cities had fallen into the hands of Royalists, who in turn had welcomed the armed intervention of British and other First Coalition (q.v.) armed forces. At Toulon Napoleon executed a successful attack on forts dominating the southwest approaches to the city, which in turn forced the British and their Allies to evacuate the port. For his success, the government in June 1794 promoted him to general of brigade. With the Thermidorian Reaction, Napoleon was arrested and incarcerated but was soon released. He went to Paris seeking a new command along with other surplus artillery officers. He even thought of offering his services to the Ottoman Army.

Napoleon, however, soon found a chance to revive his career. He met Paul Barras, a member of the new Directory (q.v.), and on 5 October 1795, Barras employed him to suppress a rightist rising in Paris. He dispersed the Royalist sympathizers with the famous whiff of grapeshot, and for his efforts the government appointed him commander of the Army of Italy. Napoleon also met Josephine Beauharnais, the widow of an aristocrat executed during the Terror (q.v.) and Barras's former mistress. He married her on 9 March 1796 and two days later left to take command of the Army of Italy. He was twenty-six.

Upon reaching the Army of Italy, he quickly established his personal ascendancy over his more experienced divisional commanders by sheer force of personality. He won the support of the rank and file by promising victory, glory, and riches on the fertile lands of Italy. His campaign was supposed to be a secondary thrust to compel the Austrians to divert troops from the main front in Germany.

The Italian campaign of 1796–1797, one of the most famous in the annals of military history, established Bonaparte's reputation not only in the France of his time, but as a military leader without peer. Yet, oddly enough, the campaign was in many ways characteristic of many of the campaigns waged by the Republic. The employment of combined arms divisions, the use of artillery as a direct support weapon for the infantry, and the employment of flexible infantry tactics combining the use of line, column, and skirmisher techniques were methods used by all Republican armies. Furthermore, rapid movement and the waging of constant battles designed to have a cumulative effect on the enemy's ability to continue to fight were additional hallmarks of Republican operational techniques. Napoleon's genius then lay not in tactical or operational innovations but in execution. He led what in many ways was a typical Republican army in terms of recruitment, organization, tactics, and battle doctrine but he did so with a style, boldness, and flair unmatched by friend and foe alike. Thus, without winning a single decisive battle, he defeated the Austrians in a whole series of lesser engagements, drove them from Italy, and, in conjunction with a successful invasion of Germany in 1797, forced them to sue for peace.

Bonaparte also indulged in a growing taste for politics during his Italian campaign. As he moved through northern Italy, he began to create satellite or sister Republics. He seems to have had a number of motives, including easing his logistical problems by establishing friendly regimes behind his army's line of march, alarming the Hapsburgs by the implied threat of spreading revolution into Austria, and enhancing his own prestige. The Directory in 1796 was, however, less interested in Italy than in Belgium and the Rhineland, and the foreign minister had a plan for peace with Austria that called for Austrian recognition of the French annexation of Belgium and the Rhineland and Austrian

compensation in Bavaria and northern Italy. In 1797 Bonaparte negotiated with the Austrians, and his peace with Austria undermined the
Directory's plan and committed France in Italy. The Directory, however, realized that public opinion demanded peace. Moreover, the government had just relied upon the army to purge Royalists who had been
elected to the legislative corps, and was unwilling to challenge the
most successful general. The government, therefore, accepted Bonaparte's settlement, thereby enhancing Napoleon's political as well as
military reputation.

Napoleon was next placed in charge of the Army of England, a force
designed to invade Britain and force London to sue for peace. Napoleon,
however, discovered that crossing the Channel was too dangerous because of the dominance of the Royal Navy (q.v.). Rejecting the idea of
renewing attempts to invade Ireland, he proposed an invasion of Egypt
as an indirect means to attacking British trade and power in India. The
Directory accepted his proposal, and in the summer of 1798 he invaded
and conquered Egypt. Britain's naval riposte, however, left him isolated
in Egypt. He thereupon decided to invade Syria and perhaps attempt an
overland march to India. Vague instructions from Paris in effect gave
him complete freedom of action, and he seems to have believed that such
a campaign was feasible. Initially, he made great progress, but in 1799
his army was unable to take by storm or siege the city of Acre (q.v.). He
returned to Egypt and concluded that his position was ultimately unten-
able and, leaving his army behind, returned to France, landing on 8 October just as France was in the process of winning the War of the Second Coalition (q.v.).

Once again luck favored his ambitions. A number of Directors were
planning a coup against other Directors and the legislature. The plotters had previously chosen a general to assist them, but the general had
died in battle in Italy. The plotters then turned to Napoleon, and the
coup of Brumaire, 9–10 November 1799, in fact made Napoleon, now
thirty years old, the master of France. In 1800 Napoleon's victory at
Marengo (q.v.), coupled with Moreau's (q.v.) victory in Germany at
year's end, forced Austria out of the war. Isolated, England decided to
sue for peace, and in 1802 France with Napoleon as its undisputed
master was finally at peace.

Of course, Bonaparte's ambition, which knew no rational limits,
guaranteed a new round of wars that would ultimately lead to his
downfall. Napoleon was a fascinating product of the Old Regime and
the Revolution. The Old Regime gave him his education and training.
The Revolution gave him his opportunity. Of course, the Revolution
gave many people their opportunity, but only Napoleon with his talent, charisma, and good fortune combined with an insatiable urge to
dominate his human and material environment could have seized the

opportunities available. Only he was able to take the forces unleashed by the Revolution and use them for his own ends.

BORGHETTO, BATTLE OF (30 MAY 1796). After taking Milan, Bonaparte (q.v.) pursued General Beaulieu (q.v.), who with 19,000 men took up a position behind the Mincio River between Lake Garda and Mantua. On 30 May 1796, the French launched a sudden attack on Borghetto and crossed the Mincio with little loss. The Austrians fell back over the Adige River and retreated toward the Tyrol, leaving Mantua isolated.

BOXTEL, BATTLE OF (13–15 SEPTEMBER 1793). On 13 September 1793 the Army of the North advanced on Boxtel in an effort to halt the Allied invasion of northern France. The French took Boxtel, capturing two German battalions. On 15 September, the Duke of York (q.v.) ordered a counterattack, but the outnumbered Allies quickly retreated in good order. Arthur Wellesley (q.v.), commanding the 33rd Regiment of Foot, covered the retreat.

BRUEYS D'AIGALLIERS, FRANÇIS PAUL, ADMIRAL (1733–1798). Brueys first went to sea in 1766 and was promoted to captain in 1792. He was arrested as an aristocrat and suspected Royalist, but was reinstated in 1795. By 1798 he was a vice-admiral. He commanded the naval portion of the Egyptian expedition and was killed on 1 August 1798 at the Battle of the Nile (q.v.).

BRUIX, EUSTACHE, ADMIRAL (1759–1805). Bruix joined the French Royal Navy and saw service in the West Indies. He became a captain in 1793, was cashiered in 1793 as a royalist, but was reinstated in 1794. He took part in the Irish expedition of 1796 and was promoted to rear admiral in 1797. In 1798–1799 he served as Minister of Marine and the Colonies and was promoted to vice-admiral. In March 1799 Bruix commanded the Brest fleet, escaped the British blockade, and entered the Mediterranean. Sickness in his fleet forced him to abandon what might have been an effort to reinforce or rescue the Army of the Orient, and he sailed back to Brest. The remainder of his career was served in administrative posts.

BRUNE, GUILLAUME MARIE ANNE, GENERAL (1763–1815). A printer by trade, Brune supported the Revolution and joined the National Guard, becoming a captain in 1789. In 1793 he became a general of brigade while serving in the Army of the North. In 1796 he was with the Army of Italy and became a general of division in 1797. In January 1799 Brune was given command of French forces in the Batavian Republic (q.v.) and led French and Batavian forces in combatting the Anglo-Russian invasion. He defeated the Allied force and compelled them to ask for terms. The Allies agreed to evacuate the Batavian Republic. After Marengo (q.v.), Brune again served in Italy, completing the campaign quite successfully. Though a Jacobin Republican, he accepted the consulate and Empire, becoming a marshal in 1804. Since he continued to express his Republican feelings, Napoleon did not employ him after 1807. He did rejoin Napoleon during the Hundred Days, but after Waterloo, he was arrested and murdered by a Royalist mob. Brune, with no formal military training, became a first-class leader of men. His greatest triumph was his 1799 campaign, which helped unhinge the strategy of the Second Coalition (q.v.).

BRUNSWICK, CHARLES WILLIAM FERDINAND, DUKE OF, GENERAL (1735–1806). Brunswick's military career began during the Seven Years' War. He served under Frederick the Great and became a Prussian field marshal. In 1780 he became the Duke of Brunswick and in 1787 led the Prussian army in an invasion of the United Provinces to crush a revolutionary movement. In 1792 he became the Allied commander-in-chief and led a Prussian force that invaded eastern France. Defeated at Valmy (q.v.), he retreated back to German territory. In 1794 he gave up his command and returned to his duchy. In 1806 he again agreed to lead the Prussian army and was killed at Auerstadt. Brunswick in the early 1790s was reputed to be Europe's premiere soldier, but his methodical style of warfare could not cope effectively with the way of war introduced by the French Republic.

BRUNSWICK MANIFESTO (25 JULY 1792). During the Austro-Prussian invasion of France the Duke of Brunswick (q.v.), on behalf of the Allied monarchs, issued a manifesto warning the French government and people that armed resistance and any threat to the safety of the royal family would be met with military punishment and total destruction. Word of the manifesto reached Paris by 28 July and stung the populace to fury. It was at least in part a cause of the storming of the Tuileries and the overthrow of the French monarchy on 10 August 1792.

-C-

CADOUDAL, GEORGES (1771–1804). The son of a farmer, he was hostile to the Revolution and became a Chouan leader in 1793. He was an effective guerrilla leader and stayed in the field for nearly seven years. The Comte d'Artois appointed him lieutenant general. He also received arms and money from the British. Cadoudal was, however, unable to pose a serious military threat to the Republic. The guerrillas ultimately laid down their arms, and Cadoudal then tried to strike directly at Bonaparte (q.v.). In 1800 a bomb nearly killed Napoleon. Cadoudal was involved in the plot. In 1804 he joined another conspiracy with General Pichegru (q.v.) to kidnap and kill Napoleon and restore the Bourbons. However, the police had infiltrated the royalist group, and Cadoudal and the others were arrested. Cadoudal was executed in June 1804.

CAFFARELLI, LOUIS MARIE JOSEPH MAXIMILIEN (1756–1799). An officer of engineers since 1775, Caffarelli supported the Revolution, although he was dismissed several times and imprisoned once because of his aristocratic origins. Serving on the Rhine front, he lost a leg and was promoted to general of brigade in 1795. He subsequently became Bonaparte's chief engineer, and served in Egypt, where he was killed during the siege of Acre (q.v.).

CALDIERO, BATTLE OF (12 NOVEMBER 1796). General Alvintizi (q.v.), in a second attempt to relieve Mantua (q.v.), led a 28,000-man force toward Verona from the east while another force moved south from Trent. The French failed to defeat Alvintizi's advance guard, and the Austrians, bringing up the main body, defeated the French near Caldiero, forcing Bonaparte (q.v.) to pull his forces back to Verona. Though defeated, Bonaparte responded quickly. Leaving a small force to block the Austrians moving south from Trent, he concentrated his forces to strike at Alvintizi thus leading to the engagement at Arcola (q.v.).

CAMPERDOWN, NAVAL BATTLE OF (11 OCTOBER 1797). A Batavian fleet of 16 vessels sailed to carry aid to Irish rebels. The Dutch were met by a British fleet of 16 ships. In bitter fighting each side had over 1,000 killed and wounded, but the Dutch also lost nine ships of the line, several frigates, and 5,000 prisoners. The battle demonstrated that the Royal Navy (q.v.) had recovered from the mutinies of 1797 and retained its naval dominance.

CAMPO FORMIO, PEACE OF (17 OCTOBER 1797). After the preliminary peace of Leoben (q.v.), Austria and France signed a formal treaty near Campo Formio. By its terms, Austria ceded Belgium to France and agreed to French occupation of the Rhineland, subject to compensation for the Rhennish princes, which was to be arranged at a subsequent conference. Austria also accepted French possession of Corfu and the Ionian Islands and recognized the Ligurian (q.v.) and Cisalpine (q.v.) republics. In return Austria received Dalmatia and Venetian territory east of the Adige. The French government was more interested in gaining recognition of their control of the Rhineland but accepted Bonaparte's treaty reluctantly. It was, after all, a peace of sorts and put Austria out of the war. Vienna, however, regarded Campo Formio as a truce rather than a permanent settlement. The treaty also enhanced Bonaparte's prestige, increased his influence at Paris, and set the stage for further ventures by the ambitious general.

CAPE OF GOOD HOPE (12 JUNE–15 SEPTEMBER 1795). In February 1795 the Prince of Orange wrote to the governors of all Dutch colonies ordering them to admit British troops. Two expeditions with four battalions of infantry sailed for the Cape, arriving in June. The Dutch governor, however, refused to capitulate. The Dutch had only 800 infantry and 2,000 militia. The British, therefore, landed and waged a number of skirmishes as they moved inland. The Dutch governor, finding his position hopeless, finally surrendered, and the British held the colony until 1802 when it was returned to the Dutch. It was recaptured again in 1806.

CARNOT, LAZARE (1753–1823). The son of a notary, Carnot, though of middle-class origin, was able to enter the military engineering school at Mézières, and became an engineer lieutenant in 1773. Carnot soon found his career stymied by his bourgeois origins since he could not be promoted above the rank of captain. In 1791 he was, along with his younger brother, elected to the Legislative Assembly, where he identified himself with leftist groups favoring a more open society and a career open to talent.

After the overthrow of the monarchy, Carnot was sent to the Army of the Rhine to ensure its acceptance of the new regime, and in September 1792 he was elected to the National Convention (q.v.), where he sat with the Mountain and voted for the death penalty for Louis XVI (q.v.). He also served as representative on mission to the Pyrenees and to the Army of the North, where he discovered Dumouriez's treason and ordered his arrest.

In August 1793 Carnot joined the Committee of Public Safety (q.v.), where he devoted himself to military affairs. Known as the Organizer of Victory, he had to supervise the organization of the nation's vast citizen armies and find able and loyal officers to lead them. Along with Prieur de la Côte d'Or (q.v.) he had to supervise the arming and equipping of the armed forces. He also had to deal with the problems of counterrevolutionary campaigns and foreign invasion. In 1793 he insisted upon vigorous attacks on all fronts to halt the enemies of the Republic. He insisted that field commanders seek out enemy forces and attack them constantly. In the following year he called for the main French effort to be directed against the Austrians and English and reinforced the area from the Channel to the Meuse as the critical operational zone. Again he called for vigor and constant offensive actions designed to wear down the Republic's enemies until French armies could win crushing victories. Though no one man made possible the French triumphs of 1793 and 1794, Carnot certainly played a major part in the Republic's victories.

Surviving Thermidor, Carnot remained on the Committee until March 1795 and then became a Director, where he continued to supervise military affairs. He opposed the Fructidor Coup of 1797 and fled to Geneva to avoid arrest. He returned to France after Bonaparte's seizure of power in 1799 and was elected to the Tribunate in 1802, where he voted against the creation of a life consulate. He also voted against the creation of the Empire in 1804 and retired to private life in 1807. In 1814 Carnot rallied to Napoleon, defending Antwerp until the first abdication. During the Hundred Days he served as the interior minister, and after Waterloo he went into exile in Germany for the rest of his life: an unrepentant Republican to the end.

CASABIANCA, JOSEPH-MARIE, GENERAL (1742–1807). A Corsican by birth, he entered the French army in 1761. He supported the Revolution and in 1792 served in the Army of the Rhine where he was promoted to general of brigade. He fought in Italy in 1794–1795 and became governor of Piedmont in 1796. In 1799 Casabianca served with the Army of Italy, suffered several serious wounds, and retired in 1801.

CASABIANCA, RAPHAEL, GENERAL (1738–1825). A Corsican of noble birth, Casabianca resisted Genoa's domination, and after France purchased the island, he joined the Royal Army. He supported the Revolution and participated in the first invasion of Belgium. He commanded the rearguard after the French panicked and held back the Austrian pursuit. Promoted to general of brigade, he participated in the occupation of Savoy. Sent to Corsica in 1793, Casabianca resisted Paoli's (q.v.) rebellion and was besieged in Calvi. He held out for more than a month and capitulated with full honors of war. Promoted to general of division, he served in Italy from 1794 to 1799 and then fought successfully against royalist insurgents in western France. He retired from active service in December 1799. His brother was a naval officer who died at the Battle of the Nile (q.v.).

CASSANO, BATTLE OF (26 APRIL 1799). Suvorov (q.v.) reached Italy in mid-April and ordered an immediate attack, in order to disrupt French offensive plans and seize Milan. His army, now bolstered by a

Russian Corps, struck the French around Cassano, seized the town, and forced the French to continue their retreat. Two days later Allied forces entered Milan.

CASTIGLIONE, BATTLE OF (5 AUGUST 1796). In July 1796 Vienna sent two armies to relieve the Mantua garrison. One force advanced west to Lake Garda while a second under Würmser (q.v.) marched from Trent on Verona. Bonaparte (q.v.), to meet the dual threat, called off the siege of Mantua (q.v.) and sent forces to repulse the force near Lake Garda, while other units repulsed Würmser's advance guard. Bonaparte took up a central position between the two Austrian forces and on 5 August near Castiglione threw the bulk of his army against Würmser. In confused and bloody fighting, the Austrians had 2,000 killed and wounded and 1,000 prisoners. The French suffered about 1,500 casualties and forced Würmser to retreat.

CASTLEBAR, BATTLE OF (27 AUGUST 1798). Having landed in Ireland at Killala in County Mayo, Humbert (q.v.) realized that his small force could survive only by rapid movement. He therefore began to move toward Dublin and encountered a force of 6,000 regulars and militia near Castlebar. With a force of 700 French and 800 Irish, Humbert attacked and shattered the British force. Some British cavalry units retreated over 60 miles in little more than a day, thus giving the battle its popular name—the Races of Castlebar. Humbert's victory reignited the Irish rebellion in some areas, but Humbert's forces were so small that their ultimate fate was a foregone conclusion. (*See also* Ireland)

CASUALTIES. During the wars of the Old Regime casualties as a percentage of the total number of troops engaged were quite heavy. At the Battle of Zorndorf, for example, the Prussians with some 30,000 men lost 40 percent of their troops. Losses for an entire war were, because of the size of armies and the relative infrequency of battles, fairly modest. France lost 50,000 men killed and wounded during the War of the Polish Succession (1731–1735). During the War of the Austrian Succession (1741–1748), French casualties amounted to 140,000 killed and wounded. The Seven Years' War (1756–1763) cost France 175,000 killed and wounded. Prisoners and desertions would expand the total casualty figures. In the War of the Austrian Succession France lost 50,000 prisoners, and during the Seven Years' War France lost about 100,000 prisoners and suffered some 70,000 desertions. In the War of the Austrian Succession total casualties as a percentage of troops engaged ranged from 44 to 3 percent. The average casualty rate per battle was about 15 percent.

By contrast, during the wars of the First French Republic casualties as a percentage of forces engaged in a particular battle were fewer than in Old Regime battles, while total losses in a war were greater since armies were larger and engagements more frequent. Battle losses between 1792 and 1802 ranged from 36 percent at Näfels and 29 percent of forces engaged at the Trebbia (q.v.) to less than 2 percent at the Pyramids (q.v.). The average loss rate as a percentage of forces engaged was a bit less than 7 percent. On the other hand, during the War of the First Coalition (1792–1797) estimates of French losses range as high as 300,000 killed and wounded and over 100,000 prisoners. Estimates of casualties between 1798 and 1802 are about 140,000 killed and wounded and a similar number of prisoners. A high percentage of the wounded did not survive their wounds because of the nature of military medicine. Wounds that would be survivable today were fatal in the 1790s, primarily because of infection. Furthermore, many of the deaths recorded were not the result of battle but of disease and generally poor conditions of sanitation. It has been estimated that for every battle death there were several deaths due to various diseases. On the other hand, most prisoners survived captivity, which was often brief because of the widespread practice of parole, wherein captured soldiers were released upon the promise of not taking up arms again for a specified period of time. Released prisoners could be and were employed against other enemies. Thus, the Mainz garrison capitulated on parole and was immediately redeployed to the Vendée (q.v.) in 1793.

CATHELINEAU, JACQUES (1759–1793). Like his father, Cathelineau was initially a mason and then became a cart driver. After 1791, because of the government's policy towards the church, he opposed the Revolution and frequently took part in nighttime services conducted by refractory priests. After the start of the Vendean insurrection, Cathelineau raised a small band of fighters from among his family and friends. He was a talented leader and soon led a band 3,000 strong. He played a major role in the capture of Samur in June. He was then elected as the commander of the Vendean army, in part because noble royalist officers realized the necessity of having a man of the people as titular leader, in order to retain the loyalty of the peasant soldiers. Cathelineau was mortally wounded in the Vendean assault on Nantes.

CATHERINE II (1729–1796). A German by birth, Catherine married the heir to the Russian throne and upon the death by murder of Peter III she became the ruler of the Russian Empire. She was quite successful in expanding the Empire, at the expense of Poland and Turkey. Ideologically, she opposed the French Revolution but always subordinated her ideology to the practical interests of state. She was in fact more concerned with seizing Polish territory than with actively joining the First Coalition (q.v.). At one point, she suggested that Berlin and Vienna deal with revolutionary movements in the west while she dealt with revolution in the east—a poorly disguised approach to get Prussia and Austria enmeshed in war with France, thereby leaving her a free hand in Poland and the Balkans.

CAVALRY. The cavalry arm was the weakest branch of the Republican armies. During the Old Regime, cavalry in the French and other European armies proved most useful in performing the tasks of reconnaissance, screening the main force, and pursuit. Despite their elevated social status, cavalry regiments rarely acted as a decisive shock arm in battle. During the Revolution, the French cavalry suffered heavily from the emigration of aristocratic officers, lack of adequate training, and a serious shortage of horses, caused in part by an epizootic epidemic. In 1793 the Republic established the strength of the cavalry at 66,000 men serving in 29 regular, 18 dragoon, 12 chasseur, and 8 hussar regiments. Occasionally, the cavalry performed useful services. Early in 1795, for example, horsemen of the Army of the North charged over ice-covered water to capture the Dutch fleet. For the most part, however, commanders confined the cavalry's activities to screening and scouting. Cavalry was a useful adjunct to the infantry and artillery but was never their equal.

Coalition cavalry was periodically effective against French infantry, especially in 1793 when French troops were new to war and only partially trained. The French ultimately learned how to fend off cavalry attacks by forming squares. By late 1794 the French could deal with Allied cavalry, and Republican infantry units were rarely shattered by cavalry shock action.

CERVONI, JEAN BAPTISTE, GENERAL (1765–1809). Cervoni joined the army in 1783. He fought at Toulon (q.v.) in 1793. In 1796 he fought in Italy, participating in the battles of Voltri (q.v.), Lodi (q.v.), Castiglione (q.v.), Arcola (q.v.), Rivoli (q.v.), and the siege of Mantua (q.v.). He became a general of division in 1798 and was killed at Eckmul in 1809.

CEVA, BATTLE OF (16–17 APRIL 1796). Ceva was a fortified position held by an Austro-Piedmontese force of about 13,000 men. An attack by the Army of Italy on 16 April failed, but on 17 April Bonaparte (q.v.) gathered 24,000 troops for a second attack. The Allied commander, however, quickly retreated to a stronger position.

CEYLON, CAPTURE OF (1795–1796). Long a Dutch colony, the British East India Company mounted an expedition to conquer Ceylon in 1795–1796. The expedition of 1,100 British troops and two Indian battalions accompanied by four warships took Trincomalee on 25 August 1795. On 7 February 1796, the British moved on Colombo, drove off an attack by 300 Malay soldiers, and bribed a Swiss mercenary regiment to capitulate. The island fell in early February 1796 with little resistance. At the Peace of Amiens (q.v.) in 1802, the British kept Ceylon, one of the few conquests that London retained.

CHABRAN, JOSEPH, GENERAL (1763–1843). Chabran was elected a captain of volunteers in 1792 and served in the 1796–1797 Italian campaign. He became a general of brigade in 1797 and a general of division in 1799. In 1800 he was in charge of the siege of Fort Bard (q.v.). Chabran later fought in Spain, and after 1814, served the Bourbons. He retired in 1827.

CHAMBARLHAC DE LAUBESPIN, JACQUES ANTOINE, GENERAL (1754–1826). Chambarlhac served in the Royal Army from 1769–1776. In 1792 he was a lieutenant colonel of volunteers. He later fought in Italy and received a battlefield promotion to general of brigade. In 1799 he crushed a counterrevolutionary revolt in the west of France. Chambarlhac later served in numerous garrison and staff posts. After the Restoration, he refused to serve the Bourbons and was retired in October 1815.

CHAMPIONNET, JEAN-ETIENNE, GENERAL (1762–1800). Championnet joined the Royal Army during the American Revolutionary War and served at the siege of Gibraltar. He supported the Revolution and in 1790 became the commander of a volunteer battalion. In 1793 he served with the Rhine army and was promoted to general of brigade; he became a general of division at year's end. In 1794 his division played a significant role in the Battle of Fleurs (q.v.). In 1797 Championnet was the equivalent of a corps commander, and with 22,000 men forced a passage of the Rhine. In the following year he was placed in charge of the Army of Rome. When Naples went to war, Championnet defeated the Neapolitan army, invaded Naples, seized the city of Naples, and despite the government's orders to the contrary proclaimed the creation of a republic. For his disobedience he was removed from command and sent back to France for a court-martial. Political shifts in Paris led to his reinstatement. He took over the French forces in Italy after the defeat at Novi, and was beaten by the Austrians at Gendala in early November 1799. He resigned his command and died while awaiting his replacement.

CHARETTE DE LA CONTRIE, FRANÇOIS ATHANASE (1763–1796). In 1790 Charette resigned from the navy because of his opposition to the Revolution. In March 1793 he joined the rebellion in the Vendée and proved to be an effective guerrilla fighter, leading a Vendean army in the swampy regions in the south. The Republican forces, however, were able to deny him access to the coast and to other bands to the east. In June and again in August Charette tried to take major towns but was defeated. He then reverted to guerrilla warfare in his own region of Bas Poitou.

Louis XVIII, in the summer of 1795, appointed him supreme commander of royalist forces in the Vendée, but this was a hollow gesture. Practical aid went to the Quiberon (q.v.) expedition, which failed. In 1796 the government hunted Charette down and executed him.

Charette was a courageous warrior and an excellent guerrilla leader. At some point in 1793, he and other Royalist chiefs posed a serious threat to the Republic, but in attempting to undertake major conventional operations the guerrillas proved unable to defeat the better organized regular forces of the Republic. (*See also* Vendée)

CHARLES IV, KING OF SPAIN (1748–1819). As king, Charles was little more than a cipher. He was dominated by his queen and her lover Prince Godoy. He declared war on France in 1793 but left the war in 1795 and formed an alliance with France in 1796. Napoleon forced him to abdicate in 1808 and he lived in exile until 1814. It was said of Charles IV that his knowledge of hunting was in inverse proportion to his knowledge of statecraft. Charles did not resume the throne after Napoleon's abdication and spent his last years in Rome.

CHARLES VON HAPSBURG (1771–1847). Charles was a younger brother of Francis II (q.v.). He was an epileptic and had a very sensitive nature, but he was also the best Austrian commander during the Revolutionary and Napoleonic wars. He entered the army in 1790 and fought at Jemappes (q.v.) in 1792. In 1793 he fought at Neerwinden (q.v.) and Wattignies (q.v.). In 1794 he served at Fleurs (q.v.).

His manifest abilities led to his promotion to field marshal in 1796, and in the ensuing campaign he defeated two French armies, driving them back over the Rhine. Transferred to Italy after the fall of Mantua (q.v.), he fought an effective rearguard action against Bonaparte (q.v.). Though he had to retreat from Italy, he managed to keep his army intact. In 1799 he again drove the French from southern Germany. Objecting to Vienna's order to invade Belgium rather than protecting the right flank of the Allied armies in Switzerland, Charles resigned his command in 1800. He returned to active duty in 1801 and continued to fight effectively against the French until his final retirement from active service in 1809.

CHASSELOUP-LAUBAT, FRANÇOIS, GENERAL (1754–1833). An engineer officer, Chasseloup-Laubat was commissioned in 1778. He became Bonaparte's chief engineer in Italy and a general of division in 1799. Later he supervised numerous sieges. After 1814 he served the Bourbons and became president of the Ecole Polytechnique.

CHERASCO, ARMISTICE OF (28 APRIL 1796). Defeated by Bonaparte (q.v.), the king of Savoy sought an armistice with the French. Approved by Paris on 21 May, the armistice required the king to turn over a number of fortified positions to the French, cease hostilities, and allow French troops free passage over the Po River.

CHOLET, BATTLE OF (17 OCTOBER 1793). From bases on the edge of the *bocage,* three Republican columns entered the Vendée (q.v.) from the east, south, and west. By 14 October the Republican forces had taken Chatillon and Vendeans were encircled on three sides around Cholet. On 16 October, Kléber (q.v.) entered Cholet and deployed 32,000 men around the town. On the 17th the Vendeans (about 35,000 strong) attacked in an effort to escape encirclement and pushed back Kléber's advanced guard. The Vendeans reached the outskirts of Cholet, but Kléber maneuvered his forces against their exposed flanks and halted their advance. Elbée (q.v.), the Vendean commander, received a fatal wound, and the shattered Vendean army and thousands of refugees fled north across the Loire into Brittany.

CHOUANNERIE. Chouans were counterrevolutionaries, mainly peasants, who operated in parts of Brittany and Normandy. Counterrevolutionary sentiment grew out of preexisting tensions in western France between town and country and owners and renters of land. The Revolution tended to benefit owners and town dwellers and, as early as the spring of 1792, armed peasant bands were in action. Later, Royalists attempted to capture the Chouans for their cause, but the peasant bands in 1793 were easily dispersed by Republican troops. The Chouans did hold out in the rough terrain of the interior but posed no major threat to the government. The Chouans never became an organized regional force.

The British and Royalists tried to revive the Chouan movement in 1795, but the failure at Quiberon (q.v.) and the influx of reinforcements from the Vendée (q.v.) defeated the Anglo-Royalist efforts. In 1797 and 1798 there was again sporadic local violence, and in 1799 the Chouans undertook a partly concerted rising with British assistance. In central Brittany, the Chouans managed briefly to occupy Le Mans and other towns, but they were soon defeated. After 1800, Chouan bands continued to operate, but they tended to be a police rather than a military problem. (*See also* Counterrevolution)

CISALPINE REPUBLIC. In 1797 Bonaparte (q.v.) joined the Cispadane (q.v.) Republic with regions north of the Po, including Milan, Mantua, and the Vallentlina, to form the Cisalpine Republic. The French government had intended to use the Italian conquests as pawns to trade with the Austrians at a future peace conference. Paris, however, could not defy their most successful general and accepted a treaty with Austria in 1797 that recognized the new republic. France then proceeded to use the Cisalpine Republic as a satellite. France provided and even altered the constitution and compelled the republic to maintain a 22,000-man army under French command and pay for the presence of 25,000 French troops.

Though objecting to French domination, the Cisalpine Republic was reasonably popular with the people. The end of internal tariffs, a fair amount of press freedom, improved local government, the confiscation of church lands, the abolition of nobility, and the introduction of the career open to talent convinced many to support the regime. The French did not, however, use the Republic as a basis for a united Italy, preferring instead either to deal with existing regimes or create separate sister republics. Swept away in the 1799 campaign, it was restored and enlarged in 1801. In 1805 Napoleon transformed the area into the Kingdom of Italy.

CISPADANE REPUBLIC (1796–1797). The Cispadane Republic was the first satellite republic created in Italy. When Bonaparte (q.v.) invaded Italy in 1796, there were rebellions in several cities south of the Po. The revolutionary movement included members of the middle class, liberal nobles, and some clergymen. Representatives of Bologna, Ferrara, Modena, and Reggio formed a league to defend themselves against a return of the Old Regime. Bonaparte urged them to form a permanent state, and an assembly proclaimed the Cispadane Republic in December 1796. Bonaparte encouraged the Italian democrats in part because he wanted to ease the Army of Italy's tasks of occupation and supply. He may also have been seeking to enhance his own position and prestige. The Cispadane Republic seems to have been reasonably popular. In the following year, however, it was merged into the Cisalpine Republic (q.v.).

CIVIL–MILITARY RELATIONS. Civil–military relations are always complex but never more so than during a time of revolution and upheaval, when the very legitimacy of the state is in question. In normal times, the fact that civilian and military authorities often disagree on a wide range of issues ranging from budgets to operations is not surprising. In fact, such differences of opinion can often be fruitful. Real problems arise when the military refuses orders from the civilian government or even takes up arms against the government. Control of the military was a perpetual problem during the Revolutionary decade, 1789–1799, and it was the failure to solve the problem that led to the demise of the First Republic.

Military disobedience to the government actually began prior to 1789. Royal efforts to reorganize government finances foundered at least in part because the government feared that the officer corps would refuse to impose the reforms by force. In 1789 Louis XVI (q.v.) did not launch an armed coup against the Assembly because he and his advisors feared that the enlisted men would not march against the Parisian populace.

With the coming of war in 1792, coupled with continued internal turbulence, problems of civil–military relations became more serious and volatile. Ambitious generals began to seek power for themselves. Other commanders often accepted the incumbent regime but sought to impose their own views of strategy or foreign policy on the political authorities.

In 1792 and 1793 a number of generals tried to strike directly at the government. Lafayette (q.v.), after the overthrow of the monarchy, sought to march on Paris. His troops, however, refused to follow him. In 1793 Dumouriez (q.v.) tried to establish himself as the ruler of an independent Belgian state. When the government foiled his intention, he too sought to march on Paris. As with Lafayette, his troops refused to follow him, and Dumouriez had to flee to the Allied lines.

During the Terror (q.v.), a period of emergency government in late 1793 to mid-1794, the government tightened its control over military leaders through the use of Representatives on Mission (q.v.), government agents who were deputies in the Convention. Officers were compelled to obey the political authorities. Armed with plenary powers, the Representatives could promote, demote, and even arrest officers they suspected of disloyalty. There were abuses. Failure or even lack of complete success was occasionally met with arrest and death. Loyal officers of aristocratic background were often removed from command simply because of the accident of their birth. Given the dangerous and chaotic conditions prevailing in late 1793, the over-zealous actions of some Representatives on Mission was unfortunate but probably inevitable. On the other hand, the Committee of Public Safety (q.v.) did find a corps of officers who were loyal, talented, and dedicated to victory. Despite its blemishes, the system of emergency government achieved notable successes.

After the Thermidorian Reaction, the Convention and the Directory (q.v.) dismantled much of the machinery of the Terror. The use of Representatives on Mission was discontinued. They were replaced by army commissioners whose powers were greatly reduced. Again, ambitious generals like Moreau (q.v.) and Pichegru (q.v.) seized their opportunity to turn against the regime. Moreover, the government often turned to the army to resolve its political problems. The coup of September 1797 placed the Directory in debt to the military. This debt, coupled with general war-weariness, enabled Bonaparte (q.v.) to dictate his rather than the government's terms at the Campo Formio Peace (q.v.). In the following year Championnet (q.v.) created a republic in Naples against the wishes of the government.

In 1799 the Directors sought to use the army again to purge the legislative and some of their own members. This extra constitutional action gave Bonaparte the opportunity to use his participation in the November coup as a stepping stone for his own seizure of power. Thus, the failure of the Republic to resolve definitively the problem of civil–military relations in large measure contributed to the regime's demise. (*See also* Committee of Public Safety)

CLAUSEWITZ, CARL VON (1780–1831). Clausewitz joined the Prussian army at age twelve and served in campaigns against the Republic in Alsace and the Saar. In 1801 he entered the War Academy in Berlin where he was associated with Scharnhorst (q.v.) and other politico-military reformers. He participated in the 1806 campaign, worked with reformers after the Jena catastrophe, took service with the Russian army, and rejoined the Prussian forces in time for Waterloo. In 1818 Clausewitz became director of the War Academy and died of cholera in 1831. His experience in the wars of the Revolution and Napoleon contributed to his understanding of the nature of war. Many of his concepts are to be found in a book, *On War,* which he began but never completed. His wife and colleagues finished the book based on his notes. Nevertheless, *On War* remains one of the most important studies on the nature of war and is still widely used today.

CLICHY CLUB (1794–1797). The Clichy Club was a loose association of deputies, newspapermen, and politicians who were essentially anti-Jacobin. Within the Club, however, there was a royalist clique that was in contact with agents representing Louis XVIII. The Clichy Royalists were primarily constitutionalists and did not support the Pretenders' political stance. The Club had some success in the 1797 elections, but the Directory's September coup effectively destroyed the group's power. The fate of the Clichy Club indicates that there were deep divisions among counterrevolutionary factions that prevented the formulation of a broad-based program.

COALITION, FIRST (1792–1797). The original members of the First Coalition were Austria and Prussia. The motives of the courts of Vienna and Berlin were mixed. Both powers feared and disliked the ideology of the Revolution and were concerned for the safety of Louis XVI (q.v.) and his family. Austria also wished to preserve the French monarchy, since France was an important Austrian ally, and Louis XVI's wife was an Austrian princess. Prussia, however, was equally concerned with using the war against France as a means of obtaining compensation at the expense of Poland (q.v.). Both powers were convinced that the war that began in April 1792 would lead to a quick victory and a restoration of Louis's position.

The overthrow of the French monarchy plus the battles of Valmy (q.v.) and Jemappes (q.v.), however, led to an expanded conflict as French forces overran Belgium and the Rhineland. The French occupation of Belgium, the opening of the port of Antwerp, and the execution of Louis XVI (q.v.) brought new powers, including Great Britain, Holland, Spain, the German princes, and the Italian states into the conflict. Coalition counterattacks in 1793 reconquered Belgium and the Rhineland and were followed by Allied invasions of northern and eastern France. On other fronts, Coalition forces crossed the Pyrenees, seized portions of the French Mediterranean coast, and threatened the line of the Alps. Coupled with counterrevolutionary risings in western France and parts of the Rhône Valley plus political turmoil in Paris, the Coalition seemed by the summer of 1793 poised on the brink of victory.

The dramatic French response—national mobilization—placed the ability of the Coalition to crush the Republic in doubt. Moreover, the Coalition was far from united. The British dispersed thousands of troops in an effort to seize French colonial possessions, while Austria and Prussia remained divided over the fate of Poland. Both powers kept thousands of men in the east to check each others' designs. Consequently, the French, in a series of desperate offensives in late 1793, halted Allied advances and reduced the threat of internal counterrevolution. French offensives in 1794 focused on Flanders and the Franco-Belgian border area. Constant French assaults from the Channel to the Meuse River were ultimately successful and once again the Republic occupied Belgium and most of the Rhineland.

In 1795 the Coalition began to fall apart. After a French invasion, the United Provinces became a sister republic. Offensives in Germany failed, but Prussia signed a treaty with France and left the war, as did Tuscany and Spain. In 1796 Spain rejoined the war, only this time as a French ally. French armies, meanwhile, campaigned unsuccessfully in Germany in 1796, but the Italian Campaign was unexpectedly and spectacularly successful. Successful operations in Germany in 1797 coupled with additional victories in Italy drove Austria to sue for peace at the end of the year, leaving only England still at war with France.

The First Coalition was motivated partly by ideological concerns, but conflicting territorial ambitions worked against the formulation of a coherent strategy. The Coalition also underestimated French capabilities and resolve and failed to react effectively to the changes in warfare wrought by the Revolution.

COALITION, SECOND. The isolation of Bonaparte's army in Egypt presented an opportunity for the enemies of France to form a new Coalition. The British devised plans to reduce France back to within the borders of 1792, restore the monarchy, restore the stadtholder in Holland, unite Holland with Belgium, and compensate Austria with provinces in Italy. Austria and Russia agreed to an alliance in August 1798, and in late December Britain and Russia signed a treaty of alliance. Prussia, however, refused to participate and remained neutral. Coalition strategy called for 17,500 Russian and 13,000 British troops to invade Holland. Some 94,000 Austrian and 24,000 Russian troops would operate in northern Italy along with 27,000 Russians and 45,000 Austrians in the Tyrol and eastern Switzerland. An additional 80,000 Austrians would advance in southern Germany. The Austro-Russian forces would advance to the Franco-Swiss border and drive the French in Italy back to the Alps. Finally, the Austro-Russian force in Switzerland, reinforced by contingents from Italy, would advance into eastern France while the Anglo-Russian army moved south into Belgium. The Allies would then proclaim the Restoration and, aided by royalist rebellions, the Allied armies would advance on Paris.

The French, with 365,000 men under arms, were outnumbered but nevertheless decided to launch a series of offensives designed to disrupt the Coalition while keeping up civilian morale at home. Initially, the Coalition enjoyed resounding success. In March 1799 Archduke Charles Von Hapsburg (q.v.) in Germany defeated Jourdan's army at the Battle of Stockach (q.v.). Jourdan's defeat in turn uncovered Masséna's left flank in Switzerland, forcing him to retreat back to Zurich. In early June Masséna (q.v.) defeated Austrian attacks on Zurich (q.v.), but suffered such heavy casualties that he pulled back to a shorter, more secure position to the west of the city. In Italy, the French attempt to advance across the Adige was hurled back with severe losses. In April the Austrians advanced, seized Rivoli, defeated the French again, and forced them to retreat. The Austro-Russian army then advanced into the Po Valley, took Brescia, and isolated a French garrison in Mantua (q.v.). By late April Coalition forces were in Milan, and within a month the Allies had occupied Turin, and the French fell back to Genoa.

The French then ordered forces in Rome and Naples to move north, unite with units in northern Italy, and mount a counterattack. The French commanders decided to launch a two-pronged assault but failed to coordinate their actions. Troops from Rome and Naples under Macdonald's command took Modena and Parma, but units in the north did not move. The Allied army was, therefore able to defeat the French in the two-day Battle of Trebbia (17–19 June) (q.v.). Remnants of the French force then joined with the forces in Genoa. The French mounted another attack in Piedmont, led by Joubert (q.v.), but the Austro-Russian army on 15 August won another victory at the Battle of Novi (q.v.). The French retreated with heavy losses, including Joubert, and sought to hold a line from Geneva to Genoa. In the north the Anglo-Russian army landed in Holland on 27 August, seized the Dutch fleet, and established a firm bridgehead. Counterrevolutionary risings also began in Brittany, the Vendée (q.v.), and southwestern France. Though not dangerous in and of themselves, the risings tied down thousands of troops desperately needed at the front.

The Coalition appeared victorious, but differences in political objectives came to the fore and disrupted Allied strategy. The Russians favored the restoration of old regime governments in Italy as well as France, a view that put them at odds with their Allies. The Austrians for their part had no intention of uniting Belgium with Holland. Rather, Vienna wanted to seize Belgium for itself and then exchange it for Bavaria while at the same time expanding its holdings in Italy. The original Allied plan required the forces in Germany to protect the right flank of the Russian forces in Switzerland by attacking Basel and Belfort. The presence of Charles's army was especially necessary while the Russians in Italy were moving north to join the Russian contingent around Zurich. Vienna, however, ordered the archduke to move north and invade Belgium in early September *before* the Russian contingents were united. Austro-Russian forces in Switzerland were, therefore, momentarily isolated.

The French government, seizing its fleeting opportunity, rushed reinforcements to Masséna (q.v.) and ordered him to attack as soon as possible. Masséna moved on 25 September, crushed the Russian force at Zurich, drove back the supporting Austrian Corps, and then turned on the Russian units moving north from Italy. The Russians escaped but suffered severe losses. The Russian defeat in turn exposed Charles's army, which in mid-October pulled back from the Rhine into central Germany. Finally, in Holland, French and Batavian forces led by General Brune (q.v.) prevented the Allied army from expanding its foothold, and forced its commander on 18 October to ask for terms. Thus, by the time Napoleon returned from Egypt and participated in the Brumaire Coup, the Directory (q.v.) had already reversed the course of the war.

Russia, feeling betrayed, left the Coalition, and for the 1800 campaign Bonaparte had only the Austrians left in the field. His victory, actually a near-defeat, at Marengo (q.v.) did not drive Austria out of the war, but a subsequent French victory at Hohenlinden (q.v.) in December 1800 convinced Vienna to sue for peace. After the treaty of Luneville (q.v.), Britain was isolated and also began peace talks with France, signing a peace treaty in 1802. As with the First Coalition, the Allies underestimated France and failed to fully coordinate their political goals and strategies. The French, after initial defeats, were thus able to mount effective counterblows and defeat the hostile alliance. (*See also* Zurich, Battle of)

COMMERCE RAIDING. Unable to challenge directly the Royal Navy (q.v.), the French (as they had done in past conflicts) resorted to commerce raiding. Well armed privateers struck at British merchant shipping in the Channel, the Mediterranean, the West Indies, and the Indian Ocean. Raiders were quite effective, seizing on average about 500 ships per year. The British use of the convoy system kept losses from rising even further. French raiders did do some damage to British commerce and drove up maritime insurance rates, but all of the privateering activity accounted for less than 3 percent of British shipping and did not seriously impede Britain's ability to wage war and finance coalitions.

COMMITTEE OF PUBLIC SAFETY (1793–1795). The deposition of the king, creation of a republic, foreign war, the outbreak of counterrevolution, and political factionalism threatened to reduce France to a state of anarchy and open the way for foreign conquest. As a response to the growing crisis, French leaders had to create a strong centralized authority. On 15 August 1792, before dissolving itself, the Legislative Assembly transferred the powers of the deposed monarch to an Executive Council of Ministers. The Council, however, could not function effectively because of the heavy workload borne by individual ministers. Consequently, the National Convention (q.v.) created on 1 January 1793 a Committee of General Defense with 24 members selected from among the elected deputies. The Committee was to assist the ministers and decide on urgent military measures. The Committee, however, was too large and unwieldy to function effectively, and the Committee of General Defense called for the creation of a smaller more efficient Committee.

On 28 March the Convention created a Committee of Public Safety, and on 6 April named the nine deputies who would compose the committee. Between 7 April and 10 July 1793 the Committee sought to reinvigorate the war effort. Gradually, the Convention eliminated socalled moderates and brought onto the Committee deputies from the Montagnard faction, who were above all things concerned with the survival of the Republic and winning the war. By 10 July 1793, the Committee of Public Safety consisted of the twelve deputies, led by

Robespierre (q.v.), who composed what future generations were to call the Great Committee of Public Safety.

The members of the Committee were largely successful middle-class lawyers and businessmen. There were also two army officers, an ex-nobleman, and an actor. They were deputies from the Convention, and their powers were renewed by the Convention each month. Some have viewed the Committee as a group of ideologues willing to use any means to create their vision of a Jacobin Republic. They were, according to this view, essentially abnormal individuals who obtained power in abnormal circumstances. Others have argued that Committee members were essentially normal people forced to cope with the near catastrophic conditions besetting France in the summer of 1793. They had, according to this view, to take extraordinary measures to cope with prevailing conditions. They had to establish a constitutional dictatorship in order to deal effectively with the foreign war and counterrevolution while simultaneously coping with political turbulence within the Republican ranks.

Ironically, most scholars and commentators have focused on the Committee's political and social policies and the Committee's relationship with society's lower classes. A crucial question, however, remains: How did the Committee deal with diplomatic and strategic issues?

Essentially, the Committee moved effectively to nationalize the people and the economy in order to win the war. The Committee created a national army by mobilizing the nation's populace, expanding the army, and abolishing distinctions among regular volunteer and conscript troops. By 1794 the nation had more than 800,000 men under arms. The Committee, despite a belief in a free market economy, established wage, price, import, and export controls to sustain the war effort and provide essential commodities at affordable prices to the lower classes. The Committee found officers to train and lead the new armies and devised a strategy for their employment.

In 1793 the Committee insisted on vigorous offensives on all fronts to halt the progress of counterrevolution and coalition advances. In the winter of 1793 France had gained breathing space. The Committee then noted that Austria and England were the powers most committed to the war, while Prussia was a reluctant partner. Moreover, the Austrian and British armies along with other contingents were located in the Low Countries and northern France, thus posing a more immediate threat to Paris than enemy forces in the Rhineland or along the Alps and Pyrenees. The Committee, therefore, decided that the Republic's main offensive operation in 1794 would take place along a front from the Channel to the Meuse, and directed reinforcements to the Army of the North. The offensive was ultimately successful, which in turn led to the Thermidorian Reaction of 27 July 1794, wherein Robespierre and his closest Allies on the Committee were removed from office and executed. During its time in power the Committee had functioned effectively. The Law of 14 Frimire (4 December 1793) and 12 Germinal (2 April 1794) had centralized power in the Committee's hands by subordinating ministers and local authorities to Committee direction. In its day-to-day operations, Committee members distributed tasks among themselves. Some, like Carnot (q.v.) and Prieur de la Côte d'Or (q.v.), dealt with military matters, others with the navy or provisions or diplomacy. Robespierre may well have been the dominant figure, but responsibility was collective and all served at the pleasure of the Convention.

After Thermidor, the Committee continued to function with limited powers. It confined itself essentially to issues of war and diplomacy, and personnel was changed each month. Nevertheless, the Committee had a number of successes: Holland was overrun, and Prussia and Spain left the war and recognized the Republic. The Convention, meanwhile, had finished writing a new constitution on 22 August 1795, and the Committee disappeared in November. It had, despite its shortcomings, organized the nation for war and enabled the Republic to survive. (*See also* National Convention)

COMPANIES OF JESUS, COMPANIES OF THE SUN. The companies were counterrevolutionary terrorist bands. Companies of Jesus operated in the Lyon area; Companies of the Sun operated in Provence. Both groups were most active in 1795. Motivation of the members was a mixture of anti-Jacobinism and personal vendettas. Ex-Jacobins were the primary targets of the bands, which in part were funded and organized by British and Royalist agents. The bands were ultimately suppressed and never posed a serious military threat, but their very existence indicated the continued existence of counterrevolutionary sentiment in France.

CONDÉ, LOUIS-JOSEPH DE BOURBON PRINCE DE (1736–1818). Condé was a cousin of the king. He was governor of Burgundy and served in the Seven Years' War. He emigrated shortly after 14 July 1789 and soon established a small émigré army in the Rhineland. The army had a staff for a force of 100,000, or close to ten times the actual number of troops. Condé himself had 30 aides de camp. Condé was a consistent supporter of pure royalism, but his army performed few useful functions except to arouse the hostility of the French public. In 1798 Condé took refuge in Russia. His army disbanded after the collapse of the Second Coalition (q.v.), and the prince went to London in 1801, where he remained until the defeat of Napoleon by foreign powers. Condé's military

efforts and political plotting with General Pichegru (q.v.) were all failures, and his actions actually served to strengthen the Republic by demon-
strating to the populace the fate of revolutionary reforms if the Bourbon
princes regained power. (*See also* Counterrevolution)

CONDÉ, SIEGE OF (APRIL–JULY 1793). The Allies in the spring and
summer of 1793 undertook a series of sieges of French fortified cities
on France's northern frontier. The Austrians were less interested in
marching on Paris than in seizing fortresses to strengthen the defense
of Belgium. The Allies blockaded Condé in April. The French were
out of food by July and capitulated on 10 July. The garrison of some
4,200 departed with the honors of war. The French surrendered some
100 guns, and the troops returned to French territory, pledged not to
fight the Allies for one year.

CONVENTION. See NATIONAL CONVENTION

COPENHAGEN, NAVAL BATTLE OF (2 APRIL 1801). The need to
counter the formation of the League of Armed Neutrality (q.v.) of the
North led the British government to order Admiral Hyde Parker
(q.v.), with Vice-Admiral Horatio Nelson (q.v.) as his second-in-
command, to take a fleet of 26 ships of the line, 7 frigates, and 23
smaller craft to the Baltic in March 1801. The fleet anchored off Danish waters while diplomatic efforts to convince the Danes to leave the
League continued. With the failure of the talks, the British fleet moved
into Danish waters outside of Copenhagen, which was protected by 18
ships and a large shore battery.

On 1 April Nelson was given command of a dozen ships of the line to
attack the Danish fleet, while Parker stood guard outside of the harbor.
Nelson, after reconnaissance, attacked on 2 April. A number of ships
went aground in the narrow channels around Copenhagen, and Parker
signaled Nelson to end the action. Nelson, however, placed his telescope
to his blind eye and pretended not to have seen the signal. He pressed on
with his attack and captured the Danish flagship, a dozen other prizes, and
2,000 prisoners. The British lost 941 men, while in addition to prisoners
the Danes lost 790 sailors killed and 900 wounded. With the British fleet
in Copenhagen's harbor, the British resumed negotiations with the Danish government. The Danes, fearing the Russians, still refused to leave
the League, but news of the Tsar's death enabled the Danes to sign a long
armistice with the British, thus effectively destroying the League.

CORNWALLIS, LORD, GENERAL (1738–1805). After being educated
at Eton and Cambridge, Cornwallis, first Marquis and second Earl
Cornwallis joined the army. He fought in Germany during the Seven

Years' War. He was a colonel by 1766 and as a major general fought in the American Revolutionary War, and was captured at Yorktown. In 1786 he was appointed governor-general of India and in 1791–1792 fought a war against Mysore. Cornwallis was successful and concluded a treaty with Tippoo Sultan (q.v.), by which Tippoo gave up half his realm. In 1798 he was appointed viceroy of Ireland (q.v.) and concluded the "pacification" of the island begun by his predecessors. In 1802 he helped negotiate the Peace of Amiens (q.v.), and in 1805 returned to India, where he died.

CORPS D'ARMÉE. The Corps d'Armée was a large, self-contained, combined arms formation consisting of two or more infantry divisions plus cavalry and artillery units. The corps could engage equal or larger numbers of enemy troops for up to a day while reinforcements moved to join them. The Republic relied primarily on divisions but on an ad hoc basis did occasionally employ corps-like formations. Napoleon made the corps a permanent fixture of the Grand Army.

COUNTERREVOLUTION. The violence of the French Revolution was not due primarily to the ideological fanaticism of Republican ideologues. Rather, it was in large measure a result of the strength and determination of the counterrevolution. Counterrevolutionaries did not form a single unified faction. Counterrevolution consisted of a wide variety of groups and individuals with an equally diverse variety of ideologies. They were unified only in their opposition to the Republic. The counterrevolutionary camp included Royalists, constitutional Royalists, peasants motivated by religion and hostility to changes wrought by the Revolution, and Republicans who were defeated in factional fights in Paris and sought to rouse the provinces against the capital.

Overt resistance took a variety of forms. Aristocratic émigrés (q.v.) in Coblenz established their own small army while their leaders called upon foreign governments to invade France and crush the Revolution. Peasant risings in the west of France involved the creation of large armed forces. The peasant rebels, initially motivated by simple hostility to Paris and attachment to their traditional religion and way of life, soon adopted Royalist leaders and ideology. The rebels in the Vendée (q.v.) originally called themselves the Catholic Army and later the Catholic and Royal Army, indicating that royalism was not their initial motive. In 1793 the rebels in the Vendée, Brittany, and Normandy posed a substantial threat to the Republic, which had to devote substantial forces to the region. The Federalist revolt also required major military operations, especially when Federalists in some regions cooperated with Royalists. The Vendée and Brittany were not pacified until 1796, although by 1794 the military threat had been reduced substantially. An attempt by Anglo-royalist forces to rekindle risings in Brittany was defeated at Quiberon Bay (q.v.) in 1795. Individual Royalists who remained in France performed acts of espionage. An agent, for example, informed the British about the destination of Bonaparte's army in 1798. Royalist agents also played a role in the insurrection of 5 October 1795 and attempted to organize another rising in 1797. Secret royalist organizations with secret British financial support also tried to win the elections of 1797 in order to restore the monarchy via a legal coup d'etat. The Directory (q.v.) in turn executed a military-backed coup against royalist deputies. In 1799 there were new military risings in the Vendée and around Toulouse. The risings were coordinated with the military campaigns of the Second Coalition, but the Royalists failed to act simultaneously, and Republican forces defeated them.

Revolts also took place in a number of satellite republics. Peasant risings in Rome and Naples were particularly effective in 1798 and 1799.

The most effective counterrevolutionary risings were spontaneous peasant rebellions, which became Royalist after the fact, but they did provide a basis of mass popular support for counterrevolution in a number of regions. Royalism by 1799 was, however, unsuccessful. Republican forces defeated Royalist risings, and royalism would triumph in France only because of the ultimate victory of foreign armies. Nevertheless, counterrevolutionaries were fairly powerful, especially in the west of France, and the forces opposed to the Republic, though divided, were nonetheless significant. The Republic had to devote substantial resources to check them.

CUIRASSIERS. Cuirassiers were a type of heavy cavalry. Troopers wore breastplates and helmets and were armed with swords and pistols. A regiment contained about 1,000 men divided into four squadrons. Their role in battle was shock action. Carabinier regiments performed a similar role. Their weapons and equipment did not differ from cuirassier units.

CUSTINE, ADAM-PHILIPPE COMTE DE, GENERAL (1740–1793). Born to an aristocratic family, Custine joined the Royal Army and served in the Seven Years' War. He then served with the French army in America and on his return was promoted to major-general. He supported the Revolution and in 1792 was appointed to command in the Army of the Rhine. After Valmy (q.v.), Custine launched a successful offensive into the Rhineland, seizing Mainz on 21 October 1792 and Frankfurt on 23 October. In March 1793 a renewed Coalition offensive forced him to retreat after leaving behind a large garrison in Mainz. After Dumouriez (q.v.) defected, he was given command of the Army of the North. Custine did an excellent job of restoring discipline and improving training in the Army of the North, which had been badly shaken by its earlier defeats. Because of his imperious command style, he was, however, unable to cooperate effectively with civilian authorities, and after the loss of the fortress of Condé (q.v.) in July 1793, he was recalled to Paris. Further defeats, including the fall of Mainz sealed his fate. He was brought to trial for treason and executed on 28 August 1793. Custine was innocent of the charges brought against him and perished because the government believed it necessary to demonstrate to the public and the officer corps alike that military men were the servants not the leaders of the Republic.

-D-

DAENDELS, HERMAN-WILLHEM, GENERAL (1762–1818). An attorney by profession, Daendels joined forces with groups opposed to the stadtholder in 1787, and was banished. He went to France and in 1793 joined the French army. He participated in operations in the Low Countries and was promoted to lieutenant general. After 1795, he served in the Batavian army and played an important role in the Helder Campaign of 1799. He later served Louis Bonaparte as governor of the East Indies. After Napoleon annexed Holland, Daendels returned to Europe and fought in the Russian Campaign. He was forced to surrender at Modlin. After 1814, he served the House of Orange as a colonial governor until his death.

DALLEMAGNE, CLAUDE, GENERAL (1754–1813). Dallemagne joined the Royal Army in 1773, served in America, and rose to the rank of sergeant major by 1786. He was commissioned in 1791 and in 1793 commanded grenadiers before Toulan (q.v.). He fought in Italy from 1794 to 1797, fighting at Lodi (q.v.) and Mantua (q.v.). He became a division commander in 1796 and served with the Army of Rome in 1798. In 1799 he removed himself from the active list and formally retired in 1802.

DANTON, GEORGES-JACQUES (1759–1794). Danton was born in Champagne. In 1780 he went to Paris as a lawyer's clerk and married, and his father-in-law purchased for him the post of advocate to the royal councils. During the early days of the Revolution, Danton came to national attention through Parisian politics. A remarkable orator, he was in 1790 elected to the Paris Commune. He opposed the war but played a significant role in the insurrection of 10 August 1792, which deposed the king, and became minister of justice in the new provisional government. Because of his vibrant personality and popularity with the Parisian populace, he was the dominant figure in the government and as such made his greatest contribution to the nation.

Coalition (q.v.) forces were advancing, and most members of the Provisional Executive Council wanted to abandon Paris and move south of the Loire River. Danton understood that Paris was the heart of the Revolution and that the loss of the city would doom the revolution. He therefore insisted that the French continue to resist in the eastern departments and defend Paris at all costs. On 2 September, the day Verdun fell to the Prussians, Danton appeared before the Assembly, where he delivered an impassioned oration calling upon the deputies to mobilize the nation for a massive effort at self-salvation. His concluding words "boldness, boldness, always boldness and France is saved" have become one of the most famous lines in French history.

The government in fact agreed to stand and fight, an essential preliminary to the Battle of Valmy (q.v.). Danton was then elected as a deputy to the National Convention (q.v.) and in March 1793 became a member of the Committee of Public Safety (q.v.). The war, however, continued to go badly, and he was removed from the Committee in July. He soon fell afoul of Robespierre (q.v.) and his Allies. Danton's shady financial contacts, secret dealings before 1792 with the court, the Orleanists, and émigrés (q.v.), and his later dealings with Dumouriez (q.v.) made the Committee suspicious of him. His willingness to engage in secret diplomacy with the Coalition deepened their suspicion. In 1794 he was arrested and executed. Opinion remains divided over Danton. Some see him as a simple opportunist. Others view him as a self-aggrandizing twister. Such judgments are essentially personal and political. What cannot be denied, however, is the crucial role he played in the summer of 1792.

DAVIDOVITCH, PAUL VON, BARON, GENERAL (FL. 1796). Davidovich was an assistant to Würmser (q.v.) during Bonaparte's Italian Campaign. He was an experienced soldier who performed well but was unable to defeat Bonaparte (q.v.) or his subordinates.

DAVOUT, LOUIS-NICHOLAS, GENERAL (1770–1823). Davout was of noble descent, the son of a cavalry officer. He was commissioned in his father's regiment in 1788, and welcomed the Revolution, but his democratic sympathies soon got him arrested in 1791. In the same year he joined the volunteers and was elected lieutenant colonel of a battalion. He fought at Neerwinden (q.v.) and tried to arrest Dumouriez (q.v.) when the general betrayed the Revolution. Davout became a general of brigade in July 1793, but resigned when the government decreed that ex-noblemen could not serve in the field. He returned to service in October 1794, fighting primarily in Germany in 1795, 1796, and 1797. He next served with the Army of the Orient. After 1800, he continued to serve Napoleon, becoming a marshal in

1804. He became one of Napoleon's best commanders, one of the few able to exercise a major independent command, although Napoleon, always reluctant to create potential rivals, never allowed Davout to exercise important initiatives. Nevertheless, in 1806 his corps of 26,000 men defeated over 60,000 Prussians at Auerstadt. Davout was a consummate professional and never suffered fools gladly—a formidable leader of men.

DEGO, BATTLE OF (14–15 APRIL 1796). After his initial victory, Bonaparte (q.v.) pursued the Piedmontese army, leaving Masséna (q.v.) to hold off the Austrians who were near Dego. Masséna attacked and took Dego on 14 April. An Austrian counterattack retook the town the next day. Bonaparte then returned with reinforcements and drove back the Austrians. With his right flank secure, he resumed his pursuit of the Piedmontese.

DELABORDE, HENRI FRANÇOIS, GENERAL (1764–1833). Delaborde joined the Royal Army in 1783. He supported the Revolution and was a general of division by 1793. He fought at Toulon (q.v.), in the Pyrenees, and in Germany. After 1799, he fought in Spain and Russia and was badly wounded in the 1813 campaign. Delaborde rallied to Napoleon in 1815, and after Waterloo retired into private life.

DELMAS, ANTOINE GUILLAUME, GENERAL (1766–1813). Delmas was first commissioned in 1784 but was dismissed for insubordination in 1788. In 1791 he was a lieutenant colonel of volunteers and by 1793 was a general of division. He campaigned in Germany and Italy. His irreligious attitudes led to his dismissal in 1802. Recalled in 1813, he was severely wounded at Leipzig and died of wounds shortly afterwards.

DEMI-BRIGADE, CAVALRY. In the French army, cavalry demi-brigades contained about 900 men divided into four squadrons of two troops each. In truth, cavalry units on campaign were usually understrength. Cavalry was broadly divided into heavy and light cavalry: one for shock action and the other for patrols, reconnaissance, and screening activities. In practice, heavy and light units acted interchangeably.

DEMI-BRIGADE, INFANTRY. The demi-brigade was an infantry formation consisting of three battalions. Originally, two demi- or half-brigades were to form a brigade and two brigades a division. In practice, however, a division usually consisted of three demi-brigades. Half-brigades were to contain 2,437 men and six light guns. By the fall of 1793 there were 198 demi-brigades and 14 light demi-brigades.

Light half-brigades employed the same tactics as the line demi-brigades. They were smaller and in theory could move more rapidly. In early 1796 the government reduced the number of demi-brigades to 110 line and 38 light units in order to combine units that had suffered heavy casualties with stronger formations. In 1803 Napoleon restored the old term "regiment" to designate a three-battalion infantry formation.

DESAIX DE VEYGOUX, LOUIS-CHARLES-ANTOINE, GENERAL (1768–1800). Desaix was one of the Republic's better generals. Of noble birth, he supported the Revolution, remained in the army, and became a general of brigade in 1793. He was promoted to general of division in 1795 and fought with the Army of the Rhine and Moselle in 1796–1797. Sent to the Army of Italy in 1798, he accompanied Bonaparte and the Army of the Orient to Egypt and successfully pacified Upper Egypt. In the Marengo (q. v.) Campaign of 1800, Bonaparte sent Desaix to block the presumed Austrian line of retreat. The Austrians, however, unexpectedly attacked and defeated the main French force. Hearing the sounds of fighting, Desaix hastened to the battle with reinforcements. His arrival enabled Bonaparte (q.v.) to counterattack, thus transforming defeat into a victory. Desaix, however, was killed during the battle. Desaix had thus enabled Napoleon to win a crucial victory although Bonaparte never fully recognized his general's contribution. (*See also* Marengo, Battle of)

DEVIL'S BRIDGE, BATTLE OF (24 SEPTEMBER 1799). In his march north to reinforce the Russian Corps at Zurich (q.v.), Suvorov (q.v.) forced the St. Gothard Pass. A French division commanded by General Lecourbe (q.v.) then took up positions at the Devil's Bridge, which spanned the Reuss River. Suvorov launched a series of costly frontal attacks and mounted a flanking movement, which finally forced Lecourbe to retreat and await reinforcements. Elements of Soult's division arrived on 28 September and Suvorov had no choice but to retreat northeast towards Germany.

DIERSHEIM, BATTLE OF (21 APRIL 1797). Moreau's (q.v.) army crossed to the right bank of the Rhine on 20 April 1797. On 21 April 14,000 Austrians counterattacked, but after hard fighting around the village of Diersheim, troops led primarily by Desaix (q.v.) and Vandamme (q.v.) defeated the Austrians. Both sides lost about 3,000 men, but the French had firmly established themselves on the right bank and launched a vigorous pursuit, supported by Hoche's (q.v.) Army of the Sambre-Meuse, which had crossed the Rhine on 18 April. News of the Leoben Armistice (q.v.) halted further operations.

DILLON, ARTHUR COMTE DE, GENERAL (1750–1794). Of Irish birth, Dillon became colonel of the family regiment in the French army in 1767. During the American Revolutionary War, Dillon served in North America and the West Indies. In April 1792 he was a lieutenant general, serving with the Army of the North. In 1793 he wrote a letter to a German prince encouraging him to withdraw into Germany. He was denounced for treason, arrested, tried, and executed in 1794.

DILLON, THEOBALD COMTE DE, GENERAL (1746–1792). Dillon was born in Dublin. He joined the French army at age 15, serving in the Dillon Regiment. He was promoted captain in 1778 and served briefly in America. In 1787 he assumed command of the family regiment. Although most of his family emigrated, he remained in the army, becoming a major-general in 1791. On 28 April 1792 Dillon led his troops into Belgium. The appearance of Austrian troops led him to order a retreat, which soon degenerated into a panicked rout. Dillon, attempting to rally his men, was shot and killed by one of his own soldiers.

DIRECTORY (1795–1799). The Directory was the five-member executive created by the Constitution of the year III (1795). Directors were elected by the actions of the Council of Ancients and Council of Five Hundred. The Directory inherited a situation of financial collapse, political schism, and foreign war. Seeking to promote a moderate political system based on republican principles, the Directory was in the unfortunate position of being viewed as an essentially temporary regime by large factions, perhaps even a majority, of the French people. Absolute monarchists, constitutional Royalists, former Jacobins (q.v.), and even proto-socialists all viewed the regime as essentially illegitimate and temporary. Consequently, the government frequently had to resort to unconstitutional means to preserve constitutional Republicanism.

Royalist electoral victories in 1797 were annulled in September (the Fructidor Coup) when the Directors, using the army arrested and deported 53 deputies and voided the electoral results in 49 departments. In May 1798 (the Floreal Coup) the Directory, without using the army, deprived 127 Jacobin deputies of their seats. In June 1799 (the Prairial Coup) the legislature in effect retaliated against the Directors by forcing several of them out of office. Finally, the Brumaire Coup (November 1799), engineered by several Directors who wanted to create a more effective conservative constitution, gave Bonaparte (q.v.) his opportunity. He was to have been the sword of the plotters but outmaneuvered them to seize power for himself.

Despite its ultimate failure, the Directory did have a number of accomplishments to its credit, including a return to a metallic currency, a reorganization and rationalization of the tax structure, and success in war. The First Coalition (q.v.) was defeated in 1797 and the second in 1799. The Directory was never able to defeat Britain, but neither was Napoleon, the Kaiser, or Hitler. The Directory was never successful at sea—nor was Napoleon. Strategic blunders did lead to the creation of the Second Coalition, but by the time Napoleon seized power the Coalition was on the verge of dissolution and was strategically on the defensive. The Directory, therefore, probably deserves a somewhat better reputation than it has enjoyed. (*See also* Coalition, Second)

DIVISION. By the later 18th century the Royal Army had divided France into 18 military divisions. These were territorial commands with permanent garrisons. Inspector generals could conduct combined arms maneuvers. It was the Republic that created combat divisions—a combined arms field formation. In 1792 some army commanders created a unit with two brigades under a single officer, but these formations had no organic artillery or cavalry elements. Other generals continued to regard the brigade as the largest subunit of a field army. The Decree of 21 February 1793 merging regular and volunteer battalions also created a two-brigade division consisting only of infantry. Divisional commanders, however, began to obtain organic artillery and cavalry elements.

Divisional strength varied. By 1794 a division might contain from two to four half-brigades with troop strength ranging from 7,800 to 13,400 men. Some divisions had no artillery while others had as many as a dozen field guns. The post-1794 division usually had three half-brigades, although the number of cannon and horsemen continued to vary widely. Divisions were generally known by the name of their commanders. A division commanded by General Lannes (q.v.), for example, would be officially known as Division Lannes. Despite the absence of uniformity, the multiarm combat division strengthened the French army. A division could march and fight on its own or as part of a larger force. An army could, therefore, move by separate routes thereby speeding movements and concentrate for battle just before or even during an engagement. Generals could, therefore, wage encounter battles or begin a battle and feed troops into the fighting according to specific tactical circumstances.

DJEZZAR, PASHA (1735–1804). A Bosnian Christian by birth, Djezzar fled to Cairo after a murder, converted to Islam, and became an executioner and killer for one of the Mameluke Beys (q.v.). He earned the name "the Butcher" for his activities. He later went to Syria, where the sultan appointed him governor of Acre. He commanded the city during the French siege, thereby inflicting one of the first defeats suffered by Bonaparte (q.v.).

DOMBROWSKI, JEAN HENRI (1755–1818). Dombrowski first served in the Saxon army. He joined the Polish army in 1791. He moved to France in 1795 and raised a Polish legion from émigrés (q.v.) that because of a French law prohibiting the use of foreign troops in the French army served in the Cisalpine Army. He fought in the 1799 campaign in Italy and served at Novi (q.v.). Under Napoleon, Dombrowski served in the Army of the Grand Duchy of Warsaw. After 1815, he returned to Poland and retired into private life in 1816.

DOMMARTIN, ELZÉAR AUGUSTE, GENERAL (1766–1799). Dommartin joined the royal artillery in 1785 and in 1793 served at Toulon (q.v.). He was promoted to general of brigade. He served in Italy from 1795 to 1797. He became the artillery commander of the Army of the Rhine in 1797 and of the Army of the Orient in 1798. Dommartin fought at the sieges of El Arish (q.v.) and Acre (q.v.). In 1799 he died of wounds received in an ambush.

DONZELOT, FRANÇOIS XAVIER, GENERAL (1764–1843). Donzelot joined the army in 1783 and was commissioned in 1792. He served in Belgium and the Rhineland, and in 1798 sailed to Egypt. He fought in numerous engagements but in June 1801 had to sign the surrender of Cairo to the British. After his return to France, Donzelot served primarily in the Ionian Islands. In 1815 he led a division at Waterloo but was later reconciled to the Bourbons. He retired after being governor of Martinique from 1817–1828.

DOUBLE COMPANY COLUMN BY DIVISION. The Double Company Column by Division was the standard battlefield maneuver formation for a nine-company battalion. The battalion would typically enter an engagement with one company deployed as skirmishers. The other companies would deploy in a formation two companies wide and four companies deep. Each company would in turn be organized in three ranks. The pairs of companies were called divisions. Thus, the column was really a rectangle 80 men across by 12 ranks deep. This formation was highly flexible and gave commanders many tactical options. A commander could order additional pairs of companies to reinforce the skirmishers. He could even order the entire battalion into action as light infantry. Alternately, he could deploy his battalion into a three-rank line for fire action or direct the troops in column to launch a bayonet charge. The precise tactical forms were in fact left to the commander, who was expected to employ his troops in the manner best suited to specific conditions. Moreover, soldiers gradually learned to shift from one formation to another while in action thereby enhancing the flexibility and battle capabilities of the battalion. (*See also* Infantry)

DRAGOONS. Dragoons were originally mounted infantry. By the late 18th century, dragoon regiments were essentially line cavalry. Armed with a sword, musket, and pistols, dragoons performed numerous functions including shock action, patrolling, raiding, and guarding the main army flanks and lines of communication. A dragoon regiment contained officially about 1,200 men, but, in practice, in all armies units were rarely up to strength after a few months of active campaigning.

DUBOIS-CRANCÉ, EDMOND-LOUIS-ALEXIS (1747–1809). The son of an intendant, Dubois-Crancé was born in Charleville, joined the army at age 15, and left ten years later. He supported the Revolution and was elected to the National Convention, where he voted for the death of the king. His main concern, however, was military affairs. He advocated national conscription and was the leading figure in the creation of the Amalgamation (q.v.). He also directed the siege of Lyon. After Thermidor, he sat in the Council of Five Hundred, was Inspector General of the Army of the Rhine, and became War Minister in September 1799. Dubois-Crancé was one of the political figures who saw the possibility of striking in Switzerland, and reinforced Masséna's (q.v.) Army of Helvetia. He was unable to do anything about Bonaparte's coup and retired in 1801.

DUGOMMIER, JACQUES COQUILLE, GENERAL (1738–1794). Dugommier was commissioned in 1757 and spent most of the Seven Years' War in the West Indies. He left the army in 1782. He returned to France in 1791, rejoined the army and in 1793 was promoted general of division. He was in command of the siege of Toulon and then transferred to the Army of the Western Pyrenees, where he was killed in action.

DUMONCEAU, JEAN-BAPTISTE, GENERAL (1760–1821). Born in Brussels, Dumonceau became an architect. He took part in an insurrection against Austrian rule in 1788 and fled to France. In 1792 he joined the French army and, with other Belgium volunteers, fought at Jemappes (q.v.). In 1794, as a general of brigade, he fought in the Low Countries. In 1795 Dumonceau became a lieutenant general in the Batavian Army and fought effectively in the Helder Campaign of 1799. In 1807 he became a marshal in the Kingdom of Holland and in 1809 helped defeat a British expedition to Walcheren Island. He fought in Germany in 1813 and was captured at Dresden. He accepted the restoration of the House of Orange and remained in military service until his death.

DUMOURIEZ, CHARLES-FRANÇOIS DU PERIER (1739–1823). Dumouriez was born into an aristocratic family: his father was a war commissioner. He joined the army in 1758. After the Seven Years'

War, where he was wounded and taken prisoner, he undertook a number of secret diplomatic missions for the government in Corsica, Poland, and Sweden. By 1788 Dumouriez was a major general. The Revolution presented his adventurous spirit with many opportunities. In his eyes the Revolution was not so much a matter of political reform as it was a career opportunity. As a lieutenant general in 1792, as well as minister of war, he favored war with Austria and advocated an invasion of Belgium. The French collapse in the opening campaign led to his appointment as commander of the Army of the North. He led his forces to join Kellermann's Army of the Center and played a significant role at Valmy (q.v.). After the Prussians retreated, he invaded Belgium again, winning the Battle of Jemappes (q.v.) and conquering most of the province.

Dumouriez planned to create a separate Belgian state with himself as its ruler. In March 1793, however, the Austrians counterattacked and defeated Dumouriez at Neerwinden (q.v.). After the battle, Dumouriez began negotiations with the Austrians, who agreed not to pursue his retreating army. In return, Dumouriez agreed to lead his army in a march on Paris, overthrow the Convention, and restore the monarchy. Dumouriez would then become the regent for the young Louis XVII. Already suspicious, the Convention sent the war minister to investigate his activities. Dumouriez arrested the minister and his aides, but his army refused to follow him on the path of counterrevolution, and on 5 April he fled to the Austrian lines.

After his treason, he travelled widely but received no welcome anywhere. The British government hired him as an advisor but never took him very seriously. After 1815, the Bourbons refused to provide him with wealth and honors, and he lived out his days in England. A modern-day Alcibiades, his own career was paramount. He lacked the charm and charisma of the original, but did survive the turmoil of his times.

DUNCAN, ADAM, ADMIRAL (1731–1804). Duncan joined the British Navy in 1755 and became an admiral in 1795. Until 1801, he was commander-in-chief of Royal naval forces in the North Sea. After the British mutinies (q.v.) of 1797, he restored order in the fleet and defeated the Dutch at Camperdown (q.v.).

DUNDAS, DAVID, GENERAL (1735–1820). Having been an artillery officer, Dundas switched to the infantry in 1756. During the Seven Years' War, he served in attacks on several French ports and Cuba. By 1790 he was a major general. He wrote a series of drill books for the army. The drill books were noted for their Prussian-style insistence on precision close-order drill. In 1799, as a lieutenant general, he served in the Batavian invasion campaign.

DUNDAS HENRY, FIRST VISCOUNT MELVILLE (1742–1811). Dundas served in Pitt's cabinet as home secretary from 1791–1794 and as secretary of war from 1794–1801. He was one of the few cabinet members to assume that in 1798 the Toulon fleet was going to Egypt. He informed Nelson (q.v.) of his views and was instrumental in convincing Pitt (q.v.) to send a fleet into the Mediterranean for the first time since 1796. In 1801 he was the leading advocate of the British invasion of Egypt. In 1806 he was impeached for negligence but was restored to the Privy Council in 1807.

DURUTTE, PIERRE FRANÇOIS JOSEPH, GENERAL (1767–1827). Durutte joined the army in 1792. He fought at Jemappes (q.v.) and in Germany. In 1799 he fought at Bergen (q.v.) and in 1800 at Hohenlinden (q.v.). Later, under Napoleon, he fought in Germany and Russia. He was wounded at Waterloo and retired.

-E-

EGMONT, BATTLE OF (2 OCTOBER 1799). Having failed to break the Franco-Batavian right in Helder Peninsula, the Allies decided to attack General Brune's left. British troops were to seize Egmont supported by the Russians. In bitter fighting, the French and Dutch held Egmont, but Russian troops managed to cut the road linking Egmont and Bergen. Consequently, on the evening of 2 October, Brune (q.v.) fell back to a strong position further south. The Allies were, therefore, still contained in the Helder.

EGYPTIAN EXPEDITION (1798–1801). Late in 1797, only Britain remained at war with France. The Directory (q.v.) wanted to force Great Britain to sue for peace before Continental powers resumed hostilities. France had three strategic options: a direct invasion of Britain, an expedition to Ireland (q.v.), or an attack on British trade in India via Egypt.

Initially, the Directory sought to invade England, but soon concluded that France lacked the naval and transport assets to attempt the risky but potentially decisive cross-Channel venture. Aiding Irish rebels and then using Ireland as a pawn in negotiations with London was never seriously considered. This left an invasion of Egypt as the most acceptable option. An Ottoman province actually controlled by local Mameluke rulers, Egypt appeared easy to take. The absence of a British fleet in the Mediterranean since Spain became a French ally in 1796 gave the French confidence that troops could be safely transported to Egypt. Once ensconced in Egypt, the French were to develop the area and send forces to French-controlled islands in the Indian Ocean, from which location they would move to India and in conjunction with the Sultan of Mysore attack British holdings in India.

On 19 May 1798, the Army of the Orient, 35,000 men strong led by Napoleon Bonaparte (q.v.), sailed from Toulon and other French and Italian ports. After capturing Malta (q.v.) on 11–12 June, the fleet reached Alexandria on 30 June. The French quickly took the city and moved on Cairo. After defeating the Mameluke army on 21 July, the French took the city the next day. Bonaparte immediately began to organize a government, including the establishment of a research institute and printing presses. Bonaparte also undertook talks with Moslem clerics about the possibility of converting his army to Islam, but this and other efforts to win popular support failed to win the loyalty of the populace.

The British naval riposte into the Mediterranean and the Battle of the Nile (q.v.) isolated his army from resupply and reinforcement from the Metropole. Thus, if Bonaparte's position in Egypt was secure, his broader mission had reached a strategic impasse. Bonaparte, therefore, decided to attempt an overland invasion of India. Following in the footsteps of Alexander the Great, he planned to march through Syria to the Euphrates and from there to Persia and India, rallying the populace of these areas to his cause.

Whether the plan was feasible or not, Bonaparte initially made substantial progress until he reached Acre (q.v.) on 20 March 1799. He besieged the city for two months but failed to dislodge the defenders. Defeated, he returned to Egypt, crushed a Turkish army at Aboukir (q.v.), and on 23 August sailed for France, leaving his army behind.

After a failed effort to negotiate an evacuation of Egypt, the Army of the Orient held out until forced to capitulate in 1801. Bonaparte brought with him on the expedition over 150 scientists, one of whom had told the British the destination of the Army of the Orient. The British ignored this information. The scientists, who among other achievements found the Rosetta Stone, founded modern Egyptology. Furthermore, it was not the French who used the Sphinx for target practice and damaged the statue's nose. The Mamelukes (q.v.) had already done this.

EL ARISH, CONVENTION OF (28 JANUARY 1801). After Bonaparte's departure from Egypt, Kléber (q.v.), his successor, and Sir William Sydney Smith (q.v.), commander of British naval forces in the eastern Mediterranean, opened negotiations for the departure of the Army of the Orient from Egypt. On 28 January an agreement that French troops would be sent back to France on Turkish ships was signed, but the British government repudiated it.

EL ARISH, SIEGE OF (8–19 FEBRUARY 1799). Bonaparte (q.v.), while marching to Syria, encountered the fort of El Arish near the border of Egypt and Palestine held by 2,300 men. He had to bring up his artillery and unleash a massive bombardment after which 900 survivors capitulated; most were paroled. Though not particularly vigorous in its defensive efforts, the garrison had delayed the French advance for eleven days.

ELBÉE, MAURICE-JOSEPH, GIGOST (1752–1794). Elbée was born in Dresden, where his father was serving in the Saxon army. He too joined the Saxon army, and then the French army. He left the army in 1783 and returned to his family estate in Poitou. In 1791 Elbée began to conspire against the Revolution with other nobles and émigrés (q.v.), but had little to do with the spontaneous revolt of the Vendée. The rebels did offer him command of a local band, which he accepted. He was an able leader and won several engagements, thus enhancing his reputation. On 19 July, after Cathelineau's death in battle, he was made general in chief. He could not withstand the renewed Republican offensive and was seriously wounded at Cholet on 17 October 1793. On 3 January 1794, the Republicans captured him and shot him.

ÉMIGRÉS. Between 1789 and 1814 about 150,000 people fled France, most of them during the period 1789 to 1794. Only about 60,000 were outside of France at any one time. Nobles made up 17 percent of the émigrés—about a quarter of the pre-1789 nobility. About 25 percent of the émigrés were clergy, or about 17 percent of the Catholic clerics in France. The remaining émigrés were from the Third Estate (less than 2 percent of that order). The aristocratic émigrés posed the greatest danger to the Republic. They called upon foreign powers to make war on France, formed émigré armies, and attempted to ignite revolts, or direct those that broke out spontaneously against the government. The émigrés were unsuccessful in their efforts to destroy the Revolution, but when their activities meshed with internal revolts and foreign invasion, they did pose a serious threat. Ironically, their efforts stiffened the resolve of those who supported the Revolution and added to the bitterness that characterized the campaigns against the internal counterrevolution. (*See also* Counterrevolution)

ENGEN, BATTLE OF (3 MAY 1800). Fought as part of the Stockach battle (q.v.), 40,000 Austrians attacked Moreau's army at Engen in Baden. The Austrians were repulsed, losing 7,000 men while the French lost 2,000. Success at Engen and Stockach forced the Austrians to retire on Ulm.

ERBACH, BATTLE OF (16 MAY 1800). Advancing through southern Germany, 15,000 French encountered 36,000 Austrian troops, who attacked in an effort to halt Moreau's (q.v.) advance. The French, though outnumbered, managed to hold until reinforcements arrived, and repulsed the Austrian attacks. The Austrians then continued their retreat.

-F-

FAMARS (23 MAY 1793). As part of the Allied invasion of northern France, Saxe-Coburg (q.v.) decided to attack the French at Famars so that he might besiege Valenciennes without interference. Advancing in six columns, a combined Austrian, British, and Hanoverian force moved forward, and the French retreated with minimal resistance. The French Commander, Custine (q.v.), was arrested and executed for his failure to offer stout resistance, although it is doubtful that the ill-trained levies could have halted the Allies.

FEDERALIST REVOLTS (1793). A split within the Republican camp led to a purge of the Convention on 31 May–2 June, 1793. The Mountain, Jacobins (q.v.) in alliance with the populace of Paris, drove their opponents from the Convention. Many were arrested. Others escaped and returned to their home districts, where they participated in a widespread rebellion involving more than 60 departments. Occurring simultaneously with Royalist revolts, the Federalist rebellion contributed to the crisis of 1793.

Federalism, however, posed less of a threat than royalism. The Federalists, as Republicans, seemed unwilling or were unable to wage a major war against Paris. Federalist armies were small. They were raised locally and with few exceptions there was little coordination among various Federalist forces. Jacobin leaders usually treated Federalists leniently when revolts collapsed. In Normandy and Brittany, for example, Federalists formed a departmental guard that broke and fled after a brief skirmish with government forces in late June. The revolt collapsed, but there were few subsequent arrests. Bordeaux also rebelled, but when the Convention passed a constitution, the revolt collapsed with almost no violence, and the city submitted to Parisian authority in September.

The most serious rebellions occurred in Lyon, Marseilles, and Toulon. In Lyon, numerous local Royalists joined the armed forces raised by Lyon. The result was a siege lasting from 8 August to 9 October. The city suffered great damage from prolonged bombardment, and after the capitulation, over 2,000 people were executed as rebels. At Marseilles, local forces began resistance on 12 June and briefly took Avignon. Government forces retook Avignon and laid siege to

Marseilles. The British offered aid if Marseilles would swear allegiance to Louis XVII, but the local government refused and began to fight with local Royalists. The internal fighting lasted until the government retook the city on 25 August. Toulon accepted British conditions and foreign troops. Thus, the Federalist revolt was transformed into a Royalist one. Sustained by British and Spanish ships and men, Toulon held out until December. The Federalist rebellions were not in and of themselves very serious military efforts, but inadvertently gave help to the forces of counterrevolution.

FERDINAND IV, KING OF NAPLES (1751–1825). Ferdinand ascended to the throne in 1767. He was married to Marie Caroline, a daughter of Maria Theresa of Austria. In 1793 he joined the First Coalition (q.v.). He was unsuccessful, but in 1798 he invaded Rome. The French rapidly defeated him, and he fled to Sicily. He recovered his mainland holdings during the War of the Second Coalition (q.v.) but had to make peace with France in 1801. In 1806 the French occupied Naples again, and Ferdinand again fled to Sicily. His restoration came as a result of the Allied defeat of Napoleon. A bigoted despot, his death in 1825 came as a relief to his subjects.

FIELD ARMIES, FRENCH REPUBLIC. The number of armies in the field varied as did their size. At one point there were 12 field armies. Armies were created and disbanded according to circumstances at particular moments. The average number of armies was ten. A field army could contain as few as 20,000 men. Alternatively, a field army could have over 100,000 men under arms. Field armies were named after the areas in which they operated. In 1794, for example, field armies included: The armies of the Sambre-Meuse, North, Moselle, Ardennes, Italy, Coast of Brest, Alps, Cherbourg, West, East Pyrenees, and West Pyrenees. The war minister in 1794 reported that, including garrisons, National Guards, and others not present for active service, there was a grand total of 1,108,000 men under arms, of whom over 800,000 were in the field—a dramatic increase over 316,000 reported in February 1793. By 1798 numbers had fallen to 387,000, not including forces in Egypt. The sporadic use of the *leveé* and the introduction of the draft law in 1798, however, gave the government the means to raise and maintain adequate numbers of soldiers. After the emergency of 1793–1794, the Republic generally kept between 350,000 to 450,000 men under arms.

FIRST OF JUNE, NAVAL BATTLE (29 MAY–1 JUNE 1794). Known as the Glorious First of June, the first major naval battle of the Revolutionary and Napoleonic wars involved a British fleet under the 69-year-old Admiral Lord Howe (q.v.) with a fleet of 26 ships of the line and a French fleet of equal strength led by Admiral Villaret de Joyeuse (q.v.), who was escorting a grain fleet of 130 ships from the United States into Brest. The fighting took place about 400 miles west of Ushant. In preliminary skirmishes on 28 May the French lost four ships. In the main engagement on 1 June, a melée, the French lost seven more ships. One was sunk and six captured. The grain fleet reached France safely, but the battle was a significant tactical victory for the Royal Navy.

FISHGUARD (24 FEBRUARY 1797). On the night of 22 February the French landed a small force, led by an American adventurer, in Fishguard, Wales. Militia and volunteers forced the expedition to surrender without a fight. Despite its failure, the "invasion" caused panic in England. There was a run on the banks, and the Bank of England even suspended specie payments.

FLEURS, BATTLE OF (26 JUNE 1794). In the spring of 1794 the French attacked along a line stretching from Flanders to the Meuse. The victory at Tourcoing (q.v.) had forced the Allies to shift reserves to the west, and the French then struck in the east crossing the Sambre River on 11 May only to be beaten back two days later. Several more crossings were also beaten back, but they forced the Allies to commit vital reserves, thereby allowing the French to advance in Flanders and take Ypres on 17 June.

The French then organized another offensive on the Sambre. General Jourdan (q.v.) received command of the right wing of the Army of the North, the Army of the Ardennes, and the Army of the Moselle. Designated the Army of the Sambre-Meuse, Jourdan led a force of some 75,000 men. After a setback on 16 June, his force crossed the Sambre on 18 June, marched on Charleroi, and invested the city in order to draw the Austrians into a major battle. Some 52,000 Austrian and Dutch troops marched to the relief of Charleroi, which capitulated on 25 June. The Austrians, nevertheless, attacked on 26 June in an effort to regain the city.

The French took up a semicircular position in front of Charleroi with their line of battle passing in front of the village of Fleurs. The Austrians advanced in five columns and broke the French center. Jourdan's artillery held up the Austrians, and Jourdan sent in reinforcements. A French division on the right broke, but its neighboring formation shifted troops to cover the open flank, and Jourdan sent reinforcements to halt the Austrian advance. By evening the Austrian thrusts had been beaten back. The French lost 7,000 and the Austrians 10,000 men, and the exhausted Austrians had to retreat, exposing Belgium to a second French conquest. Brussels fell to the French on 10 July, and before the year's end all of Belgium was in French hands.

FRANCIS II, EMPEROR OF GERMANY (1768–1835). Coming to the throne after the death of Leopold II in 1792, Francis changed Austrian policy from one of intimidation—designed to avoid war and help Louis XVI (q.v.) retain his throne—to one of threats and (if necessary) war to destroy the Revolution. Unlike his predecessor, who had a certain amount of sympathy for reform, Francis despised the Revolution and sought to crush it. He received encouragement from French émigrés (q.v.) and Louis and his queen, both of whom hoped that foreign armies would restore their power. Austrian statesman also hoped to make substantial territorial gains in any war against France.

FREDERICK WILLIAM II, KING OF PRUSSIA (1744–1797). Frederick William succeeded his uncle Frederick II as King of Prussia in 1786. A religious mystic, he was irresolute and easily influenced by court factions. He joined the First Coalition (q.v.). Although opposed to the ideas of the French Revolution, he was equally interested in using his alliance with Austria as a lever to seize Polish territory. His concern for partitioning Poland led him to fight defensively in the west after 1792 in order to concentrate on Polish issues. In 1795 he participated in the Third Partition of Poland and signed a peace treaty with the French Republic. Ironically, though Frederick William's reign is generally viewed as unsuccessful, Prussia actually did quite well. By 1797 Prussia had gained substantial territory in the east and dominated northern Germany. (*See also* Poland; Basel, Treaty of)

FREDERICK WILLIAM III (1770–1840). Frederick William III succeeded his father in 1797. In 1799 he threatened to join the Second Coalition (q.v.) if France did not turn over the Rhineland to Prussian control. The French stretched out negotiations until the military situation changed and then forced Prussia to change its policy back to one of neutrality. Prussia would pursue a similar approach in 1805, enter a disastrous war in 1806, and remain a French satellite until 1813. Though reputedly more enlightened than his predecessor, Frederick William III's policies gained little for Prussia and almost produced a total collapse of the state.

-G-

GANTEAUME, HONORÉ JOSEPH ANTOINE, ADMIRAL (1755–1818). Ganteaume went to sea in a merchant ship in 1769 and transferred to the navy in 1778. He fought in the West Indies. In 1794, as a captain, he fought at the Battle of the First of June (q.v.). In 1798 he sailed to Egypt as Brueys's chief of staff and managed to survive the Battle of the Nile (q.v.). Ganteaume served in Egypt and Syria and returned with Bonaparte (q.v.) to France in 1799. From 1800 to 1802 he commanded the Brest Fleet, sailing two times to Egypt in vain efforts to rescue the Army of the Orient. He held numerous appointments under the Empire but did not support Napoleon during the Hundred Days.

GARDANNE, GASPARD AMÉDÉE, GENERAL (1758–1807). Gardanne joined the artillery in 1779 and left the army in 1784. In 1791 he was elected lieutenant colonel of a volunteer battalion and served in the Alps and Italy and at Toulon (q.v.). In 1796 he served in the Italian Campaign and was promoted general of brigade in 1797. In 1798 Gardanne was governor of Alessandria in the Po Valley, and in July 1799 he was besieged in the city and forced to capitulate. As a general of division he fought at Marengo (q.v.). In 1807 he served in Germany, where he caught a fever and died.

GARNIER, PIERRE DOMINIQUE, GENERAL (1756–1827). The son of an architect, he joined the Royal Army in 1773 and served in the West Indies. He left the army in 1781 to return to Paris and become an architect. Garnier joined the National Guard in 1789. After 1792, he fought in the Alps, Rhineland, and Italy, becoming a general of brigade in 1793 and general of division in 1794. He then fought primarily in Italy and retired in 1801.

GASSENDI, JEAN JACQUES BAILIEN, GENERAL (1748–1828). Gassendi served in the La Fère Artillery Regiment and at one time had Bonaparte (q.v.) under his command. In 1793 he commanded the siege train at Toulon (q.v.). In 1800 Gassendi served with the Army of Reserve and managed to get some field guns over the Alps and fought at Marengo (q.v.). He retired in 1803 but continued to hold administrative posts. He rallied to Napoleon in 1815 and was not reinstated in rank until 1819.

GENOA, SIEGE OF (20 APRIL–4 JUNE 1800). In 1800 General Masséna (q.v.) with 18,000 men was besieged in Genoa by the Austrians and ships from the British navy (q.v.). Bonaparte (q.v.) was meanwhile organizing his second Italian campaign, but was unable to cross the Alps in time to rescue the garrison. Masséna conducted an energetic defense, but, running out of food, he had to capitulate. The French were allowed to leave Genoa with the full honors of war and return to France. The defense of Genoa had, however, distracted Austrian forces and attention from northern Italy, thus contributing to the surprise achieved by Bonaparte's Army of Reserve.

GEORGE III (1738–1820). George III came to the throne in 1760. An uncompromising conservative, he opposed reform at home and revolution abroad. When war came in 1793, the king viewed it as an ideological crusade, although he and his ministers were quite willing to seize French and Dutch colonies. He supported domestic repression and opposed efforts to negotiate peace with the Republic. After 1800, he suffered from repeated attacks of madness that left him incapable of governing. Although he remained popular, a Regency Bill of 1811 in effect removed him from power.

GRENVILLE, WILLIAM WYNDHAM (1759–1834). Grenville was elected to Parliament in 1782 from a district long controlled by his family. As a cousin of William Pitt (q.v.), he enjoyed rapid advancement. He became foreign secretary in 1791. He was also raised to the peerage and became Pitt's spokesman in the House of Lords. Initially, he wished to follow a moderate policy in the war with France, but by 1795 had become a leading advocate of overthrowing the Republic and restoring the Bourbons. He disagreed with Pitt over the Amiens treaty (q.v.), finding that the terms were too favorable to France. He and Pitt left office when the king opposed their efforts to obtain Catholic emancipation. He returned briefly to office in 1806–1807, and then disengaged from parliamentary affairs. A domestic reformer, his last ministry abolished the slave trade. He remained a constant foe of France.

GRIBEAUVAL, JEAN-BAPTIST VACQUETTE DE, COMTE, GENERAL (1715–1789). An artillery officer, Gribeauval served with the Austrian army during the Seven Years' War. Realizing the ineffectiveness of the French field artillery, he began in 1765 to reform the service. Despite much opposition from those who supported the old system, Gribeauval ultimately triumphed. He introduced a new series of lighter guns with standardized parts and packaged rounds. The number of gun calibers was reduced to four, thereby further enhancing efficiency. By 1789 the French field artillery was the best in Europe. (*See also* Artillery)

GROUCHY, EMMANUEL, GENERAL (1766–1847). Grouchy, a noble by birth, was commissioned in the artillery in 1781 and transferred to the cavalry in 1786. He supported the Revolution, was forced to resign his commission in 1793 because of his noble birth, but returned to service in 1794 as a general of division. He fought at Quiberon (q.v.) and participated in the Irish expedition of 1796. Separated by storms from his commander, he refused to order his troops in Bantry Bay (q.v.) ashore and sailed back to France. In 1799 Grouchy fought in Italy and was captured at Novi (q.v.). In 1800 he fought at Hohenlinden (q.v.). He later served Napoleon, fighting in Germany, Spain, and Russia. He was made a marshal by Napoleon and fought in the Waterloo Campaign. His actions at the Wavre may have cost Napoleon the battle. After 1815, Grouchy went to the United States until allowed to return to France in 1820. Though not capable of independent strategic command, Grouchy was an able subordinate.

GUADELOUPE (12 APRIL–10 DECEMBER 1794). A British expedition began its invasion of Guadeloupe, a French colony, in the spring of 1794. On 20 April the French garrison capitulated, but French reinforcements, about 1,500 men, reached the island in June. The British in turn sent two battalions to Guadeloupe. Additional French reinforcements arrived in late September and by 10 December had forced the British garrison to capitulate and leave the island.

GUIBERT, JACQUEST-ANTOINE-HIPPOLYTE DE (1743–1790). The son of an army officer, Guibert entered the army as a lieutenant in 1756 and served in the Seven Years' War. In 1775 he served in the War Ministry and continued his interest in military reform. He then served as a regimental commander, but his reputation rests on his contributions as a military reformer.

In 1772 Guibert published his *Essai général de tactique,* which advocated the creation of a patriotically motivated national militia that could live off the enemy's country and wage decisive warfare. The patriotic militia would employ flexible tactics, including aimed fire and small columns for maneuver. In 1779 he produced *Défense du système de guerre moderne,* in which he rejected the idea of a citizen army as too politically explosive and focused instead on improving current tactics. Again he advocated flexibility. He argued that the deployed linear battle order was fundamental, but small battalion columns had a significant role in combat both as a maneuver element and occasionally as an assault force. The precise use and distribution of lines and columns should, Guibert asserted, be left to field commanders in order that they might react rapidly and effectively to prevailing tactical circumstances.

Guibert's ideas had a major impact on the Drill Regulations of 1791, which became the basic drill manual of the Republican armed forces. Guibert was in fact part of a general reform effort in the post-1763 French army. The poor performance of the army in the Seven Years' War led to numerous reform plans. Some officers advocated introducing rigid linear Prussian-style tactics, others called for the use of massive assault columns. Guibert's advocacy of a combination of lines and small columns operating flexibly and allowing commanders numerous tactical options had the most significant impact influencing both the Royal Army and the forces of the First Republic. (*See also* Infantry)

-H-

HANDSCHUSHEIM, BATTLE OF (24 SEPTEMBER 1795). Pichegru's army left most of its troops behind the Rhine. Only two divisions advanced along both banks of the Necker River towards Heidelberg. Attacking on both banks, the French were outnumbered in both engagements. Their attacks failed, and Pichegru (q.v.) retreated, thereby exposing Jourdan's army to defeat in detail. Jourdan (q.v.) had no choice but to retreat back across the Rhine.

HARDY, JEAN, GENERAL (1763–1802). A volunteer of 1792, Hardy served with the Army of the Ardennes and was promoted general of brigade in 1793. In 1794 he fought in the Army of the Sambre-Meuse as a general of division. In 1798 he was captured at sea, where he was leading a force attempting to reinforce the French troops operating in Ireland. He returned to France and served in Germany in 1800, where he was seriously wounded. In 1802 Hardy was sent to Saint Domingue (q.v.), where he died of disease.

HARRIS, GEORGE, GENERAL (1746–1829). Harris served in the American Revolutionary War and fought at Bunker Hill. From 1790–1792 he led troops against Tippoo Sultan of Mysore (q.v.) and held command in Madras from 1796 to 1800. In 1799 he led British forces against Mysore and not only captured the capital but effectively destroyed the anti-British regime. Harris became a lieutenant general in 1801.

HAUGWITZ, CHRISTIAN AUGUST HEINRICH CURT, COUNT (1752–1832). In 1792 Haugwitz became the Prussian Minister of Foreign Affairs. He arranged the Second and Third Partitions of Poland, which brought Prussia much new territory but seriously undermined the unity of the First Coalition (q.v.). In 1795 he negotiated the Treaty of Basel, by which Prussia left the war and obtained de facto control of northern Germany. In 1799 he tried to force the French to make concessions, but backed down after France defeated the forces of the Second Coalition (q.v.). A similar effort in 1805 led to a similar result. Haugwitz left public life in 1806. Too clever by half, Haugwitz usually sought short-term gains at the expense of broader political and strategic approaches.

HELIOPOLIS, BATTLE OF (20 MARCH 1800). General Kléber (q.v.) had arranged a convention of allowing the Army of the Orient to leave Egypt. The British rejected it. Kléber then attacked a Turkish army that had occupied Cairo. He crushed the Turks, inflicting thousands of casualties for a loss of about 300 men, and recovered Cairo. The French position, nevertheless, remained bleak since the Army of the Orient was cut off from all aid from the Metropole.

HOCHE, LOUIS-LAZARE, GENERAL (1768–1797). Hoche was the son of a professional soldier and joined the army in 1784. He served in the French Guards, and when the unit was abolished, he joined the National Guard. He was promoted to lieutenant in 1792 and as a captain served at Neerwinden (q.v.). He was arrested, tried, and acquitted by the Revolutionary Tribunal and was then given command of the Dunkirk garrison. Hoche was promoted to general of brigade in October 1793 for his skillful defense and by late 1794 was a general of division.

In 1793 Hoche commanded the Army of the Moselle. He was unable to defeat the Prussians but scored a number of successes against the Austrians in December 1793. He was arrested again but released in the summer of 1794. He was then sent to the Vendée (q.v.) and Brittany, and defeated the British-Royalist landing at Quiberon (q.v.). Hoche also pacified the region by a combination of roving columns, fixed fortified posts, and religious concessions. By July 1796 the region was generally quiet. Placed in charge of an expedition to Ireland in December 1796, his fleet was scattered by a storm. Grouchy (q.v.), his second in command, reached Bantry Bay (q.v.) but refused to land and returned to Brest. Hoche arrived after Grouchy's departure and had to sail home. In 1797 Hoche took command of the Army of the Sambre-Meuse, crossed the Rhine, defeated the Austrians in several engagements, but had to halt upon receiving the news of the Leoben Armistice (q.v.). In September, Hoche died at his headquarters; some say he was poisoned. Others claim he died of exhaustion.

HOCHSTADT, BATTLE OF (19 JUNE 1800). In June 1800 Moreau's army advanced into Bavaria toward Ulm. Moreau (q.v.) then moved east heading for the Danube near Hochstadt. On 19 June, he attacked, and after much bitter fighting, the French took the town and secured the left bank of the Danube. The Austrians had to abandon Ulm and retreated to the Inn River, thus enabling the French to occupy Munich.

HOHENLINDEN, BATTLE OF (3 DECEMBER 1800). After Marengo (q.v.), the Austrians undertook sporadic peace talks with France. In November 1800, Bonaparte (q.v.) suspended negotiations, suspecting that the Austrians were simply playing for time. Bonaparte, therefore, directed Moreau (q.v.), who had during the summer advanced into Bavaria, to lead the Army of the Rhine, 100,000 strong, in an advance along the Danube toward Vienna. The Austrians, with 130,000 men led by Archduke John, moved first crossing the Inn River in an effort to drive the French back against the Bavarian Alps and sever their communications to France. Because of the broken terrain, the Austrians advanced in four separate columns towards Munich. The French occupied defensive positions around the town of Hohenlinden. They held the center against all attacks while Grouchy (q.v.) and Richepanse (q.v.) shattered the two left-hand Austrian columns by a flank attack. The Austrians lost 18,000 men and the French 5,000. After the battle, the Austrians retreated, and Moreau advanced rapidly to Steyr, about 100 miles from Vienna. An armistice was signed on 25 December. Hohenlinden, coupled with Brune's advance across the Adige in Italy and Macdonald's advance into Trent, forced the Austrians to sue for peace. In February, the Austrians signed the peace of Luneville (q.v.). Hohenlinden was a victory that surpassed Marengo (q.v.) in intensity and importance. Unwilling to create another military hero who might challenge his position, Bonaparte never gave Moreau the credit he deserved and gave little recognition to the importance of Hohenlinden.

HONDSCHOOTE, BATTLE OF (6–8 SEPTEMBER 1793). In the late summer of 1793, the Republic was under attack from virtually all points of the compass, while counterrevolution flared in many departments and political factionalism in Paris threatened the government's very existence. France was raising vast new armies, but it would take time to arm, equip, and train the new soldiers. The Republic desperately required breathing space, especially in the north. Fortunately for France, the Allies dispersed their efforts. The Duke of York (q.v.) with 35,000 British Hessian and Hanovarian troops besieged Dunkirk while the Austrians moved on Maubeuge. Seizing their opportunity, the French rushed reinforcements to General Houchard's Army of the North, bringing its strength to 50,000 men.

Houchard was ordered to attack immediately to relieve Dunkirk, provide security for French Flanders, and satisfy public opinion in Paris. On 6 September Houchard advanced against posts covering the siege works but failed to penetrate the enemy lines. On 8 September, supported by a sortie from Dunkirk, the Army of the North attacked again. Covered by skirmishers, assault columns moved on the village of Hondschoote, driving Hanovarian troops from the town. That evening the Duke of York abandoned the siege. Houchard, a cautious general at best, slowly followed. The Allies escaped destruction. Houchard paid for his caution with his life, but the Republic had saved Dunkirk and halted a major coalition offensive.

HOOD, SAMUEL, ADMIRAL (1724–1816). Hood entered the Royal Navy in 1741. He served under Rodney in the Seven Years' War and under Graves at the Chesapeake in 1781. He served with Rodney again in 1782, and by 1786 he was a vice-admiral. In 1793 Hood commanded the Allied force that occupied Toulon (q.v.) and in 1794 took Corsica. He was recalled to Britain, promoted to admiral, and created a viscount in 1796.

HOTHAM, HENRY, VICE-ADMIRAL (1777–1833). Hotham succeeded Lord Hood (q.v.) in the Mediterranean in 1794. After the actions of 13–14 March 1794, he remained on blockade duty until 1798 and then spent three years in the Bay of Biscay. Though not a spectacular leader, he, like many others in the Royal Navy, fulfilled his important tasks effectively.

HOTHAM AND MARTIN, NAVAL BATTLE OF (13–14 MARCH 1794). In March 1794 the French admiral Martin with fifteen ships of the line sailed from Toulon (q.v.) to escort an invasion armada of 15,000 men to Corsica. In two days of indecisive fighting with a British squadron under Admiral Hotham (q.v.), each side lost two ships, but the invasion fleet did not reach Corsica.

HOWE, RICHARD, ADMIRAL OF THE FLEET (1726–1799). Howe first went to sea in 1740 and fought in all of Britain's wars until 1778, when he resigned. He was, nevertheless, promoted to admiral in 1782. From 1783 to 1788, Howe was First Lord of the Admiralty. In 1794 he won the Battle of the First of June (q.v.) and became Admiral of the Fleet in 1796. He retired in 1797 but helped quell the naval mutinies (q.v.) of that year.

HUMBERT, JEAN JOSEPH AMABILE, GENERAL (1755–1823). Humbert joined the army as a volunteer in 1792 and was promoted general of brigade in 1794. He fought in the Vendée (q.v.) and took part in the Irish expedition of 1796. In 1798, with a force of about 1,000 men, he landed in western Ireland. Although the British had already crushed the rising, Humbert waged an effective campaign and rekindled some revolutionary spirit. Finally, surrounded by overwhelming numbers, he capitulated and was allowed to return to France, where in 1799 he fought at the Battle of Zurich (q.v.). In 1802 he fought in Saint Domingue (q.v.). He returned home in 1803. Because Humbert was an ardent Republican, Bonaparte refused to employ him. He later moved to the United States and died in New Orleans.

HUNINGUE, SIEGE OF (28 OCTOBER 1796–5 FEBRUARY 1797). After the failure of the German Campaign of 1796, the French continued to hold two footholds across the Rhine. Huningue was attacked by the Austrians in late October. The French mounted a vigorous defense including a major sortie. After the fall of Kehl, however, the Austrians brought up additional artillery. On 1 February 1797, the French agreed to evacuate their positions with full honors of war. The evacuation was completed four days later.

HUSSARS. Hussars were light cavalry. Hussar and similar chasseurs à cheval were armed with saber, carbine, and pistols. Hussars acted as advanced guards for an army. They also covered retreats or pursued defeated enemy forces. A regiment contained about 1,200 men on paper.

-I-

IBRAHIM BEY (1735–1817). A European by birth, Ibrahim was sold as a slave to the Mamelukes (q.v.). Ibrahim became a Moslem and rose to be the governor of Cairo. On the death of his owner, he became the joint Emir or ruler of Egypt with Murad Bey (q.v.). Defeated by Bonaparte (q.v.), he virtually disappeared from public life and died in obscurity.

IMOLA, BATTLE OF (3 FEBRUARY 1797). During the French invasion of the Papal States, the French encountered the Papal army near Imola. The Papal forces were entrenched behind the Senio River. General Lannes (q.v.) forded the river and attacked from the rear while General Victor (q.v.) attacked frontally. Papal troops quickly broke and fled, losing about 500 men. The French lost fewer than 100 troops. Soon after, the Pope sued for peace.

INFANTRY. During the wars of the Old Regime and French Revolution, infantry was the queen of battle. Eighty to 90 percent of an army's manpower was composed of infantry. Cavalry and artillery functioned as supporting arms. In 1791, for example, the Austrian army of 164,000 men had 13,500 gunners, and the French army of 150,000 had fewer than 10,000 gunners in 1788.

Since Old Regime armies were led by the nobility and drew enlisted personnel from conscripted serfs or society's lower orders, the recruiting base was narrow and armies were small. In the late 1780s Prussia fielded 186,000 men and Russia 200,000. Bavaria had a 15,000-man army, Saxony 23,000, Piedmont 40,000, and Britain 39,000 plus 34,000 Hanovarians.

Infantry fell into two broad categories—line and light. Line infantry fought the main engagements, using a linear order employing volley fire. Fire superiority was the key to victory. A field army would deploy in a three-rank line that, depending on the size of the force, would stretch from one to three miles. A second line would often deploy behind the first. Troops had been trained to deploy from march formation into a battle line and load and fire their muskets in unison.

Light infantry was used to screen an army's movements and pursue a beaten enemy. Light troops were kept functionally separate from regular units. The Austrians, for example, often used Croatians as light infantry and cavalry. The Russians employed Cossack horsemen. The British used Scottish Highlanders.

The French Revolution produced numerous changes in the army. Venality in commissions was abolished. The Officer Corps was opened to all on a basis of talent rather than birth, and the coming of war in 1792 led to a dramatic expansion of the army. Volunteers in 1791 and 1792 and conscripts in 1793 boosted army muster rolls to a paper strength of 670,000 by early 1794. By June 1794 the French army contained over 800,000 men. The vast majority of the troops were infantrymen.

The basic tactical unit was the nine-company battalion, which in contrast to the armies of the Old Regime, employed far more flexible tactics. Troops were taught to operate as skirmishers or as part of a firing line or assault column. *Tirailleurs* (light troops) were no longer isolated specialists performing their tasks away from the main battle force. Skirmishing became an integral part of battlefield tactics, since close order and light tactics were executed either by the same men or by subordinate units of a single tactical command. The French thus evolved an all-purpose infantryman able to act as a skirmisher, participate in a column, or take a position on a firing line.

A battalion usually moved into action in an open column. Upon reaching the battle, the French would close ranks forming closed columns by division, which was a formation two companies wide and four deep. The companies stood in three rank lines. Thus, the column actually resembled a rectangle eighty men across and twelve deep. The ninth company usually remained in the rear as a tactical reserve. The commander then had numerous options. Depending upon the tactical situation, he could detach companies and send them forward as skirmishers. He could even deploy the entire battalion as skirmishers. He could alternatively direct the companies remaining in column to deploy into a firing line, or he could order the column to deliver a charge. Moreover, French soldiers soon learned to shift from one tactical mode to another during an engagement to respond to battlefield situations.

The three-battalion half-brigade enjoyed similar flexibility. The commander could place all three battalions in line, establish a line of battalion columns, or place some battalions in line and others in columns covered by skirmishers. Bonaparte (q.v.) often used the "*ordre mixte*," which had one battalion in the center deployed in a firing line while the flanking battalions moved in column formation. Skirmishers covered the entire front. With experience, units learned to shift from one mode to another rapidly and efficiently.

Another characteristic of French infantry was high morale. Old Regime armies were held together by rigid discipline and primary unit personal loyalties. Desertion was, nonetheless, endemic. French Republican armies, of course, relied upon small unit loyalties, but French troops also knew that they were viewed by the population as the shield of the nation, a factor that greatly enhanced morale and helped produce a willingness to bear privations and face battle without massive desertions. Numbers, though important, were not the sole explanation of the growing effectiveness of the French infantry. The fact that the soldiers were citizens enabled commanders to use flexible tactical techniques and call for sacrifices unheard of in the past. (*See also* Tactics, Republican)

IONIAN ISLANDS. The Ionian Islands were initially Venetian possessions. The French took control of the islands in 1797, but in 1799 Russian and Turkish forces retook them.

IRELAND. Ireland after 1782 was in theory an autonomous state with its own parliament that recognized George III of England as the sovereign of the Kingdom of Ireland. Ireland was, however, dominated by a Protestant Ascendancy that excluded Catholics (who formed 80 percent of the population), and Protestants who were not members of the established church from political participation in political life. In 1791 the Society of United Irishmen was founded in Belfast, and lodges spread quickly throughout Ireland. The Society was essentially a middle-class organization that advocated parliamentary reform and the removal of Catholic disabilities. Though largely Protestant in membership initially, the Society soon included a large number of Catholics.

After Britain went to war with France, the small chance of reform faded, as the British began to treat lodges as criminal organizations and suspended the *habeus corpus* act. Consequently, many United Irishmen abandoned the path of moderate reform, looking instead to revolution with the aid of Republican France. France during the Old Regime had occasionally invaded or devised plans to invade Ireland. While looking to France, the Society reconstituted itself as a secret organization and adopted many of the demands of the Defenders, a peasant organization that called for lower rents and abolition of tithes paid to the established Church of Ireland. The Society decided to send one of their leaders, Theobald Wolfe Tone (q.v.), a Protestant lawyer, to France to appeal for help. Tone went first to the United States and then set out for France. Tone obtained interviews with Carnot (q.v.) and Hoche (q.v.) in 1796, and the French agreed to assist the United Irishmen. Hoche was placed in command of a 13,900-man expedition. French motives were different from those of the United Irishmen, since the Directory (q.v.) intended to use a French-controlled Ireland as a pawn in bargaining with Britain. Paris probably intended to return Ireland to London in return for peace and British recognition of French Continental conquests. In any event, storms dispersed the French fleet, and the expedition, though it reached the Irish coast undetected, did not land. The Battle of Camperdown (q.v.) foiled a Batavian attempt to an Irish landing in 1797.

After 1796, the United Irishmen continued to organize and arm themselves and renewed appeals to France for military assistance. By the spring of 1798 the Society claimed to have 278,000 members, of whom 100,000 were armed. The British responded by vastly increasing the Irish garrison to 103,000 men: 39,500 regulars, 26,000 militia, and 37,500 yeoman recruited from the Protestant gentry. The French, however, decided against a second expedition to Ireland and instead mounted the invasion of Egypt.

The United Irishmen then decided to act unilaterally setting the date of their rising for 23 May. The British, meanwhile, in addition to widespread resorts to martial law and repression, also made effective use of paid informers whose activities enabled the authorities to decapitate the Society's leadership. Thus, when the rebellion did erupt, it was initially sporadic and uncoordinated. In a wave of minor clashes, the United Irishmen were defeated.

The rebellion then took an unexpected turn when it spread to Wexford (q.v.). Initially a peasant revolt led by parish priests, it soon took on political overtones as local United Irishmen joined its ranks and transformed a Catholic peasant rising into a political movement. The rebels, however, lacked arms and, despite a number of victories at New Ross and Gorey, the British gathered 20,000 men and on 19 June defeated the Irish at New Ross and on 21 June crushed the pike-armed rebels at the Battle of Vinegar Hill (q.v.). The British then pursued the scattered remnants, showing no mercy to captured or suspected rebels. As many as 50,000 people died in the rebellion of 1798.

The French, finally, did attempt to send aid landing a battalion in western Ireland in late August. The French scored a number of local victories and raised a number of local forces but were run to earth and forced to capitulate on 8 September. Another expedition was caught at sea. The British captured several ships, and Wolfe Tone (q.v.), who commanded a battery on one of the ships, was taken prisoner. Despite the fact that Tone was a brigadier in the French army, he was condemned to death, but took his own life on 19 November.

Ireland had represented a great opportunity for France. Had the United Irishmen received adequate help, Britain's strategic position would have seriously deteriorated. Bonaparte (q.v.) had talked with Irish leaders but preferred to go to Egypt. He later noted while on St. Helena, "if instead of making the expedition to Egypt I had made one to Ireland what would England have been today . . . ?"

IRURZUN, BATTLE OF (6 JULY 1795). The Army of the West Pyrenees struck Spanish positions around Irurzun. Though losses were modest on both sides, the French split the Spanish army into two non-supporting fragments and moved on Vittoria and Bilbao. The Spanish army was soon on the verge of collapse. Spain left the war six days later under additional pressure from the Army of the East Pyrenees, which had resumed its advance into Catalonia.

-J-

JACOBINS. The Jacobins were essentially members of the middle class who supported the creation of a democratic republic and vigorous prosecution of the war. The origins of the Jacobins began in 1789, when a number of reform-minded deputies to the Estates General began to meet informally as the Breton Club. When the assembly moved to Paris, the deputies formed the Society of the Friends of the Constitution. They met in the convent of the Jacobins and soon became known as Jacobins.

Originally composed of deputies, the Jacobin Club soon admitted non-deputies. By 1790 there were about 200 deputies and 1,000 non-deputies in the Paris Jacobin Club. High dues for membership meant that members were drawn from the well-to-do middle class. Similar clubs sprang up outside of Paris and requested affiliation with the Paris Club. By late 1791 the Jacobin network included about 1,000 clubs.

The Jacobins at first favored a constitutional monarchy, but after the king's flight to Varennes as part of an attempt at counterrevolution, more and more club members came to favor the creation of a republic. The public was admitted to debates in the Jacobin Club of Paris, which began to propose decrees, criticize ministers, receive petitions, and draft addresses and circulars.

The Jacobins were internally divided on the issue of declaring war on Austria. Robespierre (q.v.), for example, warned against going to war. Nor did the Jacobins support the insurrection of 10 August 1792, which deposed the king. The Jacobins did accept the creation of the Republic and after 22 September 1792 encouraged well-to-do members of the lower middle class to join the club.

In 1793 Jacobin members of the National Convention (q.v.) were known as the Mountain. Non-deputies supported them and, via the network of clubs, spread their views throughout the nation. Jacobin ideology was a blend of militant Republicanism coupled with a willingness to sacrifice particular interests to the general interest of public safety and a coherent national war effort. The Jacobin clubs favored the centralization of the war effort and the mobilization of the nation's human and economic resources in order to defeat foreign and domestic enemies. In 1793 and 1794 the Jacobins were the watchdogs of the Revolution and mobilized public opinion throughout France in support of the government's economic and military measures. In August 1794 deputies in the Convention turned against the Mountain and the Jacobins. Robespierre and his closest Allies were executed, and in November 1794 the Paris Jacobin Club was permanently closed. There followed a purge of leading Jacobins, and in the provinces counterrevolutionaries assaulted and often murdered members of local Jacobin clubs. The Jacobins, however, survived and were often influential during the Directory (q.v.). The Jacobin spirit, of course, persisted down to the 20th century. (*See also* National Convention; the Terror)

JAFFA, STORM OF (3–7 MARCH 1799). Advancing into Syria in February, 1799 the French took Gaza and moved to invest Jaffa. After three days of preparation, Bonaparte's men stormed the city. Upon learning that the garrison contained 3,000 Turks, who had recently been released on parole from El Arish (q.v.), Bonaparte (q.v.) ordered the entire garrison executed. Although his action was technically legal, the executions revealed a ruthless streak in Bonaparte's personality and tarnished his reputation.

JELLACIC VON BUZIN, FRANZ BARON VON, GENERAL (1746–1810). An Austrian officer, he fought successfully against Moreau (q.v.) in Germany in 1796. In 1799 he again fought effectively in southern Germany but was defeated in Switzerland in September. Like many Hapsburg generals, he was experienced and effective but ultimately unable to cope with Revolutionary and Napoleonic armies.

JEMAPPES, BATTLE OF (6 NOVEMBER 1792). After Valmy (q.v.), Dumouriez (q.v.) convinced the government to invade Belgium. With 40,000 men he began to advance on Mons in early November. The 14,000 Austrian defenders decided not to hold the rundown fortress of Mons and entrenched themselves on nearby high ground that ran through the village of Jemappes. The French attack involved a brutal frontal assault by several columns. Despite initial setbacks, the French persisted and finally took Jemappes. After the loss of the village, the Austrians retreated, exposing all of Belgium to French occupation. The victory was one of élan rather than skill and was the first major Republican success in offensive operations.

JERVIS, JOHN, ADMIRAL, EARL OF SAINT VINCENT (1735–1823). Jervis began his naval career as a seaman and midshipman. In 1755 he became a lieutenant and in 1759 participated in the campaign to capture Quebec. During the American Revolutionary War he participated in the relief of Gibraltar. By 1793 Jervis was a vice admiral. He fought in the West Indies in 1794 and in 1795 became an admiral and commander-in-chief in the Mediterranean. In February 1797, he won the Battle of Cape Saint Vincent. Ill health caused his resignation in 1799, but he reentered active duty to command the Channel Fleet and, as First Lord, planned the attack on Copenhagen in 1801. He retired from the active list in 1807 and was promoted to Admiral of the Fleet in 1821.

JOUBERT, BARTHÉLEMI-CATHERINE, GENERAL (1769–1799). Joubert attended law school and joined the army in 1791. Initially, he served on the Rhine and in Italy, and in 1795 was promoted colonel. He served in Bonaparte's Italian Campaign, gaining a reputation for courage and leadership and earning promotion to general of division. In 1798 Joubert was in command in Holland and Italy. Some members of the Directory (q.v.) intended to employ him in a coup against the government. To enhance his prestige, he was appointed to command the Army of Italy in the summer of 1799, but was killed during the Battle of Novi (q.v.). Bonaparte (q.v.) ultimately played the role intended for Joubert.

JOURDAN, JEAN BAPTISTE, GENERAL (1762–1823). Jourdan was the son of a surgeon, worked as a clerk in the silk trade, and enlisted in the army in 1778. He fought in America, was discharged in 1784, and became a haberdasher. He returned to military service via the National Guard and in 1791 became a National Volunteer and was elected lieutenant colonel. Jourdan fought at Jemappes (q.v.) and Neerwinden (q.v.) and was promoted general of division. He led the center of the French Army at Hondschoote (q.v.). In October he won the battle of Wattignies (q.v.). In 1794, as Commander of the Army of the Sambre-Meuse army, he won the Battle of Fleurs and went on to occupy eastern Belgium and part of the Rhineland.

Jourdan campaigned in Germany in 1795 and 1796, but was defeated primarily because Pichegru (q.v.) and then Moreau (q.v.) failed to coordinate operations with him. He became a deputy in 1797 and introduced a Conscription Act in 1798. Jourdan returned to active service but in 1799 lost the Battle of Stockach (q.v.) to a larger Austrian army. He left the army and was reelected to the Council of Five Hundred, where he opposed Napoleon's coup. He nevertheless served Bonaparte who made him a marshal in 1804.

Jourdan later served in Naples and Spain, retiring in 1813. He rallied to the Bourbons, supported Napoleon during the Hundred Days, and after Waterloo supported the Bourbons again. He refused to preside over the Council of War that tried Marshal Ney, became a peer of

France, supported the Revolution of 1830 and ended his career in command of Les Invalides.

Like many Republican generals, Jourdan began his career as an enlisted man in the Royal Army, but left because of limits on his ability to advance into the officer corps. He resumed his military career via the National Guard, and the Republican system of promotion based on loyalty and talent rather than birth provided him with opportunities for rapid promotion. As a general, Jourdan was competent and persistent. He was at his best on the field of battle in large-scale frontal engagements. Not a strategic thinker, he nevertheless served the Republic well at the important battles of 1793 and 1794.

JOURDAN LAW (5 SEPTEMBER 1798). The *levée en masse* (q.v.) was an emergency conscription act designed to meet the crises of 1793. As the war continued, the *levée* was only sporadically applied, and the size of France's armies began to decline because of casualties and desertion. By 1798 the French army numbered only about 365,000 men. To raise new troops and to place the conscription process on a rational basis, the government adopted a conscription law proposed by General Jourdan (q.v.), who in 1797 had become a deputy.

The Jourdan Law called for Frenchmen between 20 and 25 years of age to register for conscription. If medically fit, they would be placed on lists maintained by local authorities, and the central government could call individuals to the colors according to specific requirements. Voluntary enlistments were encouraged, but when insufficient, the government could and did rely upon conscription. Entire year groups could be called to the colors, or portions of a given year group could be drafted depending upon prevailing requirements. The Jourdan Law was applied throughout the Republican and Napoleonic periods to supply the army's manpower needs.

-K-

KAISERSLAUTERN, BATTLE OF (28–30 NOVEMBER 1793). Hoche (q.v.), leading the Army of the Moselle with some 30,000 troops, attacked the Prussians around Kaiserslautern. The French attacked without success on three successive days. The French lost 3,000 men and the Prussians, along with a Saxon contingent lost 1,300. Despite the defeats, the French were by late 1793 on the offensive, thereby securing the eastern frontiers of the Republic. Constant French attacks, moreover, wearied the Allies who retired to the right bank of the Rhine.

KASTRIKUM, BATTLE OF (6 OCTOBER 1799). A Russian force moving towards Brune's new battle position, taken up after the battle of Egmont (q.v.), encountered French forces at an advanced post at Kastrikum. A battle developed when the French reinforced their forward troops and pushed the Russians back to Bergen (q.v.). British troops arrived and with the Russians began a second advance on Kastrikum. Brune (q.v.) then led reinforcements forward and halted the Anglo-Russian advance. After additional fighting, the Allies, having lost some 3,000 men, fell back. Brune's victory foiled the last Allied effort to break out into open country before bad weather made resupply efforts impossible.

KEHL, SIEGE OF (22 NOVEMBER 1796–6 JANUARY 1797). After recrossing the Rhine, Moreau's (q.v.) army continued to retain a foothold on the right bank at Kehl across from Strasbourg. The Austrians besieged the town. The French maintained a vigorous defense, but after the Austrians fired about 100,000 cannon rounds and 25,000 howitzer rounds at the defense works, the French withdrew from the town across bridges to the French side.

KEITH, GEORGE, ADMIRAL (1746–1823). Keith first went to sea in 1767 and in 1770 became a lieutenant. He served in American waters in 1780 and at Toulon (q.v.) in 1793. He became a rear admiral in 1794 and in 1795 commanded forces sent to seize the Cape of Good Hope from the Dutch. In 1796 Keith participated in the capture of Ceylon. He served in the Mediterranean from 1798 to 1801, landing in Genoa in 1800 and landing Abercromby's army in Egypt in 1801. Promoted to admiral in 1801, Keith commanded in the North Sea from 1803–1807 and in the Channel from 1812–1815. He was on board the *Bellerophon* when Napoleon, after Waterloo, surrendered to the British. In 1797 he was made Baron Keith and was made a viscount in 1814.

KELLERMANN, FRANÇOIS-ETIENNE-CHRISTOPHE, GENERAL (1735–1820). Born to Alsatian gentry, Kellermann joined the Royal Army at 15 and was a colonel by 1784. He served in the Seven Years' War, undertook a diplomatic mission to Poland in 1765 and helped train Polish cavalry in 1770. Kellermann supported the Revolution and the Republic. At the Battle of Valmy (q.v.), 20 September 1792, he played a major role in halting the Prussian advance on Paris. In 1793 he conducted the siege of Lyon while at the same time protecting the Alpine frontier. In 1794 he was arrested and imprisoned, as were many officers of aristocratic background, but was acquitted in November. Later, Kellermann commanded the Army of the Alps and of Italy. After the army was split, he continued to command the Army of the Alps but retired from active service in 1797. In 1804 Napoleon made him a marshal and later the Duke of Valmy. His promotion was, however, honorary, a reward for past services, and he exercised no further active commands. In 1814 he accepted the Restoration.

KELLERMANN, FRANÇOIS ETIENNE, GENERAL (1770–1835). The son of the victor of Valmy (q.v.), he served in the Army of Italy in 1796 and 1797. In 1797 he served in the Army of Rome and Naples. Kellermann became a general of brigade in 1797 and in 1800 fought at Marengo (q.v.). Later he served in Spain and in 1815 rallied to Napoleon and fought at Waterloo. He was then reconciled to the Restoration, held a number of administrative posts, and retired in 1831.

KILLALA (AUGUST 1798). After the beginning of the Irish Rebellion, the Directory (q.v.) tried to organize several expeditions to Ireland (q.v.). Administrative inefficiency and shipping shortages prevented all but one expedition from sailing. In August, a battalion of the 70th half-brigade landed at the small town of Killala in western Ireland. The rebellion, however, had already been crushed. Led by Colonel Humbert (q.v.), the French, nevertheless, recruited a number of Irish, defeated British troops at Castlebar, and moved east. The British soon brought overwhelming numbers to bear and forced the French to capitulate in early September. Humbert had waged a brilliant little campaign and survived to participate in the Battle of Zurich (q.v.). He had, however, arrived in Ireland too late and with too small a force to be really effective. The Killala expedition does indicate what the French might have accomplished had they seriously tried to intervene in Ireland.

KILMAINE, CHARLES EDOUARD, GENERAL (1751–1799). Kilmaine was born in Dublin and entered French service in 1774. He fought in America. He supported the Revolution, fought at Jemappes (q.v.), and after a brief arrest, fought in Italy from 1795 to 1797. In late 1798 Kilmaine tried to organize an expedition to Ireland (q.v.). but ill-health forced him to leave active duty and he died of dysentery in 1799.

KLÉBER, JEAN-BAPTISTE, GENERAL (1753–1800). An Alsatian, Kléber served in the Austrian army from 1776–1783. Returning to France, he supported the Revolution, fought in the Vendée (q.v.), and in 1794 was a general in the Army of the Sambre-Meuse. He participated in the Egyptian expedition and played a major role in Bonaparte's victory at Mount Tabor (q.v.). In August 1799, Bonaparte (q.v.) returned to France, leaving Kléber in charge of the French forces in Egypt. He defeated the Turks at Heliopolis (q.v.) in March 1800 and crushed a revolt in Lower Egypt. Moslem fanatics killed him on 14 June 1800. Kléber was a dedicated Republican with a quarrelsome personality. He never liked Napoleon and viewed Bonaparte's return to France as desertion.

KORSAKOV, ALEXANDER MIKHAILOVITCH RIMSKI, GENERAL
(1753–1840). An experienced soldier, Korsakov commanded the Russian contingent in Switzerland. Masséna (q.v.) defeated him at Zurich (q.v.) in September 1799, before Suvorov (q.v.), who was moving up from Italy, could join him. After 1800, Korsakov served in civil posts and was governor of Lithuania for almost thirty years.

KOSCIUSZKO, ANDRZEJ TADEUSZ BONAWENTURA (1746–1817). A member of a minor noble family, Kosciuszko had to leave school after his father's death in 1758. In 1765, with the patronage of one of Poland's leading families, he entered a newly created military school, graduated, and stayed on as an instructor. In 1769 he was sent to France for an advanced military education and volunteered for the American Army. From 1776 to 1782 he served in the Continental Army as an engineer, distinguished himself in battle, and in 1783 was promoted to brigadier general.

Kosciuszko returned to Poland in 1784, participated in fighting against Russia in 1792, and after the armistice left the country. He went to Paris and appealed for aid, but France could do little for Poland because of the War of the First Coalition (q.v.). In Poland, an insurrection was being prepared. Since the Russians were taking steps to crush it, Kosciuszko returned to Poland, and on 24 March at Cracow he began the fight against foreign domination. He won some peasant backing by suppressing serfdom and forbidding the expulsion of peasants from their holdings. The small regular Polish army and peasant levies won a number of victories against Prussian and Russian forces, but in October 1794, the Polish forces were defeated and Kosciuszko was captured. The rising collapsed soon afterwards.

After two years' imprisonment, he made his way to the United States and then to France, where he represented Polish interests to the Directory (q.v.). He opposed Napoleon's coup and thereafter refused to cooperate with the French. After Waterloo, he refused overtures from the Russians to return to Poland and spent his remaining years in Switzerland. His demands for a truly independent Poland and for social reforms made Kosciuszko the most respected figure in the pantheon of modern Polish nationalism, a place he holds to this day. (*See also* Poland)

KRAY, PAUL BARON, GENERAL (1735–1804). Of Hungarian birth, Kray earned an excellent reputation during the Seven Years' War. After a successful campaign against the Turks, he was promoted to major general. In 1799 in Italy he defeated the French at Magnano and recaptured Mantua (q.v.). In 1800 he briefly commanded Austrian troops in Germany but was forced to retreat and was removed from command.

-L-

LAFAYETTE, MARIE JOSEPH PAUL MOTIER, MARQUIS DE (1757–1834). Born into a wealthy aristocratic family, Lafayette joined the army in 1771. In 1777, with a small volunteer force, he sailed to America and became a major general in the Continental Army. He returned to France in 1779, but went back to America in 1780, where he played an active role at Yorktown. His military exploits were less important than his mere presence, which boosted American morale by showing the people that they were not alone.

Lafayette supported the early phases of the Revolution at least in part because he believed that his wealth and fame would guarantee him political power in a more democratic society. In 1789 he helped form the National Guard and in 1791 ordered the arrest of Louis XVI (q.v.) when the king tried to flee the country. In 1792 he commanded the Army of the Center and in August protested the suspension of the king. He also decided to mount a coup against the Revolution, which he believed had gone too far. He convinced General Luckner (q.v.), who commanded an army located near Paris, to shift armies so that he and his troops would be better placed to march on the capital. He arrested the government's representatives at Sedan and ordered his troops to march on Paris. The soldiers, however, refused to follow him, and on 19 August 1792, Lafayette fled to the Allied lines. Instead of welcoming him, the Prussians arrested him and then turned him over to the Austrians. The Austrians imprisoned Lafayette until 1797, when the Leoben Armistice (q.v.) secured his release.

Unable to return to France, Lafayette lived east of the Rhine until the Bourbons permitted him to return home in 1814. After Waterloo, he resumed his political career, as well as making a long voyage to the U.S.A., where he was still popular. In 1830 he became the head of the National Guard and was instrumental in the Revolution of that year. He helped bring the Orleanist monarchy to power. The hero of two worlds remains popular in America. The same cannot be said about views of Lafayette in France, where many view him as an unsuccessful political meddler.

LAKE, GERARD, GENERAL (1744–1808). Lake entered the army in 1758 and by 1792 was an army general officer. Lake served in a Guards unit where ranks were lower than in the line army. Thus, a Guards major was the equivalent of an army lieutenant colonel. He served in Germany from 1760 to 1762 and in the Yorktown Campaign of 1781. In 1793 he commanded the Guards Brigade in Flanders, serving until 1794. Lake then sold his commission in the Guards and became a colonel of an infantry regiment in Ireland. In 1797 he was promoted to lieutenant general. In 1798 he commanded the forces that crushed the Irish rebellion, exercising great severity towards all rebels and their sympathizers. He was in direct command of the forces that forced Humbert (q.v.) to surrender in September 1798. In 1801 Lake became commander-in-chief in India and was promoted to full general in 1802. He served in India, took a leading role in the Mahratta War, and then returned to England.

LANCERS. Equipped with lances, lancer formations acted as shock formations. Lancers also carried pistols. Cossacks and some Polish units were the best known lancer units. The Republic initially did not have lancer units. Napoleon later introduced them into his Grand Army.

LANNES, JEAN, GENERAL (1769–1809). Lannes as a youth was apprenticed to a dyer. In 1792 he entered the army as a volunteer, served in the Pyrenees, and obtained rapid promotion. He then transferred to the Army of Italy in 1795. Between 1796 and 1797 he fought in most of Bonaparte's major battles. His courage and leadership qualities led Bonaparte (q.v.) to promote him to general of brigade. Lannes accompanied the Army of the Orient to Egypt and Syria, and he returned to France in 1799. After Napoleon's seizure of power, Lannes served the Consulate and Empire, becoming a marshal in 1804. A Republican, he was opposed to the establishment of the Empire, to the point of nearly disrupting the coronation ceremony by swearing loudly throughout the festivities. Despite his views, Napoleon continued to employ him because he was such a talented leader. Lannes served in Germany and Spain, dying of wounds received at Aspen Essling. Lannes had few equals as a battlefield commander.

LA ROCHEJAQUELIN, HENRI DU VERGIER, COMTE DE (1772–1794). A member of a noble family from Poitou, La Rochejaquelin joined the King's Constitutional Guard and retired to his home after the Revolution of 10 August 1792. The Vendean rebellion began the following year. Initially a spontaneous peasant rising, the rebels soon found noblemen to organize and lead their forces. La Rochejaquelin soon took a leading military role in actions against Republican forces and earned a reputation for valor. He became a member on the controlling council of the rebel army, which was defeated in several major battles in the winter of 1793. La Rochejaquelin and other officers then returned to guerrilla warfare, mounting numerous raids and ambushes. In the course of a raid, he was killed on 28 January 1794. His courage and ability, however, made him a Royalist legend. (*See also* Vendée)

LARREY, DOMINIQUE-JEAN (1766–1842). Larrey studied medicine at Toulouse. In 1792 he was attached to French troops in the Rhineland, where he devised a system of mobile field hospitals in order to render more rapid assistance to the wounded. Larrey was promoted to chief surgeon of the army, and was named professor of the school of military medicine at Val-de-Grace in Paris. In 1796 and 1797 he organized medical services for the Army of Italy and accompanied Bonaparte's expedition to Egypt. After his return from Egypt, Larrey assisted at all of Napoleon's subsequent campaigns. He was present at Waterloo, where he was taken prisoner. By modern standards, military medicine in the 18th century was primitive. Wounded soldiers often perished from infection after reaching hospitals, but given the limitations of military medical care, Larrey developed a system that for its time was one of the best in Europe. Moreover, Larrey understood that the sooner a wounded soldier received medical care, the better his chances of survival, and worked constantly to provide rapid and effective medical aid.

LA TOUR D'AUVERGNE, THEOPHILE MALO CORRET DE (1743–1800). The son of a Breton lawyer, La Tour d'Auvergne joined the army in 1767. In 1784 he was promoted to captain. He supported the Revolution and in 1792 he served in the Army of the Alps. In 1793 he fought in the Pyrenees with singular bravery. His health broke down, forcing him to retire in 1795. Returning to Brittany by sea, he was captured by the British and was a prisoner for two years. In 1797 La Tour d'Auvergne rejoined the army and served on the Rhine and later in Switzerland. His courage led Bonaparte (q.v.) to name him the premier grenadier of France in April 1800. Two months later La Tour d'Auvergne was killed in Germany.

His legendary courage became famous in the French army. His embalmed heart became a treasured possession of the 46th Regiment. Even after the fall of Napoleon, La Tour d'Auvergne's name was retained on his company's roster, and when it was called at parades an NCO would reply "dead on the field of honor."

LATOUR DU PIN GOUVERNET, JEAN-FREDERIC (1727–1794). La-Tour du Pin was a lifelong soldier, first serving in 1741. He later commanded several infantry regiments and by 1789 was a lieutenant general. Louis XVI (q.v.) appointed him war minister, and he presided over a number of major reforms of the Royal Army. A convinced monarchist, he swiftly crushed a mutiny at Nancy in 1790, and the National Assembly forced him from office. He retired from political life, but in 1793 he testified on behalf of the queen, with the result that in April 1794 he was tried by the Revolutionary Tribunal and condemned to death.

LECLERC, VICTOR EMMANUEL, GENERAL (1772–1802). In 1791 Leclerc enlisted as a volunteer and was elected lieutenant. He served at Toulon (q.v.) in 1793 and fought in the Italian Campaign of 1796–1797. In 1797 he married Bonaparte's sister and became a general of brigade. He served with the Army of Rome, became a general of division and fought at Hochstadt (q.v.) in the German Campaign of 1800. Leclerc was, in 1802, given command of an expeditionary force to Santo Domingo. He arrived in early 1802, and after several successful battles against Toussaint L'Ouverture (q.v.), Leclerc caught yellow fever and died.

LECOURBE, CLAUDE JOSEPH, GENERAL (1760–1815). Lecourbe served in the Royal Army, but left because advancement was blocked. In 1792, however, he became commander of a volunteer battalion, and in 1793–1794 fought at Hondschoote (q.v.), Wattignies (q.v.), and Fleurs (q.v.). From 1795 to 1797 he fought in Germany, and by 1799 he was a general of division. Lecourbe fought against Suvorov (q.v.) in Switzerland in 1799 and, though forced to retreat, inflicted heavy losses on the Russians and delayed their advance. In 1800 he fought again in Germany. His Republican sentiments and loyalty to Moreau (q.v.) did not endear him to Napoleon, who refused to employ him in field commands. He accepted the Restoration and did not support Napoleon during the Hundred Days. He did, however, accept a command at Belfort to protect France against foreign invasion. Lecourbe died at Belfort several months after Waterloo.

LEFEBVRE, FRANÇOIS JOSEPH, GENERAL (1755–1820). Lefebvre joined the Royal Army in 1773 and by 1789 was a sergeant. In 1792, as a captain, he fought in the armies of the Center and Moselle. In December 1793 he was promoted to general of brigade. Lefebvre played a crucial role in the Battle of Fleurs (q.v.) in 1794. He fought in Germany for the next five years. Wounded in 1799, he became commander of the Paris military area and supported Napoleon's coup. In 1804 he became a marshal. During the Empire, Lefebvre fought in Germany, Spain, Austria, and Russia. He accepted the Restoration, joined Napoleon during the Hundred Days, and again accepted the Restoration. Lefebvre was a loyal, blunt-spoken soldier. Not a strategist, he was an able leader of troops on the battlefield.

LEGRAND, CLAUDE JUSTE ALEXANDRE, GENERAL (1762–1815). Legrand enlisted in the Royal Army in 1777 and by 1786 was a sergeant major. In 1790 he joined the National Guard and soon became a lieutenant colonel. Legrand fought at Fleurs (q.v.) and on the Rhine front. By 1799 he was a general of division, and fought at Stockach (q.v.) in 1799 and Hohenlinden (q.v.) in 1800. He later fought in Germany, Austria, and Russia, where he was seriously wounded. He fought in France in 1814, but died in January 1815, probably from the effect of wounds suffered in Russia.

LEOBEN ARMISTICE (18 APRIL 1797). After taking Mantua (q.v.), Bonaparte (q.v.) advanced into Hapsburg territory reaching the town of Leoben in Styria on 7 April. The French were nearly exhausted, but so were the Austrians, who agreed to an armistice on 7 April. Bonaparte immediately launched into peace negotiations, and the Austrians signed the Preliminaries of Leoben on 18 April. The terms, including Austrian acceptance of French annexation of Belgium and recognition of the Cisalpine Republic (q.v.) in return for Venice, were later incorporated with some changes into the Peace of Campo Formio.

LEVÉE EN MASSE (23 AUGUST 1793). The *levée en masse* was the culmination of efforts to create a mass citizen army and to place the whole process of conscription and military organization on a coherent, well-organized basis. The French army had already grown substantially by early 1793. Volunteers from 1791 and especially those of 1792 had led to the creation of hundreds of new battalions. At the same time, thousands of recruits had joined the ranks of the regular army. By the early summer of 1793, nearly half a million men were under arms, organized into more than 500 battalions. Nevertheless, the military situation faced by the Republic was nearly catastrophic, and the government needed to organize and direct the entire nation in a coherently organized war effort. Therefore, on 23 August 1793, the National Convention declared:

> From this moment and until all enemies are driven from the territory of the Republic the French people are in permanent requisition for army service. Young men shall go to battle; the married men shall forge arms and transport provisions; the women shall make tents and clothes and shall serve in the hospitals; the children shall turn old linen into lint; the old men shall repair the public places to stimulate the courage of the warriors and preach the unity of the Republic and hatred of Kings.

The decree further declared that national buildings would be converted into barracks and workshops, that citizens had to turn over to the government arms, saddle horses for the cavalry, and non-essential draught horses for the artillery. The Committee of Public Safety (q.v.) was also empowered to create arms factories and requisition workers. Representatives were to be sent to localities to oversee the implementation of the decree. They were invested with unlimited powers.

Typically, requisitioned troops gathered at the canton or district level, where they were given a physical check by a review council. Before moving, the draftees often received rudimentary military training by ex-soldiers or non-commissioned officers sent from active formations.

Contingents then moved towards the battle zones under the control of "conductors," who made arrangements for each night's lodging either in churches, public buildings, and if necessary in private dwellings. The conductors also sought to keep up the morale of the young men, who were leaving home for the first time. The long marches hardened the draftees and showed them that they were part of the nation.

Some 300,000 draftees ultimately reached their destinations, where they were assigned as replacements to understrength battalions and demi-brigades. The *levée* increased the overall strength of the French army to about 800,000 men present under arms. The paper strength of the army, including men in convalescent depots, missing, or prisoners of war was even higher. Whatever the final figure, France by 1794 had created an enormous citizen army drawn from all segments of the populace and all geographical areas. France had a national army rather than a collection of regional forces, and the national army of the Republic was destined to change the nature of warfare. (*See also* Committee of Public Safety)

LIGURIAN REPUBLIC (1797–1805). In May 1797 Genoese radicals rose in rebellion against the entrenched rulers of the ancient Republic of Genoa. Defeated, the rebels, who called for a democratic constitution, appealed to Bonaparte (q.v.), who had already established sister republics in Italy. Bonaparte supported them and compelled Genoa to agree to a democratic constitution in June 1797. In November the new constitution was approved by a large majority. Allied troops did not invade the new Ligurian Republic in 1799, but in 1800 laid siege to Genoa (q.v.), which was held by French troops commanded by Masséna (q.v.). Running out of supplies, the French had to capitulate. The Republic was reconstituted in 1802 and annexed to France in 1805 as a logical extension of Napoleon's annexation of Piedmont.

LILLE NEGOTIATIONS (1796–1797). In October 1796, the British, alarmed by the strategic situation in Europe, opened secret talks with the French at Lille. Neither side was, however, willing to make significant concessions, and the Directory (q.v.) ended the discussions in December.

When Austria agreed to leave the war, Pitt (q.v.) and his cabinet decided that, in the absence of a Continental ally, Britain would once again have to negotiate. Pitt hoped that the growing strength of royalism in France would force the Directory to make significant concessions. Talleyrand (q.v.), who had become foreign minister in 1797, encouraged the British to hold out for major concessions, which would be granted in the wake of a Royalist electoral victory in forthcoming elections.

The original French diplomatic plan was to have London recognize the annexation of Belgium and the satellite republics. Moreover, Paris wanted Britain to return captured Dutch and Spanish colonies. In return, Britain would obtain part of Portuguese Brazil or retain several Dutch overseas possessions, and the Batavian Republic would take part of Brazil.

Encouraged secretly by Talleyrand and by the Royalists, the British rejected the French plan, and even put pressure on Portugal to prevent the conclusion of a peace between Paris and Lisbon. The Coup of September 1797, however, put the Republicans firmly back in power. The Directory then reasserted its original position, and negotiations ended on 15 September 1797. Pitt officially ended the talks on 11 October. (*See also* Directory; Pitt)

LINDET, JEAN-BAPTISTE-ROBERT (1746–1825). The son of a prosperous merchant, Lindet studied law in Paris. In 1791 he was elected to the Legislative assembly, and in 1792 he was elected to the National Convention (q.v.), where he voted for the death of the king. Lindet supported the Mountain against the Girondins and was also elected in April 1793 to the Committee of Public Safety (q.v.), where he served until 1795.

During the crisis months of 1793, Lindet specialized in the areas of provisioning the armies, finding transport for the army, and enforcing the General Maximum Law. With a staff of over 500, Lindet ran the Subsistance Commission, which supervised agriculture and industrial production, imports and exports, price controls, and the drafting of workers for service in arms and munitions factories. In 20th-century terms, he was in charge of the nation's logistics efforts. He worked closely with Carnot (q.v.), who regarded Lindet's efforts as essential.

Lindet survived the coup against Robespierre (q.v.) in 1794, and defended his actions and those of several of his colleagues on the Committee when they were tried by the Convention in 1795. After 1795, Lindet was elected to the Legislative Assembly twice, but both times his election was overturned by the Directory (q.v.). In 1799 he became minister of finance, but he opposed Bonaparte's coup, resigned, and refused to serve under Napoleon. In private life he became a successful lawyer until his death in February 1825. (*See also* Committee of Public Safety; National Convention)

LINTH RIVER, BATTLE OF (1 OCTOBER 1799). In his retreat from Switzerland, Suvorov (q.v.) reached the Linth River on 1 October. Helvetian and French troops in vicious fighting prevented the Russians from establishing a foothold across the river. The Franco-Helvetian forces beat back six Russian attacks. Each side lost some 2,000 men, and Suvorov changed his line of march from northeast to due east into the Grissons in eastern Switzerland.

LOANO, BATTLE OF (23 NOVEMBER 1795). General Scherer (q.v.), commander of the Army of Italy, attacked the Austrian supply base of Loano. He struck, after the Austro-Sardinian forces had gone into winter quarters, by launching a two-pronged surprise attack; leaving 8,000 casualties behind, the Austrians pulled back to Genoa. The French lacked the troops to mount an effective pursuit, but had gained a position from which to mount further assaults in the following year.

LODI, BATTLE OF (10 MAY 1796). To outmaneuver the Austrian army defending Lombardy, Bonaparte (q.v.) crossed the Po River at Piacenza and advanced to Lodi, which was defended by a rearguard of 8,500 men covering the retreat of the main body. The French took Lodi, and the Austrians retreated across a wooden bridge that spanned the Adda River. While French cavalry forded the river, infantry stormed the bridge, forcing the Austrians to retreat after a loss of 2,000 men. The French, having lost 1,000, pursued and occupied Milan.

LOGISTICS. Broadly defined, logistics means the production or procurement of weapons, munitions, food, and clothing for the army, and the delivery of these supplies to the troops. During the Old Regime, troops depended upon a series of fixed magazines containing necessary supplies for the army. The Revolution and subsequent expansion of the armed forces rendered the traditional system largely irrelevant.

The Republic did a fairly good job in supplying weapons. At the start of the war there was a severe shortage of firearms. There were only some 150,000 pattern '77 muskets available, and the government arsenals produced only 42,000 pieces a year. In 1793 a number of arsenals were captured by coalition troops. Carnot (q.v.) and Prieur de la Côte d'Or (q.v.) proceeded to meet the emergency by centralizing musket production in Paris. Eventually, some 258 public workshops were established, which by 1794 employed more than 5,000 men and turned out some 750 muskets per day. Moreover, private forges and workshops were pressed into public service. Thus, in contrast to early 1793, when serious thought was given to arming troops with pikes, armies by the end of the year were armed with standard muskets.

Saltpeter, an essential element in the manufacture of gunpowder, was also in short supply in 1793, a situation made worse by the fact that major imports of saltpeter from Turkey were cut off. By August 1793, the army had only 14 million tons of gunpowder on hand against a requirement of 80 million. In September the Committee of Public Safety reinstated the right of search of private property and encouraged citizens to search houses, cellars, stables, and caves for saltpeter. Saltpeter was ground in flour mills and a new factory was set up at Grenelles. Eventually, France produced over 30,000 pounds of gunpowder per day.

In 1793 Monage estimated that France needed an additional 6,000 cannons and invented a simplified casting method. Furnaces were built in converted churches, and workers were taught the new methods in special classes. Copper for bronze guns was found by requisitioning church bells and roofs. In 1793 nearly 7,000 cannons were cast, and by 1795 France had about 4,800 bronze siege and fortress guns, 2,800 iron siege guns, and 2,500 field guns.

Uniforms, shoes, and other clothing presented a more difficult problem. At the start of the war the Line Army was equipped as were the volunteers of '91. In 1792 new waves of volunteers were occasionally outfitted by their villages, but the situation rapidly deteriorated. Bouchotte, the war minister, tried to remedy the situation by setting up public workshops in the sections of Paris to make uniforms. He also ordered that every shoemaker in the country had to provide five pairs of boots every ten days for each person he employed, and in the winter of 1793–1794 he ordered that shoemakers produce only footwear for the army. Such measures were not sufficient, and local commanders and Representatives on Mission (q.v.) often resorted to requisitions. Still, despite all government efforts, Republican troops always looked remarkably scruffy both at home and in the field.

Food supply for the armies was an especially difficult problem. Troops were officially supposed to receive one and a half pounds of bread per day, as well as half a pound of meat, an ounce of rice or two ounces of dried vegetables, a quart of wine, and small amounts of brandy and vinegar. To provide for 7–800,000 men was a daunting task that was never fully accomplished.

At the start of the war, the government tried to leave supply to private contractors. Failing this approach, the Committee of Public Safety (q.v.) ordered commanders to procure what they required from the peoples of conquered territories or even from local French resources.

In 1793 the Convention (q.v.) created a group of *commissaires ordonateurs.* A commissary official must have served as a commissary in the old line army or as a serving soldier with experience as a quartermaster or sergeant-major. The original 390 commissaires, therefore, included a large number of veterans. Many others were new to the military, but they were often notary clerks, teachers, lawyers, or local government officials in their previous civilian occupations and soon became fairly competent supply officers.

The *commissaires,* working with field armies and military districts, had sweeping powers. They could buy supplies anywhere they could find them, and if owners were reluctant to sell, supplies could be seized. If no local transport was available, they could requisition horses and carts. *Commissaires* were generally responsible for collecting, storing, and issuing rations. The government generally hired private contractors to supply food and clothing, and *commissaires* had to deal with the contractors, exercising overall quality control. The system did produce a good deal of graft and corruption. Moreover, it was unable to supply the armies with a consistent flow of rations. In turn, many units resorted to requisitions, and Republican armies learned to supplement their official supply system by living off the country, preferably an enemy's country.

Perhaps the major benefit derived from logistics difficulties was that Republican armies travelled light. An Old Regime army allocated over fifty pack animals to carry tentage. Officers were entitled to travel in carriages and to bring with them large retinues of personal servants. An army of 50,000 men required 100 wagons to haul supplies. Republican armies, perhaps making a virtue of necessity, had a much shorter "logistical tail." Troops did not carry tents and slept in the open whenever possible. Battalions had but a few carts for essential items. Consequently, the citizen soldier of the Republic could march farther and faster than his Old Regime counterparts, thereby enhancing the operational capabilities of the field armies.

LOISON, LOUIS HENRI, GENERAL (1771–1816). Loison received a commission in 1791, and after 1792 fought in the armies of the North, the Rhine, and Moselle. As a general of brigade, he fought in the Army of Helvetia and was promoted to general of division. Loison retook the St. Gothard Pass in 1799, joined the Army of Reserve in 1800, and took part in the siege of Fort Bard. After 1800, he served the Empire, fighting in Germany and Spain. Relieved of command in 1813, he retired from military service.

LONATO, BATTLE OF (5–6 AUGUST 1796). After taking Milan in May 1796, Bonaparte (q.v.) advanced on Mantua (q.v.) and began to lay siege to the city with its 12,000-man garrison. General Würmser (q.v.), however, moved south from the Alps to relieve the garrison with a force of more than 50,000 men. Outnumbered, Bonaparte had to raise the siege and abandon numerous siege guns. Würmser was able to resupply the city. On 5 August Bonaparte attacked one of Würmser's columns advancing down the banks of Lake Garda. At Lonato on 5 August Masséna's division repulsed the Austrians, inflicting heavy casualties in the fighting. Augereau (q.v.), meanwhile, held off Würmser's main force at Castiglione. The Austrians attacked again at Lonato on 6 August and were again repulsed with heavy losses. Würmser then retired toward Trent, and Napoleon resumed the siege of Mantua.

LOUIS XVI (1754–1793). The grandson of Louis XV, he became king in 1774. A reasonably intelligent man, he lacked willpower and political acumen. Many have said that he would have made an excellent village postmaster or a first-rate locksmith, but these are hardly qualifications for a ruling monarch. Had Louis followed the Bourbon tradition of Henry IV, Louis XIII, and Louis XIV of appealing to the middle levels of French society while not overly antagonizing the nobility, he might well have survived. However, in the 1780s he abandoned efforts at fiscal reform in the face of aristocratic opposition, agreed to call an Estates General for the first time since 1614, and then antagonized the delegates of the Third Estate, who should have been his natural Allies. When the Third Estate, supported by a substantial portion of the clerical estate, proclaimed that they were going to write a constitution for the nation, Louis decided upon a military counterrevolution but delayed acting for too long. The storming of the Bastille on 14 July 1789 put an end to the idea of an armed coup.

Louis opposed the subsequent reforms of the National Assembly and in June 1791 tried to flee the city of Paris to join troops on the frontier for another effort at counterrevolution. Caught at Varennes, he was brought back to Paris under virtual arrest. Louis then accepted the Constitution of 1791, which reduced his power but left him numerous prerogatives. He then supported the drift to war and at the same time secretly encouraged the Austrians to strike at France. He hoped either that the threat of foreign intervention would force the French people to rally around him for protection, or failing that, he desired that foreign armies destroy the Revolution and restore his power. Secret correspondence with the Allies continued even after the declaration of war.

Overthrown on 10 August 1792, Louis was brought to trial early in 1793. At the trial, instead of maintaining the absolute Royalist position that the monarch can do no wrong, he based his defense on the Constitution of 1791 and claimed that he was innocent of the charges levied against him. He was found guilty, condemned to death, and executed on 21 January 1793. In the days before his execution, he displayed courage and dignity, and perished with no overt fear or remorse. Had his courage been matched by his intelligence, he might well have survived as a constitutional monarch.

LOUIS-PHILIPPE, DUC DE CHARTRES, DUC D'ORLÉANS (1773–1850). A descendent of the second son of Louis XIII, Louis-Philippe became the duc de Chartres when his father in 1785 became the duc d'Orléans. Both father and son supported the Revolution, perhaps in the hope that the French would depose the Bourbons and place the Orleans family on the throne as constitutional monarchs.

The duc d'Orléans, as a deputy to the National Convention (q.v.), voted for the death of Louis XVI, while the duc de Chartres joined the army, became a lieutenant-general, and fought heroically at Valmy (q.v.) and Jemappes (q.v.). Louis-Philippe, however, became hostile to the Convention and after the Battle of Neerwinden (q.v.), joined Dumouriez (q.v.) in deserting to the Austrians. This action in turn led to the execution of the duc d'Orléans and Louis-Philippe obtained his title. Louis-Philippe subsequently lived in Switzerland, the United States, and England. Though reconciled to the Bourbons, he always refused to bear arms against France. He returned to France in 1814 and became king after the Revolution of 1830.

LUCKNER, NICHOLAS COMTE DE, GENERAL (1722–1794). Born in Germany to a noble family, Luckner became a professional soldier, entering the Bavarian army in 1737. He next joined the Dutch and then the Hanovarian army. In 1763 he joined the French army as a lieutenant general and in 1784 became a count. Luckner supported the Revolution and was appointed to command the Army of the Rhine. Roget de Lisle even dedicated the "La Marseillaise" to him in 1792. In the same year he agreed to move his entire army to positions held by Lafayette's army so that Lafayette (q.v.) could bring his forces closer to Paris in order to execute a coup. Luckner was then given internal commands and allowed to retire in September 1792. He was arrested in October 1793 and executed in January 1794. Luckner was a brave soldier but lacked intelligence and competence. He had never conspired with Lafayette, but his noble birth, association with Lafayette, and lack of success cost him his life.

LUNEVILLE, PEACE OF (8 FEBRUARY 1801). After the Battle of Hohenlinden (q.v.), the Austrians reopened peace talks with France. Anxious to end the war, Napoleon gave the Austrians fairly reasonable terms that were essentially the same as the 1797 Campo Formio treaty (q.v.). Austria recognized French gains in Belgium, the Rhineland, and Northern Italy. France also controlled Swiss affairs, and Austria kept Venice. The Duke of Parma was given Tuscany in return for the loss of his state to the Cisalpine Republic (q.v.). The King of Naples was restored to his kingdom. Britain was thus isolated and forced to contemplate an end to hostilities.

LUXEMBOURG, SIEGE OF (JANUARY–JUNE 1795). Luxembourg was one of the great fortress cities of Western Europe. It was held by a 10,000-man garrison. Too strong to be taken by assault, the French starved it into submission. The garrison capitulated on 24 June 1795.

-M-

MACDONALD, JACQUES-ETIENNE-JOSEPH ALEXANDRE, GENERAL (1765–1840). Descendant of a Jacobite family, Macdonald joined the Royal Army in 1784. A supporter of the Revolution, he rose to the rank of general by 1794. In 1799 he fought in Italy but suffered defeat at the Trebbia (q.v.), in part because Moreau (q.v.) failed to coordinate operations with him. In 1800 he fought successfully in Germany. He supported Napoleon, who made him a marshal and a duke; after 1814, he served the restored monarchy. A competent commander, Macdonald had a reputation for being unlucky.

MACK, KARL, BARON (1752–1828). Mack entered the Austrian army in 1770. Most of his career was spent as a staff officer. During a war with Turkey in 1788–1789 he was aide-de-camp to the emperor and then military tutor to Archduke Charles (q.v.). During the War of the First Coalition (q.v.) he was a brigadier general and chief of staff to Saxe-Coburg (q.v.). He helped arrange the defection of Dumouriez (q.v.), but resigned in 1794 when his plan of operations failed. In 1797 he returned to active duty as a major-general. In 1798 he was sent to command the Neapolitan army, but the French defeated his forces and captured him. Mack achieved lasting fame (or infamy), in 1805, when he and 27,000 men capitulated to Napoleon at Ulm. Mack was subsequently court-martialed and sentenced to two years' imprisonment plus loss of rank and medals. In 1819, however, the emperor restored his rank and honors. Mack was in fact a talented 18th-century officer, who had the misfortune to face the new style of warfare introduced by the French Republic.

MAINZ, SIEGE OF (MARCH–JULY 1793). Mainz contained a French garrison of 23,000 men. A Prussian army with Hessian and Austrian contingents blockaded Mainz in late March and opened siege operations in June. Several French sorties were repulsed as approach trenches and artillery were pushed forward. When food and forage was exhausted, the French capitulated on 24 July 1793. Leaving its artillery, the garrison returned to France after pledging not to fight the Allies for a year. The government sent the garrison forces to the Vendée (q.v.), where it played a major role in the defeat of the Catholic and Royal Army (q.v.).

MAINZ, SIEGE OF (SEPTEMBER–NOVEMBER 1795). In an effort to drive Austria out of the war, two French armies, the Sambre-Meuse under Jourdan (q.v.) and the Rhine and Moselle under Pichegru (q.v.) invaded Germany in September 1795. The campaign was ill-conceived, since the two armies were too far apart to offer mutual support. Moreover, Pichegru, engaged in secret talks with the Royalists, refused to cooperate with Jourdan. Acting alone, Jourdan crossed the Rhine, turned south, and invested Mainz from the right bank. Pichegru finally moved on Heidelberg, but the Austrians defeated him near the city on 24 September. The Austrians, under the command of Archduke Charles (q.v.), then turned north and forced Jourdan to recross the Rhine on 16 October and abandon his siege. The Austrians then reinforced Mainz, and in late October, struck into the Rhineland. When both sides agreed to a truce on 15 December, the Austrians were not only firmly in control of Mainz but also had significantly widened their foothold in the Rhineland.

MALAVILLY, BATTLE OF (2 MARCH 1799). While marching on Seringapatam, the British were attacked by Tippoo Sultan (q.v.). The better-disciplined British easily routed the Mysore army, which lost over 1,000 men.

MALTA (1798–1800). On his way to Egypt, Bonaparte (q.v.) occupied Malta in early June. There was only marginal resistance. Bonaparte left a 4,000-man garrison under General Vaubois (q.v.) and went on to Egypt. After the Battle of the Nile (q.v.), Nelson (q.v.) blockaded Malta, and a small British force landed on the island. In June 1800 a larger force arrived and serious siege operations were undertaken. The garrison eventually ran out of food and capitulated. The French obtained free evacuation back to France.

MAMELUKES. The effective rulers of Egypt at the time of the French invasion, the Mamelukes were descendants of warriors who had come to Egypt from the Caucasus in the 13th century. Ibrahim (q.v.) and Murad Bey (q.v.) ruled Egypt. In theory, a pasha from Constantinople was their superior, but the Mamelukes had long since reduced the role of the pashas to that of figureheads. Bonaparte (q.v.) easily defeated the Mamelukes in 1798, for although they displayed great personal courage, their tactics were outmoded, and they were no match for the French. Admiration for the courage of the Mamelukes, nevertheless, led Bonaparte to take one, Roustan, as his personal bodyguard and to organize a squadron of Mameluke cavalry, which served him until 1814.

MANHEIM, BATTLE OF (18 OCTOBER 1795). Having forced Jourdan's (q.v.) army to retreat, the Austrians attacked Pichegru's army around Manheim. Outnumbered, the French were still holding positions on both sides of the Necker River, and the Austrians were able to defeat them in detail. Leaving 9,000 men in Manheim, Pichegru (q.v.) retreated to the west. The Manheim garrison was short of munitions and had to capitulate on 22 November.

MANTUA, SIEGE OF (1796–1797). With an initial garrison of 13,000 men and 500 guns, Mantua held out against the Army of Italy for eight months. The siege began in June 1796, but Würmser's first advance forced Bonaparte (q.v.) to raise the siege. He defeated Würmser (q.v.), who nevertheless managed to slip about 2,000 reinforcements into the city. The siege was reestablished until Würmser's second advance caused the French to abandon operations. Würmser, though defeated again, managed to enter Mantua with 12,000 men on 13 September. Bonaparte moved quickly to reestablish the siege and defeat additional relief expeditions. Würmser finally capitulated on 2 February 1797 with 16,000 survivors.

MARABOUT, BATTLE OF (17 AUGUST 1801). Having taken Cairo in June, the British attacked the French at Marabout on 17 August. The British carried a French redoubt, and General Menou (q.v.) surrendered.

MARENGO, BATTLE OF (14 JUNE 1800). In the spring of 1800, Bonaparte (q.v.) with the Army of the Reserve crossed the Alps into northern Italy. Most of the Austrian army was besieging Genoa (q.v.) which, however, fell on 4 June. Napoleon, still convinced that he had taken the Austrians by surprise, divided his army to cut off the Austrian retreat routes. He thus reduced the force under his command to about 24,000. Far from retreating, General Melas (q.v.) with 31,000 troops decided to attack the French near the village of Marengo.

Outnumbered, the French were forced to give ground, and after several hours of fighting, the French had no more reserves and were running low on ammunition. Meanwhile, Desaix (q.v.), who had initially been sent north to watch Po River crossings, heard the sounds of the fighting at Marengo and returned to the battlefield just as Bonaparte's troops were on the verge of collapse. Desaix led a counterattack supported by field guns firing at close range. Desaix was killed, but his troops were successful. It was the Austrians who broke. The French lost 7,000 and the Austrians 14,000. Northern Italy was again in French hands.

The war itself went on until the end of 1800. Marengo, however, was important to Napoleon not just as a military victory but also as a political triumph. Having just seized power by a coup, he had to produce a victory in his first campaign as the effective head of state or expose himself to the possibility of a coup against his regime. Napoleon, therefore, doctored reports of the battle sent back to Paris to make it appear as if he had ordered Desaix to reverse his march and return to the battlefield. He made it appear as if everything had gone according to plan rather than being a near-defeat. Later, Napoleon's favorite horse was named Marengo.

MARESCOT, ARMAND SAMUEL, GENERAL (1758–1832). In 1778 Marescot joined the engineers. In 1793 he served at Toulon (q.v.) and in 1794 took part in numerous sieges including Charleroi and Condé (q.v.). By 1795 he was a general of division and from 1796 to 1800 served in Germany and Switzerland. In 1800 he commanded the engineers in the Army of Reserve and fought at Marengo (q.v.). Marescot served the Empire, but was disgraced and imprisoned for participating in the surrender of a French force in Spain in 1808. Released in 1814, he took no further part in military affairs.

MARMONT, AUGUSTE FRÉDÉRIC LOUIS VIESSE DE, GENERAL (1774–1852). The son of an officer, Marmont was commissioned in the artillery in 1792. He fought at Toulon (q.v.) in 1793 and Mainz (q.v.) in 1795. He became Bonaparte's aide-de-camp in 1796. He went to Egypt in 1798, served in several battles, and in 1799 returned to France with Napoleon. In 1800 he handled the artillery at Marengo (q.v.) and was promoted to general of division. After 1800, Marmont continued to serve Napoleon, becoming a marshal in 1809. He served in Spain, Germany, and France, where in April 1814 he surrendered his corps to the Allies, an action for which Napoleon never forgave him. Marmont then served the Bourbon regime and left the country in 1830. He settled in Venice for the rest of his days. A talented commander, his action in 1814 earned him widespread unpopularity.

"MARSEILLAISE, LA". "La Marseillaise" was written on the night of 25–26 April 1792 by Roget de Lisle, an army captain in the engineer corps. In 1792 Roget de Lisle was in Strasbourg. At a social gathering on 25 April the mayor of the city commented that the army that was preparing for war had no marching song of its own. The mayor asked de Lisle, who was an amateur musician, to write a song for the volunteers. He wrote the tune and lyrics, originally called "War Song of the Rhine Army," in a single night. The mayor in turn distributed the song to local army units.

The song was an immediate hit and by late summer was known throughout France. The song received the name "La Marseillaise" because a battalion of volunteers from Marseilles, while storming the Tuileries on 10 August 1792, sang the song. From that time the song became the unofficial national anthem of French Republican regimes.

The lyrics describe essentially the idea of citizens leaping to the defense of the nation to protect it from the forces of the Old Regime. The song displays militance and determination but is still in orientation defensive. The famous last verse, for example, states in literal translation: "To arms, citizens. Form your battalions. March, march. Their impure blood will water our furrows." France, according to the anthem, is not trying to wage a war of conquest but is defending itself from invasion. Plato once noted "Let me write the songs people sing and you may write the laws." Though not perhaps universally true—what can one say about "You ain't nothing but a hound dog"?—popular songs often express the attitudes and aspirations of a population.

MARTINIQUE (5 FEBRUARY–16 MARCH 1794). A British expedition of five ships of the line commanded by Vice-Admiral Jervis (q.v.) arrived at Martinique on 5 February 1794. Troops were put ashore at three locations and soon captured the island except for two forts. Cannon were sent ashore and the forts capitulated on 16 March. The island was returned to the French by the Peace of Amiens (q.v.) and was retaken in 1809. In 1814 Martinique was again restored to French rule.

MASSÉNA, ANDRÉ, GENERAL (1758–1817). Masséna was the son of a small merchant who died when Masséna was six. He went to sea as a cabin boy at 13 and four years later joined the army. After fourteen years of service, he was an NCO, but because of his humble status could advance no further. He left the army to become a grocer and perhaps a smuggler. In 1791 Masséna joined the National Guard, volunteered for active service, and was elected lieutenant-colonel.

In 1793 he was rapidly promoted to general of division after service at Toulon (q.v.). In 1795 he played a crucial role at the Battle of Lonato (q.v.). In the Italian campaign of 1796–1797 Masséna earned a well-deserved reputation for personal courage and tactical brilliance. He led the assault on the bridge at Lodi (q.v.) and his division played a major role at Castiglione (q.v.), Bassano (q.v.), Arcola (q.v.), and Rivoli (q.v.). Napoleon gave him the nickname "l'enfant chéri de la victoire." In 1798 Masséna commanded the French troops occupying Rome and was recalled because of extensive looting by his forces. He was then given command of the Army of Helvetia and waged an effective defensive campaign in 1799 against Austrian and Russian troops.

By September 1799, his army was the only French force that had not suffered a major defeat. The Directory (q.v.), reacting to Masséna's report that Austrian troops were moving into Germany while Russian reinforcements had not yet arrived to replace them, reinforced his army and ordered him to launch a counter-offensive. At the Battle of Zurich (q.v.) in late September, 1799 Masséna scored a major victory. He then turned on Suvorov (q.v.), who managed to escape his clutches but suffered heavy casualties. Zurich and the subsequent operations in the Alps in turn convinced the Tsar to leave the coalition—a major turning point in the war. In 1800 Masséna led the defense of Genoa. He had to capitulate when supplies ran out but had tied down a large Austrian force for three months, thereby contributing to the success of Napoleon's second Italian campaign.

In 1804 Masséna became a marshal and fought for the Empire in Italy, Germany, Austria, Spain, and Portugal. Broken in health, he was recalled from Iberia in 1811 and took no further part in active operations. Masséna was one of the most able generals of the Republic and the Empire. He was one of the few Napoleonic marshals who understood strategy as well as tactics and operations.

MAXIMUM, LAW OF (29 SEPTEMBER 1793). In 1793 the Convention (q.v.) established price and wage controls. The Maximum of 4 May 1793 fixed prices on wheat and flour. The General Maximum Law of 29 September 1793 fixed both prices and wages over a wide variety of primary commodities and production activities. A third law of 24 February 1794 replaced the local prices of the General Maximum with a schedule of national prices. The controls were a temporary retreat from the free market economic views of the revolutionary leaders. They were war emergency measures designed to pacify the Parisian populace and simultaneously deal with the provisioning of the enlarged armies of the Republic.

MEDICINE, MILITARY. Survival of wounded personnel is a function of the nature of an individual's wound and the speed and efficiency of medical care. In any war a certain number of wounded will survive in almost all circumstances because the wounds are superficial. At the other end of the scale, certain wounds are so serious as to be beyond medical help. It is the range between minor and mortal wounds where the medical services play their essential role.

In 1792 there were 4,000 doctors, surgeons, druggists, and assistants in the army. The numbers soon fell due to battle casualties, illness, arrest, and emigration. They were soon replaced by volunteers, and at the start of 1793 there were some 2,800 surgeons and physicians serving with the armies. Despite the fact that the Convention (q.v.) had closed down all universities and medical schools, the number of medical personnel continued to grow. The Convention authorized the training of assistant surgeons in military hospitals, appointed anybody with any medical knowledge as a military surgeon, and ordered the creation of three national schools of health. By the end of 1793 the number of medical officers had grown substantially. There were 4,000 medical officers in 1793 and by 1794, the number had risen to about 9,000.

A number of doctors realized that rapid treatment of wounds improved chances of recovery. In 1792 Larrey (q.v.), a leading medical man, began to devise field ambulances, while others introduced teams of stretcher bearers to collect wounded from the battlefields. Numbers were, however, always insufficient, and many wounded perished where they fell.

If collected, the wounded were brought to collection points where surgeons wielded knives, probes, saws, and needles in an effort to save them. Aside from opium and alcoholic spirits, there were no anesthetics, and the idea that germs caused infection and death had yet to be discovered. A seriously wounded soldier's best chance for survival was amputation, usually done at the joint above the injured limb, because the process of cauterization acted as an effective, though painful, antiseptic. Stomach and chest wounds were often fatal; wounds of the spine were almost invariably fatal. During the Vietnam War, about 95 percent of wounded American soldiers survived, a much higher rate than the 50 percent survival rate of French wounded during the Wars of the First Republic.

Disease—typhus, dysentery, cholera and malaria—was a far more lethal killer than musket and artillery fire. During the Valmy (q.v.) campaign, for example, the Prussian army lost several hundred men a day from dysentery, and the British army in the West Indies lost more than 40,000 from disease. Hospitals, lacking medical knowledge, were unable to cope with the ravages of disease, and what care was given amounted to little more than home remedies. The poor condition of hospitals was not unique to the Revolutionary period. Hospitals during the Crimean War, after all, became a public scandal.

MELAS, MICHAEL FRIEDRICH BENEDIKT, GENERAL (1729–1806). Melas joined the Austrian army at age 16 and served in the Seven Years' War. During the First Coalition (q.v.) he fought in Italy and in 1796 was severely wounded in the attempts to relieve Mantua (q.v.). During the Second Coalition (q.v.), he commanded the Austrian army in Italy and defeated the French at Cassano (q.v.) and Novi (q.v.). In 1800 he prepared to invade France, but Napoleon unexpectedly crossed the Alps into Northern Italy. Instead of retreating, Melas attacked, surprised Napoleon at Marengo (q.v.) and nearly defeated him. Melas retired from service in 1803, having earned the respect of his opponents. Napoleon even gave him a sword as a token of respect for Melas's bravery at Marengo.

MENIN, BATTLE OF (13 SEPTEMBER 1793). After his victory at Hondschoote (q.v.), General Houchard with 40,000 men advanced on Menin, which was held by 20,000 Dutch troops. Houchard drove back the Dutch but was unable to defeat the Austrian forces further east and he retreated. His army simply lacked the training to sustain a major advance, but Houchard was, nevertheless, removed from command and executed.

MENOU, JACQUES-FRANÇOIS, GENERAL (1750–1810). Menou was the son of an officer and joined the army in 1766. By 1787 he was a lieutenant colonel. He supported the Revolution and by 1793 was a general of division. He retired in 1793 because of wounds suffered in fighting in the Vendée (q.v.), but was recalled to service in 1795. Menou rose to command the Army of the Interior. In 1798 he joined the Army of the Orient, fighting at Alexandria (q.v.) and Aboukir (q.v.). He also married in Egypt and became a Moslem convert, adding Abdallah to his name, no doubt to the great amusement of his men. He replaced Kléber (q.v.) in command after Kléber's assassination and, after his defeat by the British, capitulated in August 1801. After his return to France, he served in a series of administrative posts in Italy. He died in Venice in 1810.

MERLIN DE THIONVILLE, ANTOINE-CHRISTOPHER (1762–1833). Merlin came from a middle-class family and in 1788 became a lawyer. He was elected to both the Legislative Assembly and the National Convention (q.v.). He spent a good deal of time as a Representative on Mission. In 1792 he went to northern France to help raise troops and encourage patriotism. In 1793 Merlin went to the Army of the Rhine, which was soon besieged in Mainz (q.v.) by the Prussians. Merlin helped organize the defense and helped sustain morale by personally participating in combat. While at Mainz, he sent a letter to Paris calling for a death sentence for the king. After Mainz capitulated, Merlin served in the Vendée (q.v.) and in 1794–1795 he was again with the Army of the Rhine. He survived the fall of Robespierre (q.v.), with whom he was closely associated, by turning on him and other Jacobins (q.v.). He then served in the Council of Five Hundred under the Directory (q.v.) and retired from public life in 1802. Merlin also acquired much wealth as a legislator by suspicious means. His role as a Representative on Mission was important. Representatives on Mission (q.v.) were not only political watchdogs but also by their direct participation in military affairs they demonstrated to the troops that the government was concerned for their welfare and their success, thereby sustaining morale.

MILET DE MUREAU, LOUIS-MARIE-ANTOINE, GENERAL (1756–1825). Milet de Mureau was of noble origin and joined the army engineers at age 15. By 1789 he was a captain. In 1792 he participated in the occupation of Nice. Suspect because of his origins, Milet de Mureau, now known as Milet Mureau, left the army until 1795. He became a general of brigade in 1796. In 1799 he became the War Minister between February and July and again later in the year. He also became a general of division. In his second term as war minister, he played a role in reinforcing Masséna's forces in Switzerland. He retired from active service after Napoleon's coup, although he occupied a number of civil administrative posts. He left the army permanently in 1816.

MILLESIMO, BATTLE OF (14 APRIL 1796). At the start of the Italian campaign, General Augereau (q.v.) defeated an Austro-Piedmontese force at Millesimo in Liguria. He then advanced toward Ceva (q.v.), but his division was halted at Cosseria.

MIRANDA, FRANCISCO DE (1750–1816). Miranda was born in Caracas. He joined the Spanish army, serving in Spain and the Mediterranean. In 1780 he fought in the Caribbean and Gulf of Mexico. He was a lieutenant colonel in 1782 when he was arrested for plotting against continued Spanish control in South America. He escaped from Havana in 1784 and travelled widely to places including the United States and Russia.

Miranda went to France in 1792 where his connections with a number of leading politicians made it possible for him to obtain a commission as a major general. He served at Valmy (q.v.) in 1792 and later captured Antwerp. At Neerwinden (q.v.) in March 1793, Miranda commanded the left wing of Dumouriez's army. Miranda's troops, mainly new levies, broke under fire and retreated, and probably cost the French the battle. Miranda was then sent to Paris where he was tried and acquitted by the Revolutionary Tribunal. His military career was over, but because he was associated with Girondin politicians, he was arrested and sent to jail until 1795. After his release, he was again placed under suspicion and fled France in 1798. He then went to England and briefly back to France seeking aid for a South American rising without success. In 1810 along with Bolivar, he returned to South America, where in 1812 he was captured by Spanish forces. He died in prison in Cadiz in 1816.

MOLITOR, GABRIEL JEAN JOSEPH, GENERAL (1770–1849). Molitor served as a volunteer in 1791. By 1799 he was a general of brigade. He fought in Switzerland and defeated Suvorov (q.v.) at Näfels in October. In 1800 he fought at Stockach (q.v.). He then campaigned in Italy, Austria, and France. Molitor accepted the Restoration and by 1823 was a corps commander in the Spanish Campaign. In 1847 he was appointed governor of Les Invalides.

MOLLENDORF, RICHARD J. H. VON, GENERAL (1724–1806). Mollendorf entered the Prussian army and fought in the Seven Years' War. He became a general in 1762 and a field marshal in 1793. In 1794 he commanded the main Prussian army. He defended Kaiserslauten (q.v.) in a siege that lasted almost four months. In 1806 he died of wounds received at Auerstadt.

MONCEY, BON ADRIEN JANNOT, GENERAL (1754–1842). Moncey joined the army in 1769 and was commissioned in 1779. He became a captain in 1791. From 1793 to 1795 he fought in the Pyrenees, where he played a major role in defeating the Spanish. In 1794 he was promoted to general of division and captured San Sebastian. He was suspended from command after the September 1797 coup as a suspected Royalist. In 1800 Moncey was back in action, serving in the Army of Reserve. In 1804 he became a marshal and later served in Spain. He then held primarily administrative posts. He supported Napoleon passively, during the Hundred Days, refused to preside over Ney's court-martial, and was jailed for a brief period. The Bourbons restored his rank in 1816, and in 1823 he commanded a corps in the Spanish campaign. In 1824 he was appointed governor of Les Invalides.

MONDOVI, BATTLE OF (21 APRIL 1796). After the battles of Dego (q.v.) and Ceva (q.v.), Bonaparte (q.v.) advanced into Piedmont while Masséna (q.v.) held back the Austrians. On 21 April the French with 25,000 men stormed Mondovi held by 13,000 Piedmontese. Bonaparte then prepared to march on Turin, but the King of Sardinia asked for terms, signing an armistice on 28 April that allowed the French to occupy Piedmont.

MONGE, GASPARD (1746–1818). Monge displayed an early talent for physics and mathematics. He attended the Royal Engineering School at Mézières in 1765 and taught there until 1784. In 1775 he became a professor, and, in 1780, he was admitted to the Academy of Sciences. Between 1784 and 1792 he was an inspector of naval schools. He also conducted numerous scientific studies. In 1792 Monge was appointed minister of marine, holding the position until April 1793.

During the Terror (q.v.), Monge worked to improve military production methods. He wrote studies of how to use bronze from church bells to cast cannons and how to gather and refine saltpeter for the production of gunpowder. Pamphlets describing his methods received wide distribution. In 1794 he helped found a school that would become the Ecole Polytechnique. In 1795 he helped found the Institut National.

Monge then went on missions to Italy, helped found the Roman Republic, and in 1798 was one of the savants who accompanied Bonaparte (q.v.) to Egypt. In Egypt, he established a printing press and helped create the Institute of Egypt. He returned to France with Bonaparte in 1799 and resumed his work at the Polytechnique. After the second Restoration, Monge was dismissed from his posts by the Bourbons. (*See also* Egyptian Expedition)

MONTEBELLO, BATTLE OF (9 JUNE 1800). While advancing into Piedmont, a French advance guard of 6,000 troops encountered 17,000 Austrians. Initially repulsed, Lannes (q.v.) was reinforced by Victor's division of 6,000. Lannes then pushed the Austrians back, inflicting 4,000 casualties while losing 500 men.

MONTENOTTE, BATTLE OF (12 APRIL 1796). Bonaparte (q.v.) advanced from the Ligurian coast to split Piedmontese and Austrian forces. With 9,000 men Bonaparte attacked a 6,000-man Austro-Piedmontese force near Montenotte. A turning movement led to the rout of the Austro-Piedmontese force, which lost 2,500 men, the remnants scattering. This was Bonaparte's first victory in the Italian campaign.

MONTREJEAU, BATTLE OF (20 AUGUST 1799). After foiling Royalist efforts to take Toulouse, Republican columns moved to finish off the counterrevolutionary bands. Six columns surrounded the Royalists at Montrejeau and shattered them. Out of a force of 4,000, the Royalists lost 2,000 killed and 1,000 prisoners. Remnants fled toward the Spanish frontier. Isolated bands continued to resist, however, and small-scale fighting continued for many months.

MOORE, SIR JOHN, GENERAL (1761–1809). Moore was born in Glasgow, entered the army in 1776, and served in the American Revolutionary War. In 1790 he became a lieutenant-colonel and in 1794 participated in the British capture of Corsica. Recalled to England in 1795, he was promoted to colonel and served in the West Indies. He became a major general in 1798. In 1799 Moore fought in Holland. In 1801 he took part in the reconquest of Egypt and played a major role in the night battle of Aboukir (q.v.). After 1802, he introduced light infantry training to the British army at a special training camp at Shorncliffe. British soldiers were taught skirmishing techniques and were trained to operate in direct support of the line infantry. In 1808 Moore went to Portugal, moved into Spain and was, in the face of overwhelming numbers of French troops, forced to retreat to Corunna, where the Royal Navy (q.v.) extracted his army. Moore was, however, killed outside of the town while directing rearguard operations against the French.

MORALE. Morale is a crucial factor in war. In the 18th century it was the factor that enabled soldiers to trade volley fire with an enemy at a range of 100 yards or less. Morale enabled soldiers to overcome their fear of death or mutilation.

In Old Regime armies, the basis of troop morale was loyalty to their primary group—a squad or platoon. The wish to be well-regarded by their immediate companions and the fear of embarrassing themselves were crucial elements in troop morale. It allowed soldiers to submerge their human fears by mechanical obedience to orders. Beyond primary group loyalty, pride in the larger unit, respect for superior officers, and occasionally admiration for senior commanders contributed to effective morale. Soldiers, however, received little or no support from civil society. Civilians tended to view soldiers as agents of repression drawn from the dregs of society.

Soldiers of the Republic, though motivated by primary group loyalty, had the added advantage of being viewed in a heroic mold by society at large. Soldiers were seen as the shields of the Republic and saw themselves as defenders of liberty. Drawn from the full range of the population, Republican fighting men were part of, not separate from, the civil social order. Consequently, military leaders could rely on the enthusiasm of the individual fighter in addition to discipline to enhance battle performance. Republican officers could demand more of their men than could officers in Old Regime armies. The French could also employ innovative tactics and rely on individual initiative to a degree not possible in traditional armies.

Old Regime soldiers were good and usually fought well. They won many battles and when defeated rarely broke and fled in disorder. What they lacked was tactical flexibility, since officers simply could not imagine giving private soldiers a large measure of individual initiative. French soldiers were not always triumphant, although they improved with training and experience. French Republican soldiers were occasionally subject to panic, despair, and desertion. Nevertheless, with their morale sustained by the knowledge that the country looked upon them as protectors and that citizenship included the obligation to serve the nation, French troops evolved a style of warfare—aggressive, persistent and flexible—that gave them inherent advantages over their enemies.

The growth of literacy in the late 18th century meant that many Republican soldiers were able to write, or have written for them, letters home. These letters reveal that troops—although suffering severe privations due to strains in the logistics system, and feeling homesick—

were genuinely convinced that they were fighting for a good cause and that the nation as a whole appreciated their efforts.

MORAND DE GALLES, JUSTIN BONAVENTURE, VICE-ADMIRAL (1741–1809). Morand de Galles joined the French navy in 1757 and became a first lieutenant in 1777. In 1781 he was promoted captain. By 1792 he was a rear admiral and became a vice-admiral in 1793. He was arrested as a nobleman but released in 1795. In 1796 Morand commanded the naval portion of an expedition to Ireland (q.v.). His ships became separated from the main body of the fleet due to fog and rough weather. By the time he arrived at Bantry Bay (q.v.), the rest of the expedition had sailed for France. He later held shore commands, but the 1796 expedition was his last operational effort.

MOREAU, JEAN-VICTOR, GENERAL (1763–1813). Moreau's father was a Breton lawyer, and Moreau studied law at Rennes. He supported the Revolution, joined the National Guard, and was elected captain in an artillery company. He fought with the Army of the North, and deputies on mission promoted him to general of brigade for gallantry in late 1793. In 1794 he led a division in the campaign that conquered the Low Countries, and in 1796 received command of the Rhine and Moselle Army. His campaign in Germany, however, was unsuccessful and the Austrians drove him back across the Rhine. Ambitious and somewhat Royalist in his political views, he was slow to denounce Pichegru's treasonous activities and in 1797 was placed on the inactive list. Recalled in 1798, Moreau served in Italy, but suffered several defeats during operations in 1799. He assisted Napoleon's coup, and Bonaparte (q.v.) sent him to the Army of the Rhine. In the Campaign of 1800 Moreau advanced into Germany and defeated the Austrians at the Battle of Hohenlinden (q.v.) in December 1800. He retired from active duty in 1801, conspired with Pichegru (q.v.) against Napoleon, and was arrested. Between 1804 and 1813 he lived in exile in the United States. He returned as an advisor to Alexander I in the German campaign and at the Battle of Dresden suffered mortal wounds from French artillery fire.

MORTIER, ADOLPHE-EDOUARD-CASIMIR-JOSEPH, GENERAL (1768–1835). General Mortier was the son of a cloth merchant. He was educated at Douai and joined the National Guard in 1789. He fought at Jemappes (q.v.), Neerwindin (q.v.), and Fleurs (q.v.). He next campaigned with the Army of the Rhine, and in 1799 fought at the Battle of Zurich (q.v.). He became a general of division in October 1799. He continued to serve Napoleon, becoming a marshal in 1804. He fought in Germany, Spain, and Russia, and in the 1814 campaign in France.

Mortier supported Napoleon during the Hundred Days. He lost his rank under the Bourbons, but was reinstated by the Orléanist monarchy, which he served until 1835 when he was killed by a bomb at a parade.

MÖSKIRCH, BATTLE OF (5 MAY 1800). Moreau's army, advancing into southern Germany, encountered 60,000 Austrians around Möskirch in Bavaria. Moreau (q.v.) attacked immediately but without success. Reinforcements then arrived, and the French forced the Austrians to retreat. The Austrians lost 5,000 men and the French 3,500. The French were then able to continue their advance into Germany.

MOULIN, JEAN-FRANÇOIS (1752–1810). The son of a grocer, Moulin served a brief tour in the army and became a geographer and engineer, serving at Caen and Paris. A supporter of the Revolution, he joined the National Guard. In 1793, as an army officer, Moulin campaigned successfully in the Vendée (q.v.) and by year's end had been promoted to general of division. He served briefly with the Army of the Alps, until poor health forced him to assume several administrative posts. He fought in Germany in 1796 and in 1798 repressed revolts in Brittany and Belgium. In 1799 Moulin became a Director and opposed Napoleon's Brumaire Coup. Placed briefly under arrest, he continued to oppose Napoleon until poverty led him to come to terms with the new regime. He served in several administrative posts until ill health forced his retirement. He returned to France in 1810 and died a few weeks later.

MOUSCRON, BATTLE OF (29 APRIL 1794). The Army of the North advanced on Menin (q.v.). Saxe-Coburg (q.v.) sent a relief column, but it encountered a superior French force. The Austrians lost 2,000 men and had to retreat, which sealed the fate of Menin. The garrison escaped on 30 April, but the French had gained the strategic initiative.

MURAD BEY (1750–1801). With Ibrahim (q.v.), Murad was one of the Mameluke rulers of Egypt. He was defeated by the French at the Battle of the Pyramids (q.v.) in 1798 and retreated south into Upper Egypt. He eluded his pursuers. He refused to support the Turkish efforts to recapture Egypt and entered into talks with both the French and the British. On his way to Cairo, he died of plague.

MURAT, JOACHIM, GENERAL (1767–1815). Murat was the son of an innkeeper with a large family. He joined the cavalry in 1787. In 1792 he became a second lieutenant and served with the Army of the North. In early October 1795 he assisted Bonaparte (q.v.) in crushing a Royalist rising in Paris. He became Bonaparte's aide during the Italian campaign and was promoted general of brigade in 1796. Murat fought in Egypt in 1798 and 1799 and was promoted to general of division. He returned to France with Napoleon and in 1800 married Bonaparte's sister. He fought at Merengo (q.v.) and then reoccupied central Italy. Murat became a marshal in 1804 and, as a cavalry commander, fought in the campaigns of 1805 and 1806. In 1808 he became King of Naples. He served in the Russian campaign but in 1813 deserted Napoleon in order to retain his kingdom. In 1815 he switched sides again, but was defeated and fled to France. After Waterloo, he went back to Italy, where he was arrested, tried, and executed. Murat was a dashing figure and a first-rate cavalry commander. He was, however, vain, ambitious and not overly bright. His ill-considered political initiatives led to his doom.

MUSKET. The standard infantry weapon of French Republican infantrymen was the Charleville 1777 musket, a smoothbore flintlock weapon, about 50 inches long, firing a .70 caliber lead ball. The official range of the weapon was over 1,000 meters, but in practical terms the range against formed bodies of troops was about 250 meters. The range against individual targets was about 100 yards. Fouling required the barrel to be cleared after 50 rounds, and the flint to be changed after 10 to 12 discharges. The average rate of fire was one or two rounds a minute, although expert marksmen could do better. Aimed fire was not, however, tactically important since muskets were not particularly accurate. Commanders, therefore, relied upon volley fire delivered at close range—usually 100 yards or even less.

French infantrymen also carried a 15-inch triangular-shaped socket bayonet for shock action. The havoc caused by "cold steel" tended to be more moral than physical. Fear of the bayonet rather than its actual use caused units to break. Considering the fact that after the Battle of the Pyramids (q.v.) in 1798, French infantrymen easily bent their bayonets into hooks to fish Mameluke corpses out of the Nile, the relatively rare use of the bayonet in actual combat was quite practical.

Rifled weapons were available. They had a longer range and greater accuracy, but because of the rifling took longer to load. A few soldiers carried rifled carbines, but the vast majority of the soldiers used the musket. Other European armies were armed with similar weapons. Later, the British army made more extensive employment of rifled weapons.

MUTINIES. See Nore; Spithead.

-N-

NARBONNE-LARA, LOUIS, COMTE DE (1755–1813). Narbonne was born in Parma. His father was a Spanish nobleman, and his mother was a maid of honor to a daughter of Louis XV. Rumor asserted that Narbonne was the illegitimate son of the monarch. Narbonne entered the French army, and because of his court connections was a colonel by the time he was 25. In 1791 he was named war minister. A loyal monarchist, he supported Louis XVI's policy of getting France into war. He even assured the Legislative Assembly that in early 1792 the army was ready for battle. Because of political disputes with the Assembly, he resigned from office in March 1792. After the fall of the monarchy, Narbonne fled to London. When Britain joined the First Coalition (q.v.), Narbonne went to Switzerland and then Germany, but refused to bear arms against France. In 1801 he returned to France and served Napoleon loyally. He died of typhus at Torgau in November 1813.

NATIONAL CONVENTION (1792–1795). The National Convention consisted of 749 deputies elected in September 1792. The Convention was supposed to write a new constitution for the nation and govern the country as a provisional government until the constitution could be put into effect. The Convention faced daunting tasks, for in addition to its assigned role it had to deal with the foreign war, domestic counterrevolution, factional conflicts among the deputies, and direct pressure from the Parisian populace.

The deputies were drawn primarily from the middle class. The largest occupational group were lawyers, but there were also clergymen, doctors, soldiers, businessmen, farmers, and even a few noblemen. Many of the deputies had political experience—191 of them had served in the former Legislative Assembly, and 83 had been members of the Constituent Assembly. Others had been local officials. Only a small minority had no prior experience in government.

The Convention was divided into factions: about 25 percent of the deputies were anti-Parisian Girondins. Montagnards—who favored the creation of a strong central government, at least for the duration of the war emergency, and were willing to make some concessions to the demands of the Parisians, including price controls and a vigorous war effort—comprised slightly more than 30 percent of the deputies. Known as the Mountain because they occupied highest seats in the convention hall, most Montagnards were also members of the Jacobin Club. The remaining members of the convention were known as the Plain, whose members tended to react on an issue-by-issue basis. During the Crisis of 1793, however, the plain, more often than not, tended to support the Montagnards. The Mountain, therefore, had the support of about two-thirds of the deputies by late 1793.

The Convention to meet immediate threats to the new Republic created a highly centralized regime, including controls over the nation's manpower and economy. A series of committees, including the Committee of Public Safety (q.v.), and Representatives on Mission (q.v.), armed with plenary powers, were created in order to conduct an efficient and unified war effort.

Ironically, most studies of the Convention focus on issues of politics and social policy rather than on the issues that beset the Republic. The later political right has accused the Convention of being composed of leftist ideologues trying to impose abstract political ideas on reality. Marxists tended to claim that the Convention was an arm of the bourgeois that sought to crush the aspirations of the lower classes. A few have argued that extraordinary circumstances drove the deputies to take extraordinary measures to deal with problems that, if unsolved, might have led to the collapse of the Republic.

The achievements of the Convention were impressive. A war emergency government was created, and its powers were renewed each month by the Convention until the emergency was resolved. After July 1794, much of the power of the Committee of Public Safety was reduced. Foreign invasion was defeated. Counterrevolutionary forces, though not eliminated, were greatly reduced in power. The nation was effectively mobilized. On the other hand, the Convention did not succeed in creating a smoothly functioning democracy, and the government created by the constitution of 1795 was quite weak. The Convention did turn the tide of the war but never ended hostilities successfully. Foreign and internal stability ultimately eluded the Convention, but the deputies by their efforts did enable the Republic to survive the crisis of 1793 and turned the tide of battle against both foreign and domestic enemies.

NATIONAL VOLUNTEERS. "National Volunteers" is a term used to describe the waves of troops volunteering or conscripted between 1791 and 1793. In 1791 the government raised over 100,000 men from National Guard members, who volunteered for active military service for one campaign. New volunteers, some 220,000 men, were raised in 1792. A *levée* in early 1793 produced about 150,000 men, about half of what the government desired, and the *levée* (q.v.) of August 1793 raised over 300,000 troops. The various waves of troops plus the regular army (which also absorbed over 50,000 recruits) produced Europe's largest force, which numbered by 1794 about 800,000 active troops.

NAVY, BRITISH. Throughout the Revolutionary and Napoleonic wars, the Royal Navy (q.v.) dominated the seas. Between 1793 and 1802, the Royal Navy destroyed or captured 56 French, 10 Spanish, 25 Dutch, and 5 Danish ships of the line with a loss of 26, mostly due to storms and other hazards of the sea. Quantatively and (more critically), qualitatively, the

Royal Navy was superior to the naval forces of any power or combination of powers on the European continent.

In 1793 the Royal Navy possessed 141 ships of the line and 165 smaller warships including frigates. Moreover, the navy possessed bases and dockyards capable of supporting and enlarging the fleet. By 1797 the Royal Navy contained 161 ships of the line and 209 other war vessels, and by 1799 the numbers had increased to 176 and 221, respectively. By 1800 the Royal Navy contained 180 ships of the line and 233 other warships. Of course, the navy had numerous tasks to perform, ranging from the blockade of French and later Spanish Atlantic and Mediterranean ports to the protection of overseas bases and the escort of convoys. Nevertheless, the British won every major naval engagement.

Superior numbers were not the explanation of British dominance at sea. At the Glorious First of June (q.v.), numbers of British and French ships were equal. At Cape Saint Vincent (q.v.), 15 British vessels defeated 28 Spanish ships, while at Camperdown (q.v.) the numbers of British and Dutch ships were equal. At the Battle of the Nile (q.v.) numbers were again equal.

The quality of the officers and seamen made all the difference. By 1793 Royal naval officers were in essence professionals. Typically, an officer came from a middle-class background and had gone to sea as a youth, serving at least six years as a midshipman before being promoted to lieutenant. Afterwards, further advancement was a function of longevity or bravery and, frequently, a combination of both. There was in the navy no purchase of commissions.

Crews consisted of a small percentage of volunteers and large numbers of impressed men, often not even British. In peacetime, warships were not fully manned to save expenses. When war came, press gangs would be unleashed in seaport towns, merchant vessels would be stopped at sea, and able-bodied men would be dragged into the navy. Thus in 1790 the Royal Navy had fewer than 20,000 sailors, but by 1800 there were about 120,000 men in the fleet. Crews were ill-paid, ill-fed, and subject to brutal discipline, although life afloat was probably not much more brutal than civilian life ashore.

Officers were, however, able to turn impressed seamen into highly effective fighters. British warships typically spent months—even years—at sea, and officers had more than ample time to train their crews not only in the handling of a single ship but also in the methods of working in squadrons and fleets.

Finally, it is worth noting that British naval commanders were very aggressive. They were constantly seeking battle and opportunities to crush their foe. The traditional tactics of fighting in strict linear order had in practice by the late 1790s given way to more flexible tactics that called for a mêlée. British vessels would seek to break through an enemy battle line and then wage a series of single- or multiple-ship engagements. Nelson (q.v.), for example, typically encouraged his subordinates to seize tactical opportunities and exploit them. The flexible aggressiveness of the Royal Navy was in a sense a naval parallel to the tactical and operational methods of the French army, with the striking exception that no British fleet was ever defeated at sea.

Naval superiority had a number of significant strategic consequences. The Royal Navy effectively prevented a hostile invasion of Britain. The navy also virtually eliminated French seaborne commerce and, despite the activities of privateers, protected British commerce. This in turn helped provide the wealth that Britain required, both for its own war effort and for subsidies to enable coalition partners to put armies in the field against France. The navy could also transport armies to crucial fighting fronts. Alone, the supremacy of the Royal Navy did not guarantee the defeat of France. The fate of two coalitions between 1793 and 1802 is evidence enough that sea power alone could not defeat a land power. Nevertheless, for Britain, the navy was necessary but not sufficient. Necessary in that it was the essential element in Britain's survival and prosperity; not sufficient in that to defeat France, Britain, along with a number of great power Allies, had to defeat the French on the ground. Naval supremacy however, guaranteed that even a defeat on land would not be ultimately catastrophic and that Britain could always try again to form new coalitions. In wars against the Republic, Britain failed to defeat France, but was ultimately successful against Napoleon.

NAVY, FRENCH. Despite much sacrifice and heroism, the Republic's navy was no match for the British fleet. French warships, 76 in 1793, were well-designed and well-constructed. The officers were highly trained and the crews no worse than the human matériel used by the British. The turmoil of the Revolution did have an impact on the navy, especially in terms of the loss of experienced leaders through emigration or execution. The abolition of the specialist gunnery corps also produced much turbulence in the enlisted ranks. The British destruction of naval facilities at Toulon (q.v.) plus the destruction of ten and seizure of three French ships of the line further weakened the Republic's fleet. Between 1793 and 1802 the French lost 56 ships of the line and over 150 frigates. On the other hand, the Revolution's excesses were temporary, and there is evidence that the impact of Republican beliefs actually enhanced crew morale. There are after all numerous examples of warship crews fighting on against terrible odds rather than striking their flag. Moreover, considering the fact that the Bourbon navy did not have a stellar record against the British in wars of the Old

Regime, the loss of Royalist officers may not have been that harmful. During the Seven Years' War, for example, the French lost 45 ships of the line and 19 during the American Revolution. Perhaps the weakness of the Republic's navy was in other areas.

In the first place, France faced the best navy in the world: the British Royal Navy (q.v.), sustained by a country that understood that sea power was the crucial component of their national power. By contrast, France was a land power. Mortal threats to France came only from the land. The British understood that in the process of resource allocation the navy had to have first priority. Similarly, the French had first to build up their armies. A second factor was that the Royal Navy had more training than the French navy. At the start of the war in 1793, the Royal Navy put to sea and stayed there. Consequently, officers trained not only crews of a single vessel but also learned to operate as part of a larger force. The French constantly faced an almost insoluble problem: they could remain in port and be safe or attempt to put to sea to gain proficiency in fleet evolutions and face defeat. Consequently, throughout the Revolutionary Wars, French ships often fought brilliantly while fleets did badly. The French simply could not overcome a legacy of defeat that stretched back to the days of monarchy in the face of the world's best fleet.

NEERWINDEN, BATTLE OF (18 MARCH 1793). On 17 February 1793, General Dumouriez (q.v.), with 18,000 men, invaded the United Provinces while General Miranda (q.v.) covered his right flank. By the beginning of March, Dumouriez had taken Breda, but the Austrians had defeated Miranda, throwing his army back over the Meuse and taking Liege in early March. To protect Brussels, the government ordered Dumouriez to return to Belgium. To halt the Austrians, Dumouriez, with his and Miranda's combined army of 45,000 men, attacked 39,000 Austrians near the village of Neerwinden. The French failed to take the town, lost 4,000 men, and had to retreat to Louvain. His defeat at Neerwinden (q.v.), coupled with the Convention's decision to annex Belgium, ended Dumouriez's hopes of creating a Belgian state with himself as ruler. He therefore decided to mount a coup against the Republic in cooperation with the First Coalition (q.v.). His troops, however, refused to follow him, and he had to flee the Allied lines.

NELSON, HORATIO, VICE-ADMIRAL (1758–1805). Nelson, the son of a clergyman, went to sea as a midshipman in 1771. In 1777 he took his lieutenant's exam and was commissioned. In 1779 he became a post captain in command of a frigate. By 1787 he was ashore on half-pay, but with the advent of war in 1793 Nelson was recalled to active duty in command of a ship of the line.

He served in the Mediterranean and took part in the conquest of Corsica in 1794, losing the sight in his right eye in a minor action. From 1795–1797 he led a squadron off the French and Italian coasts. He was promoted to commodore and played an important role at the Battle of Saint Vincent (q.v.), earning a promotion to rear admiral. In July 1797 Nelson lost his right arm in an attempt to capture a Spanish treasure ship. In April 1798, however, he was put in charge of the blockade of Toulon. When the French fleet nevertheless escaped from port, Nelson, convinced that Egypt was their destination, sailed to the eastern Mediterranean—a bold decision, since the French might have intended to sail to Portugal or Ireland. Nelson actually beat the French to Egypt, sailed off in search of the enemy fleet, and returned to Egyptian waters in late July. On 1 August he found the French in Aboukir Bay, and attacked and virtually destroyed Bonaparte's fleet at the Battle of the Nile (q.v.). He then operated in Italian waters, assisting the Bourbons of Naples in the recovery of the mainland portion of their kingdom. Since the Bourbons had promised safe passage out of Italy to local democrats, Nelson took it upon himself to seize the head of the Neapolitan Republic's navy and hang him on a British ship.

Nelson returned to England in 1800 and was promoted to vice-admiral in 1801, the same year in which he successfully crushed the Danish fleet at Copenhagen (q.v.). In 1805 he defeated a Franco-Spanish fleet at the Battle of Trafalgar, but lost his life during the engagement.

Nelson was the most famous British admiral of his day, but in some respects he was a product of, not a cause of, British naval supremacy. His courage and boldness, his willingness to fight, and his efforts to annihilate his enemies were characteristic of many naval officers. Nelson, of course, did it better than most. His famous "Nelson Touch," wherein he would assemble his captains before a battle, explain to them his general concept of operations, and encourage them to act innovatively to fulfill the overall goal, was not exclusively his own approach or invention. Nelson was part of a superior system and used what he had with courage, dash, and brilliance.

NERESHEIM, BATTLE OF (11 AUGUST 1796). The Rhine and Moselle Army with Moreau (q.v.) in command advanced into southern Germany and marched for the Danube. On 11 August, 65,000 French troops faced 56,000 Austrians at Neresheim. Both the Archduke Charles (q.v.) and Moreau ordered attacks. After hard fighting, in which each side lost about 3,000 men, the Austrians retreated. Moreau's advance in turn enabled Jourdan's Sambre-Meuse Army to cross the Rhine a second time.

NEUMARCK, BATTLE OF (21 AUGUST 1796). Archduke Charles (q.v.) concentrated his army against Jourdan's (q.v.) Army of the Sambre-Meuse. He encountered a French advance guard at Neumarck and threatened to turn their right flank. Fighting was minimal, but the French retreated.

NEUWIED, BATTLE OF (18 APRIL 1797). Hoche's Sambre-Meuse Army crossed the Rhine and occupied Neuwied. The Austrians intended to attack before the entire army had crossed the river, but Hoche (q.v.) attacked first. A frontal attack sustained by a turning movement led by Lefebvre and Richepanse was successful, and the Austrians had to retreat, leaving their supply wagons behind. The Austrians lost some 5,000 men. Hoche then launched a vigorous pursuit. The French occupied Frankfurt, but the Leoben Armistice (q.v.) ended further operations.

NEW ROSS, BATTLE OF (5 JUNE 1798). Irish rebels, about 30,000 strong, attacked the British garrison of New Ross. The rebels were marching on Dublin in hopes of seizing the arsenal and encouraging the French to send aid. The rebels, lacking muskets, were defeated and lost over 2,500 killed. After the battle, the Irish had to retreat back into Wexford. (*See also* Ireland)

NEY, MICHAEL, GENERAL (1769–1815). Ney was the son of a cooper. He joined the army in 1787 and became a sergeant major. The Revolution offered expanded opportunities, and after the overthrow of the monarchy, Ney became an officer. He fought effectively in numerous campaigns and by 1799 was a general of division. He played a significant role in the battle of Hohenlinden (q.v.). He continued to serve Napoleon, who made him a marshal, a prince and a duke. He accepted the Restoration in 1814, but joined Napoleon during the Hundred Days. After Waterloo, the Bourbons had him arrested, tried, and—stories of his escape to the United States notwithstanding—shot. Ney had a volatile temper and was incredibly brave. He, like many generals of the Republic and Empire, had no real grasp of strategy but was a fine operational and tactical commander.

NILE, BATTLE OF THE (1 AUGUST 1798). In the early spring of 1798 the French government decided to invade Egypt as part of a strategic plan to weaken the British economy and force London to sue for peace. Bonaparte (q.v.) was to conquer Egypt and use the country as a stepping stone for a thrust at India where, in cooperation with the Sultan of Mysore, the French would attack British holdings in the subcontinent, thereby dealing a severe blow to British trade. The French presumed that they could safely traverse the Mediterranean because no major British fleet units had been stationed in the area since Spain had declared war on Britain in 1796.

In May a force of 32,000 men led by General Bonaparte left Toulon, occupied Malta, and landed successfully in Egypt. The British had learned of the Toulon expedition, but at first had no precise idea as to its ultimate destination. The Cabinet presumed that the French expedition might strike at Naples, Portugal, or Ireland. Only Dundas (q.v.) guessed at Bonaparte's actual destination. Pitt (q.v.), nevertheless, decided to send a fleet back into the Mediterranean to counter French designs, whatever they were, and to encourage other powers to resume the war with France.

A British fleet under Nelson's command entered the Mediterranean, only to find that the French had sailed from Toulon in late May. Nelson (q.v.), like Dundas, believed that the French were intending to strike at India using Egypt as an advanced base and sailed for Alexandria (q.v.). Upon reaching Alexandria he found no French forces—he had, in fact, beaten them to the Egyptian coast—and sailed off to continue his search. Finding nothing, Nelson returned to the Egyptian coast, and on 1 August 1798, he found the French fleet anchored in Aboukir Bay. Bonaparte had insisted that the fleet remain near his army, and when the British attacked, the French were unprepared. Many sailors were ashore procuring water, and the ships did not cover the entire bay, leaving a gap through which a number of British ships could sail to take the French in a deadly crossfire. The ensuing engagement was a complete victory for the Royal Navy (q.v.), which sank or captured 11 of 13 French ships of the line, inflicting over 8,900 casualties for a loss of 900 men.

The strategic impact of the battle was as disastrous for the French as the tactical results. The Army of the Orient was isolated in Egypt and unable to obtain reinforcements or supplies from the Metropole. Moreover, the battle set in motion a chain of events that would lead to the formation of a Second Coalition (q.v.).

NORE MUTINIES (12 MAY–13 JUNE 1797). British warship crews anchored off the Nore in the Thames Estuary mutinied against conditions of service, including inadequate pay that was often late, bad food, and the brutality of certain officers. Some rioting and looting spread ashore. After order was restored with the promise of early reforms, the leader of the mutiny, Richard Parker, an educated man who had been jailed for debt and then sent to sea, was hanged. Several of his lieutenants were also executed. The navy recovered quickly, and a few months later the Royal Navy (q.v.) won a major victory at Camperdown (q.v.). (*See also* Spithead Mutinies.)

NOVI, BATTLE OF (15 AUGUST 1799). General Joubert (q.v.), with 59,000 men, advanced on Novi, faced by a 68,000-man force led by Suvorov (q.v.). The French were attempting to reverse earlier defeats and maintain a foothold in northern Italy. Early in the battle Joubert was killed by a stray bullet. Moreau (q.v.) took over. In vicious fighting, the French lost 6,500 killed or wounded and 4,000 prisoners. Suvorov suffered 8,000 casualties, took Novi (q.v.), and forced the French to retreat back to Genoa. A number of Directors were at this time planning a coup to purge the legislature, and they intended to use Joubert as their "sword." His death forced the conspirators to seek another military man. A few months later they would choose Bonaparte (q.v.).

-O-

OPERATIONS, FRENCH MILITARY. The operational level of war may be broadly defined as the employment of engagements for the purpose of a campaign. After 1792, the armies of the Republic developed a distinctive operational style based upon the size, motivation, and capabilities of the field armies and the political requirements of the government. French armies by 1793–94 were large, on the whole well-motivated, and organized tactically to wage flexible, aggressive battlefield engagements. The government needed victory to survive the onslaught of foreign and domestic enemies and to retain the support of the Parisian populace, who demanded vigorous prosecution of the war. Thus, in 1793, the government called for offensives on virtually all battlefronts and, in 1794, instructed commanders to avoid sieges whenever possible, mask enemy garrisons with a minimum number of troops, seek major field engagements, and follow every victory with a relentless pursuit. Moreover, defeats in the field were not to be the signal for a retreat. Rather, they were to be the cause of renewed attacks. Republican armies were to attack constantly, exhaust the enemy, and ultimately defeat the nation's foes on the field of battle.

In 1794 Jourdan's operations provide an excellent example of the evolving Republican operational style. Jourdan (q.v.) led the right wing of the Army of the North, plus the Moselle and part of the Army of the Ardennes. Jourdan's force, ultimately known as the Army of the Sambre-Meuse, first crossed the Sambre River on 12 May only to be driven back. Renewed attacks on 20 May, 25 May, and 29 May were also defeated. Jourdan advanced again on 12 June. He was defeated and attacked again on 18 June and finally secured a firm lodgement across the Sambre. He advanced rapidly on Charleroi and brought the coalition army to battle at Fleurs (q.v.) on 26 June. After the victory, the Sambre-Meuse army moved rapidly into Belgium, taking Namur in mid-July.

The French operational technique of constant offensives did not always succeed. In 1795 and 1796 operations in Germany failed. In 1799 French offensives in Germany were also defeated. In Italy, by contrast, Bonaparte's campaign of 1796–1797 was strikingly successful. Using Republican operational techniques, Bonaparte (q.v.) moved rapidly and attacked constantly, keeping his enemies off-guard and on the defensive. In 1799, though on the defensive, the French were constantly seeking opportunities to attack.

French armies rarely sought to annihilate their enemies in a single engagement. They were instinctively too clever to think that a single battle would decide a campaign or a war. Rather, the French employed a combination of attrition and annihilation. Constant assaults would wear down enemy strength and morale until an engagement would produce a victory of some magnitude. Operational style, then, was a process, not a search for a simple decisive solution.

Napoleon as ruler of France did seek decisive victories and won a number of battlefield triumphs between 1805 and 1807 that many viewed as decisive victories. He failed to profit from these triumphs, raising serious doubts about the nature of his so-called decisive battles. After all, if a battle, no matter how successful, does not produce beneficial long-term political results, can it in fact be labelled decisive? Soldiers and scholars, however, became mesmerized by Napoleonic victories and tended to define the object of war as the effort to wage a single, war-winning decisive engagement or campaign. In so doing they ignored the experience of the Republic, whose leaders by accident or design learned that battles were the culmination of a process and that operational techniques could enhance the prospects of victory, but could not in and of themselves guarantee success.

OTT, PETER CARL, BARON, GENERAL (1738–1809). Ott was born at Gran and had a distinguished career in the Austrian army. He fought against the Turks in 1789 and the French in the Low Countries in 1793 and 1794. In 1799 he served under Suvorov (q.v.), fighting at Novi (q.v.) and Ancona. In 1800 he successfully besieged Genoa (q.v.). He fought at Marengo (q.v.) and, though defeated, withdrew his troops in good order. This was his last active command. Ott was a typical Hapsburg general—well-trained and experienced, but ultimately unable to deal effectively with Republican military innovations, especially when combined with Bonaparte's talents.

OUDINOT, NICHOLAS CHARLES, GENERAL (1767–1847). Oudinot was the son of a brewer who joined the army in 1784. He joined the National Guard in 1789, and from 1792–1794 served with the Rhine and Moselle armies as a lieutenant-colonel. In 1794 Oudinot became a provisional general of brigade. In 1795 he was wounded several times and briefly taken prisoner. In 1799 he was promoted to general of division and played a major role in the Battle of Zurich (q.v.). In 1800 he fought at the siege of Genoa (q.v.). Later Oudinot served in Germany and on the Danube, and in 1809 he became a marshal. He fought in Russia in 1812, Germany in 1813, and France in 1814. He accepted the Restoration, did not join Napoleon during the Hundred Days, and in 1823 led a corps into Spain. He spent the last five years of his life as governor of the Les Invalides. Oudinot was above all a fighting general. He sustained more wounds, 22, than any other senior commander.

-P-

PAOLI, PASCAL (1725–1807). Paoli was a Corsican, educated at a military school in Naples and commissioned into a regiment of Corsican refugees commanded by his father. He soon became the leader of Corsicans seeking independence from Genoa. Paoli, after France took possession of Corsica, continued to resist foreign control. He was, however, defeated and went into exile. He returned to Corsica in 1789, initially accepting French sovereignty—but in 1793 he turned against the Republic. In 1794 Paoli accepted and encouraged British occupation of Corsica, but broke with them, retired to London, and died in obscurity. Bonaparte (q.v.) viewed Paoli as his hero until the break with France in 1793, and the Bonaparte family that had remained in Corsica left the island.

PARKER, SIR HYDE, ADMIRAL (1739–1807). The son of a vice-admiral, Parker served in North American waters during the American Revolutionary War and later commanded naval forces stationed at Jamaica from 1796 to 1800. In 1801 he commanded the fleet sent to attack Copenhagen. He was, however, rather timid, and Nelson won the naval engagement against the Danes. After Copenhagen, Parker was recalled and received no other active commands.

PARTHENOPEAN REPUBLIC. After the French defeat at the Battle of the Nile (q.v.), the King of Naples, with British encouragement, attacked French troops stationed in the recently created Roman Republic. On 27 November 1798, Neapolitan troops led by General Mack (q.v.) took Rome. The French army, led by General J. E. Championnet (q.v.), after receiving reinforcements, counterattacked and retook Rome in mid-December and proceeded to invade Naples. The king fled to Sicily and, in January 1799, Mack asked for an armistice which left the French in control of the kingdom except for Sicily and the city of Naples.

The Directory (q.v.) had initially no intention of creating new commitments in Italy, but Championnet, on his own initiative, entered the city of Naples in late January and proclaimed the existence of the Parthenopean Republic (after the Greek name for Naples). The Directory dismissed Championnet for disobeying the instructions of the army commissioner to refrain from creating a Republican regime.

The new republic was accepted by the people of the city of Naples, but an agent of the king, Cardinal Ruffo, raised a peasant rebellion. On 5 May 1799 the French evacuated the city to deal with the Austro-Russian forces in the north. Small garrisons held some forts, but they capitulated in June and were allowed to return to France. Neapolitan democrats were supposed to be allowed to accompany them, but the king broke his word, hanged 120 of them, and more than 1,100 received long prison terms.

PASTRENGO, BATTLE OF (26–27 MARCH 1799). Scherer (q.v.) advanced on Verona on 26 March in order to disrupt a planned Austrian offensive and relieve pressure on Jourdan's army, which had just been defeated in Germany. Scherer ordered his army to cross the Adige River. His forces took Pastrengo on the western side of the river, but were unable to cross to the Austrian side. Nor were other units able to take Verona. Each side lost about 8,000 men, but the French offensive had failed on the first day.

PAUL I, TSAR OF RUSSIA (1754–1801). Coming to the throne upon the death of Catherine II in 1796, Paul brought his own circle of courtiers to power. Those excluded soon circulated rumors that Paul was mad, but eccentricities not withstanding, there is no real evidence of insanity. In foreign affairs, Paul sought to prevent Russian involvement in the wars of the Revolution, in order to focus upon the restoration of the state's finances and the absorption of the new Polish provinces gained by the partitions of 1792 and 1795.

The French invasion of Egypt, however, seemed to pose a threat to Russian interests. Bonaparte's seizure of Malta (q.v.) alienated Paul, who was the Grand Master of the Order of the Knights of Malta, and the subsequent invasion of Egypt inserted French power into a region long regarded by Russia as an important area of Russian interest. Paul, therefore, decided to take up arms against the Republic. At the end of 1798 he concluded an alliance with the Ottoman Empire and joined the Second Coalition (q.v.).

Paul agreed to send Russian forces to fight in Italy, Switzerland, and Holland. His objective was the same as Pitt's: the overthrow of the Republic, the reduction of France to the frontiers of 1792, and the restoration of the pre-1789 status quo in the Italian peninsula. The campaign of 1799 began with a series of Allied victories. The Austrians, however, betrayed their partners in pursuit of their own particular ambitions. Vienna intended to seize and retain northern Italy. Austria also intended to take Belgium and exchange it for Bavaria. Consequently, Austrian forces that were to guard the right flank of the Russian army in Switzerland moved away to prepare for the attack into the Rhineland and Belgium. They moved before the Russian army in Italy had arrived to support the corps in Switzerland, which was momentarily isolated and crushed at the Battle of Zurich (q.v.) in September 1799. The French then turned on the forces that were moving into Switzerland. The Russians escaped annihilation but suffered heavy losses. Shortly after, the Russians in Holland had to surrender along with the British expeditionary corps.

Angered by the disloyalty of his Allies, Paul left the coalition at the end of 1799 and adopted a pro-French policy. He formed a League of Armed Neutrality (q.v.) and began to plan an invasion of India. Before his policy had time to have a major impact, he was murdered on 23 March 1801 by a clique of aristocrats, who acted with the knowledge of Alexander, his son and heir.

PECH DAVID, BATTLE OF (7–8 AUGUST 1799). By the spring of 1799 Royalists in southwestern France had created armed bands numbering about 20,000 men. Toulouse had, in effect, become a Republican island in a Royalist sea, and Royalists were prepared to launch a massive rising to aid the advance of the Allies.

On 2 August, Louis XVIII issued orders for a general rising to begin on 8 August. Republican agents, however, had penetrated some of the Royalist organizations and helped disrupt Royalist plans. Consequently, the rebellion began sporadically on the night of August 4–5.

The Royalists, nevertheless, managed to concentrate a large force at Pech David, a hill dominating Toulouse. On 7 August they attacked Toulouse, but the Republicans were mobilized and drove off the attack. On 8 August, 11 National Guard battalions attacked and routed the rebels, killing over 300. On 9 August the Republicans shattered another Royalist force that was moving on Toulouse from the west. The Royalists lost 400 killed and 800 prisoners out of a force of about 5,000.

PELLEW, EDWARD, ADMIRAL (1757–1833). Pellew joined the Royal Navy in 1770. In 1793 he captured the first French frigate of the war. In 1797, along with another frigate, he captured a French 74-gun ship of the line. He entered Parliament in 1802. Later, Pellew held commands in the East Indies, the North Sea, and the Mediterranean. He became an admiral in 1814. From 1817 to 1821, he was the commander at Plymouth. A "Nelsonian" type, Pellew was a colorful figure and an inspiring leader in the Royal Navy's tradition.

PÉRIGNON, DOMINIQUE, MARQUIS DE, GENERAL (1754–1818). A member of the old sword nobility, he became an officer in the Royal Army in the 1780s but retired early. A supporter of the Revolution, he took a commission in the National Guard and was elected to the Legislative Assembly in 1791. In 1792 he returned to active service, fighting in the Pyrenees against the Spanish army. He was promoted to major general in 1794 and became commander of the army in Spain in 1794–1795. After Spain made peace with France, Pérignon returned to civilian life and served as ambassador to Spain from 1795 to 1797. During the War of the Second Coalition (q.v.) he returned to active service, fought in Italy, and was captured at Novi (q.v.). Napoleon made him a senator in 1802 and one of the original marshals in 1804. His promotion was primarily a reward for past services, and he never again exercised a field command. Pérignon served in administrative posts under the Empire, supported the Bourbon Restoration, and became a peer of France in 1814. He did not join Napoleon during the Hundred Days.

PERPIGNAN, BATTLE OF (17 JULY 1793). After several defeats, the Army of the Eastern Pyrenees established a fortified camp in front of Perpignan. The Spanish, about 15,000 strong, attacked 12,000 French, who drove off the attack. The two sides then entrenched themselves and waged a series of small encounters. Although neither side scored a major victory, the French managed to retain control of the city and block further Spanish advances.

PERRÉE, JEAN-BAPTISTE EMMANUEL, REAR ADMIRAL (1761–1800). Perrée first went to sea as a cabin boy in 1773 and worked his way up to the command of a merchant ship. In 1793 he transferred to the navy and was promoted to captain in 1794. In 1795 he conducted a successful commerce raiding expedition in the Mediterranean, and in 1798 he took part in the Egyptian expedition. Perrée successfully commanded gunboats on the Nile and was promoted to rear admiral. He was captured while attempting to return to France but was quickly exchanged. In 1800 he attempted to resupply the French garrison on Malta (q.v.)—the British fleet intercepted him. Perrée accepted battle against hopeless odds to permit other French ships to escape. He was mortally wounded in the engagement, and his ship had to strike its flag.

PHÉLYPEAUX, ANTOINE LE PICARD (1768–1799). Of aristocratic birth, Phélypeaux attended the military school in Paris at the same time as Napoleon. He entered the artillery but opposed the Revolution and became an émigré (q.v.). He served in Condé's (q.v.) army until 1795, when he tried and failed to raise a Royalist rebellion in Berry. He also helped Sir William Sidney Smith (q.v.) escape captivity, and Smith obtained for him a commission as a colonel in the British army. He played a leading part in organizing the defense of Acre (q.v.) in 1799, but after defeating the Army of the Orient, he caught the plague and died.

PICHEGRU, JEAN-CHARLES, GENERAL (1761–1805). Born to a peasant family, Pichegru was educated in church schools. He enlisted in the army, fought in America, and rose to be a sergeant major by 1789. By the summer of 1792 he was a lieutenant. He left the army only to be elected commander of a battalion of volunteers. Pichegru served in the Rhine army and by August 1793 was a general of brigade. His abilities led to rapid promotion, and in 1794 he became commander of the Army of the North and played a crucial role in the conquest of Belgium and Holland. In August 1795, however, he began dealing with Royalist agents. He was attracted by the money they offered and the promise of high position if he helped destroy the Republic. His defeat in 1795 in Germany may well have been the product of secret dealings with the Austrians. Pichegru, however, lacked the courage to take the final step of outright rebellion and resigned his commission in 1796. Using English money, he got himself elected to the Council of Five Hundred in 1797, but in September was arrested and deported to Guyana. He escaped in 1798 and in 1799 advised Allied forces in Holland. In 1803 he secretly returned to Paris as part of a Royalist plot to kidnap or kill Napoleon. He was arrested in February 1804 and on 5 April was found strangled in his cell, possibly at Bonaparte's direction.

PILLNITZ, DECLARATION OF (27 AUGUST 1791). Leopold II of Austria was initially sympathetic to the French Revolution, believing that a constitutional monarchy would strengthen France and enhance its value as an Austrian ally. Louis XVI's refusal to accept a constitution and his failed attempt to flee the country forced Leopold to act. He wanted to strengthen moderate factions in France and avoid war. To do so, he decided to issue a threat, which in theory would preserve the French monarchy and silence the radicals. On 27 August 1791, Leopold and the King of Prussia issued the Declaration of Pillnitz, named after a town in Saxony where they had met. The declaration asserted that the position of the French king was a matter of common concern to all the rulers of Europe. The declaration invited other powers to join Berlin and Vienna in employing the most effective means to strengthen the Bourbons, in which case Austria and Prussia would be prepared to act promptly.

Leopold, of course, knew full well that the powers would never agree on a common policy, and the notion of "in which case" would never come to pass. The impact of the declaration, however, was very different from Leopold's intentions. Frenchmen viewed it not as a hollow gesture but as a real threat. The declaration, coupled with émigré (q.v.) agitation for action against the Revolution, strengthened the radicals and weakened the moderates in France and made people more suspicious than ever of the king's motives and actions. Thus, an effort to preserve the peace became a step on the road to war and revolution.

PIRMASENS, BATTLE OF (14 SEPTEMBER 1793). To protect Alsace, 12,000 French troops of the Army of the Moselle attacked a fortified encampment that was defended by Prussian troops led by the Duke of Brunswick (q.v.). The attack failed. The French suffered 4,000 casualties. The Prussians, however, did not mount a vigorous pursuit.

PITT, WILLIAM (1759–1806). Pitt became prime minister in 1783. He was Britain's youngest prime minister, and an expert manager of parliamentary politics. After 1789, in foreign affairs he initially did not view the Revolution in France as a threat. In fact, he seems to have felt that the French concern for domestic politics would reduce the possibility of serious international rivalries between London and Paris. When France went to war with Austria and Prussia in 1792, Pitt continued to believe that Britain could remain neutral. However, when France overran Belgium and opened the Scheldt to navigation in order to win the support of Belgian merchants, Pitt realized that Britain would have to enter the war to prevent French domination of the Low Countries.

Britain entered the war in 1793 and organized the First Coalition (q.v.). Pitt's wartime strategies were typical British responses to a great power that sought to control the Low Countries. Pitt intended to subsidize Allied armies on the Continent, seize French colonial possessions, support counterrevolutionary movements within France, and send an army to the Continent to fight alongside Allied forces. The British had done something like this in the War of the Spanish Succession, the War of the Austrian Succession, and the Seven Years' War with reasonable success. Pitt, however, failed.

He has been blamed for being a poor war leader, but it is hard to see how he could have done much better. Britain's Allies in Europe were feckless and self-absorbed. They were unwilling to subordinate their particular objectives to a common coalition policy and strategy. Moreover, France on land was dramatically stronger than ever before and more than a match for Continental adversaries. Britain was victorious at sea and in colonial warfare but could not defeat France on land. Pitt could not energize the First Coalition, which collapsed by 1797. He then sought to negotiate with France, but talks in Paris in 1796 and at Lille (q.v.) in 1797 were unsuccessful. Pitt was willing to recognize the French conquest of Belgium, but the French insisted that the British also return colonies that Britain had taken from the Dutch, and the talks collapsed. Pitt then fought on alone until the formation of a Second Coalition (q.v.), which also failed due to a combination of Allied disunity and French land power.

Pitt then left office, and his successor did conclude a treaty with France that granted Britain a few colonial concessions coupled with British recognition of French Continental conquests. Pitt supported the treaty. When war was renewed in 1803, Pitt returned to office and organized a Third Coalition, which was quickly defeated by Napoleon. Exhausted by his efforts, Pitt died in 1806.

Throughout the wars with Revolutionary and Napoleonic France, Pitt was a determined foe. He introduced an income tax to sustain the war effort, but also suppressed civil liberties and refused to push for parliamentary reform. He pursued a logical and coherent strategy. Pitt failed to defeat the Republic and the Empire due to circumstances well beyond his control. He nevertheless held the country together, garnered respect even from his political rivals, and set an example of dogged persistence in the face of adversity.

PIUS VI, POPE (1717–1799). Giovanni Angelo Braschi, from a noble family in the Roagna, was elected pope in 1775. Before 1789 he concerned himself with efforts to improve the government of the Papal States and sought to fend off efforts of Catholic monarchs who sought to bring ecclesiastical authorities more directly under their control. The reforms of the French church, including the nationalization of church lands and the introduction in 1790 of the Civil Constitution of the Clergy, initiated by the Revolution after 1789, quickly turned Pius into an enemy of the Revolution. In March and April 1791 he condemned not only the Civil Constitution of the Clergy but also the regime's support of religious toleration and freedom of the press. After 1792, the pope declared war on the Republic and supported counterrevolution in France. The French church split, and many clerics opposed the Revolution and even took up arms against it. Hostility between the church and the Republic became a political fact of life in France that in a more muted form still persists. In 1798 French troops occupied Rome and placed Pius under arrest when he refused to leave the city. Pius spent the rest of his life as a French prisoner. He died at Valence in France in August 1799.

POLAND. Poland was a large state with a weak central government and no military capability. Poland was also surrounded by rapacious great powers. An effort to strengthen the government in 1791 was defeated by Russian intervention. In 1793, Prussia and Russia executed the Second Partition, and the remainder of the state was occupied by Russians. The Poles offered no effective resistance. Seeing that the extinction of their independence was only a matter of time, the Poles rebelled in March of 1794. The Poles held out for six months against Russian and Prussian forces, but the Russians took Warsaw in November, and a final partition followed in 1795. The French, though sympathetic, could offer little practical assistance, absorbed as they were with warfare in the west. Many Poles fled to the west, and thousands of them fought with the Republic against the eastern powers. Poland's obliteration, however, helped the Republic in an oblique way. Prussian and Austrian hostility over the terms of the 1793 and 1795 partitions led both powers to retain substantial forces in the east, away from the crucial battlefield in Belgium. Moreover, Austro-Prussian rivalry over Poland was a significant factor in convincing Berlin to leave the First Coalition (q.v.) in 1795.

PRIEUR DE LA CÔTE-D'OR, CLAUDE-ANTOINE (1763–1832). Prieur Duvernois was born in Auxonne. His father was a royal receiver of finances, a low-ranking post of nobility of the robe. Claude-Antoine was, however, able to claim noble birth and obtain admission to the school of military engineering at Mézières in 1781. He supported the Revolution from the outset and was in 1791 elected to the Legislative Assembly from the Côte-d'Or. He supported the overthrow of the monarchy and was elected to the National Convention (q.v.) in 1792. He made numerous trips to inspect frontier defenses, but in early 1793 was back in Paris for the trial of Louis XVI. He voted for the death penalty.

Prieur de la Côte-d'Or was elected to the Committee of Public Safety (q.v.) in August 1793 and devoted his major efforts to organizing the production of arms and munitions for the Republic's greatly expanded army. He became the government's de facto minister of armaments, establishing factories in Paris and in the provinces to produce weapons and munitions. He established a military proving ground at Meudon to test new weapons and created "Courses on the Revolutionary Production of Weapons and Explosives" to teach workers throughout France how to improve and increase production. Though not well known, Prieur played a crucial role in the development of the Republic's armed forces.

Prieur survived the fall of Robespierre (q.v.) and continued to serve on the Committee of Public Safety (q.v.) until October 1794. He returned to the Convention, where he helped establish the school that became the Ecole Polytechnique. Under the Directory (q.v.), he served in the Council of Five Hundred until May 1798. He later became a successful wallpaper manufacturer and spent his last years in Dijon.

PROMOTION SYSTEM, FRENCH. During the early days of the Revolution, the Constituent Assembly attempted to reform and rationalize the army promotion system. In 1790 venality was abolished, and all ranks were open to all citizens. The Assembly declared that three-quarters of entering sub-lieutenants would obtain commissions via examinations, while the remainder would be drawn from NCOs. Promotion to lieutenant and captain would be based on seniority. For lieutenant colonels and colonels, two-thirds of the commissions were to be based on seniority and one-third by nomination of the king, who also selected half of those promoted to general officer grades. The other half was based on seniority.

Officer emigration upset the efforts to create a systematic promotion system in the line army. In June 1791, in order to fill vacancies rapidly, generals were authorized to nominate any suitable candidate to sub-lieutenancies. One-half of the nominees were to be NCOs from the unit in which vacancies occurred. Examinations were suspended in late 1791, and promotions to junior officer grades would come from NCOs and National Guards. Beyond sub-lieutenant, promotion was based on seniority.

Volunteer battalions of 1791 and 1792 elected their officers. A law of 4 August 1791 decreed that company grade officers and NCOs were to be selected from among individuals with some prior military service in the line army or National Guard. Each battalion was to elect two lieutenant colonels, one of whom must have commanded a company.

The amalgamation decree of 21 February 1793 eliminated distinctions between the line and volunteer units. A decree of 26 February 1793 created a single promotion system. All ranks from sergeant to lieutenant colonel (chief of battalion) were to be filled by a combination of election and seniority. Two-thirds of the vacancies would be filled by seniority. The rest were to be elected. Soldiers selected three candidates, and the final choice was made by soldiers serving in the rank to which the nominees aspired. Promotion to chief of brigade was based upon seniority in grade or total length of service of the eligible battalion commanders. The central government named general officers. A decree of 19 July 1794 established that officers up to and including chief of battalion would be selected for promotion by a combination of election, nomination, and seniority. One-third would obtain promotion based on election, another third would be promoted by seniority, and the final third would be selected by the Convention, which would make its selection from three nominees submitted by battalion administrative councils, which included the commander, one officer, one NCO from each grade, and five privates.

In December 1793, as an emergency measure, Representatives on Mission (q.v.) were authorized by the Convention (q.v.) to make field promotions. A law of 15 February 1794 stipulated that only individuals who could read and write could become officers or NCOs. The Republican promotion system was a combination of military efficiency, democratic practice, and ultimate civilian control. A law of 3 April 1795 regularized the promotion system, eliminating the emergency measures while retaining the basic methods of seniority, nomination, and election as the basis of promotion. The system enabled the Republic to expand rapidly the officer corps and reward loyalty, longevity, and talent.

PROPAGANDA DECREES (1792). On 19 November 1792, the Convention (q.v.) issued the First Propaganda Decree, promising aid and friendship to all peoples who sought liberty. The decree sounded like a call to universal revolution, and the Girondin-dominated government had a definite internationalist tinge. Brissot, the foreign minister, had lived abroad for many years, and volunteer legions from Belgium, Holland, Switzerland, and Germany served in the French army. The decree also sought to assure the French public that the people of Europe would greet the Republic's armies as liberators.

In reality, however, the decree had more specific intents related to French national interests. The decree was a response to requests from Belgian and Rhennish democrats, who were assisting the French and wanted protection from counterrevolutionary reprisals, that it was safe to collaborate with France. Moreover, the French told foreign governments not yet at war with the Republic that the decree excluded neutrals from its scope.

On 15 December 1792, the Convention issued the Second Propaganda Decree, stating that when French forces entered enemy territory, commanders would proclaim the abolition of titles and feudal dues, abolish aristocratic privileges, convoke primary assemblies that would in turn organize interim governments, and confiscate the property of the ruling prince, the church, and aristocrats. Generals were to use assignats for the purchase of supplies, using confiscated property as security. The decree was in part a response to the activities of General Dumouriez (q.v.) in Belgium. Dumouriez, who had ambitions to become the ruler of Belgium, had followed his own occupation policy, including raising loans from the Belgian clergy and promising them that they would retain their manorial dues and titles. The decree, by establishing a clear occupation policy, sought to prevent Dumouriez and other generals with political ambitions from acting against the interests and orders of the Convention. The decree also sought to secure cooperation from pro-Republican groups in occupied territories and force groups most opposed to France to bear the costs of the war.

The second decree was not a proclamation of class war, and it did not apply to neutrals. It was designed to serve French interests in specific circumstances. It established a clear occupation policy, limited the independence of the military, and made the Republic's foes pay for the French war effort. The decree also served as a warning to enemies and neutrals of what lay in store for them if they continued the war or joined the ranks of the Coalition.

PROVENCE, LOUIS-XAVIER, COMTE DE (1755–1824). Provence was a younger brother of Louis XVI (q.v.). Before 1789 he was known as a liberal and an admirer of the philosophes. In 1789 he declared his support for the Revolution in ambiguous terms, but in June 1791 fled to Brussels. He then moved to Coblenz, where he presided as regent over a shadow government and denounced the Constitution of 1791, despite the fact that Louis XVI had accepted it. After the failure of the Prussian invasion in 1792, Provence moved to Westphalia. Upon receiving news of Louis XVI's execution, Provence declared himself regent for Louis XVI's son. Upon the death of the son, who Royalists regarded as Louis XVII, Provence declared himself king as Louis XVIII.

Provence then followed a peripatetic existence, moving to Verona, and from there to Mittau in Courland. After Mittau, Provence and his court went to Warsaw, back to Mittau, and finally in 1807 to London. Throughout his sojourn, Provence lived upon the largesse of his hosts. Throughout the Revolutionary and Napoleonic periods, Provence actually did little to inspire counterrevolutionary activity. Artois (q.v.) and Condé (q.v.) were far more active. Provence, unlike most Bourbons after Louis XIV, appears to have learned something and in January 1814 issued a proclamation announcing his willingness to accept some of the changes wrought by the Revolution. Napoleon's defeat in 1814 paved the way for the Charter of 1814, which in fact preserved much of the legacy of the Revolution. Provence, thanks to the exertions of Allied arms, was in fact restored to the throne as Louis XVIII in 1814, and again after Waterloo in 1815. He ruled until 1824. While in exile, Provence did little to strike at the Republic and Empire. The Allies, not his own efforts, restored him to the throne, but during his years outside of France he did manage to keep alive the Royalist idea.

PUISAYE, JOSEPH-GENEVIÈVE, COMTE DE (1755–1827). Puisaye initially accepted the Revolution, but in 1793 sided with the Girondins. He briefly led a Federalist army in Normandy, but was defeated. He fled to Brittany, where he tried to transform the various Chouan (q.v.) bands into an effective army. Defeated in August 1794 he went to London where the British and Artois (q.v.) were planning the Quiberon (q.v.) invasion. Artois suspected Puisaye of being a constitutionalist rather than an absolute Royalist but, nevertheless, placed him in command of Brittany. After the failure of the Quiberon expedition in 1795, Pruisaye in 1796 tried to recreate a guerrilla force in Brittany and link it with guerrilla bands in the Vendée (q.v.) and Anjou. Defeated again, he went into hiding and escaped back to Britain. He was removed from command and efforts to justify his actions in print led to a permanent split with the Bourbons. He never returned to France.

PYRAMIDS, BATTLE OF THE (21 JULY 1798). After landing in Egypt, Bonaparte (q.v.) advanced along the west bank of the Nile toward Cairo. Nearing the city, the Army of the Orient encountered the Mameluke army. Some 18,000 peasant soldiers were on the east bank. On the west bank the Mamelukes (q.v.) placed 15,000 infantry plus 6,000 elite cavalrymen. Bonaparte drew up his forces into large squares six ranks deep with artillery at the corners. The French advanced in square formation. The Mameluke cavalry charged and were crushed. The French also attacked the Egyptian infantry, and the peasant troops quickly broke and fled. About 3,000 Mameluke horsemen were killed or wounded plus an unknown but large number of footsoldiers. The next day the French occupied Cairo as the garrison withdrew without offering battle. Bonaparte effectively controlled Lower Egypt. (*See also* Egyptian Expedition)

-Q-

QUASDANOVITCH, PETER GENERAL (CA. 1796). Quasdanovitch commanded the western column of Würmser's (q.v.) army, which was trying to relieve Mantua (q.v.). Near Lake Garda, Masséna (q.v.) repulsed him at Lonato (q.v.). He played a significant role in Alvintizi's 1797 operations. He fought at Rivoli (q.v.) but was again defeated.

QUIBERON (JULY 1795). In 1795 the British attempted to open another front against France, since the Allied forces in the Low Countries had collapsed. A landing in western Brittany would, the British and émigrés (q.v.) hoped, respark Royalist insurrections in western France. On 27 June 100 transports protected by a dozen warships put a force of 3,000 émigrés ashore on the Quiberon peninsula, plus arms and equipment for 70,000 men. Some 5,000 Chouans (q.v.) rallied to the invaders, but General Hoche (q.v.) moved quickly to halt an advance inland. On 16 July and again on 21 July Hoche attacked and defeated the Royalists. About 300 Royalists were killed and 1,000 captured. The rest escaped to sea. Additionally, 5,000 Chouans were captured. The French showed clemency to the Chouans but shot 640 émigrés. The defeat of the expedition enabled Hoche to force a general pacification of western France in 1796. (*See also* Counterrevolution)

-R-

RANKS. The terminology for various ranks changed during the Revolution.

Royal Army ranks:

Sub-lieutenant
Quartermaster
Lieutenant
Captain
Major
Lieutenant colonel
Colonel
Brigadier
Maréchal de camp
Lieutenant general
Maréchal of France

In 1791 the grade of major was suppressed. In 1793 the title chief of battalion (squadron in the cavalry) replaced the rank of lieutenant colonel, and chief of brigade replaced the designation colonel. The rank of brigadier was also eliminated. The title general of brigade replaced the rank of maréchal de camp. The grade of general of division replaced that of lieutenant general.

Republican army ranks:

Sub-lieutenant
Captain
Chief of battalion
Chief of brigade
General of brigade
General of division

General of the Army was a title given to an army commander but was not a permanent rank. It went with the job but not with the individual. A general of brigade was a general officer who was entitled to command combined arms formations. A chief of brigade commanded only troops from his own service: i.e. infantry, cavalry, artillery, or engineers.

REGULATION OF 1 AUGUST 1791. The drill regulations of 1 August 1791 were the culmination of reform efforts undertaken by the

Royal Army after 1763. The Regulations, strongly influenced by the work of Guibert (q.v.), described how to form firing lines and small columns and how to move from a marching column into a battle formation. Moreover, the Regulations allowed commanders a large degree of tactical flexibility. The drill book described formations but did not prescribe when and where to use the various battle forms. It was left to commanders to select the precise battle order according to specific situations. Both the Republican and Imperial armies employed the 1791 Regulations as the basic drill manual. In fact, the manual was not substantially modified until 1831. The simplicity of the drill and the wide discretion left to commanders made the 1791 Regulations, written for the line army, well-suited for use by the citizen-soldiers of the Republic. (*See also* Infantry; Republican Army, French)

REPRESENTATIVES ON MISSION. Representatives on Mission were deputies to the National Convention (q.v.) assigned to oversee the armed forces, enforce the laws in the departments, supervise conscription, and organize the war economy. The Convention first sent deputies on mission on 22 September 1792 when deputies went to Orléans and the north to restore order. On 9 March 1793, the Convention divided France into 41 regions each of two departments, assigning two deputies to each region. Other deputies were assigned to field armies. Members of the Committee of Public Safety (q.v.) also undertook missions, and in 1793–1794, as many as 130 deputies might be on mission at any one time.

A law of 4 December 1793 that codified the conduct of the revolutionary government provided the Representatives on Mission with virtually plenary powers. A Representative on Mission could arrest suspects, establish special courts, and have convicted suspects executed. They could issue decrees, fix prices, requisition private property, and levy taxes. They could dismiss or promote army officers, and try and execute officers suspected of disloyalty. Representatives on Mission were responsible for their actions and were required to report to the Committee of Public Safety on a regular basis. Representatives could be punished for going beyond the letter and intent of the law.

A minority of the Representatives were corrupt; others were fanatics. On the whole, however, the system worked effectively. The authority of the Convention was brought into the countryside. The Federalist revolt was broken and the Vendean revolt was contained. Armies were raised, war factories established and the nation effectively mobilized. The system did not work perfectly—few systems do—but the Representatives on Mission did extend the authority of

Paris into the departments. They played a major role in organizing France for total war. (*See also* Committee of Public Safety)

REPUBLICAN ARMY, FRENCH. Revolutionary France created between 1791 and 1794 an army that was authentically representative of the nation. The Royal Army in 1789 was a force led by aristocrats and staffed by society's lower orders. The enlisted ranks had a representation from urban backgrounds far out of proportion to the population as a whole. About 63 percent of the troops came from artisan or shopkeeper backgrounds, although peasants composed the vast majority of the population. Although France was only 15 percent urban, over 30 percent of the troops were from urban areas. Moreover, volunteers from frontier provinces supplied more recruits than other areas.

During the first year of the Revolution, the composition and size of the Royal Army changed only marginally. The army's strength remained at about 150,000, growing to 180,000 by 1793. The number of troops with origins as artisans and shopkeepers fell, but remained high—48 percent—while the number of peasant soldiers grew from 19 to 39 percent. Thus, the number of soldiers from urban areas remained much higher than the overall urban population percentage. Frontier provinces continued to supply a disproportionate number of men.

In 1791, however, the Legislative Assembly called for volunteers from the National Guards, a bourgeois militia established two years earlier to keep order and check any governmental attempt to use the army in a coup. The Volunteers of 1791 formed their own battalions. About 101,000 men volunteered. They were overwhelmingly urban in origin, with only 15 percent coming from rural areas. The volunteers were from fairly well to do backgrounds. Although mainly artisans and shopkeepers, they were from the upper levels of these occupations. The troops elected their own officers, many of whom had previous service in the line army. The volunteer battalions fought in the 1792 campaigns, but in the winter of 1792–93 most men left their units, since they had signed on for only one campaign and were legally free to leave the army two months after notifying their officers.

In July 1792 the Legislative Assembly called for 42 more battalions of volunteers. The response was massive, far greater than the government demanded. The Volunteers of 1792, in fact, formed over 250 battalions and reached a total strength of about 220,000 men. The force was 69 percent rural and 31 percent urban, with peasants appearing in greater numbers than ever before.

In February 1793 the Convention called for 300,000 new troops. Each department was assigned a quota of troops, and if a department did not meet its quota, compulsory enlistment would be used to raise necessary manpower. The February *levée* also permitted the hiring of replacements. Unfortunately, the *levée* did not work well. It produced only about 150,000 men, and attempts to enforce it sparked off counterrevolutionary rebellions in the Vendée (q.v.). Troops of the February 1793 *levée* contained a high percentage of peasants. Urban recruits came from social levels lower than those who had volunteered in 1792.

The *levée en masse* (q.v.) of 23 August 1793 imposed universal conscription. The hiring of substitutes was forbidden. The *levée en masse* produced about 300,000 men. The troops were reflective of the population at large. About 84 percent of the *levée* came from rural areas and 16 percent from towns and cities, a population distribution representative of the nation at large. The *levée* was both geographically and socially representative of the nation's population. Thus, in 1791, France raised an essentially bourgeois force. In 1792 the volunteers were a *sansculotte* force drawn from the lower middle classes. In February 1793 the volunteers came from among the young and poor, and in August the recruits represented with reasonable accuracy the social and demographic distribution of the nation at large.

The government sought to enhance the national as opposed to regional nature of the army. The amalgamation (q.v.) eliminated distinctions between the regular and volunteer units. The creation of half-brigades ordered in 1793, but because of the exigencies of war not completed until 1794 placed a line unit alongside two volunteer battalions. Moreover, no two volunteer or conscript battalions from the same department served together in the same half-brigade. Finally, the conscripts from the February and August 1793 levies did not form new battalions. Rather, they were used as replacements for existing formations, thus further ensuring that fighting units consisted of Frenchmen from every part of the nation.

The composition of the officer corps also changed dramatically. In 1789 about 85 percent of the officers were noble and 15 percent nonnoble. By 1795 the percentages had been reversed. Nobles who supported the Revolution continued to serve, although their presence was often greeted with suspicion. The majority of the officers were drawn from the middle class and artisan ranks, and the number of officers from peasant backgrounds climbed dramatically. In 1794 about 44 percent of company-grade officers had bourgeois backgrounds. Some 26 percent had artisan origins, and 24 percent were of peasant background.

Officers tended to be young. More than half the generals in 1793–94 were under 45 years old. Napoleon Bonaparte (q.v.), for example, was an army commander at age 26. The officers had a fair amount of military experience. About 21 percent of the officer corps had joined the army with the volunteers of 1791 and 28 percent with the volunteers of 1792. About half the officer corps had been in the army before 1789, usually as enlisted men or NCOs. Among the general officers, 87 percent had been in the army before 1789, and half of them had been officers prior to the Revolution. About 87 percent of the colonels had also been in the army before 1789; half of them had been officers and 30 percent had been NCOs. Among infantry captains, 60 percent had pre-Revolutionary military experience, usually as enlisted men or NCOs. The percentage of officers with prior experience in the Royal Army was higher in the cavalry and artillery than in the infantry. The Revolutionary concept of the career open to talent and the pressures of military expansion and war had thus fundamentally changed the officer corps. The leadership cadre of the French Republican army, in contrast to the officers of the Old Regime army, bore a much closer resemblance to the army's rank and file then ever before.

The size of the French Republican army also grew dramatically. From a force of about 150,000 in 1789, the army grew to a strength of more than 600,000 men by the end of 1793. By 1794 there were about 800,000 active troops. Additionally, there were troops in garrisons training camps, hospitals, prisoners, and National Guardsmen, thereby expanding the paper strength of the army even further.

REYNIER, JEAN-LOUIS, GENERAL (1771–1814). Reynier was trained as a civil engineer and volunteered for the artillery in 1792. He fought at Jemappes (q.v.) and was promoted to general of brigade in 1795. He fought in Germany in 1796 and became a general of division. In 1798 Reynier fought in Egypt, but was sent home after quarreling with General Menou (q.v.). He was exiled from Paris after killing a fellow officer in a duel and subsequently served in Naples. In 1809 he fought against Austria and in 1810 and 1811 served in Spain. He fought in Russia and Germany, was captured in 1813, and exchanged in 1814. Reynier died shortly after returning to France.

RICHEPANSE, ANTOINE, GENERAL (1770–1802). The son of a professional soldier, Richepanse joined the Royal Army, supported the Revolution, and by 1796 was a general of brigade. Two days after his first promotion, he received a battlefield promotion to general of division for bravery during the campaign in Germany. He played a major role at Hohenlinden (q.v.) and pursued the Austrians toward Vienna until the armistice of 25 December 1800. In 1802 Bonaparte sent him to Guadeloupe (q.v.) to reestablish French authority over rebellious blacks. Richepanse restored order in the major towns but died of yellow fever.

RICHERY, JOSEPH, REAR ADMIRAL (1757–1799). Of noble but impoverished birth, Richery sailed on merchantmen for nine years and transferred to the navy in 1774. He served under Admiral Suffren, returning to France in 1785. Richery supported the Revolution, becoming a captain in 1793. He was suspended for a year because of his aristocratic background, but in 1795 he was given a squadron at Toulon. He successfully attacked a British Levant convoy, capturing thirty merchantmen; in March 1796 was promoted to rear admiral. He sailed to Newfoundland waters in 1796 and successfully attacked the British fishing fleets. After returning to France, Richery took part in the unsuccessful Bantry Bay (q.v.) expedition, which was his last active command.

RIVOLI, BATTLE OF (14 JANUARY 1797). In 1796 Bonaparte (q.v.) had surrounded a large Austrian force in Mantua (q.v.). The Austrians sought to rescue the garrison, but the French defeated them at Bassano (q.v.) and Arcola (q.v.). In January 1797 the Austrians launched another thrust toward Mantua. The Austrians advanced in two separate columns. Ignoring the weaker of the two forces, Bonaparte attacked and defeated the larger contingent at Rivoli. He then rushed back and defeated the other force near Padua. Starving, the Mantua garrison capitulated in February, freeing the Army of Italy for a continued advance into Hapsburg territory.

ROBESPIERRE, MAXIMILIEN (1758–1794). Robespierre was a lawyer who was elected as a delegate to the Estates General in 1789. At the Estates General and Constituent Assembly, Robespierre became a spokesman for democratic principles. Although out of office in 1792, he denounced the drift to war, claiming that the conflict would be long and brutal, and would lead to a military dictatorship. He was right, and on 27 July 1793 he entered the Committee of Public Safety (q.v.), which did indeed establish an emergency dictatorship that lasted until July 1794.

Historians have, according to their political views, pictured Robespierre as everything from a bloodthirsty dictator to a proto-socialist or a timid representative of the French bourgeoisie. Few of these views take into account the prevailing military situation or offer judgments as to Robespierre's abilities as a war leader.

A few scholars, such as R. R. Palmer, have recognized that Robespierre and the Committee faced serious problems and that failure to solve them would lead to defeat, collapse, and anarchy. Robespierre and the Committee in fact organized the nation and turned the tide of the war. Nor did Robespierre act alone. He may have been the first among equals on the Committee and the Committee's chief spokesman, but the work of transforming France into a state that had to wage total war was a collective effort.

There were, of course, cruelties and injustices committed. This is often the case in a revolutionary situation compounded by a foreign war. The British in Ireland (q.v.) in 1798–1799 can hardly be said to have acted with decorum and impartial justice. The point remains that under Robespierre's guidance and leadership France turned the tide against enemies both foreign and domestic. Far from being a bloodthirsty fanatic, Robespierre may well have been a normal person forced to cope with grossly unusual circumstances. French victories in 1794 allowed Robespierre's enemies to turn against him. He was arrested and executed just as Republican armies were completing the conquest of Belgium. (*See also* Committee of Public Safety)

ROCHAMBEAU, JEAN-BAPTISTE-DONATIEN DE VIMEUR, COMTE DE, GENERAL (1725–1807). Rochambeau entered the Royal Army at age 16. He fought with distinction during the War of the Austrian Succession and by 1748 was a colonel. During the Seven Years' War he earned new honors, emerging from the conflict as a maréchal de camp. After 1763, he became the inspector general of infantry and then led the French expeditionary corps to America, where he worked effectively with George Washington. He then commanded a series of military divisions in France and was promoted marshal in 1790. In 1792 he commanded the Army of the North. He was reluctant to invade Belgium because his troops lacked discipline. Dumouriez (q.v.), at that time the foreign minister, forced him to act. He managed to avoid complete disaster and resigned in disgust. He was arrested during the Terror (q.v.) but released in 1794, and lived the rest of his life as a quiet observer of events.

ROMAN REPUBLIC (1798–1799). In 1796 the Army of Italy occupied Bologna and Ferrara, which were part of the Papal States. The pope in turn went to war, was rapidly defeated, and early in 1797 made peace with France. The Papal States were badly governed and unstable, and in early 1798 the Directory (q.v.) sent troops to Rome, exiled the pope, and with the cooperation of local Jacobins (q.v.) established a Republican regime. The Roman Republic never gained much popular support, but there were no serious counterrevolutionary rebellions. Looting by generals and soldiers did not endear either France or the local regime to the inhabitants. In November 1798 the British and Austrians convinced the rulers of Naples to invade the Roman Republic. Led by General Mack (q.v.), the Neapolitan army quickly took Rome but was then defeated north of the city. The Neapolitans withdrew, and the French followed and invaded Neapolitan territory, forcing the rulers to flee to Sicily. Austro-Russian advances in the spring of 1799 forced the French to abandon Rome, and the short-lived republic collapsed.

ROVEREDO, BATTLE OF (4 SEPTEMBER 1796). During the second Austrian attempt to relieve Mantua (q.v.), an Austrian force moved down the Brenta Valley while a smaller contingent guarded the approaches to Trent. Masséna (q.v.), with 10,000 troops, attacked the 14,000-man Hapsburg force guarding Trent, striking at an important road junction at Roveredo. Masséna captured the Austrian position, taking 6,000 prisoners; he then advanced and captured Trent. Leaving forces to hold the city, Bonaparte (q.v.) turned to pursue the main Austrian force.

ROYAL ARMY, FRENCH. In the late 18th century the French Royal Army consisted of the Royal Household Troops, the regular forces, and the militia. The Household Troops included the Bodyguard, the Swiss Guards, and the French Guards, for a total of some 7,278 men. The regular forces comprised 79 French and 23 non-French regiments with about 113,000 men. There were 62 cavalry regiments with 33,000 men and seven artillery regiments with about 7,000 troops. There were also some 75,000 men in the militia. The militia were mainly peasants chosen by lot. They received little training and in wartime served in depots and forts.

To fill its ranks the regular army relied upon volunteers who signed up for eight-year enlistments. Young men signed up for a variety of reasons, including economic hardship, escape from dead-end lives, and a search for adventure. Sometimes enlistment was offered to debtors, vagabonds, and criminals as an alternative to imprisonment. Town dwellers were overrepresented in the army because the presence of permanent garrisons in many cities made recruitment easier. French society in the 1780s was 80 to 85 percent rural, but 35 percent of the soldiers came from places with a population of 2,000 or more. Whether rural or urban, artisans and shopkeepers made up a majority of the soldiers. Only about 15 percent of the regular army was of peasant origins, while 63 percent were former artisans and shopkeepers, 13 percent day laborers, and ten percent bourgeois. Border provinces along the northern and eastern frontiers supplied more recruits than other areas of France, probably because of the presence of numerous garrisons and depots, which made recruiting easier.

The officer corps was overwhelmingly of aristocratic background. Ranks of colonel and above were reserved for nobles who had been presented at court. Most officers, however, came from the provincial nobility. A series of military schools established in the 1750s admitted only the sons of poor noblemen who could prove four generations of nobility, and a law of 1781, known as the Ségur decree, required four generations of nobility of anyone who wanted to enter the army as an officer, thus excluding commoners and nobles of recent origin. By

1789, of some 10,000 officers, over 90 percent were noblemen, and between 1781 and 1789 fewer than 50 men rose from the enlisted to officer ranks. Provincial noblemen wanted to reduce the special privileges of the court nobility and create a more professional officer corps, but a profession that remained closed to new nobles and commoners.

After 1763, there was a good deal of thought and action given to improving the capabilities of the Royal Army, but the army was still far from being a truly national citizen force. With the coming of the Revolution, the army suffered much turmoil. Troops were reluctant and at times unwilling to act against popular uprisings, and there was much desertion from both enlisted ranks and the officer corps. By the end of 1790 army strength had declined from about 150,000 to less than 130,000 men. In 1791 and 1792 some 5,000 officers left their posts, and by the spring of 1794, out of some 10,000 officers in 1789, 6,693 had abandoned their commissions and over 3,000 left the service in some other manner, including death in battle. About 87 percent of the officers on duty in 1789 had left active service by 1794. After war was declared, the old Royal Army expanded again to about 180,000 men by early 1793 when the amalgamation (q.v.) decreed the creation of a single national force.

ROYAL NAVY, BRITISH. See NAVY, BRITISH

-S-

SAINT-ANDRÉ, JEANBON (1749–1813). Saint André was born into a Protestant family. As a young man he went to sea and became a captain in the merchant marine. In 1771 he attended a Protestant seminary in Switzerland and was ordained as a Calvinist minister in 1773. From 1773 to 1788 he was a pastor. In 1789 Saint-André supported the Revolution and in 1792 was elected to the National Convention (q.v.). He voted for the death of Louis XVI (q.v.) and went on missions to organize military recruitment. On 10 July he became a member of the Committee of Public Safety (q.v.). In August he went on mission to the armies of the North, Moselle, and Ardennes, where he and another member of the Committee worked to reinforce and supply the armies.

Saint-André's maritime experience led to his being sent to Brest to reorganize the weak and dispirited fleet. He secured food and supplies, hastened the construction of ships, and improved the morale of the sailors. His efforts were successful, and in 1794 the fleet gave a good account of itself at the Battle of the First of June (q.v.). Saint-André was aboard one of the warships and, though defeated, an important grain convoy did reach Brest. In July he went to Toulon and began to rebuild a Mediterranean squadron.

He was arrested as a result of Thermidor but released at the end of

1795. He then went into the diplomatic service, where he was arrested by the Turks in 1798 and not released until 1801. Under the Consulate and Empire, Saint-André served effectively in a number of administrative posts until his death from typhus at Mainz in 1813.

SAINT-CYR, LAURENT GOUVION, GENERAL (1764–1830). Saint-Cyr was an artist who joined the army in 1792. By 1794 he was a general of division. He played important roles at the siege of Mainz (q.v.) in 1795 and in the German campaign of 1796. In 1799 Saint-Cyr fought at Stockach (q.v.) and Novi (q.v.). He fought in Germany in 1800 and from 1801 to 1803 was ambassador in Madrid. He fought in Italy in 1805 and then in Spain. He participated in the Russian campaign, and Napoleon appointed him marshal. In 1813 Saint-Cyr fought in Germany and was captured. He accepted the Restoration and served as Minister of War, retiring in 1819.

SAINT DOMINGUE. In 1789 Saint Domingue, now Haiti, was one of France's wealthiest and most important overseas possessions, occupying about a third of the island of Hispaniola. With the advent of the Revolution, the white population sent delegates to the Estates General, while indulging in internal political debates at home in which the plantation aristocracy was ranged against the poorer whites of the cities. Free mulattos rose in arms in 1790 demanding equality, but the planters crushed them using armed Negro slaves. When the planters then tried to re-enslave the Negroes, they rebelled in 1791 and soon gained control of the northern part of the colony. Many whites fled to British colonies in the Caribbean. France sent reinforcements to Saint Domingue, but the commanders and civilian commissioners were not sympathetic to the planters.

When Britain and Spain joined the war against France, Pitt's government saw an opportunity to grab French Caribbean colonies. Moreover, the French planters actually called for and welcomed British intervention. British and Spanish forces invaded the colony in 1793 and British forces took Port-au-Prince by March 1794. In response, the Republic's commissioners in Saint Domingue proclaimed the abolition of slavery. The Convention (q.v.) approved their action and abolished slavery in all French colonies. The Convention's action was only partly idealistic. The Committee (q.v.), having nothing to lose, hoped that their action would encourage the Negro rebellion and tie down British and Spanish troops away from Europe.

The Convention's action was successful in that it convinced Negro leader Toussaint L'Ouverture (q.v.) to switch sides. Toussaint had earlier joined the slave revolt and had joined the Spanish army in 1793. The French abolition of slavery plus the belief that, if victorious, Britain and Spain would restore slavery convinced him to support the Republic. He proved to be a very able military leader, forcing the Spanish to retreat back to their part of the island and waging an effective guerrilla war against the British, which eventually caused the British well over 50,000 casualties. The casualty list was actually greater when losses from disease were included. By 1796 the French army commander in Saint Domingue recognized Toussaint as the de facto ruler of the colony, and in February 1798 he recaptured Port-au-Prince.

At the end of 1798 the British decided to disengage from Saint Domingue, to free troops for use on the continent. In October, in return for a promise by Toussaint to remain neutral in the European war, the British agreed to leave the island. In June 1799 Toussaint and the British signed a second agreement by which Toussaint agreed to refrain from spreading slave revolts to British colonies and to the United States in return for a commercial agreement with both nations.

The Directory (q.v.), however, wanted to keep war raging in the Caribbean, and shifted French support from Toussaint to Rigaud, a mulatto leader who ruled the western part of Saint Domingue and was willing to spread slave rebellions in order to convince Paris to support him as the ruler of Saint Domingue. Toussaint in turn decided to crush his rival and, with the support of American warships, defeated Rigaud. By 1800 Toussaint was the sole ruler of Saint Domingue, and in the following year, he captured the Spanish colony of Santo Domingo (the other part of the island).

Napoleon, after the War of the Second Coalition (q.v.), evolved grandiose plans for creating an empire in the New World based on Hispaniola. In 1802 he sent General Leclerc (q.v.) to recapture the island. The French were initially successful, forcing Toussaint to capitulate. Toussaint was sent to France as a prisoner and died in 1803.

Toussaint's subordinates, who had initially accepted French authority, upon learning that Bonaparte (q.v.) had restored slavery on French Caribbean islands rebelled again. Effective black leadership and disease decimated the French army, and in 1803 Bonaparte gave up plans to subdue Saint Dominque. Remnants of the French army left the country and sailed to Jamaica, where they surrendered to the British. Saint Domingue thus emerged as the second independent republic in the New World and the first black republic in the Western Hemisphere.

SAINT JEAN D'ACRE, SIEGE OF (18 MARCH–20 MAY 1799). Isolated in Egypt as a result of the Battle of the Nile (q.v.), Bonaparte (q.v.) decided to pursue the strategy of attacking British possessions in India by land. He intended to march through Syria, Mesopotamia, and Persia in order to reach India, while mobilizing the local populations of the Middle East to support his endeavor. Some felt the plan was fantastic, but Bonaparte pointed out that it had been done before. The British, at any rate, took the threat seriously.

At first the French advance went well, but the fortress of Acre (q.v.) was an obstacle that could not be ignored or by-passed, since it contained a formidable garrison that was supported by a British naval squadron that managed to capture Bonaparte's siege guns that were moving along the coast. Bonaparte, therefore, laid siege to the city while the British sent marines and guns ashore to bolster the defenses.

The French launched eight assaults against the city, all of which failed. Plague also broke out in the French lines, and in late May Bonaparte abandoned the siege and began to retreat back to Egypt. Acre was Bonaparte's first major defeat. The defenders also foiled his plans for campaigns into the Middle East and seriously weakened the Army of the Orient, which suffered about 5,000 casualties. Bonaparte began to contemplate leaving his army and returning to France. (*See also* Egyptian Expedition)

SAINT-JUST, LOUIS-ANTOINE-LÉON DE (1767–1794). Saint-Just was the youngest member of the Convention (q.v.) and a close ally of Robespierre (q.v.). He joined the Committee of Public Safety (q.v.) on 30 May 1793. He was a leading spokesman for the creation of a centralized emergency government. His role in the war was important, and he travelled as a Representative on Mission (q.v.) to several armies in 1793 and 1794.

In October 1793 Saint-Just joined a colleague on Mission to the Army of the Rhine in Alsace. He visited the troops, found food and supplies for them, and removed incompetent officers and ineffective local officials in Strasbourg. He played a significant role in restoring the army's morale. In January and February 1794 he was with the Army of the North, where he helped reorganize the army's transportation and supply system in preparation for the forthcoming offensive. From April to June he was again with the army. Saint-Just accompanied the Sambre-Meuse army during the offensive and encouraged Jourdan (q.v.) to keep attacking despite several defeats. The French finally succeeded at the Battle of Fleurs (q.v.).

As a close ally of Robespierre, he perished along with him in July 1794. Saint-Just's character and actions have been subject to a wide variety of interpretations, almost none of which deal with him in terms of his military achievements, which were significant.

SAINT VINCENT, CAPE, BATTLE OF (14 FEBRUARY 1797). Admiral Sir John Jervis (q.v.), with 15 ships of the line, was blockading Cadiz. His fleet was located off Cape Saint Vincent when it sighted a Spanish fleet of 27 warships. The Spanish fleet was, however, strung out for about twenty miles. Jervis ordered an immediate attack against the van. He led his fleet between two portions of the Spanish fleet and proceeded to attack the larger segment. Nelson (q.v.), leading three ships and acting on his own initiative, blocked the Spanish effort to escape. The rest of the British fleet then caught up with the Spanish. A general melée followed. The British captured four Spanish ships of the line and took more than 2,500 prisoners for a loss of some 300 seamen. Once again the Royal Navy (q.v.) demonstrated its superiority even against superior numbers.

SAMUR, BATTLE OF (9 JUNE 1793). Bands of Vendeans reached and attacked Samur on 9 June 1793. Republican forces, largely untrained volunteers, broke and fled. The Vendeans took 8,000 prisoners, thousands of muskets, and 30,000 barrels of powder. Fortunately for the Republic, the Vendeans had no strategy, since they were essentially a confederation of local bands without an effective supreme command. Moreover, the troops were concerned primarily with local defense and resistance and did not view their actions within a broader strategic context. Though in position to move on Paris, the leaders could not agree among themselves on the next moves, and had no contact with Coalition (q.v.) powers. Vendean disarray gave the Republic a chance to reorganize its forces. (*See also* Vendée, The.)

SANTERRE, ANTOINE-JOSEPH (1752–1809). Santerre was the son of a brewer and had a large establishment in Paris. In 1789 he participated in the attack on the Bastille and in 1791 was chief of a National Guard battalion. In 1792 he became commandant of the Paris National Guard and in May 1793 he was given command of a force of Parisian volunteers assigned to fight in the Vendée (q.v.). His campaign in the Vendée was a disaster. He failed to defend Samur (q.v.) in June and was defeated again in September. Santerre was arrested in April 1794, since the authorities concluded that his defeats were a result of treachery rather than incompetence. He was released in October. His military career was over; he lived quietly and made a great deal of money in real estate. In 1800 Bonaparte (q.v.) restored his rank as a general and promptly retired him.

SAUMAREZ, JAMES, ADMIRAL (1757–1836). Saumarez became a lieutenant in the Royal Navy in 1776 and served in the Channel Fleet and in the West Indies. After 1793, he served on blockade duty off Brest. He fought at Cape Saint Vincent (q.v.) and at the Nile (q.v.). He became a rear admiral in 1801 and continued to serve on blockade duty off Brest and in the Mediterranean. From 1808 to 1813 Saumarez commanded a squadron in the Baltic and became a full admiral in 1814.

SAXE-COBURG, FREDERICK-JOSIAS, DUKE (1737–1815). Saxe-Coburg took part in the Seven Years' War and the war against the Turks in 1788 to 1789. In 1792 he was placed in command of Austrian troops in Belgium. In 1793 Saxe-Coburg defeated the French at Neerwindin (q.v.) and took the frontier fortress of LeQuesnoy, Landrecies, and Valenciennes (q.v.). He failed to cooperate with the British, who insisted on taking Dunkirk rather than advancing into the heart of northern France, and his insistence upon taking the numerous fortresses in northern France prevented a concentrated drive on Paris. Halted in 1793, his plans for an offensive in 1794 were disrupted by a French offensive. Defeated at Tourcoing (q.v.) and Fleurs (q.v.), Saxe-Coburg gave up both Belgium and his command.

SCHARNHORST, GERHARD JOHANN DAVID VON, GENERAL (1755–1813). Scharnhorst was born in Hanover and entered the army in 1788. In 1793 he fought at Hondschoote (q.v.) and Menin (q.v.). He transferred to Prussian service in 1801 where he taught at the War Academy and was tutor to the crown prince. Scharnhorst understood that the basis of French success was essentially political, since only the social, political, and economic changes wrought by the Revolution enabled France to create a well-motivated citizen army. He advocated, in a military journal that he edited, similar reforms for Prussia. Prior to 1806, his ideas had little impact on the Prussian regime. After Jena, he and other reformers did gain influence, but Napoleon forced the king to dismiss him. Returning to service in 1812, he was mortally wounded in the German campaign of 1813. Scharnhorst was one of the first to comprehend the impact of the Revolution on warfare, and understood the necessity of transforming passive subjects into active citizens to create an army that could cope with Napoleon.

SCHERER, BARTHELEMY LOUIS JOSEPH, GENERAL (1747–1804). Scherer began his career in the Austrian army during the Seven Years' War. He then transferred to the French army, and from 1785 to 1790 served in the Dutch Army. He retired, but rejoined the French army in 1792. Scherer served with the Army of the Rhine, where he was promoted to general of brigade in 1793, and then to general of division in the same year. In 1794 he conducted numerous sieges on the northeast frontier and briefly became commander of the Army of the West Pyrenees and the Army of Italy. He left active service in 1796 but held several administrative posts, including that of War Minister from 1797 to 1799. Scherer returned to command in 1799 in Italy, where he launched several unsuccessful attacks against the Austrians in an effort to disrupt the projected Austro-Russian offensive. He again left active service, and after Napoleon's coup in November he was not reemployed.

SEELBACH, BATTLE OF (17 NOVEMBER 1793). After their victory at Wattignies (q.v.), the French reinforced the Army of the Moselle. General Hoche (q.v.), with 35,000 men, attacked the Prussian lines on 17 November. The Prussians drove back the French attacks but, fearing additional French assaults, retreated towards Kaiserslautern the next day.

SEMAPHORE. Claude Chappe (1763–1805) was a scientist. In 1792, the government adopted his invention of a semaphore system consisting of an upright post with a cross-bar. At the end of the bar were two wooden arms on pivots. The position of the arms represented various letters. A series of semaphore posts, each visible to the next one, enabled messages to be transmitted rapidly. By 1793 semaphores were in use in northern France. The system was extended in the years following, thereby facilitating the rapid transmission of orders, news, and information.

SERINGAPATAM, SIEGE OF (MARCH 1792). In 1790 Tippoo Sultan (q.v.), the ruler of Mysore, invaded Travancore. Lord Cornwallis (q.v.), governor-general of India, declared the region to be under British protection, and invaded Mysore. In March, he laid siege to Tippoo's capital, Seringapatam, which fell on 19 March 1792. Tippoo had to give up half his lands and pay a large indemnity. Tippoo's hostility to Britain grew, and he soon began to seek an alliance with the French Republic.

SERINGAPATAM, STORMING OF (4 MAY 1799). Tippoo's efforts to undermine and perhaps destroy British influence in India convinced Lord Richard Wellesley (q.v.), the governor-general, to eliminate him. Despite orders from London to follow a non-aggressive policy, Wellesley first eliminated Tippoo's local Allies and then invaded Mysore. On 4 May 1799, British and East India Company troops stormed Seringapatam. Tippoo died defending his capital. The British took over Mysore, restoring a former Hindu dynasty that was obedient to British wishes, thus solidifying their control of southern India.

SÉRURIER, JEAN MATHIEU PHILBERT, GENERAL (1742–1819). Sérurier joined the army in 1755 and fought in the Seven Years' War. By 1791 he was a lieutenant colonel in the Royal Army; by 1795, he was a general of division. He fought at Loano (q.v.) and in the Italian campaign of 1796–1797. He was in charge of the siege of Mantua (q.v.). In 1799 Sérurier was besieged by Russian forces at Verderio, surrendered, and was released on parole. He retired from active service in 1800. Napoleon rewarded his services by making him a marshal in

1804. He also became a governor of Les Invalides. In 1814, as the Allies closed in on Paris, he burnt over 1,400 banners that had been earlier captured by French armies.

SERVAN DE GERBEY, JOSEPH (1741–1808). Servan was a career officer who became minister of war in May 1792. He had violent disputes with Dumouriez (q.v.) over the issue of creating a special volunteer force to protect Paris not only from foreign invasion but also from internal counterrevolutionary conspiracies. The dispute led to his dismissal in June. After the insurrection of 10 August, Servan returned to office and again had serious disputes with Dumouriez. Dumouriez wanted to invade Belgium, while Servan wanted to concentrate on the defense of the eastern approaches to Paris threatened by Brunswick's army. Dumouriez refused to cooperate with Servan, which led the government to contemplate moving the seat of government south of the Loire. Danton's oratory and threats, however, put an end to this scheme. Moreover, with the fall of Verdun on 2 September, Dumouriez realized that he had to cooperate with Servan, who was able to move Kellerman (q.v.) and Dumouriez into positions from which they could challenge Brunswick's advance.

Exhausted by his efforts, Servan left office in October and became a general in the Army of the Pyrenees. He was arrested in 1793 because of prior associations with the Girondins, coupled with accusations of corruption. Released after Thermidor, his rank was restored in 1795. Servan served in various administrative posts until his retirement in 1803.

SIEGE WARFARE. During the Old Regime, siege warfare played a vital role in military campaigns. Carl von Clausewitz (q.v.), with some exaggeration, wrote that "The plan for a given campaign was to take an enemy fortress or prevent the capture of one's own. No battle was ever sought or fought unless it were indispensable for that purpose" (*On War*, p. 591).

Fortified cities represented a valuable economic and strategic prize, and generals who would not usually risk combat would fight to protect a major fortified city. Fontenoy, Lanfelt, Prague, Kohn, Leuthen, and Québec form but a partial list of battles fought to take, protect, or relieve a garrison city.

There were several forms of sieges. An attacking force might simply contain and observe an enemy garrison, attacking only if the defenders mounted a major sortie. Blockade was a more elaborate form of containment, designed to deny a garrison food and supplies from the outside until shortages force the defenders to capitulate. Finally, there was the formal attempt to break into the city. The attacking force brought up a besieging detachment with heavy siege guns, munitions, and entrenching equipment, while other formations covered the siege against attempts to relieve the garrison from outside. The besiegers would proceed by digging a parallel with positions for heavy artillery. Approach trenches would then be pushed forward, and another parallel dug with additional batteries established. A third parallel would then be constructed. Parallels and approach trenches were not dug all around a fortress. Rather, activity was concentrated against one particular sector. When the parallels were complete, the artillery would commence a heavy sustained bombardment. Once a breach was blasted in the enemy position, the attackers could launch an assault, although in many cases the garrison would capitulate once the breach was made. Garrisons might also surrender before a breach was made if the defenders had run out of food and munitions. Full-scale assaults were in fact quite rare. Sieges were time-consuming and expensive but were viewed as crucial to the success of a major campaign.

The First Republic sought to place emphasis on open field engagements that would lead to the destruction of enemy field armies. In 1793 Carnot (q.v.), in fact, instructed his field commanders to place less emphasis on geographical objectives and concentrate on seeking battle with enemy armies. Sieges, nevertheless, continued to play a significant role in Republican campaigns. Republican armies often besieged a city in order to force Allied relief armies to offer battle. The battles of Hondschoote (q.v.), Wattignies (q.v.), and Fleurs (q.v.), for example, were fought in large measure to resolve a siege operation. The Italian campaign of 1796–1797 hinged on the siege of Mantua (q.v.), and Bonaparte's failure in the siege of Acre (q.v.) helped determine the outcome of his Syrian campaign. As in the days of the Old Regime, sieges were rarely ended by direct assault. Garrisons capitulated when they ran low on food and munitions. Sieges did play a lesser role in Republican campaigns, but, nevertheless, remained an important form of military operations.

SISTER REPUBLICS (1795–1799). France established a series of sister or satellite republics in Holland, Switzerland, and Italy. The sister republics provided money, troops, and territorial buffers for the Republic. Some of the republics enjoyed local popular support, as was the case in the Batavian and Cisalpine republics. In other cases, the populace was divided, as in Liguria and Switzerland. Finally, a number of republics, including Rome and Naples, were imposed by French arms and enjoyed support from a very narrow range of people.

The idea of imposing a government on another state was not unique. The French monarchy had often supported Stuart pretenders to the British throne and, earlier, Spain had attempted to put its own candidate on the French throne. What was new in the case of the Republic was that Paris created democratic satellites. On the whole, the satellite states enhanced France's strategic position, although the existence of sister republics did complicate French diplomacy. (*See also* Batavian Republic; Cisalpine Republic; Roman Republic)

SMITH, SIR SIDNEY, ADMIRAL (1764–1840). Smith joined the Royal Navy in 1777 and served in the West Indies. In 1793 he served under Admiral Lord Hood (q.v.) at Toulon (q.v.). He served briefly in the Swedish navy, but in 1796 he was back in British service, where he was captured off Le Havre. Imprisoned in Paris, he made a daring escape. In 1798 Smith operated under Nelson (q.v.) in the Mediterranean. In 1798 and 1799 he commanded a squadron that played a vital role in the siege of Acre (q.v.). British marines, gunners, and ships bolstered the Turkish defense of the city, thus halting Bonaparte's advance into Syria. Smith continued to operate in the Mediterranean and in Iberia. He was present at Waterloo, where he helped organize the evacuation of the wounded after the battle. In 1821 he was promoted to admiral.

SOUHAM, JOSEPH, GENERAL (1760–1837). Souham enlisted in the Royal Army in 1782 and enjoyed rapid promotion during the Revolution, rising from an elected lieutenant colonel in a volunteer battalion in August 1792 to a general of division in September 1793. He served with the Army of the North and played a crucial role in the Battle of Tourcoing (q.v.). He continued to serve with the Army of the North and the Army of the Rhine, but when Moreau (q.v.) was disgraced, Souham was imprisoned because of his association with Moreau. He resumed active duty in 1807, serving mainly in Spain and Germany. He rallied to the Bourbons in 1814 and held a variety of posts, including governor of Strasbourg, before retiring from active duty in 1832.

SOULT, NICOLAS-JEAN DE DIEU, GENERAL (1769–1851). Soult's father was a small-town notary. In 1785 Soult, despite a club foot, enlisted in the army and by 1791 was a sergeant. The Revolution's policy of opening military careers to talent, coupled with the emigration of aristocratic officers, enabled Soult to advance rapidly. He was a lieutenant in 1792 and a colonel soon afterwards. In 1794 at the Battle of Fleurs (q.v.) he served as General Lefebvre's chief of staff and in the same year was promoted to general of brigade.

Soult next fought in the Rhine campaigns from 1795 to 1797. In 1799 he fought at Stockach (q.v.) and was promoted to general of division. He transferred to Switzerland and played a crucial role of the Battle of Zurich (q.v.). An Austrian force was stationed on the Russian left, and

Soult attacked and shattered it, thereby denying reinforcement to the Russians, who fell victim to Masséna's assault. In the following year he served with Masséna (q.v.) at the defense of Genoa (q.v.).

Soult continued to serve the Consulate and Empire, becoming a marshal in 1804. Later he participated in Central European campaigns from 1805 to 1807 and fought in Spain from 1808 to 1813. He campaigned in Germany, the Pyrenees, and southern France in 1813 and 1814. Though defeated, he had fought well and delayed Wellington's advance into France.

Soult accepted the Restoration, joined Napoleon as Chief of Staff during the Hundred Days, and was exiled after the second abdication. He returned to France in 1819. He then held office under the Orléans monarchy as minister of war. He represented France at Queen Victoria's coronation, where he met Wellington (q.v.) for the first time. He then served as minister of foreign affairs, president of the Council of Ministers, and minister of war for a second time. The government proclaimed him marshal general of France in 1847, a rank previously held only by Turenne, Villars, and Saxe, and he retired the same year.

Soult had found in the Revolution a path that enabled him to exploit his talents. He was an able military leader on the tactical level and also displayed a high level of ability at the operational level of war.

SPITHEAD MUTINIES (16 APRIL–15 MAY 1797). British sailors had long-standing grievances over low pay, bad food, and generally bad conditions at sea. The admiralty ignored the problems until the sailors of the Channel Fleet refused to sail from port. Lord Howe (q.v.) undertook talks with the mutineers, who were generally quite restrained, and Parliament increased the pay of seamen. A royal pardon was granted, and there were no reprisals. The sailors then returned to duty. The mutiny had no political agenda and was motivated almost completely by poor conditions. (*See also* Nore Mutinies.)

STAFFS. All armies require a staff system to bring order to what otherwise might become chaos. During the Old Regime and Revolutionary period, the French staff system was designed to translate the intentions of the commander into a practical set of directives to subordinates. Staff officers also had to keep track of the supply system, numbers of men available, and the other reams of paperwork that articulate a mass of individuals into a functioning organism.

In 1783 the French monarchy established a staff corps in which officers were specially trained for staff work. In October 1790 the Assembly established a system including a number of adjutant generals, who with their subordinates would compose the staffs of active field armies. By 1799 there were over one hundred adjutant generals. In

1792 the Convention (q.v.) decreed that each field army would have a chief of staff assisted by four adjutant generals. The adjutant generals in turn had a number of aides assigned from active units. The aides served on a rotating basis. Adjutant generals also served as chiefs of staff for active divisions. Desaix (q.v.), Kléber (q.v.), Saint-Cyr (q.v.), Soult (q.v.), and Ney (q.v.) were among leading figures in the French army, who at some point in their careers served as adjutant generals.

In 1796 P. A. Berthier, as chief of staff of the Army of the Alps, wrote an important manual on staff organization. The chief of staff was the center of all staff organizations. The four adjutant generals were charged with specific duties. The first section was responsible for staff records, organization, inspections, and troop movements. The second section dealt with armaments, artillery, engineers, subsistence, and hospitals. The third section dealt with reconnaissance, operational plans, communications, and employment of the guide company. The fourth section controlled the establishment and organization of the headquarters.

Not all armies followed Berthier's method of organization until Napoleon imposed a standardized system after 1802. Berthier's approach was, however, widely used, and Republican armies all employed some form of staff system designed to assist the army commander.

STENGEL, HENRI CHRISTIAN MICHAEL, GENERAL (1744–1796). Stengel, after service in the Palatine Guards, joined the French army in 1760. By 1792 he was a cavalry officer and served under Dumouriez (q.v.). In 1793 he was arrested, tried, and acquitted by the Revolutionary Tribunal and retired in 1795. In the same year, Stengel was recalled to active service, promoted to general of division, and sent to command the cavalry in the Army of Italy. He was killed in 1796 while leading a crucial charge at Mondovi (q.v.).

STOCKACH, BATTLE OF (25 MARCH 1799). As the Austrians moved through south Germany towards the Rhine, General Jourdan (q.v.) tried to halt the advance of Archduke Charles's army. Some 40,000 French faced 60,000 Austrians. Jourdan was defeated and forced back over the Rhine with a loss of 5,000 men.

STOCKACH, BATTLE OF (3 MAY 1800). In 1800 General Moreau (q.v.) invaded south Germany with 50,000 troops, while Bonaparte (q.v.) struck into northern Italy. On 3 May Moreau attacked a smaller Austrian force and compelled it to retreat to Ulm. The Austrians lost over 4,000 men as well as their depot of stores and munitions.

STOFFLET, JEAN-NICHOLAS (1751–1796). A former soldier and forest guard, Stofflet was one of the first to join the Vendean insurrection.

After the crushing of the Vendean army in December 1793, Stofflet escaped and with a number of survivors. He returned to the Vendée (q.v.) and waged a guerrilla war throughout 1794. He rejected the Republic's offer of an amnesty and threatened the lives of those who came to terms with the government. In mid-1795, he did undertake talks with the Republic, but he was also in contact with Royalist agents. Artois (q.v.) appointed him lieutenant-general and called upon him to resume fighting. In June 1796 he took up arms again but was soon captured and executed.

STRATEGY, FRENCH. Strategy is the art and science of using campaigns to attain the military and political goals of the state. Depending upon the nature of the war, strategy may aim at the complete destruction of an enemy's ability and will to resist. Such a strategy would most likely be pursued in an unlimited war; i.e., a war in which the complete conquest of the enemy was the political objective. In other cases, strategy might call for inflicting sufficient defeats upon an enemy until the enemy decided that further fighting would be more expensive and dangerous than making territorial and economic concessions. Such a strategy, designed to increase the costs of the war to an opponent, is usually followed in a limited conflict where belligerents seek concessions rather than overthrow.

The First French Republic fought limited wars in that Paris did not seek the destruction of its most powerful enemies. France essentially sought survival, recognition as a legitimate regime, and a victorious peace involving some annexations (although the nature and extent of the annexations varied from political faction to faction and over time). To obtain survival, recognition, and a victorious peace, France had to mobilize the full range of the country's human and economic resources, thus fighting a total war for limited aims.

To achieve the national objectives, the Republic had to devise a strategy to force its enemies to sue for peace. Paris, engaged in what amounted to a multifront war, had to decide where and against whom to deploy its armies, which armies to reinforce, and where to place the main emphasis of operations.

In 1792 the French had to wage a defensive strategy to halt the Allied advance on Paris. Subsequent attacks, after Valmy (q.v.), produced initial victories in Belgium and the Rhineland, but political problems at home and in occupied territories prevented the government from devising a coherent national strategy.

Allied counterattacks and internal counterrevolution in 1793 threw France on the defensive. The advance of Coalition powers forced the Republic to introduce national mobilization and to mount desperate counterattacks in Flanders and northern Alsace simply to stabilize the situation. On other fronts, French armies also struggled to halt Allied armies, while major offensive operations were organized against counterrevolutionary forces in the Vendée (q.v.), Brittany, Lyon, and the coastal enclaves on the Mediterranean. The strategy of 1793 was essentially defensive. The Republic emphasized halting the Allies in northern and eastern France, since the main Allied armies operated there and because the enemy forces in Flanders and northern France posed a direct threat to Paris. Counterrevolutionary movements also had to be crushed, or at least reduced in strength, to provide for the Republic's internal security. By the end of the year, the Republic had blunted both internal and external offensives and won a breathing space in which to devise a more coherent strategy for the following year.

In late 1793 the Committee of Public Safety (q.v.) decided to wage its major campaigns in 1794 along the Franco-Belgian frontier. The Committee had concluded that Britain and Austria were the Republic's most determined foes, their armies were the largest coalition forces, and they were closer to Paris than the Prussian forces in the Rhineland. Furthermore, it was clear to Paris that Prussia was more interested in Poland than Paris and might be convinced to leave the war, whereas only military defeat would force London and Vienna to come to terms. The Committee, therefore, reinforced its armies in the north and ordered operations in Flanders and on the Sambre. Attacks on the wings of the Coalition forces would compel the Allies constantly to shift reserves and wear down the enemy forces to a point where French forces could defeat them.

The strategy of striking Allied forces on opposite wings ultimately succeeded, and by the late summer French forces, victorious in Flanders and on the Sambre, were advancing into Belgium. The pursuit lasted until the following year when, in the winter of 1795, the Republic's armies occupied Holland and most of the Rhineland. Prussia and Spain left the war soon after, but a drive into Germany, designed to force Austria to sue for peace, was unsuccessful.

In 1796 the French decided to focus on the defeat of Austria. The government called for two advances into Germany and a spoiling attack into Italy. Paris also tried to mount an invasion of Ireland in order to use the island as a bargaining chip in peace talks with England. All campaigns except the Italian campaign, however, failed, and neither England nor Austria felt sufficiently threatened to seek peace. Consequently, French strategy in 1797 focused primarily on Austria. Bonaparte (q.v.) advanced from Italy into southern Austria, while renewed campaigns in Germany achieved initial success. The Austrians finally concluded that the costs and risks of continued fighting were too great and sued for peace. Britain, isolated from Continental allies, also entered peace talks with the Directory (q.v.), but the talks failed.

In 1798 the French faced only one opponent and initially contemplated an invasion of the British Isles to force London to accept peace. The risks of a cross-Channel invasion, however, appeared too great, and instead, the French decided to strike at British holdings in India via Egypt. The French assumed that the loss of valuable colonies in India would force the British to sue for peace, but Britain's effective use of sea power, although it failed to stop the invasion of Egypt, isolated the Army of the Orient in Egypt and stymied French strategy. Moreover, the British naval victory set off a chain of events that led to the formation of a Second Coalition (q.v.).

In the opening phases of the new or renewed war, the French attempted a repetition of their earlier strategy of mounting campaigns in Germany and Italy to split Allied forces and threaten the Hapsburg crown lands. The offensive, however, failed, and France was soon thrown on the defensive in Germany, Switzerland, Italy, and Holland. The Republic then sought an opportunity for a counterblow, which they found in Switzerland. The Directory (q.v.) reinforced Masséna's (q.v.) army, which enabled him to launch an offensive in September 1799. The victory also had the effect of convincing Russia to leave the coalition. In the following year the French conducted operations in Italy and Germany, winning victories in both areas and forcing Austria out of the war. Once again isolated, England concluded a peace with France in 1802.

Throughout the wars of the First French Republic, France fought for extensive but still limited aims. The French, often faced with threats on several fronts, constantly had to select which battle areas were the most critical and organize coordinated campaigns to compel their enemies to seek peace. The Republic was reasonably successful staving off invasion in 1793 and shifting the tide of the war in 1794–1795. Campaigns in 1796 and 1797 were not as effective, but by 1797 the combination of operations in Germany and Italy were sufficient to force Austria to end hostilities. Efforts at overseas operations failed in the face of British naval power. The initial campaigns of 1799 were also a failure, but as in 1793, the French designated a vital area and mounted an effective counter-offensive. In 1800 the dual thrust in Italy and Germany produced the desired results. By 1802 French strategy had driven the nation's enemies out of the war and enabled the Republic to attain its goals of survival, recognition, and a victorious peace. (*See also* Coalition, First; Coalition, Second)

STUART, SIR JOHN, GENERAL (1759–1815). Stuart was born in Georgia, educated in London and served in the British army during the American Revolution. He served in Flanders from 1793 to 1795, and in 1801 he commanded a division at the Battle of Alexandria. Later, Stuart fought in Italy and held Sicily until his retirement from active service in 1810, after a dispute with London over support for his garrison.

SUCHET, LOUIS GABRIEL, GENERAL (1770–1826). The son of a silk manufacturer at Lyons, Suchet joined the National Guard in 1791 and in 1792 was elected to command a volunteer battalion. In 1793 he fought at Toulon (q.v.). Suchet next served in the Army of Italy, fighting in many of the major engagements, including Arcola (q.v.) and Rivoli (q.v.). In 1798 he was promoted to general of brigade and in 1799 became a general of division, serving as Joubert's chief of staff. In 1800 Suchet fought in Italy and, in the years following, fought at Ulm and Austerlitz. From 1808 to 1814 he operated in Spain and became a marshal in 1811. After 1814, he served the Bourbons, joined Napoleon during the Hundred Days, and was restored to his rank by the Bourbons in 1819 but took little part in public affairs.

SUVOROV, ALEXANDER VASILIEVITCH, PRINCE OF ITALY, GENERAL (1729–1800). The son of a general, Suvorov joined the army as a youth and read widely about military campaigns and battles. He fought in the Seven Years' War and was promoted to colonel in 1762. During a series of wars with Poland (1768–1772) he became a major general. He fought against the Turks in 1773–1774, helped crush the Pugachev revolt in 1775, and again fought the Turks in 1787–1788. In 1794–1795 he helped crush the Polish rising, thereby completing the extermination of the Polish national independence.

In his years of combat, Suvorov developed his own operational style, closely resembling French Republican methods. He advocated aimed fire, constant attacks, and use of bayonet charges. He also learned the importance of troop morale, and his religious observances and rough-hewn manners may well have been designed to win the loyalty of his peasant soldiers. Suvorov would often label bayonet practice dummies as "French Atheists," and in Vienna in 1799 he refused to sleep in a palace because Christ was born in a manger. When the Austrians insisted that he occupy a palace, Suvorov had all the mirrors covered and slept on straw placed on the palace floors. Both acts could not but appeal to the common soldiers of his army.

In 1799 Suvorov was given command of the Austro-Russian army in Italy and proved himself to be one of the Republic's most dangerous opponents. In the space of six weeks he defeated Moreau (q.v.), Macdonald (q.v.), and Joubert (q.v.), thereby undoing all of the French achievements in the Italian peninsula. For his successes, Tsar Paul created for him the title Prince Italiysky (Prince of Italy).

In the summer of 1799 Suvorov wanted to invade France, but Austrian ambitions frustrated his designs. The Russians wanted to restore former Italian princes, but the Austrians intended to keep northern Italy for themselves. To get Suvorov out of Italy, they insisted that he join Russian forces operating in Switzerland. Austrian forces in southern Germany and northern Switzerland were then moved north to invade Belgium from the east, leaving the Russians momentarily isolated at Zurich save for a small Austrian supporting corps. The French in late September defeated the Russians at Zurich before Suvorov could join them and then moved to attack Suvorov's army.

Suvorov conducted a masterful retreat. He lost baggage, artillery, and over 5,000 men, but he brought the bulk of his army to safety. He won great renown for his heroic feat, but was unable to influence the course of the war. In January 1800 the Tsar ordered Suvorov and his armies to return to Russia, and Suvorov, exhausted by his efforts, died soon afterwards. (*See also* Zurich, Battle of)

-T-

TABOR, MOUNT, BATTLE OF (16 APRIL 1799). During the siege of Acre (q.v.), Bonaparte (q.v.) sent forces to investigate reports of Turkish movements. After a number of skirmishes, Kléber (q.v.), with about 2,000 men, encountered 25,000 Turkish troops. He formed two squares and fended off Turkish attacks until Bonaparte arrived with reinforcements of 3,500 troops. Attacking from the rear, the French quickly shattered the army of Damascus. The French lost only two killed and sixty wounded. Turkish losses are unknown.

TACTICS, REPUBLICAN. Flexibility became the hallmark of French Republican tactics as French soldiers learned to fight in line for fire action, in column for maneuver and shock action, and in skirmish order. The Republican army developed the all-purpose soldier. Commanders learned to employ the various modes of combat according to circumstances and to shift from one mode to another during combat.

A nine-company battalion usually marched to action in an open column. Upon entering combat, French infantry usually formed double company columns by division, a formation two companies wide and four deep. Since the companies stood in three rank lines (q.v.), the column resembled a rectangle eighty men wide by twelve deep, with the ninth company in reserve.

The battalion commander then had numerous options. Depending upon a particular situation, he could detach companies forward as skirmishers. He could then reinforce his skirmish line using the entire battalion in open order if appropriate. Alternatively, he could order the companies remaining in column to deploy into line for fire action, or he could order the column to deliver a bayonet charge.

The half-brigade enjoyed similar flexibility. The commander could place all three battalions in a firing line or establish a line of battalion columns or place some battalions in line and others in column. A fairly common initial deployment was the *ordre mixte*, wherein the center battalion deployed in a firing line while battalions on either flank moved in a double company column. Skirmishers would cover the entire formation.

The precise combination of line column and skirmish order varied widely. At Hondschoote (q.v.), for example, Jourdan's (q.v.) division advanced in a line of columns, and then, after coming under fire, the entire division moved forward in open order. At Toulon (q.v.), battalion columns covered by skirmishers stormed British entrenchments. At Tourcoing (q.v.), several battalions fought in line while skirmishers fired at the flanks of advancing coalition columns. At Fleurs (q.v.), Kléber's division fought in linear order with skirmishers covering the flanks. Lefebvre's (q.v.) division also fought in line, and when the Austrians fell back, several battalions pursued in column.

Initially the French periodically had problems shifting formations during a battle, and Allied commanders often launched effective counterblows while the Republican troops were in the midst of moving from one mode to another. By mid-1794, however, the French had learned by hard experience to execute shifts rapidly and cohesively. The ability to fight in close order or tight formations and the capacity to shift rapidly from one mode to another provided the French with the means to combat Old Regime armies on better than even terms. (*See also* Republican Army, French)

TALLEYRAND-PERIGORD, CHARLES-MAURICE (1754–1838). The eldest son of a noble family, Talleyrand had a club foot, which precluded a military career. In 1779 he was ordained a priest, rose rapidly in the church due to family influence, and became a bishop in 1789. Indifferent at best to religion, Talleyrand supported the early reforms of the Revolution, including the nationalization of church property.

His diplomatic mission to London in 1792 failed to stem growing British hostility to the Revolution. After the fall of the monarchy, Talleyrand stayed in London for two years and then visited the United States. He returned to France in 1796 and was named foreign minister in 1797.

His tenure as foreign minister in 1797 was marked by corruption and, even worse, lack of positive achievement. He sabotaged peace talks with Britain by assuring the British that elections in September 1797 would produce a government willing to make a greater concession than the incumbent government was offering. The British, consequently, refused serious negotiations and ended talks when the Directory (q.v.)

purged Royalists from the government and insisted upon its initial offer. His venality in the XYZ Affair (q.v.) produced an undeclared naval war between the United States and France, and he supported the idea of an Egyptian expedition (q.v.), which ended in disaster.

Talleyrand, in November 1799, played a significant role in Bonaparte's coup and returned to office as minister of foreign affairs, serving until 1807.

Out of office, he continued his intrigues and played a minor role in the Bourbon Restoration of 1814. He was the French delegate to the Congress of Vienna, where he played a significant but secondary role. He retired in 1815, but after the Revolution of 1830, he served the Orléanist monarchy as ambassador to London.

Talleyrand was intelligent, venal, and corrupt. He was also a survivor, who, according to his own account, served thirteen different governments.

TEIL, JEAN DE BEAUMONT, CHEVALIER DU (1738–1820). The younger brother of Jean Pierre du Teil, the chevalier first served in the artillery in 1745. In 1784 he was promoted to lieutenant colonel in the Metz artillery regiment. He supported the Revolution and in February 1792 became the artillery commander in the Army of the Rhine. In 1793, as a general of brigade, he commanded the artillery at the siege of Toulon (q.v.). Du Teil was suspended because of his noble birth, but was recalled in 1799. He later served as commandant of the Metz garrison until his retirement in 1813. During the Old Regime, du Teil had called for a more active tactical role for field artillery which, he argued, should, whenever possible, avoid counterbattery fire and instead support the infantry by firing against the enemy foot soldiers. Field artillery should also move in battle in order to respond to tactical circumstances and bring its fire to bear more effectively. During the Revolutionary wars, commanders frequently employed du Teil's suggestions.

TEIL, JEAN PIERRE DU, GENERAL (1722–1794). Du Teil was an artillery officer. He fought in the Seven Years' War and later became commander of the La Fère Artillery Regiment, where he put into practice the ideas of his younger brother. Bonaparte (q.v.) was a cadet in the regiment and learned the most advanced field artillery techniques of his day. In 1793 du Teil supported the Royalist cause, fought in the south, and was captured and executed at Lyon.

TERROR, THE (1793–1794). As a response to foreign invasion, rebellion, and internal subversion, the Convention (q.v.) established what amounted to a centralized instrument of national defense. The structure of the Terror involved a number of incremental steps.

On 10 March 1793, the Convention established a Revolutionary Tribunal to punish crimes against the Revolution. A law of 21 March gave legal status to local Committees of Surveillance that had formed spontaneously in many departments and ordered areas without Committees to establish them. The Committees had the power to arrest suspects. A law of 19 March called for the rapid execution of rebels taken in the field, while a law of 23 April called for the deportation of refractory priests; if they returned, they were subject to immediate execution. The Law of Suspects of 17 September 1793 defined crimes against the revolution to include both political and economic crimes, such as hoarding and counterfeiting.

On 10 October 1793, the Convention declared that the French government was, until the end of hostilities, a revolutionary regime. The constitution was suspended, and the Committee of Public Safety (q.v.) received the authority to nominate generals, regulate the activities of ministers, and exercise control over local officials. On 14 December 1793 the Convention further extended the Committee's powers. Ministers were to report on their activities to the Committee every ten days. Local authorities were forbidden to alter or ammend decrees emanating from Paris, and locally elected officials in districts and communes were replaced with national agents responsible directly to the Committee. Finally, the decree placed the conduct of foreign affairs directly in the hands of the Committee.

A final step in the centralization of governmental authority came on 1 April 1794, when the Convention abolished the council of ministers and replaced it with a dozen commissions reporting directly to the Committee. The Committee of Public Safety quickly emerged as the locus of power in the Republic.

Known as the Republic of Terror and Virtue, the regime was designed to deal with a near-catastrophic emergency situation. *Terror* in theory was directed at the enemies of the Revolution. *Virtue* did not mean a puritanical system of morality. Rather, the use of the word "virtue" derived from a Latin term, meaning a willingness to subordinate personal interests to the good of society during a crisis. Justice was not, of course, fully even-handed. Many people were arrested for what others perceived as disloyalty. Political rivals occasionally fell victim to the Revolution not for disloyalty but for disagreements, legitimate for the most part, over policy.

The Terror did not turn France into a charnel house. The total number of people executed during the Terror numbered about 40,000. The vast majority of those executed were rebels taken with arms in hand waging war against the government. The Terror fell most heavily in the Vendée (q.v.), Brittany, Lyon, Toulon, and Marseilles, all areas of major counterrevolutionary insurrection. By the summer of 1794, as the tide of war turned, the Convention turned and destroyed the leaders of the Terror, some of whom had come to believe that opposition to their views was tantamount to treason. The Terror, nevertheless, worked in that it enabled the government to organize the nation for total war, defeated the internal rebellions, and turned the tide of battle against the nation's external enemies. (*See also* Committee of Public Safety; National Convention)

THREE RANK LINE. The three rank line for fire action was the standard formation for fire action. Initially, armies sought to have all three ranks delivering fire simultaneously, which required the front rank to kneel. It proved difficult, however, to get the front rank to stand up and advance. Kneeling soldiers felt safe and were reluctant to stand upright and expose themselves to enemy fire. By the 1770s the third rank was supposed to load muskets for the front ranks. Soldiers would fire, pass their weapons back and receive loaded weapons from the rear line. Soldiers, however, proved reluctant to relinquish their personal weapons. Consequently, the third rank of the deployed firing line tended to act as a tactical reserve, with individuals moving forward to replace casualties in the first two ranks.

THUGUT, FRANZ-MARIA (1736–1818). Thugut began his diplomatic career as interpreter for the Austrian ambassador to Constantinople. He later held a number of ambassadorial posts. In 1793 he became the director-general of foreign affairs. His main goals were to prevent the final partition of Poland and to enlarge the Austrian Netherlands (Belgium) at the expense of France. He favored an alliance with Britain and joined the Second Coalition (q.v.). His goals were to acquire additional provinces in Italy and to reconquer Belgium and exchange it for Bavaria. His policies brought him into conflict with the Russians, and were in large part responsible for the Allied defeat at Zurich (q.v.). He retired from office in 1800.

THURREAU, LOUIS-MARIE, GENERAL (1756–1816). A member of the Royal Army, Thurreau supported the Revolution and in 1794 commanded the Army of the West Pyrenees. Transferred to the Vendée (q.v.), he successfully used mobile columns against the rebels. His suppression of resistance was brutal and effective. He was arrested on charges of misconduct, but acquitted in 1795. He then served in Switzerland and Italy. From 1803 to 1811 he was minister to the United States. He served in the campaigns of 1813–1814 and retired from service the following year.

TIPPOO SULTAN (1749–1799). Having lost a major war to Britain in 1792, Tippoo began to seek the support of a European power in order to renew hostilities. In May 1797, a French privateer was shipwrecked on the coast of Mysore. He was brought to the capital and claimed to be a representative of France. Tippoo realized he was a fraud but decided to use him in order to gain access to the French. Tippoo sent a delegation with the privateer to the Ile-de-France in the Indian Ocean with a proposal for an alliance. The governor refused to ratify a treaty but did send Tippoo's proposals on to France. The British were aware of Tippoo's schemes: they sent reinforcements to India, and informed Richard Wellesley (q.v.), the governor-general, to watch Tippoo closely and attack if the Sultan initiated hostile preparations. In November 1798, Wellesley told Tippoo to abandon his pro-French policies. Tippoo attempted to open negotiations that would last until the advent of the monsoon season made operations unfeasible. Wellesley, however, struck first. On 3 February 1799, 25,000 European and 13,000 native troops invaded Mysore. Poor roads and slow moving pack animals slowed the advance, but by the second week of April the British had siege works in front of the capital. On 4 May the British stormed Seringapatam. Tippoo died fighting. Wellesley put a new dynasty in place and forced it to sign a binding alliance with England.

TOLENTINO, TREATY OF (19 FEBRUARY 1797). After the fall of Mantua (q.v.), Bonaparte (q.v.) led 9,000 men into the Papal States. He soon forced Pope Pius VI (q.v.) to sign a peace treaty, in which the pope agreed to pay the Directory (q.v.) 30 million francs as an indemnity.

TONE, THEOBALD WOLFE (1763–1798). Tone was born in Dublin to an Anglo-Irish Protestant family. Educated in Dublin and London, he became a lawyer in 1789. He soon became involved in politics, advocating parliamentary reform and Catholic emancipation. In 1791 he was a founder of the United Irish Society, which advocated political reform. Tone soon concluded that reform was impossible without the creation of an Irish Republic; by 1794, Tone was in contact with French agents urging France to invade Ireland (q.v.). His negotiations were discovered by the authorities, and he had to flee the country, going first to the United States and then to France, where he continued to urge the French to invade Ireland. He participated in Hoche's (q.v.) abortive expedition in 1796, and despite its failure, he and other agents from the Society continued to urge the French to invade Ireland. The French, however, decided that their main venture in 1798 would be the Egyptian expedition (q.v.) and the Irish rebellion erupted without outside aid. The Directory (q.v.), after the British had crushed the major rising, did mount several small expeditions to Ireland. Tone sailed with one of them and was captured at sea on 12 October 1798. Sentenced to hang, Tone escaped the noose by slashing his throat in his cell. After lingering for a week, he died on 19 November 1798. (*See also* Bantry Bay; Ireland)

TOULON, SIEGE OF (7 SEPTEMBER–19 DECEMBER 1793). With a population of some 20,000 and the base of the Mediterranean fleet, Toulon was a city of great strategic importance. In July 1793 a Federalist rebellion took control of the city, but Royalist influence in the rebellion was strong, and Royalists soon took control, proclaimed allegiance to Louis XVII, and in late August opened the city to the British fleet under Lord Hood. British, Spanish, Neapolitan, and Piedmontese troops soon occupied a number of forts that protected the city.

The Committee of Public Safety (q.v.), realizing the importance of the city, ordered its rapid recapture. A lengthy siege ensued, and during the operations, a young artillery captain, Napoleon Bonaparte (q.v.), planned and executed an assault on two forts that dominated the harbor. The assault succeeded on 14 December, and the Allies abandoned the city five days later. They burned the French fleet and destroyed arsenals and dockyards. They also evacuated some 10,000 Royalists, but the city was again in the hands of the Republic, a success of great psychological importance. For his part in the siege Bonaparte was promoted to general of brigade. He was 24 years old, and his name had for the first time been brought to public notice.

TOURCOING, BATTLE OF (17–18 MAY 1794). Having decided to make their major military effort in Flanders and Belgium, the Committee of Public Safety (q.v.) reinforced the Army of the North. In early May, General Pichegru (q.v.) seized Menin (q.v.) and Courtrai. The Allies counterattacked in an effort to crush the French forces that had occupied the two towns. The Allies advanced with 73,000 men organized into six converging columns against 60,000 French commanded by General J. Souham (q.v.), who in Pichegru's absence was in command of the threatened sector. Souham deployed his forces to defeat the advancing columns in detail. He left a small force to hold off the largest column and concentrated the bulk of his troops against two of the weaker formations. After hard fighting around Courtrai and Tourcoing, the Allied advance was halted. The battle raised French morale, demonstrated that the new Republican armies were rapidly gaining tactical proficiency, and prepared the way for a French offensive on the Sambre.

TOURNAI, BATTLE OF (22 MAY 1794). After his victory at Tourcoing (q.v.), Pichegru (q.v.), with some 62,000 men, attacked Allied troops around Tournai. Fighting raged from 5 a.m. until 9 p.m., but the Allied forces drove off the French attacks with heavy losses. The

French lost 6,000 men and the Allies 4,000. Though defeated, the Army of the North was not routed and was able to continue offensive operations. Moreover, Allied troops were pinned down in Flanders and thus not available to fight against Jourdan's (q.v.) forces on the Sambre.

TOUSSAINT L'OUVERTURE, FRANÇOIS DOMINIQUE (1743–1803). The son of a slave, Toussaint was raised as a Christian and learned to read. He became a coachman and ultimately a steward on the plantation of Saint Domingue. Initially, he took no part in early slave rebellions, but when France and Spain went to war in 1793, he joined the Spanish forces. He displayed a talent for attracting followers and waging irregular warfare, and the Spanish made him a general and a knight in the Order of Isabella. He soon led a force of some 4,000 men.

In 1794 Toussaint switched sides. The National Convention (q.v.), with nothing to lose, had abolished slavery on 4 February 1794, while the British and Spanish were intent on retaining and restoring the institution of human bondage. Toussaint killed the Spanish officers serving with his forces, joined the French, and soon drove the Spanish back to their portion of the island.

Toussaint was also an able politician and rapidly established himself as the dominant power in the French colony. He soon clashed with Paris. Toussaint had inflicted heavy losses on the British and, at the end of 1798, London agreed to evacuate its footholds in Saint Domingue. The Directory (q.v.) wanted the war to continue in order to tie down British resources in the West Indies. The Directory, therefore, supported Rigaud, a mulatto, who ruled a semi-independent state in the southwestern part of the colony. Rigaud wished to replace Toussaint and to win French backing agreed to spread slave rebellions to British Caribbean colonies. Toussaint, with American aid, turned and crushed Rigaud, killing over 10,000 of Rigaud's mulatto followers in the process. By 1800 he was supreme within the colony.

In 1801 Toussaint occupied the Spanish portion of the island, issued a constitution that made him governor-general for life with the right to name his successor, and gave little more than lip service to French rule.

Bonaparte (q.v.) had vast schemes for Hispaniola and Louisiana, and could not achieve them unless the island were firmly in his possession. He, therefore, invaded the island in 1802. French forces captured Toussaint, who was taken to prison in France, where he died in the following year.

Toussaint was an able, ambitious leader. He wanted to rule an independent state that was not a pawn in French political schemes. He came close to success, and even his defeat did not end the hopes of the former slaves for an independent regime. (*See also* Saint Domingue)

TRAINING, FRENCH. Recruits in Republican armies received rudimentary training on their way to depots. If time permitted, there was additional training at the depots. At Famars in 1793, for example, demi-brigades maneuvered daily, and at Maubeuge several half-brigades trained together. Occasionally, army commanders established special schools to instruct soldiers drawn from many units in the fundamentals of drill. The soldiers then returned to their units and passed on the information to others. Essentially, training was done "on the fly." Lulls in operations allowed commanders the opportunity to train their soldiers not only in drill but also in musketry. If time were lacking, new soldiers would learn the essentials from NCOs and comrades in their unit. It was not until after the Peace of Amiens (q.v.) that Napoleon was able to devote a great deal of time to extensive troop training.

TREBBIA, BATTLE OF (17–19 JUNE 1799). To reverse their defeats in Italy, the French ordered Macdonald's Army of Naples, 29,000 men strong, to move north and join Moreau's Army of Italy around Genoa. Macdonald (q.v.) suggested instead that his army move on Modena and Parma while Moreau (q.v.) advanced to meet him at Parma. Moreau agreed. Meanwhile, Macdonald moved north, taking Modena on 13 June and Parma on 15 June. Moreau, however, did not advance, leaving Macdonald to face a combined Austro-Russian force under Suvorov (q.v.) of some 36,000 men between the Trebbia and Tidone rivers. In vicious fighting on 17 June Suvorov halted the French. Fighting resumed the next day. The Allies lost 12,000 men and the French 8,000. Macdonald, consequently, concluded that in the absence of Moreau's support he had no choice but to retreat to Genoa, which he reached on 12 July.

TRINIDAD (17 FEBRUARY 1797). A British expedition of four ships of the line, joined by another ship of the line and transports arrived off Trinidad on 16 February 1797. A Spanish squadron of four ships of the line was anchored in Port of Spain. Troops under the command of Sir Ralph Abercromby (q.v.) landed and began to move inland. The Spanish scuttled their ships and destroyed their shore batteries and then surrendered without a fight. At the Peace of Amiens (q.v.), Britain kept the island.

TUSCANY, GRAND DUCHY OF. The French occupied Tuscany in 1799 but were driven out during the War of the Second Coalition. After Marengo, the French returned. In 1801, by the Peace of Luneville (q.v.), Tuscany became the kingdom of Etruria, ruled by the Duke of Parma, who was the son-in-law of the king of Spain. In exchange,

Spain gave Louisiana back to France. In 1808 Napoleon annexed Tuscany.

-U-

UKERATH, BATTLE OF (19 JUNE 1796). While retreating to the Rhine, Jourdan's (q.v.) troops at Ukerath mounted a counterblow against the Austrian advance. Kléber (q.v.), Ney (q.v.), and Richepanse (q.v.) attacked, but after some initial success were driven back by General Kray's (q.v.) Austrian battalions.

-V-

VALENCIENNES, SIEGE OF (MAY–AUGUST 1793). As part of a series of sieges, on 24 May Allied forces opened approach trenches against the 9,500-man French garrison. The Allies had 30,000 troops engaged in the siege, covered by an additional 20,000 men. The Allied army included Austrian, British, and Hanovarian troops. After weeks of bombardment and a major assault, the remaining French troops (about 5,000 men) surrendered on 1 August. The French left behind 180 guns and returned to French territory after a pledge not to fight the Allies for a year. The Allies had fired over 150,000 rounds against Valenciennes and suffered about 1,750 casualties. The Austrians then announced that French territory up the Somme River would be annexed to Belgium.

VALMY, BATTLE OF (20 SEPTEMBER 1792). In the summer of 1792 Austrian and Prussian armies were everywhere victorious. Leading a force of some 35,000 men, the Duke of Brunswick (q.v.) took the fortresses of Longway on 23 August and Verdun on 2 September. He then advanced through the Argonne Forest on his way to Paris. To protect Paris, Dumouriez (q.v.) pulled his army out of Sedan and General François-Etienne-Christophe Kellermann (q.v.) marched from Metz. Together the two forces included 50,000 men, many of whom were recent volunteers with little training or battle experience. The two armies united around the small village of Valmy east of the Prussian army. There was no organized force between the Prussians and Paris, but Brunswick feared that if he marched directly on the city, the French might strike his flank and rear echelons. He therefore ordered his regiments to turn and destroy the last organized French units before advancing on Paris.

On the morning of 20 September French artillery drove back the Prussian advanced guards. The main Prussian force then came up and, after a short artillery barrage, moved forward, only to face another barrage from the French field artillery, which soon forced the

Prussians to retire. The Prussians in turn laid down a barrage of their own. One shell struck a French munitions wagon. The ensuing explosion caused a momentary panic in the ranks of Kellermann's troops, who were holding the front line. Officers managed to restore order, and Dumouriez, whose army was in reserve, sent additional field guns forward. Brunswick, meanwhile, sent forward a second attack, which was again met by heavy artillery fire and fell back. There were few casualties in the battle. The French lost fewer than 200 men and the Prussians 300. Nevertheless, the Prussian attack was halted, and bad weather and disease convinced Brunswick to retreat eastward ten days later. Stories that Dumouriez bribed Brunswick to retreat with Marie Antoinette's jewelry are without foundation. The new French armies did not break. They halted a major Allied offensive, and two days after the battle, France became a republic.

VANDAMME, DOMINIQUE JOSEPH RENÉ, GENERAL (1770–1830). Vandamme joined the army in 1791 and in 1792 fought in Belgium and Holland. In 1793 he was promoted to general of brigade, and fought at Tourcoing (q.v.) and in several sieges. By 1799 he was a general of division and fought at Stockach (q.v.). Transferred to Holland, he played a major role in defeating the Anglo-Russian invasion, fighting brilliantly at Alkmaar and Bergen (q.v.). After 1800, he served Bonaparte (q.v.) loyally, fighting at Austerlitz, in the Prussian campaign of 1806, and in the Austrian campaign of 1809. He served in Russia in 1812 and Germany in 1813, where he was captured and interviewed by the Tsar. Alexander accused him of looting and serving a tyrant, to which Vandamme replied that he at least had never been accused of murdering his father. He returned to France in 1814 and served Napoleon during the Waterloo campaign, commanding a corps under Grouchy (q.v.). He then commanded the rear guard after the battle. From 1816 to 1819 he lived in the United States; he returned to France and was granted retirement in 1825. Vandamme was a tough, outspoken soldier. He was an able leader of men, whose most effective performance was on the field of battle rather than in the realm of strategy.

VAUBOIS, CHARLES HENRI, GENERAL (1748–1839). Vaubois joined the artillery in 1770. In 1791 he was a lieutenant colonel of volunteers. In 1793 he was promoted general of brigade and served at the siege of Lyon. As a general of division in 1796, he served at the siege of Mantua (q.v.). As part of the Army of the Orient, Vaubois took part in the occupation of Malta (q.v.) and became the garrison commander. Besieged by the British, he had to surrender in September 1800. He returned to France but took no further part in active operations.

VENDÉE, THE. The Vendée is located south of the Loire, which forms its northern boundary. To the west, the Vendée's approximate border ran through the towns of Samur and Thouars. The southern boundary was sixty miles south of the Loire, following a road connecting the small port of Les Sables with Fontenay.

Topographically, the Vendée consisted of the *marais* and the *bocage*. The *marais*, near the coast, was flat and marshy and sparsely populated. Further inland, the *bocage* consisted of fields, small villages, and buildings enclosed by thick hedges and crisscrossed by sunken roads. The *bocage* covers most of the Vendée; to the east, the *bocage* gives way to rich agricultural districts.

In 1790 about 800,000 people lived in the Vendée. The vast majority of the population worked on the land. Most peasants were tenant farmers, sharecroppers, or day laborers. There was also a large number of drifters, who were unemployed or only seasonally employed. The nobles in the region were on the whole quite poor and their estates not much different from neighboring farms. The small towns were largely administrative centers and contained small textile businesses. The peasantry was also quite religious, and parish priests were important and influential figures in the peasant communities.

Even before the Revolution, there was considerable tension between the peasantry and the middle classes in the towns. The middle class was not subject to militia service, and the peasants, who often worked for textile makers during the winter season, felt they were being exploited.

The middle classes accepted the Revolution and were the chief beneficiaries of Revolutionary reforms, including access to local offices and the sale of church lands. The peasants also disliked the church reforms of 1790 and continued to follow priests who refused to accept the Civil Constitution of the Clergy.

Into this explosive brew came the war, the execution of the king, and the disastrous military situation of early 1793. In late February the Convention (q.v.) introduced a *levée* of 300,000 men. Word of the new law reached the Vendée in early March. By 3 March young peasants and artisans banded together and pledged to resist conscription. There were riots in many towns. On 11 March riots spread to towns throughout the region, as peasants attacked constitutional priests and local officials. By 13 March the Vendée was in open revolt, and hundreds had been killed. The rebellion initially was a popular spontaneous uprising against the Parisian government and local officials and individuals who supported the Republic. By the middle of March, the insurgents controlled most of the Vendée.

The government's response was to push small detachments into the Vendée to restore order, but the small columns were rapidly crushed.

In early April the government sent 20,000 men, organized into four columns, into the Vendée. Republican troops, who were drawn from the National Guard, lacked training and had little knowledge of the terrain. In a series of engagements between 19 and 22 April, government troops were defeated and pushed back with heavy losses. In May the Vendeans defeated additional Republican offensives.

The Vendeans also began to give their rebellion a permanent organization. The original bands of rebels were led by a wide variety of individuals — peasants, artisans, former soldiers, and local nobles. The Vendeans established a Grand Council for civil administration, located at Chatillon in the center of the Vendée, and parish councils including a local priest who maintained morale. For military affairs a Supreme Council of 30 officers was appointed, although there was no supreme commander. The armed bands were loosely organized. In the *bocage* the largest band, known as the Catholic and Royal Grand Army of Anjou and Haut Poitou, could mobilize 40,000 men. In the western *bocage* the Catholic and Royal Army of the Center contained 10,000 men, and the Army of Retz and Bas Poitou in the *marais* had about 12,000 men. The three armies retained a total of 7–8000 men permanently under arms, while the remainder worked their fields until the regional commands ordered mobilization, which was transmitted from parish to parish by the ringing of church bells.

On 9 June the Army of Anjou and Haut Poitou stormed Samur (q.v.), and on 12 June, the Vendeans chose Cathelineau, a wagoner and leader of one of the earliest bands, as supreme commander. Senior leaders then decided to attack Nantes. Forces from the *marais* would advance north while the Army of Anjou and Bas Poitou moved from Samur to the west. The dual offensive against Nantes failed because the two columns did not coordinate their attacks. The Army of Retz and Bas Poitou attacked and was driven back on 28 June. The Army of Anjou and Haut Poitou attacked a few days later. It too was driven back, and Cathelineau died in the fighting.

The Vendeans withdrew to the *bocage,* where they drove back Republican probes and elected Elbée, a former soldier, as the new supreme commander. The Vendeans had thus managed to hold their own but had failed to break out and spread their rebellion to other regions. Nor had they taken a port in order to receive weapons and perhaps troops from England.

The Republicans, who had been employing primarily National Guardsmen and untrained recruits in the Vendée, in August sent the veteran Mainz garrison of 12,000 men to the west. In September the Republic launched another offensive into the *bocage,* but the Vendeans ambushed and defeated individual columns. The Republicans retreated. They were not, however, completely defeated and soon organized another offensive.

Under Kléber's command, three large columns moved into the bocage, converging on Chatillon. On 16 October 1793, Kléber (q.v.) entered Cholet (q.v.) and organized its defense with 32,000 men. The Vendeans were cornered and, with 35,000 men, launched a massive counterattack on 17 October. The Vendeans sustained a major defeat, Elbée was killed, and the Vendean army, accompanied by thousands of women, children, and elderly people, retreated to the Loire. On 19 October 65,000 Vendeans crossed the river into Brittany. Only a few thousand men under Charette in the *marais* held out in the Vendée.

In Brittany the Vendeans decided to move north to Laval and from there to the coast to capture a port where they could obtain support from the British. On 13 November the Vendeans tried and failed to storm Granville on the Channel and retreated back to the Vendée. They attacked and failed to take Angers, moved back north, took Le Mans on 10 December and were defeated upon leaving the town on the 12th. Unable to cross the Loire back into the Vendée, they moved west, where Kléber caught them at Savenay on 23 December. The Republicans annihilated the desperate Vendeans, and only small groups made their way back to the *bocage*.

By the end of 1793 the Vendeans were broken as a military force. In 1794 Republican forces, using roving columns, kept up pressure on guerrillas, who operated in small scattered bands. The war of ambush and reprisal went on throughout the year. In February 1795, after the Republic promised amnesty, exemption from conscription, and the free practice of religion, Charette (q.v.) made peace with the regime. In May Stofflet (q.v.) also concluded a truce.

A third insurrection broke out in 1795 in conjunction with the abortive Quiberon (q.v.) expedition. It lasted until early 1796, ending with Stofflet's death and Charette's capture and execution. A fragile peace was established, but insurrection erupted again in 1799 in a less effective form. A tenuous peace was restored in 1800, but throughout the Imperial period, the government's writ was not complete in the Vendée.

The rising of 1793 was a broad-based popular insurrection. The ensuing war and pacification was, as is the case in most guerrilla conflicts, terribly brutal. Both sides committed atrocities, and the murder of prisoners and noncombatants was common. It is estimated that approximately 15 percent of the population of the Vendée perished in battle or as the result of blue and white reprisals. Well into the 20th century, the Vendée was known for its deep political divisions, with the town voting Jacobin-Republican and the countryside clerical conservative. (*See also* Counterrevolution)

VERONA, BATTLE OF (5 APRIL 1799). Having failed at Pastrengo, Scherer (q.v.) advanced on Verona a second time. In vicious fighting, the French lost 10,000 men. The Austrians suffered about 5,000 casualties. As a result, the French had to fall back from the Adige and retreat to the Adda, leaving garrisons in Mantua (q.v.) and Peschiera to hold up the Allied advance.

VIAL, HONORÉ, GENERAL (1766–1813). Vial joined the army in 1792, serving in Corsica, the Army of the North, and the Army of the Alps. In 1796 he was promoted to general of brigade while serving in the Army of Italy. Vial fought at Arcola (q.v.) and at Rivoli (q.v.) and in 1798 became the governor of Rome. He fought in the Egyptian campaign, returning to France at the end of 1800. He became a general of division in 1803 and held a number of diplomatic posts. In 1813 Vial participated in the German campaign and was killed at Leipzig.

VICTOR, CLAUDE, GENERAL (1764–1841). The son of a notary, Victor enlisted in the Royal Army and rose to the rank of sergeant. Denied further promotion because of his social status, he left the army and became a grocer. He supported the Revolution, and in 1791 reentered the army via the National Guard. In 1793 he fought at Toulon (q.v.) and became a general of brigade. Victor campaigned in Italy in 1796–1797, in Egypt, and in the Italian campaign of 1800. A loyal and reliable commander, he served Napoleon, became a marshal, and after Waterloo held posts in the restored Bourbon regime.

VICTOR AMADEUS III, KING OF SARDINIA-PIEDMONT (1773–1796). Coming to the throne in 1773, Victor Amadeus enlarged his army but also dismissed reforming ministers and restored clerical influence. He was bitterly opposed to the French Revolution. In 1790 he closed Masonic societies throughout his kingdom, and in 1791 allowed Turin to become a center for French émigrés (q.v.). In 1792 he joined the war against France after rejecting a French offer of alliance. He soon lost Nice and Savoy, and in 1796 Bonaparte (q.v.) defeated his army and a contingent of Austrian troops. He left the war and had to accept the French annexation of Savoy and Nice and allow France to maintain garrisons in several cities in Piedmont. His successors remained neutral until 1799, when they began to prepare to join the Second Coalition (q.v.). The French struck first and annexed Piedmont; they held it until 1814.

VILLARET DE JOYEUSE, LOUIS THOMAS, VICE-ADMIRAL (1748–1812). Villaret de Joyeuse went to sea in 1765 and served in the East Indies. In 1793 he was promoted to captain and became a rear admiral in the same year, after successfully escorting a grain convoy to Brest. In 1794 he was defeated at the Battle of the First of June (q.v.) but again managed to get a grain convoy safely to Brest. Villaret de Joyeuse became a vice admiral in 1794 and in 1795 became a member of the Council of Five Hundred. He was forced from office after the coup of September 1797 and went into retirement. He was reemployed in 1800, and in 1802 escorted Leclerc's army to Haiti. He then became the military governor of Martinique and St. Lucia until 1809, when he was forced to surrender to the British. In 1811 he became governor of Venice.

VILLENEUVE, PIERRE CHARLES, VICE-ADMIRAL (1763–1806). Villeneuve joined the Bourbon navy in 1778 and served in the West Indies. In 1793 he became a captain, but was suspended as a former aristocrat. He was restored to service in 1795, and in 1796 was promoted rear admiral. He took part in the expedition to Ireland. In 1798 he sailed to Egypt, survived the Battle of the Nile (q.v.), and escaped to Malta (q.v.) with two ships of the line and two frigates. He was captured in September 1800 when the British took Malta. In 1804 Villeneuve was promoted to vice-admiral. In 1805 he commanded the Toulon fleet in the ill-fated attempt to invade England. Nelson (q.v.) defeated him at Trafalgar, and he was taken prisoner. In 1806 he committed suicide.

VILLERS-EN-CAUCHIES, BATTLE OF (24 APRIL 1794). The Austrian General Ott (q.v.), with a force of two Austrian and two British cavalry squadrons, marched to investigate the advance of a French force northeast of Cambrai. The Allies soon discovered a large French force. News then reached Ott that Emperor Francis (q.v.) and his entourage were close by and might be captured. Ott, therefore, ordered a desperate charge that completely surprised the French, who fell back in disorder, losing 1,200 men. The emperor later issued a special medal to Austrian and British officers present at the engagement and, in 1801, conferred Austrian knighthoods upon them. The enlisted men, of course, received no recognition.

VINEGAR HILL, BATTLE OF (21 JUNE 1798). After the Irish rebellion spread to Wexford, the British sent over 20,000 men to crush the Irish. After a series of preliminary engagements, the British encountered the main Irish force at Vinegar Hill. Armed mainly with pikes, the Irish were no match for the British, who broke the Irish force and pursued the fleeing remnants, giving no quarter even to wounded rebels. After the battle, the British continued to hunt down fleeing rebels in a campaign that was as vicious as the French operations in the Vendée (q.v.). (*See also* Ireland)

VOLLEY FIRE. Volley fire was a standard tactical device in both Old Regime and Republican armies. Volley fire was, however, more complex than often thought. A battalion, regiment, or entire deployed firing line did not in fact fire their muskets simultaneously. Most armies employed a rolling fire wherein companies within a battalion fired sequentially from right to left. By the time the last company fired, the first, in theory, would have reloaded and would resume the process. The Prussian army used a slightly different method, wherein a company on one flank of a battalion fired, followed by the unit on the opposite flank. Alternate units would take up the firing working inward, while the other formations reloaded and prepared to resume the process. In combat after the first few rounds, noise, smoke, casualties, and the chaos of battle made it almost impossible for soldiers to hear commands. Soldiers then loaded and fired individually to continue the fire fight. There was also a tendency for troops to lose their initial alignment as soldiers were hit and others moved up to take their places, while others either fled or sought cover. Consequently, battle alignment often changed into groups of soldiers shifting about. Nevertheless, well-trained troops would continue to load and fire their weapons with the mechanical methods learned on the drill fields.

VOLTRI, BATTLE OF (10 APRIL 1796). At the start of the 1796 Italian campaign, the Austrians attacked a French half-brigade at Voltri near Genoa. Cervoni (q.v.), the French commander, successfully avoided the Austrian effort to trap his force. A minor setback, the engagement convinced Bonaparte (q.v.) to hasten his own offensive.

-W-

WARREN, SIR JOHN, ADMIRAL (1753–1822). Warren entered the navy in 1771 as a seaman, became an officer in 1777, and obtained his first command in 1779. In 1794, as a squadron commander, he captured three French frigates. For several years he attacked French merchant ships and destroyed or captured over 100 vessels. In October 1798, Warren defeated a French expedition that was attempting to land troops in Ireland. He became an admiral in 1810 and commanded in American waters in 1813–1814.

WARSAW, SIEGE OF (AUGUST–NOVEMBER 1794). To crush the Polish rising, 25,000 Prussians and 65,000 Russians marched on Warsaw. The Polish garrison of 35,000 withstood two assaults and the siege was temporarily abandoned. Additional Prussian and Russian reinforcements arrived in September. Some 50,000 Prussians and 50,000 Russians plus 5,000 Austrians resumed the offensive. The Poles lost a number of engagements, and on 4 November, a Russian force under Suvorov (q.v.) stormed the Praga, a suburb of Warsaw on the east bank of the Vistula. The Russians took the Praga and slaughtered not only the garrison but also the civilian population. The Poles then abandoned Warsaw, and by the end of the month the rising was over. In 1795 the eastern courts carried out the final partition of Poland. The failure of the Polish rising, however, tied down many Coalition (q.v.) troops in the east, thus materially aiding the French Republic. (*See also* Poland)

WARSHIPS. The primary ship of war of the 18th century and early 19th century was the full-rigged wooden sailing ship. Ships were classified according to their armament. The largest, mounting 100–120 guns, were called first rates; those with 90–98 guns were second rates; ships with 64–84 guns were third rates. Ships with 80 guns or more had three gun decks, while the rest had two decks. First, second, and third rate vessels were the capital ships of the fleet. In the 18th century ships usually fought in a linear formation and were called ships of the line.

Of ships below the line, those with 50–60 guns were termed fourth rates; those with 32–44 cannon were fifth rates; those with 20–28 guns were sixth rates. Armament on ships below the line was carried on a single deck. The smaller warships were called frigates and served as scouts, convoy escorts, and merchant raiders.

Ships' guns were a mixture of 32-, 24-, and 12-pounders. A 32-pounder was 8½ feet long with a 6½-inch caliber. It weighed two tons and had a crew of 15. Guns normally fired solid shot but could also fire chain, grape, and canister. The maximum range for solid shot was 2,500 yards, but more damage was caused by firing at about 400 yards, where a round could penetrate up to three feet of timber and cause splinters that were lethal to anybody in their path. By the late 18th century British ships carried one or more carronades, a short-barreled gun that fired a 68-pound shot. The French navy also adopted them.

The 74-gun ship of the line was the most common warship in many fleets. The 74-gun ship was 160 feet long and 45 feet wide. It had a draught of nearly 20 feet and weighed over 2,000 tons. It carried a crew of 590 officers and men, and in good sailing weather had a speed of about seven knots. Battle tactics in the 18th century involved fleets deployed in line trading broadsides. The British ultimately came to prefer the mêlée, where individual ships or small groups of vessels fought individually, supplementing broadsides with musket fire from snipers in the rigging. Ships were rarely sunk in an engagement. Rather, a ship battered beyond endurance capitulated to its opponent. During the Revolutionary wars, the British Royal Navy was generally dominant at sea. French warships were better designed than British vessels, but the British had the advantage of numbers and experience.

WATTIGNIES, BATTLE OF (15–17 OCTOBER 1793). Having halted the Coalition's (q.v.) advance in Flanders at the Battle of Hondschoote (q.v.), the French turned their efforts to the Sambre River area, where the Austrians were attacking Maubeuge, an important fortress useful as an advanced base for a march on Paris. The Committee of Public Safety (q.v.) attached great importance to Maubeuge's relief, since the fortress was critical to the defense of northern France. Failure to relieve it might well produce an outburst of public anger in Paris. Carnot (q.v.), therefore, personally went to the front to assist General Jourdan (q.v.), who had recently replaced Houchard. While Carnot requisitioned supplies, Jourdan, with 45,000 troops, advanced on Wattignies, a fortified village in the Austrian siege lines.

Jourdan attacked on 15 October, but the Austrians drove back the poorly coordinated French assault columns with heavy losses. Encouraged by Carnot, Jourdan reorganized his troops and attacked again on 16 October. Again the French attacks were poorly coordinated due to the inexperience of many of the commanders, but one of the columns battled its way into the village. Supported by a 12-gun artillery battery, the French repulsed Austrian counterattacks. On 17 October, shaken by the fury of the French attacks, Saxe-Coburg (q.v.) gave up the siege and withdrew back into Belgium. Jourdan did not gain a complete victory at Wattignies. The Austrian forces withdrew intact. The French had, however, blunted a second Allied offensive and gained security from invasion for the rest of the year. The French had also won the time needed to complete the national military and economic mobilization.

WEISSEMBOURG, BATTLE OF (13–14 OCTOBER 1793). The French, to protect Alsace, held a series of fortified posts centered on Weissembourg. An Austro-Prussian army attacked the Army of the Rhine on 13 October. The Austrian assaults were generally unsuccessful, although the French did give up several advanced positions. The Prussians, however, outflanked the Army of the Rhine on 14 October. The French retreated towards Strasbourg in reasonably good order. Reinforcements from the Army of Moselle enabled the French to halt the Austrians at Saverene. The Allies then undertook a number of sieges, thus giving the French a much needed respite.

WELLESLEY, ARTHUR, GENERAL (1769–1852). The fourth son of the Earl of Mornington, Wellesley was born in Dublin and educated at Eton, Brussels, and Angers. Initially, he was a fine violin player. He joined the army in 1787 and served as aide-de-camp to the Lord Lieutenant of Ireland. Due to his ability to purchase commissions, he was a lieutenant colonel in 1793 and a regimental commander in the same year. He fought in Flanders and the Low Countries, learning what not to do in military operations.

In 1797 he went to India, where his older brother was governor-general. In 1799 Wellesley commanded a division in the invasion of Mysore and became governor of Seringapatam. In 1802 he became a major general. He returned to England in 1805 and participated in the siege of Copenhagen in 1807.

In 1808 he became a lieutenant general and was sent to Portugal, thus beginning a military career that would make him one of the most famous military leaders of all time. Emerging from the Napoleonic Wars as the Duke of Wellington, he then began a political career that lasted until the early 1850s.

His experience in Flanders and India may well have established the foundations of his future generalship. He perhaps learned the importance of logistics and sea power. He may also have learned to work effectively with foreign armies. Nonetheless, his genius for war cannot be reduced to a simple enumeration of previous experiences. Genius is unique and cannot be reduced to formulas. Wellington moved beyond the realm of the scientific aspects of war, which he readily mastered, into the art of war in which individual intelligence and will are dominant.

WELLESLEY, RICHARD, EARL OF MORNINGTON (1760–1842). Born into a wealthy Anglo-Irish family, Wellesley in 1797 was sent to India as governor general. Although the government desired a non-expansionist policy in order to save troops and money for the war against France, Wellesley presumed that he could eliminate French influence in southern India without undue risk. The French in the late 1790s had attained much influence in Hyderabad and Mysore. Both states were anti-British and had begun to deal with local French adventurers who had remained in India after 1763 and the loss of remaining French possessions in 1793. Mysore was attempting to conclude an alliance with France. Wellesley moved first against Hyderabad, forcing the ruler to get rid of French officers in his army. Having isolated Mysore, he invaded and conquered the region in 1799, replacing the sultan with a compliant ruler. Wellesley's younger brother Arthur commanded a division in the Mysore campaign. Arthur, of course, was to go on to become the Duke of Wellington.

WELLINGTON, DUKE OF. *See* Wellesley, Arthur, General

WESTERMANN, FRANÇOIS-JOSEPH, GENERAL (1751–1794). Westermann joined the Royal Army in 1766, and by 1773 was a sergeant. He supported the Revolution and, on 10 August 1792, played a leading role in the storming of the Tuileries. He was promoted to colonel and fought at Jemappes (q.v.). He then served in the Army of the North. Investigated and cleared after Dumouriez's treason, Westermann next campaigned in the Vendée, where he was victorious in two grim battles at Le Mans and Savaney. In July 1793 he was court-martialed but acquitted on charges of brutality and pillage. Throughout his career, he demonstrated great personal courage, but his fiery personality made it almost impossible for him to work with the civil authorities. He was arrested, tried, and executed along with Danton.

WETZLAR, BATTLE OF (15–16 JULY 1796). After the defeat at Altenkirchen, the Austrians sent reinforcements to the Lahn. On 15 July the Austrians attacked Jourdan's troops. Austrian and Saxon troops took Wetzlar. Further attacks on 16 July threatened the French flanks, and Jourdan (q.v.) fell back across the Rhine.

WEXFORD REBELLION (1798). Wexford is a city in southeastern Ireland (q.v.). It was the scene of the most serious rising during the Irish Rebellion of 1798. The Wexford Rising began as a Catholic peasant rebellion led by parish priests. Soon, however, it took on political overtones, as a number of Protestant United Irishmen joined and began to direct the rebel forces. A Protestant led the rebel army and another Protestant commanded the Wexford garrison. The rebels also appealed to France for aid. The French were, however, already committed to the Egyptian venture, and with the rebels sorely lacking arms, the British soon crushed the rebellion.

WICKHAM, WILLIAM (1761–1840). Wickham held a law degree from the University of Geneva, married a Swiss national, and became a secretary in the Home Department. Late in 1794, the British government sent him to Switzerland to act as an intelligence agent and paymaster for Royalist efforts against France. In 1795 he spent nearly 100,000 pounds to assist counterrevolutionary military efforts, including bribes to Pichegru (q.v.). The approach of supporting military action having failed, Wickham next backed constitutional Royalists in France in the hope that they would win sufficient power in elections to restore the monarchy by legal means. The Directory's (q.v.) coup of September 1797 undid efforts to execute a "legal" counterrevolution. In 1799 Wickham was again instructed to provide financial assistance for Royalist military uprisings, but France defeated the Republic's internal and external enemies before Wickham could accomplish anything. After 1800, Wickham served briefly in Parliament and on the Treasury Board, retiring in 1807.

WILLIAM V (1747–1806). William was the prince of Orange Nassau and stadtholder of the United Provinces (commonly called Holland or the Netherlands). In the 1780s he resisted demands for political reform and, in 1787, accepted Prussian intervention to destroy the reformist "Patriot" movement. He joined the First Coalition (q.v.) and fled to England when the French overran the United Provinces in 1795. When the French invaded the United Provinces, there was a good deal of support for the creation of the Batavian Republic (q.v.) and very little for the stadtholder. William's refusal to promise any political reforms and his invitation to the British to take over Dutch colonies further undermined what little popularity and support William had left. He died in exile in 1806.

WIMPFFEN, LOUIS-FÉLIX, BARON DE (1744–1814). Wimpffen retired from the Royal Army as a marshal in 1788. He was a veteran of the American Revolutionary War, having served at the siege of Gibraltar. He reentered the army in 1792 and successfully defended Thionville against the Prussians. In 1793 he supported the Federalist revolt and was appointed head of the Federalist army organized by Federalists at Caen. Republican forces easily defeated the half-hearted Federalists of Normandy, and Wimpffen retired to his estates and took no further part in military affairs.

WÜRMSER, DAGOBERT SIGMUND VON, COUNT (1724–1797). Born in Strasbourg, Würmser served in the French army during the Seven Years' War. In 1763 he joined the Austrian army, becoming a major general during the War of the Bavarian Succession. During the War of the First Coalition (q.v.), he commanded the Imperial army in the Rhineland and in 1795 again commanded successfully Imperial forces in the Rhineland. In the following year he was promoted to field marshal and placed in charge of the Austrian army in Italy. Though an experienced and courageous soldier, Würmser was no match for Bonaparte (q.v.), who defeated the Austrians in detail and drove Würmser with 24,000 men into Mantua (q.v.). Würmser held Mantua for seven months. His garrison shrank to 7,000 effectives due to losses and disease, but he capitulated in 1797 only after several efforts to relieve the city had been halted by the French.

WURZBURG, BATTLE OF (3 SEPTEMBER 1796). In 1796 the French again launched a two-pronged attack into Germany. Jourdan (q.v.) again commanded the Army of the Sambre-Meuse, while Moreau (q.v.) replaced Pichegru (q.v.) in the Rhine and Moselle Army. As in 1795 the two generals failed to coordinate their operations. By August 1796, Moreau was advancing on Munich, but he moved so slowly that

Archduke Charles (q.v.) moved quickly and concentrated over 60,000 men against Jourdan. Jourdan wished to retreat, but the government ordered him to remain on the right bank of the Rhine as long as possible to support Moreau. On 3 September the Austrians attacked and forced Jourdan to retreat to the Lahn. Another Austrian attack on 16 September forced Jourdan back across the Rhine where he resigned in disgust at Moreau's failure to assist him. Jourdan's defeat in turn forced Moreau to retreat, and by 24 October the Rhine and Moselle Army was back on the French side of the Rhine.

-X-

XYZ AFFAIR (1797–1798). Anglo-American talks in the 1790s led to the Americans implicitly accepting British interpretations of the laws of blockade and neutrality. The French, convinced that the United States was siding with Britain, launched a virtual war on American commerce, seizing hundreds of U.S. merchant vessels. President Adams sent three representatives to France to try to resolve outstanding issues.

The delegates first met unofficially with Talleyrand (q.v.), the foreign minister, in October 1797. Talleyrand then sent four emissaries to the Americans. They demanded a bribe of 1.2 million francs and a commitment to purchase Dutch bonds prior to opening formal talks. The American position was that the United States, following normal diplomatic procedures, would pay a bribe and discuss a loan after but not before the conclusion of negotiations. One of the American delegates stated that the United States would not pay a sixpence, which soon became transformed into the phrase "millions for defense but not one cent for tribute," a ringing slogan that was of no relevance to the issue at hand.

Adams, meanwhile, published reports from his representatives referring to Talleyrand's agents as "XYZ" (he left out one agent, or the affair would have been known as the WXYZ affair). The result was an undeclared naval war in which American frigates defeated a number of French warships. Alexander Hamilton and his followers sought a full-scale conflict, including the seizure of French and Spanish colonial possessions. Adams, however, sought peace—which was concluded, to nobody's full satisfaction in 1800. Talleyrand's policy and venality had come close to adding another power, albeit a minor one, to the list of the Directory's enemies. (*See also* Talleyrand)

-Y-

YORK, FREDERICK AUGUSTUS, DUKE OF (1763–1827). The Duke of York was the second son of George III. He entered the British and

Hanoverian armies in 1784 and, from 1793 to 1795, commanded the British army in Flanders. He was unsuccessful. He failed to take Dunkirk and was defeated at Hondschoote (q.v.) and ultimately driven from the Continent. In 1799 Frederick Augustus commanded the Anglo-Russian invasion of Holland and was again defeated. York was also commander-in-chief of the British army, and as an administrator, he introduced a number of significant reforms including the improvement of light infantry tactics, reducing punishments, and founding the Royal Military Academy at Sandhurst. He resigned his position in 1809 but was reinstated in 1811. He became George's guardian during the monarch's last years.

-Z-

ZURICH, BATTLE OF (25 SEPTEMBER–5 OCTOBER 1799). In the summer of 1799 the armies of the Second Coalition (q.v.) drove the French from southern Germany, eastern Switzerland, and Italy. Allied forces also landed successfully in Holland. The Allies initially planned to invade France in the spring of 1800. Forces in Holland were to advance south, while armies in Switzerland moved west. In Switzerland the Coalition had a force of 27,000 Russian and 22,000 Austrians located around Zurich. A force of 30,000 Russians under Suvorov (q.v.) was to move out of Italy and join the Allied forces in Switzerland for the invasion. An Austrian army in southern Germany was to cover the right flank of the invasion force. The Austrians, however, failed to cooperate and ordered the army in southern Germany to move north in order to invade and seize Belgium before the Anglo-Russian army in Holland captured the province. The Austrian move momentarily isolated the Coalition army in Switzerland, since the Austrians began to move before Suvorov could arrive with his reinforcements. Both the French government and General Masséna (q.v.) recognized their opportunity.

The government reinforced Masséna's Army of Helvetia to a strength of 80,000 men. On 25 September Masséna attacked, driving back both the Russian and Austrian forces. French forces struck north across the Limmat River, splitting the Russian front in half while blocking Russian forces on their left. The main assault pivoted to the right and seized the Zurichberg just north of the city in costly fighting. Further south, Soult (q.v.) defeated the Austrian corps, thus preventing them from reinforcing the Russians who were still fighting in the city. Masséna continued his assault the next day. After vicious fighting he succeeded in forcing the Russians from Zurich with the loss of 2,000 killed and 5,000 prisoners. He also forced the Austrians to continue their retreat after losing 5,000 men. Masséna then shifted his forces south in an effort to trap and destroy Suvorov in the Alps. After several bitter engagements, Suvorov managed to escape to Germany but lost his artillery, baggage train, and about 5,000 men. Zurich was a brilliant tactical victory. It saved France from invasion. Moreover, the Russian defeat, coming as a result of Austrian perfidy, convinced Tsar Paul (q.v.) to leave the Second Coalition.

ZURICHBERG, BATTLE OF (3–4 JUNE 1799). After defeating Jourdan (q.v.) at Stockach (q.v.), Archduke Charles (q.v.) attacked Masséna's army in Switzerland, which had taken positions covering Zurich. Austrian attacks on 3 June failed. Charles attacked on 4 June. The key to the battle was Zurichberg, a height dominating the roads around the city. In bitter fighting, Charles lost over 3,000 men and failed to dislodge the French. Masséna's army, however, had also suffered heavily. Consequently, Masséna (q.v.) abandoned Zurich and took up a shorter, stronger position further west.

Bibliographic Essay

Carl von Clausewitz noted that the manner in which armies were organized, trained, and fought was not simply a military phenomenon. Armies resembled and reflected the societies that created them. An Old Regime state could not seriously contemplate the creation of a citizen army because the populace were subjects, not citizens. The Revolution, on the other hand, could unleash the full range of the people's energies, precisely because the Revolution produced citizens, who had a personal stake in the Republican regime. The French Revolution changed substantially the political and social basis of the state, and only these changes enabled the government to introduce significant military changes. As Clausewitz noted:

> It follows that the transformation of the art of war resulted from the transformation of politics. So far from suggesting that the two could be disassociated from each other, these changes are a strong proof of their indissoluble connection. (*On War*, p. 610)

The Revolution in France indeed changed the size, organization, social composition, tactics, operational style, and strategy of the French army. Other powers had to try to cope with a government that was far stronger than its Bourbon predecessor. The history of the military reforms of the Republic and the military operations of the Republic's armies has, not surprisingly, generated a tremendous number of scholarly and popular books and articles. Memoirs, documentary collections, and studies began to appear even while the Republic's armies were engaged on the battlefields of Europe, the Near East, and the Caribbean. The flood of studies continues even today, and no bibliography can hope to be complete. Consequently, this bibliography is designed to provide guidance for further reading, while attempting to cover some of the more important aspects of the Wars of the Revolution. The primary focus will be on Revolutionary France. The bibliography will also include material on the armies, navies, and campaigns of countries that fought against the Republic.

185

French scholars have compiled a number of bibliographies that are essential guides to the collections held by the army archives and the National Archives. The War Archives administration has produced multivolume catalogues listing manuscripts and documents. These official publications are basic guides to the holdings located at the Chateau de Vincennes, where the government has centralized document collections from both the army and the navy. The Austrians have also produced bibliographical guides to the Military Archives in Vienna.

The French National Archives and individual scholars have published guides to manuscript source holdings. The National Archives contains a wealth of data on the organization and administration of the armed forces.

Numerous bibliographies cover the history of France. Emile Bourgeois and Louis André did an eight-volume bibliography on the sources of French history. Though an older work, it still retains its importance. Pierre Caron has compiled a useful bibliography covering works published between 1866 and 1897. The Bibliothèque Nationale has issued a multivolume guide to modern French history. These works include studies of French military affairs.

There are also a number of important bibliographies dealing with the Revolutionary period. S. A. Berville and F. Barrière edited a massive work of 60 volumes on memoirs dealing with the Revolution. They include works by individuals involved with military issues. Caron, André Martin, and Gerhard Walter each produced a bibliography on the Revolution. Gustave Davois and Frederick Kircheisen have each done bibliographies on Napoleon. Both bibliographies include works on Napoleon's military education and early campaigns. Finally, the National Center of Scientific Research publishes an annual bibliography of French history. The series began in 1955, with retrospective volumes covering the years 1931 to 1955.

Bibliographies dealing with military history cover a wide range of subjects. Some focus on the broad sweep of military evolution. Others focus on a particular national army or a specific aspect of military development. Professor Robin H. Higham edited a very useful study of official histories from many nations. Pierre Chalmin's bibliographical guide, though dated, still covers a wide spectrum of military history and is still useful, as is Hardin Craig's bibliography of military encyclopedias and dictionaries. The French Army Historical Service has compiled an excellent bibliography covering French military and colonial history.

Studies on particular aspects of military history include an excellent article by John Lynn, which describes the publications of the Army Historical Section; R. R. Palmer wrote an article on studies of the Committee of Public Safety. These and other bibliographical studies provide essential guides for additional research and exploration.

Historical studies of France and Europe provide a basic framework for a closer examination of military matters. Among the most important historical surveys is the Peuples et Civilisation series, written between 1926 and 1961 and edited by Louis Halphen and Philippe Sagnac. Georges Lefebvre wrote the volume on the French Revolution, and his explanations of the causes and development of the Revolution still influence current scholarship. Lefebvre, of course, deals with diplomatic and military issues. R. R. Palmer, in his two-volume study of democratic revolutions in the Western world, places the French Revolution in a global context. Jacques Godechot has also written a study on the revolutions of the 18th century as well as a history of counterrevolutionary thought and action. An older study by Albert Sorel, a multivolume work that appeared between 1885 and 1904, provides a detailed history of European diplomacy during the Revolutionary and Napoleonic Era. His view that there was much continuity between Old Regime and Revolutionary diplomacy has been challenged but is still worthy of serious consideration. *The New Cambridge Modern History* and *The Cambridge History of the British Empire* both have volumes dealing with the revolutionary period and provide useful overviews. Pierre Renovin's series on international relations and Ernest Lavisse's series on the history of France are also very useful, detailed overviews of the history of the period and include wealth of information on military affairs. More recently, Samuel F. Scott and Barry Rothaus edited a two-volume encyclopedia of the French Revolution that includes numerous articles on the French army, major battles, and leading military figures. Moreover, each article includes a brief bibliography of major works on the particular subject. David Chandler's dictionary of the Napoleonic wars contains many entries on battles and leaders of the Republican period.

General histories of the art of war also focus on the Revolutionary era. Theodore Ropp's history of warfare in the modern world places the wars of the French Republic within the overall context of the evolution of modern warfare. Edward M. Earle's work on strategy, a collective study, has an excellent chapter by R. R. Palmer dealing with the impact of the Revolution on warfare. An older work by Jean Colin, a professional soldier, deals with the relationship between social and technological change and the unchanging principles of strategy. David Chandler, the leading scholar of Napoleonic military history, produced a general history of warfare covering major military campaigns.

Numerous monographs deal with specific aspects of military history. At the turn of the century, a number of British soldiers and scholars carefully examined the evolution of tactics. F. R. G. Henderson, Gerald Gilbert, E. B. Hambley, and E. M. Lloyd all deal with the history and evolution of tactics. W. Rustow wrote a major study of the history of infantry, and T. Dennison has an old but still useful history of cavalry. F. G. Herr and O. F. G. Hogg have produced carefully detailed studies of the history of artillery. Christopher Duffy, a prolific military historian, has written an excellent history of fortress warfare and sieges, while Fairfax Downey has produced a first-rate study of major artillery actions. S. Toy and A. de Zastrow have each written useful studies on the history and evolution of permanent fortifications.

Among older studies of the history of the French army, General Bardin's eight-volume dictionary of battles and leaders is still useful. Marshal Oudinot assisted Bardin in compiling the 1841 study. Dussieux's three-volume history of the French army published in 1884 is still a mine of valuable information. I. Favé's 1845 history of tactics remains a classic, and A. Pascal's six-volume history contains detailed accounts of engagements of the Old Regime and Revolutionary period. Among more modern works, J. Revol's 1929 semi-official history is excellent, while Marshal Weygand's history, though containing useful basic information, is more defensive and propagandistic. Eugene Carrias's study by contrast is illuminating and interesting.

During the Revolutionary wars, France fought all of Europe's great powers. Histories of the armies of French rivals add depth and perspective to any study of French operations and are useful for comparative purposes. Sir John Fortescue's massive study of the British army published between 1910 and 1930 remains the basic examination of the British army and its campaigns. More recently, Correlli Barnett has done a shorter but insightful history. For the Prussian army, Carl Jany's four-volume study is essential. H. Bleckween's more recent study of the Prussian army between 1713 and 1807 is a well balanced appraisal that incorporates much recent research on the Hapsburg army. Herman Meynert and A. von Werede have each done multivolume histories. D. Buturlin's four-volume study of Russian campaigns is sound but dated, while Christopher Duffy's study is an excellent overview of the operations and evolution of the Russian army.

Histories of the individual French service arms provide not only a detailed picture of how armies operated, but also a vital explanation of how segments of the armed forces responded to the impact of the Revolution. Lieutenant Colonel Belhomme's five-volume history of the infantry, published between 1893 and 1902, is especially useful for a detailed compilation of infantry orders of battle during the wars of the Old Regime and the Revolution. Jean Colin's history of 18th-century infantry is especially useful for an examination of tactics in the Old Regime and efforts of the Crown to enhance the efficiency and effectiveness of the infantry arm. Quimby's more recent study provides a wealth of detail on the ideas of post-1763 reformers and their efforts to create a more effective tactical system.

Edouard Desbrière and Maurice Sautai, between 1899 and 1910, produced a five-volume study of the French cavalry. Their first volume deals with cavalry during the Old Regime. The next two volumes carry the history to 1795, and the final volumes cover the development and use of cavalry during the period of the Directory. Henri Choppin and Louis Picard have each written valuable studies on cavalry organization and tactics. Among the better studies of the French artillery are Susane's older study of 1874. Matti Laurema's work, which appeared in 1956, not only deals with French field artillery during the Old Regime and Revolutionary period, but also supplies a wealth of information on the artillery systems of other European powers.

The French engineer corps was periodically a separate service arm and at other times it was part of the artillery. The Revolution made the engineer corps permanently a separate service. Henri Berthaut and Colonel Augoyat each produced detailed studies of the engineer corps. Though written at the end of the 19th century, both studies retain their utility. Pierre Chalmin has done a number of excellent articles on military schools, and E. H. Ackernect has written a fine book on military medicine in France, while Emile Knorr's older work examines military medicine in many European states.

Military uniforms, heraldry, and music have symbolic, political, and social significance. The introduction of the tricolor flag and the blue uniform, for example, were vivid indications of the development of a national army. Revolutionary songs provide an indication of the changing attitudes towards the role of the army and its relation to the nation. P. Barbier and F. Vernillat in the 1950s produced a seven-volume study of the history of French popular songs. E. Fonclare and Fred and Liliane Funken produced histories of French military uniforms. Henry Lachoque also did a first-rate history of military uniforms.

Navies played an important role in both Old Regime and Revolutionary warfare. E. H. Jenkins wrote an excellent history of the French navy. His book is based on the previous works of French naval historians and is a sound reliable survey. Earlier works include studies by E. Chevalier and R. Jouan, as well as Charles de la Roncière's six-volume history completed in 1934. There are numerous studies of the British Royal Navy. Michael Lewis has written several useful studies on British naval history. Paul Kennedy's history of the rise and fall of British sea power places the evolution of British naval power within a broad social, political, and economic framework. Oliver Warner and Geoffrey Bennett have each done excellent books of particular battles and leaders. C. J. Marcus has a fine study of the Royal Navy during the Revolutionary and Napoleonic wars.

The impact of the Revolution on the structure and tactics of the French army has been examined by numerous scholars. Most recently, Jean Paul Bertaud, Samuel F. Scott, and John Lynn have produced indispensable examinations of the army's response to the Revolution. Bertrand's study describes in detail changes in numbers, organization, social composition, and above all morale in the new armies raised between 1791 and 1794. Scott examines the Royal Army and how it adjusted to changing political conditions. By 1793, just before it was merged with the volunteer and conscript formations, the Royal Army, now the army of the Republic, was a very different force from the pre-Revolutionary army. John Lynn's work not only describes the changes in size, structure, morale, and composition of the army but relates these changes to the evolution of Republican morale and tactics. He clearly shows that the morale of France's new armies was a crucial element in the creation of new flexible tactics.

Campaign and battle studies form an important part of any study of the wars of the French Revolution. Like it or not, war involves fighting and campaigns, and battles are essential elements in war, since wars are not in fact decided only by long term trends or assessments of economic capabilities. The results of wars in many cases are contingent. States and leaders must use the assets available to them effectively, and fighting does in fact determine the results of a conflict.

Among the more useful studies of campaigns between 1792 and 1799 is Edmond Bonnal's history of Republican armies between 1792 and 1800. Hurbert Camon produced numerous studies on Napoleon, in which he examines Bonaparte's Italian campaign. David Chandler's book on Napoleon's campaigns also examines operations in Italy and Egypt. Older works by Theodore Dodge and Mathieu Dumas provide detailed histories of Republican military operations, as does Baron Jomini. B. Nabonne and R. Guyot examine the diplomacy of the period. Their works are essential in order to place military operations in a strategic context. Gunther Rothenberg has dealt with the Austrian army's operations, and the Austrian official histories are also useful for this purpose. C. von der Goltz performed a similar study on the Prussian army.

For operations between 1792 and 1797, the works of Arthur Chuquet, though written in a patriotic vein, are still useful. Jean Paul Bertaud's work on Valmy is excellent, as is Jean Colin's older study of the 1793 campaign in Alsace. H. Coutanceau and C. De la Jonquière did a five-volume work on the 1794 campaign that was published between 1903 and 1908 and is still a basic study. Paul Foucart and Jules Finot wrote an excellent study of the operations in northern France in 1793–94, and Jean Hennequin's book on the 1794 campaign in the northeast remains one of the best explorations of the subject. Louis Jouan's book on 1794 operations in the Low Countries is equally valuable. J. H. Rose and Albert Sorel each have interesting studies on specific operations.

The counterrevolution has generated a great deal of literature that is often quite polemic. Charles-Louis Chassin's older studies are, however, fairly dispassionate and provide a wealth of detail on the war in the Vendée. Godechot's study of the counterrevolution is an exemplary work that deals with both doctrine and military efforts. Charles Tilly has done excellent work on the social and economic background of the Vendean revolt, and Peter Paret wrote a fine study in which he treats the Vendée as a case study in guerrilla and counterinsurgent warfare. J. de Roince, Bertrand Lavigne, and Joseph Lacoutre have each done sound treatments of Royalist movements in Brittany and other parts of France, while Harvey Mitchell and John Sherwig have written first-rate studies of Britain's involvement with and aid to counterrevolutionary movements.

Bonaparte's Italian campaign of 1796–1797 has been extensively explored. Hubert Camon's study of the opening moves of the campaign remains a classic, as does Clausewitz's earlier study of operations in 1796. Gabriel Fabry, in a three-volume study, provides a wealth of detail not only on operations, but he also gives focus to issues of organization and logistics. Leonard Chodzko did an excellent, though now dated, study of the Polish Legions in Italy, whose marching song later became the national anthem of Poland. Spencer Wilkinson in his book published in 1930 also provides an excellent study of the 1796 campaign.

Bonaparte's Egyptian Expedition has also been the subject that has attracted much scholarly attention. Among the most important works are those of François Charles-Roux. He has written about the origins of the expedition, Bonaparte's activities as ruler of Egypt, and British responses to the French invasion. J. C. Herold, P. Elgood, and J. Benoist-Méchin have all written solid accounts of the expedition, while Alfred Boulay de la Meurthe has done an excellent work on the French government's overall strategy for the eastern venture. J. Holland Rose wrote a solid appraisal of the consequences of the Battle of the Nile, and George Douin did a fine book on French operations in Syria. Christopher Lloyd and Lee Winograd each wrote excellent monographs on the siege of Acre.

The Irish rebellion of 1798 has also received extensive attention. Charles Dickson has written several useful narrative histories, as have H. F. B. Wheeler and M. A. Broadley, whose collaborative work is older but remains useful. Thomas Pakenham's history of the rebellion is detailed and well-written, as is his article on Humbert's expedition.

Among the more modern works on the War of the Second Coalition is A. B. Rodger's study, which provides a solid guide to the strategy of the entire conflict. Piers Mackesy has written an excellent, detailed study of British strategy and operations in 1799, with particular attention to the Anglo-Russian invasion of the Batavian Republic.

Between 1903 and 1906 Edouard Gachot produced three first-rate monographs dealing with the 1799 campaign. He dealt with Suvorov's operations in Italy and Switzerland, Jourdan's operations in Germany, and Brune's operations in Holland. Between 1856 and 1858 D. A. Miliutin, who later became Russia's minister of war, did a five-volume staff study on the operations of the Russian army in 1799. Though dated, it is replete with detail and indispensable for an examination of the Russian role in the Second Coalition. Herman Hueffer did a number of important articles and a two-volume book on the campaigns of 1799. Otto Hartman and Lawrence Shadwell have each done first-rate books on the Swiss campaign, while Alfred von Vivenot and Leon Hennequin each produced well-researched monographs on the Battle of Zurich. Operations in Italy and Germany in 1800 are well covered in numerous biographies of Napoleon. David Chandler's splendid history of Napoleon's campaigns had an excellent chapter on the 1800 Italian campaign and the Battle of Marengo. T. A. Dodge does a first-rate job on operations in Germany.

Given the drama and violence of the Revolutionary wars, there are naturally numerous biographies of leading political and military figures. Virtually every important general has his biographers, and biographies of Napoleon would fill entire libraries. A French scholar, Georges Six, has produced a two-volume dictionary of generals and admirals of the Revolutionary and Imperial periods. The dictionary contains over 1,500 separate biographical sketches, and any biographical study should begin with Six's work. A general study by Six on generals and admirals deals with the social origins and career patterns of general officers. Biographies of individual commanders are numerous, and scholars still find biographies are a rich field of exploration.

Collections of official documents, sets of army regulations, and manuals written by officers on active service help explain the complex and difficult process of raising, organizing, and training a national citizen army. Alphonse Aulard compiled a 25-volume collection of the decrees of the Committee of Public Safety, including the Committee's decisions on military matters and strategy. A. Debidour's five-volume collection covers the acts of the Directory, including decisions on military organization and operations.

Army regulations reveal the inner workings of the army. The Republican armies not only had to expand their numbers, but also devise an effective tactical system and train the new soldiers. The French army has published numerous sets of documents dealing with the organization, training, and operations of the various service arms. The army has also published numerous orders of battle, describing the size and location of the various units of the army at particular periods.

The Revolutionary period is also rich in collections of correspondence and memoirs. If used carefully, such collections can be of great value. Carnot's correspondence (edited by E. Charavay) and Robespierre's correspondence (edited by Bouloiseau, Lefebvre and Soboul) contain much useful information on military and strategic issues. Napoleon Bonaparte, of course, left an enormous amount of correspondence, and there is a 32-volume set of his military directives compiled by the government of the Second Empire. The War Ministry between 1876 and 1897 compiled a ten-volume set dealing exclusively with Napoleon's military correspondence.

Most leading generals including Soult, Masséna, Davout, Jourdan, Macdonald, Marmount, Saint-Cyr, and Murat either wrote memoirs or had their papers collected and published. Of course, many lesser-known officers also left memoirs or papers. Equally interesting are the memoirs of junior officers and enlisted men. Arthur Chuquet has edited a two-volume set of letters from volunteers. Gunner Bricard and infantrymen Coignet, Bourgogne, and Joliclerc wrote of their experiences and provide a useful view from the bottom of the organization of the motivation of a soldier in the battles of the First Republic.

No bibliography covering the wars of the first French Republic can ever hope to be complete. Consequently, this bibliography is designed to provide a general overview of the period and a guide to further reading and research.

Bibliography

Bibliographic Guides to Archives

Army Archives

Austria, Direktion des Kriegsarchiv Wien. INVENTAR DES KRIEGS ARCHIVS WIEN. Vienna Staatsarchiv, 1953. 2 vols. in 1.

Cambier, A. INVENTAIRE DES ARCHIVES CONSERVEES AU SERVICE HISTORIQUE DE L'ETAT-MAJOR. Paris, n.d.

Fabre, Marc-André, and Jean-Claude Devos. SUPPLEMENT A L'INVENTAIRE DES MANUSCRITS DES ARCHIVES DE LA GUERRE ETABLI PAR LOUIS TUETEU. Paris: Ateliers d'impressions de l'armée, 1954.

France. Archives de la guerre. INVENTAIRE SOMMAIRE DES ARCHIVES HISTORIQUES (ARCHIVES ANCIENNES). Paris: Imprimerie nationale, 1898–1905.

————. Archives de la guerre. CATALOGUE GENERAL DES MANUSCRITS DES BIBLIOTHEQUES PUBLIQUES DE FRANCE. ARCHIVES DE LA GUERRE. 3 vols. Paris: Plon-Nourrit, 1912–1920.

————. Archives nationales. ETAT SOMMAIRE PAR SERIE DES DOCUMENTS CONSERVES AUX ARCHIVES NATIONALES. Paris: Administration des Archives, 1891.

————. Archives nationales. INVENTAIRE SOMMAIRE ET TABLEAUX METHODIQUES DES FONDS CONSERVES AUX ARCHIVES NATIONALES. Paris: Imprimerie nationale, 1871.

————. Archives nationales. CATALOGUE DES MANUSCRITS CONSERVES AUX ARCHIVES NATIONALES. Paris: Plon-Nourrit et Cie, 1892.

————. Archives nationales. LES ARCHIVES DE LA FRANCE PENDANT LA REVOLUTION. Paris: J. Claye, 1866.

————. Archives nationales. LES PAPIERS DES ASSEMBLEES DE LA REVOLUTION AUX ARCHIVES NATIONALES. INVEN-

TAIRE DE LA SERIE C (CONSTITUANTE, LEGISLATIVE, CON-VENTION). Paris: E. Cornély, 1908.
————. Ministère de la guerre. INVENTAIRE DES ARCHIVES CON-SACRES AU SERVICE HISTORIQUE DE L'ETAT-MAJOR DE L'ARMEE (CHATEAU DE VINCENNES) (ARCHIVES MOD-ERNES). Paris: Ateliers d'impressions de l'armée, 1954.
————. Ministère de la guerre. INVENTAIRE SOMMAIRE DES ARCHIVES HISTORIQUES (ARCHIVES ANCIENNES). 7 vols. Paris: Imprimerie nationale, 1898–1930.
————. Ministère de l'instruction publique. CATALOGUE GENERAL DES MANUSCRITS DE BIBLIOTHEQUES PUBLIQUES EN FRANCE. ARCHIVES DE LA GUERRE PAR LOUIS TUETEU. 3 vols. Paris: Plon-Nourrit, 1912–1920.
Langlois, Charles, and H. Stein. LES ARCHIVES DE L'HISTOIRE DE FRANCE. Paris: A. Picard, 1891.
Laurencin-Chapelle, Pau. LES ARCHIVES DE GUERRE HIS-TORIQUES ET ADMINISTRATIVES, 1688–1898. Paris: Berger-Levrault, 1898.
Picard, Alphonse. LES ARCHIVES DE L'HISTOIRE DE FRANCE. Paris: Picard, 1891.
Rousset, contrôleur-général. "Les archives du département de la guerre." REVUE DE L'INTENDANCE MILITAIRE, no. 18 (1950), pp. 69–92.
Schmidt, Charles. LES SOURCES DE L'HISTOIRE DE FRANCE DEPUIS 1789 AUX ARCHIVES NATIONALES. Paris: Librairie Champion, 1907.

History of France

Berville, S. A., and F. Barrière, eds. LES MEMOIRES RELATIFS A LA REVOLUTION FRANCAISE. 60 vols. Paris: Boudoin, 1820–1828.
BIBLIOGRAPHIE ANNUELLE DE L'HISTOIRE DE FRANCE DU Ve SIECLE A 1945. Paris: Centre nationale de Recherche scientifique 1955– (Since 1964, has a retrospective series for period 1931–1955.)
BIBLIOGRAPHIE CRITIQUE DES PRINCIPAUX TRAVAUX PARUS SUR L'HISTOIRE DE FRANCE DE 1660 A 1914. 3 sections. Paris: Comité de direction de la Revue d'histoire moderne, 1933–35.
Bibliothèque impériale. Département des imprimés. CATALOGUE DE L'HISTOIRE DE FRANCE. 10 vols. Paris: Didot, 1855–1861.
Bouloiseau, Marc. "Sources de l'histoire de l'émigration et de la contre-révolution dans les archives étrangères." BULLETIN D'HISTOIRE ECONOMIQUE ET SOCIALE DE LA REVOLUTION FRAN-CAISE (1967), pp. 77–123.
Bourgeois, Emile, et Louis André. LES SOURCES DE L'HISTOIRE DE FRANCE. 8 vols. Paris: Picard, 1913–1935.

Brière, G., and Pierre Caron. REPERTOIRE METHODIQUE DE L'HIS-
TOIRE MODERNE ET CONTEMPORAINE DE LA FRANCE. 11
vols. Paris: Picard, 1899–1913.

Bromley, J. S., and A. Goodwin. A SELECT LIST OF WORKS ON EU-
ROPE AND EUROPE OVERSEAS, 1715–1815. Oxford: Clarendon
Press, 1956.

Caron, Pierre. BIBLIOGRAPHIE DES TRAVAUX PUBLIES DE 1866
A 1897 SUR L'HISTOIRE DE FRANCE DEPUIS 1789. Paris: Cor-
nely, 1912.

————. MANUEL PRATIQUE POUR L'ETUDE DE LA REVOLU-
TION FRANCAISE. Paris: Picard, 1947.

Caron, Pierre, and Henri Stein. REPERTOIRE BIBLIOGRAPHIQUE
DE L'HISTOIRE DE FRANCE. 5 vols. Paris: Picard, 1923–31.

Comite français des sciences historiques. LA RECHERCHE HIS-
TORIQUE EN FRANCE DE 1940 A 1965. Paris: Centre national de
la recherche scientifique, 1965.

Davois, Gustave. BIBLIOGRAPHIE NAPOLEONIENNE FRANCAISE
JUSQU'EN 1908. 3 vols. N.P.: L'édition bibliographique, 1909–1911.

France. Bibliothèque nationale. Département des imprimés. CATA-
LOGUE METHODIQUE DE L'HISTOIRE DE FRANCE. 12 vols.
Paris: Firmin-Didot, 1855–1895.

Goby, J. E. "Les travaux d'un siècle en Egypte sur l'expédition française de
1798–1801." REVUE DE L'INSTITUT NAPOLEON (January 1955).

Horward, Donald D. THE FRENCH REVOLUTION AND
NAPOLEON COLLECTION AT FLORIDA STATE UNIVERSITY:
A BIBLIOGRAPHICAL GUIDE. Tallahassee: Friends of the Florida
State University Library, 1973.

Horward, Donald D., ed. NAPOLEONIC MILITARY HISTORY: A
BIBLIOGRAPHY. New York: Garland Publishing, 1986.

Kircheisen, Frédéric. BIBLIOGRAPHIE NAPOLEONIENNE, COL-
LECTION DES SOURCES CLASSEES PAR ORDRE DES
MATIERES. Paris: n.p., n.d.

Lemière, Edmond. BIBLIOGRAPHIE DE LA CONTRE-REVOLUTION
DANS LES PROVINCES DE L'OUEST. 5 sections. Paris: H. Champion, 1905–35.

Lenoir, Madeleine. "Les bibliothèques dépots d'archives et musées militaires en France." REVUE INTERNATIONALE D'HISTOIRE MIL-
ITAIRE 4 (1953–1955), pp. 351–431.

Martin, André, and Gérard Walter. CATALOGUE DE LA REVOLU-
TION FRANCAISE. Paris: Bibliothèque nationale, 1936–1943.

Monglond, André. LA FRANCE REVOLUTIONNAIRE ET IMPERI-
ALE: ANNALES DE BIBLIOGRAPHIE METHODIQUE ET DE-
SCRIPTIVE DES LIVRES ILLUSTRES . . . 9 vols. Grenoble: B.
Arthaud, 1929–1963.

Palmer, R. R. "Fifty Years of the Committee of Public Safety." JOURNAL OF MODERN HISTORY 13 (1941), pp. 375–397.

REPERTOIRE BIBLIOGRAPHIQUE DE L'HISTOIRE DE FRANCE. 5 vols. Paris: Picard, 1923–1934. (Works published from 1923–1929.)

REPERTOIRE METHODIQUE DE L'HISTOIRE MODERNE ET CONTEMPORAINE DE LA FRANCE. Paris: Société nouvelle de librairie et d'édition, 1899–1914. (Works published between 1898–1913.)

Ross, Steven T. FRENCH MILITARY HISTORY, 1661–1799. A GUIDE TO THE LITERATURE. New York: Garland Publishing, 1984.

Schmidt, Charles. LES SOURCES DE L'HISTOIRE DE FRANCE DEPUIS 1789 AUX ARCHIVES NATIONALES. Paris: Libraire H. Champion, 1907.

Walter, Gérard. REPERTOIRE DE L'HISTOIRE DE LA REVOLUTION FRANCAISE TRAVAUX PUBLIES DE 1800 A 1940. 2 vols. Paris: Bibliothèque nationale, 1941 and 1951.

Military History

Basset, Mc.-A. "Bibliographie de l'artillerie technique jusqu'en 1825." MEMORIAL DE L'ARTILLERIE FRANCAISE (1934), vol 2. pp. 529–588.

Buttet, lieutenant-colonel de. "Les méthodes de travail du Dépôt de la Guerre." REVUE HISTORIQUE (Oct.–Dec. 1961), pp. 421–26.

Chalmin, Pierre. GUIDE BIBLIOGRAPHIQUE SOMMAIRE D'HISTOIRE MILITAIRE A L'USAGE DES OFFICIERS ET DES CHERCHEURS. Paris mimeo. 1951.

Cornelius, John C. Special Bibliography 15. THE MILITARY FORCES OF FRANCE. Carlisle Barracks, PA: U.S. Army Military History Institute, 1977.

Craig, Hardin. A BIBLIOGRAPHY OF ENCYCLOPEDIAS AND DICTIONARIES DEALING WITH MILITARY, NAVAL, AND MARITIME AFFAIRS, 1577–1965. Houston: Fondren Library, Rice University, 1965.

France. Etat-major de l'armée de terre: Service Historique. GUIDE BIBLIOGRAPHIQUE SOMMAIRE D'HISTOIRE MILITAIRE ET COLONIALE FRANCAISE. Paris: Imprimerie nationale, 1969.

France. Ministère de la guerre. BIBLIOTHEQUE DU DEPOT DE LA GUERRE: CATALOGUE. 9 vols. Paris: Imprimerie nationale, 1883–1896.

————. Ministère de la guerre. CATALOGUE GENERAL DES MANUSCRITS DES BIBLIOTHEQUES PUBLIQUES EN FRANCE: BIBLIOTHEQUES DE LA GUERRE. Paris: Plon-Nourrit, 1911.

————. Ministère de l'instruction publique. CATALOGUE GENERAL DES MANUSCRITS DES BIBLIOTHEQUES PUBLIQUES EN FRANCE: BIBLIOTHEQUES DE LA GUERRE. Paris: Plon-Nourrit, 1911.

Girard, Georges. "Bibliographie et sources de l'histoire des institutions militairies. Etat de la question." BULLETIN DE LA SOCIETE D'HISTOIRE MODERNE (1923), pp. 409–29.

Hanoteau, Jean, and Emile Bonnot. BIBLIOGRAPHIE DES HISTORIQUES DES REGIMENTS FRANCAIS. Paris: Champion, 1913.

Higham, Robin, ed. OFFICIAL HISTORIES, ESSAYS AND BIBLIOGRAPHIES FROM ALL OVER THE WORLD. Manhattan: Kansas State University Library, 1970.

Lamière, E. BIBLIOGRAPHIE DE LA CONTRE-REVOLUTION DANS LES PAYS DE L'OUEST OU DES GUERRES DE VENDEE ET DE LA CHOUANNERIE (1793–1815). Saint-Brieux: Guyon, 1904–1914.

Liskenne, François Charles, comp. BIBLIOTHEQUE HISTORIQUE ET MILITAIRE DEDIEE A L'ARMEE ET A LA GARDE NATIONALE DE FRANCE. 7 vols. Paris: Administration, 1853–1865.

Lynn, John. "The Publications of the SECTION historique, 1899–1915." MILITARY AFFAIRS (April 1793), pp. 56–59.

Spain. Servicio historico militar. CAMPAXAS EN LOS PIRINEOS A FINALES DEL SIGLO XVIII, 1793–1795. 4 vols. in 5. Madrid: 1949–1954.

Tournes, René. "Notions de bibliographie pour l'étude de l'histoire militaire." REVUE MILITAIRE FRANCAISE (April 1924), pp. 70–91.

General Histories

General Histories: France and Europe

Bourgeois, Emile. MANUEL DE POLITIQUE ETRANGERE. 2 vols. Paris: Firmin-Didot, 1901.

————. MANUEL HISTORIQUE DE POLITIQUE ETRANGERE. 4 vols. Paris: Belin Frères, 1820–1926.

Calvert, Michael. A DICTIONARY OF BATTLES, 1715–1815. New York: Mayflower Books, 1979.

Dodwell, H. H. THE CAMBRIDGE HISTORY OF INDIA. New Delhi: New Era Offset Printers and Cambridge University Press, 1963.

Godechot, Jacques. LA GRANDE NATION: L'EXPANSION REVOLUTIONNAIRE DE LA FRANCE DANS LE MONDE 1789–1799. Paris: Aubier, 1956.

————. LES INSTITUTIONS DE LA FRANCE SOUS LA REVOLUTION ET L'EMPIRE. Paris: Presses Universitaires de France, 1951 and 1968. (The 1968 edition has chapters dealing with army and navy.)

Halphen, Louis, and Philippe Sagnac, eds. PEUPLES ET CIVILISA-TIONS. 20 vols. Paris: Presses Universitaires de France, 1926–1961. (In this set, the following works are included:
Lefebvre, Georges. LA REVOLUTION FRANCAISE. Paris: Presses Universitaires de France, 1957.
Sagnac, Philippe. LA FIN DE L'ANCIEN REGIME ET LA REVO-LUTION AMERICAINE (1763–1789). Paris: Presses Universitaires de France, 1952.)
Hanotaux, Gabriel, ed. HISTOIRE DE LA NATION FRANCAISE. 15 vols. Paris: Plon Nourrit, 1920–29.
————. HISTOIRE DES COLONIES FRANCAISES ET DE L'EX-PANSION DE LA FRANCE DANS LE MONDE. 6 vols. Paris: Société de l'histoire nationale, Plon, 1929.
Lavisse, Ernest, ed. HISTOIRE DE FRANCE CONTEMPORAINE DEPUIS LA REVOLUTION JUSQU'A LA PAIX DE 1919. 10 vols. Paris: Hachette, 1920–22.
(In this set, the following works are included:
Sagnac, P. LA REVOLUTION (1789–1792). Vol. I.
Pariset, G. LA REVOLUTION (1792–1799). Vol. II.)
Louis-Jaray, Gabriel. L'EMPIRE FRANCAIS D'AMERIQUE, 1534–1803. Paris: Colin, 1938.
Marion, Marcel. DICTIONNAIRE DES INSTITUTIONS DE LA FRANCE AU XVIIe ET AU XVIIIe SIECLES. Paris: A. Picard, 1923.
————. HISTOIRE FINANCIERE DE LA FRANCE DEPUIS 1715. Paris: A. Rousseau, 1914–24.
Martineau, A. HISTOIRE DES COLONIES FRANCAISE, INDE. Paris, 1932.
(In this set, the following work is included:
Hanotaux, Gabriel. HISTOIRE DES COLONIES FRANCAISES ET DE L'EXPANSION DE LA FRANCE DANS LE MONDE. Paris: Société de l'histoire nationale, Plon, c.1929.)
NEW CAMBRIDGE MODERN HISTORY, THE. 13 vols and atlas. Cambridge: Cambridge University Press, 1957–70.
(In this set, the following works are included:
Crawley, C. W. WAR AND PEACE IN AN AGE OF UPHEAVAL, 1793–1830. Vol. IX. Cambridge: Cambridge University Press, 1965.
Goodwin, A., ed. THE AMERICAN AND FRENCH REVOLUTIONS. Vol VII. Cambridge: Cambridge University Press, 1957. Vol. VII.
Lindsay, J. O., ed. THE OLD REGIME. Vol. VIII. Cambridge: Cambridge University Press, 1957.)
Palmer, R. R. AGE OF THE DEMOCRATIC REVOLUTION, 1760–1800. 2 vols. Princeton: Princeton University Press, 1959–64.
Reddaway, W. F., et al. CAMBRIDGE HISTORY OF POLAND. 2 vols. Cambridge: Cambridge University Press, 1941–50.

Renouvin, Pierre, ed. HISTOIRE DES RELATIONS INTERNA-
TIONALES. 8 vols. Paris: Hachette, 1953–58.
(In this set, the following works are included:
Fugier, André. LA REVOLUTION ET L'EMPIRE NAPOLEONIEN.
Paris: Hachette, 1954.
Zeller, Gaston. DE LOUIS XIV A 1789. Paris: Hachette, 1955.)
Rose, J. H., A. P. Newton, and E. A. Benians. THE CAMBRIDGE HIS-
TORY OF THE BRITISH EMPIRE. 8 vols. Cambridge: Cambridge
University Press, 1929–30.
Ross, Steven T. EUROPEAN DIPLOMATIC HISTORY 1789–1815:
FRANCE AGAINST EUROPE. New York: Doubleday, 1969.
Sagnac, Philippe. LA FORMATION DE LA SOCIETE FRANCAISE
MODERNE. 2 vols. Paris: Presses Universitaires de France, 1945–1946.
Scott, Samuel F., and Barry Rothaus. HISTORICAL DICTIONARY OF
THE FRENCH REVOLUTION 1789–1799. 2 vols. Westport, CT:
Greenwood Press, 1985.
Smith, Vincent Arthur. THE OXFORD HISTORY OF INDIA. Ed. by
Percival Spear. 3rd ed. Oxford: Clarendon Press, 1958.
Sorel, Albert. L'EUROPE ET LA REVOLUTION FRANCAISE. 8 vols.
Paris: Plon-Nourrit, 1885–1904.
Villat, Louis. LA REVOLUTION ET L'EMPIRE. Paris: Presses Uni-
versitaires de France, 1936.
Ward, A. W., and G. P. Gooch. CAMBRIDGE HISTORY OF BRITISH
FOREIGN POLICY. 3 vols. Cambridge: Cambridge University Press,
1922–23.

General Histories of Warfare

Bernard, H. DE MARATHON A HIROSHIMA: VINGT-CINQ
SIECLES DE L'ART ET DE PENSEE MILITAIRES. 3 vols. Brus-
sels: Impr. médicale et scientifique, 1948–1949.
Bernard, Henri. LA GUERRE ET SON EVOLUTION A TRAVERS
LES SIECLES. 2 vols. Brussels: Impr. médicale et scientifique,
1955–1957.
Bodart, Gaston. LOSSES OF LIFE IN MODERN LIFE: AUSTRIA-
HUNGARY, FRANCE. Oxford: Clarendon Press, 1916.
Bonnal, Henri. L'ESPRIT DE LA GUERRE MODERNE: DE ROS-
BACH A ULM. Paris: Chapelot, 1903.
Bourdeau, Emile. CAMPAGNES MODERNES. 3 vols. Paris: H.
Charles Lavauzelle, 1912–1921.
Brunet, Jean Baptiste. HISTOIRE GENERALE DE L'ARTILLERIE. 2
vols. Paris: Maison Angelin, 1842.
Carman, W. Y. A HISTORY OF FIREARMS FROM EARLIEST
TIMES TO 1914. London: Routledge and Kegan Paul, 1955.

Chandler, David. THE ART OF WARFARE ON LAND. London and New York: Hamlyn Publishing Group, 1974.

————, ed. A GUIDE TO THE BATTLEFIELDS OF EUROPE. Philadelphia: Chilton, 1965.

Colin, Jean. LES GRANDES BATAILLES DE L'HISTOIRE. Paris; Flammarion, 1915.

————. LES TRANSFORMATIONS DE LA GUERRE. Paris: E. Flammarion, 1911.

Delbruck, Hans. GESCHICHTE DER KRIEGSKUNST IN RAHMEN DER POLITISCHEN GESCHICHTE. 4 vols. Berlin: Walter de Gruyter, 1964.

Denison, T. A HISTORY OF CAVALRY FROM THE EARLIEST TIMES WITH LESSONS FOR THE FUTURE. London: Macmillan, 1877.

Downey, Fairfax. CANNONADE: GREAT ARTILLERY ACTIONS OF HISTORY; THE FAMOUS CANNONS AND THE MASTER GUNNERS. Garden City, NY: Doubleday, 1966.

Dubail, E. PRECIS D'HISTOIRE MILITAIRE. 2 vols. Paris: J. Dumaine, 1879.

Duffy, Christopher. FIRE AND STONE: THE SCIENCE OF FORTRESS WARFARE, 1660–1860. London: The Trinity Press, 1975.

Dumas, Samuel, and K. O. Vedel-Petersen. LOSSES OF LIFE CAUSED BY WAR. Oxford: Clarendon Press, 1923.

Dupuy, R. Ernest, and Trevor N. Dupuy. THE ENCYCLOPEDIA OF MILITARY HISTORY FROM 3500 B.C. TO THE PRESENT. New York: Harper and Row, 1977.

Earle, Edward M. MAKERS OF MODERN STRATEGY. Princeton: Princeton University Press, 1943.

Eggenberger, David. A DICTIONARY OF BATTLES. New York: Thomas Y. Crowell, 1967.

Gilbert, Gerald. THE EVOLUTION OF TACTICS. London: Hugh Rees, 1907.

Hamley, E. B. THE OPERATIONS OF WAR EXPLAINED AND ILLUSTRATED. London: Blackwood, 1907.

Henderson, G. F. R. THE SCIENCE OF WAR. London: Longmans, Green, 1912.

Herr, F. G. L'ARTILLERIE, CE QU'ELLE A ETE, CE QU'ELLE EST, CE OU'ELLE DOIT ETRE. Paris: Berger-Levrault, 1923.

Home, Robert. A PRECIS OF MODERN TACTICS. London: W. Clowes, 1873.

Howard, Michael. WAR IN EUROPEAN HISTORY. Oxford: Oxford University Press, 1976.

Hughes, Maj-Gen. B. P. FIREPOWER: WEAPON'S EFFECTIVENESS ON THE BATTLEFIELD, 1630–1850. New York: Charles Scribner's Sons, 1974.

Hughes, Quentin. MILITARY ARCHITECTURE. New York: St. Martin's Press, 1974.

Johnstone, H. M. A HISTORY OF TACTICS. London: Hugh Rees, 1906.

LaBarre-Duparcq, Edouard de. HISTOIRE DE L'ART DE LA GUERRE. 2 vols. Paris: Tanera, 1860–1864.

Laffont, Robert. HISTOIRE UNIVERSELLE DES ARMEES. 4 vols. Paris: Editions Robert Laffont, 1965.

Lloyd, E. M. A REVIEW OF THE HISTORY OF INFANTRY. London: Longmans, Green, 1908.

Manucy, Albert C. ARTILLERY THROUGH THE AGES. Washington, D.C.: Government Printing Office, 1949.

McNeill, William. THE PURSUIT OF POWER TECHNOLOGY, ARMED FORCES AND SOCIETY SINCE A.D. 1000. Chicago: University of Chicago Press, 1982.

Paret, P. "Colonial Experience and European Military Reform at the End of the Eighteenth Century." BULLETIN OF THE INSTITUTE OF HISTORICAL RESEARCH 37 (May 1964).

Peterson, H. L. ENCYCLOPEDIA OF FIREARMS. New York: E. P. Dutton, 1964.

Peterson, Harold. ROUND SHOT AND RAMMERS. Harrisburg, PA: Stackpole Books, 1969.

Pichené, R. HISTOIRE DE LA TACTIQUE ET DE LA STRATEGIE JUSQU'A LA GUERRE MONDIALE. Paris: Editions de la pensée moderne, 1957.

Pope, Dudley. GUNS: FROM THE INVENTION OF GUNPOWDER TO THE TWENTIETH CENTURY. London: Weidenfeld and Nicolson, 1965.

Preston, Richard, and Sydney F. Wise. MEN IN ARMS: A HISTORY OF WARFARE AND ITS INTERRELATIONSHIPS WITH WESTERN SOCIETY. New York: Holt, Rinehart and Winston, 1979.

Redlich, Fritz. DE PRAEDA MILITARI; LOOTING AND BOOTY 1500–1815. Weisbaden: F. Steiner, 1956.

Rocolle, Pierre. 2000 ANS DE FORTIFICATION FRANCAISE. 2 vols. Limoges: Charles Lavauzelle, 1973.

Rogers, Col. H. C. B. ARTILLERY THROUGH THE AGES. London: Seeley Service, 1971.

Ropp, Theodore. WAR IN THE MODERN WORLD. Durham, NC: Duke University Press, 1959.

Ross, Steven T. FROM FLINTLOCK TO RIFLE: INFANTRY TACTICS, 1740–1866. Rutherford, NJ: Fairleigh Dickinson University Press; London: Associated University Presses, 1979.

Rustow, Wilhelm. GESCHICHTE DER INFANTERIE. 2 vols. Gotha: H. Scheube, 1957–58.

Schneider, Fernand. HISTOIRE DES DOCTRINES MILITAIRES. Paris: Presses Universitaires de France, 1957.

Shields, Joseph W. FROM FLINTLOCK TO M1. New York: Coward-McCann, 1954.

Spaulding, O., H. Nickerson, and J. W. Wright. WARFARE: A STUDY OF MILITARY METHODS FROM THE EARLIEST TIMES. Washington, D.C.: Infantry Journal Press, 1939.

Stevens, Phillip. ARTILLERY THROUGH THE AGES. New York: F. Watts, 1965.

Turner, Gordon B., ed. A HISTORY OF MILITARY AFFAIRS IN WESTERN SOCIETY SINCE THE EIGHTEENTH CENTURY. New York: Harcourt, Brace, 1953.

Vial, J. HISTOIRE ABREGEE DES CAMPAGNES MODERNES. 2 vols. Paris: L. Baudein, 1886.

Wagner, A. L. ORGANIZATION AND TACTICS. Kansas City, MO: Franklin Hudson Publishing, 1912.

Wintringham, Thomas. MUTINY. New York: Fortnoy's, 1936.

Wright, Quincy. A STUDY OF WAR. Chicago: University of Chicago Press, 1942.

Zastrow, A. de. HISTOIRE DE LA FORTIFICATION PERMANENTE. Translated by E. de la Barre-Duparcq. Liege: D. Avanzoet, 1846.

French Army Histories

Agauche, Guy d'. LE RECRUTEMENT DE L'ARMEE FRANCAISE. Mayenee, 1894.

Ambert, Joachim. ESQUISSES HISTORIQUES DES DIFFERENTS CORPS QUI COMPOSENT L'ARMEE FRANCAISE. Samur: A. Degouy, 1835.

Amiot, A. P. J. PANORAMA MILITAIRE, OU PRECIS DE L'HISTOIRE DES TROUPES FRANCAISES, DEPUIS LA FOUNDATION DE LA MONARCHIE JUSQU'A NOS JOURS. Paris: Corby, 1830.

Audouin, Xavier. HISTOIRE DE L'ADMINISTRATION DE LA GUERRE. Paris: Didot, 1811.

Blin, E.-C -H. HISTOIRE DE L'ORGANISATION ET DE LA TACTIQUE DES DIFFERENTES ARMES DE 1610 A NOS JOURS. Paris: Charles Lavauzelle, 1931.

Carrias, Eugène. LA PENSEE MILITAIRE FRANCAISE. Paris: Presses Universitaires de France, 1957.

Coquelle, P. LES PROJETS DE DESCENTE EN ANGLETERRE D'APRES LES ARCHIVES DES AFFAIRS ETRANGERES. Paris: Plon-Nourrit, 1902.

Courtot, A. QUELQUES NOTES SUR L'ETAT MILITAIRE DE FRANCE DE 1730 A 1830. Paris: Victor Rozier, 1888.

Dervelle, G. "Aperçu historique sur les fabrications d'armement en France." REVUE HISTORIQUE DE L'ARMEE. 12, no. 4 (1956), p. 89–101.

Dubail, E. CARTES-CROQUOIS DE GEOGRAPHIE MILITAIRE AVEC UN EXPOSE SOMMAIRE DES PRINCIPALES CAMPAGNES DEPUIS LOUIS XIV JUSQU'A NOS JOURS. Paris: Chapelot, 1881.

Dufourt, Général. "La mobilisation industrielle, 1793–1870–1914." CARNET DE SABRETACHE (March 1967), p. 271–90.

Dussieux, L. L'ARMEE EN FRANCE: HISTOIRE ET ORGANISATION. 3 vols. Versailles: L. Bernard, 1884.

Favé, Ildephonse. HISTOIRE ET TACTIQUE DES TROIS ARMES ET PLUS PARTICULIEREMENT DE L'ARTILLERIE DE CAMPAGNE. Paris: J. Dumaine, 1845.

France. Ministère de la guerre. DICTIONNAIRE MILITAIRE ENCYCLOPEDIE DES SCIENCES MILITAIRES. Paris: Berger-Levrault, 1894.

————. HISTOIRE DE L'ARMEE ET DE TOUS LES REGIMENTS DEPUIS LES PREMIERS TEMPS DE LA MONARCHIE FRANCAISE JUSQU'A NOS JOURS. 5 vols. Paris: Barbier, 1847–1850.

————. HISTORIQUES DES CORPS DE TROUPE DE L'ARMEE FRANCAISE (1569–1900). Paris: Berger Levrault, 1900.

Fremont, Paul. LES PAYEURS D'ARMEES. HISTORIQUE DU SERVICE DE LA TRESORERIE ET DES POSTES AUX ARMEES, 1293–1870. Paris: Plon, 1906.

Gaulle, Charles de. LA FRANCE ET SON ARMEE. Paris: Plon, 1938.

Giguet, P. HISTOIRE MILITAIRE DE LA FRANCE. 2 vols. Paris: Hachette, 1849.

Grimoard, Philippe-Henri. RECHERCHES SUR LA FORCE DE L'ARMEE FRANCAISE ET LES SECRETAIRES D'ETAT OU MINISTRES DE LA GUERRE DEPUIS HENRI IV JUSQU'A 1806. Paris: Treuttelet Wurtz, 1806.

Guinard, Pierre. REPERTOIRE DES ABREGES DE LA CARTE GENERALE MILITAIRE DE LA FRANCE DE LA CAISSE DES ETATS MILITARES DE FRANCE ET DES EMPLACEMENTS DES TROUPES. Paris: Manuscrit du Service historique de l'armée.

Hardy de Périni, Edouard. BATAILLES FRANCAISES. Paris: 1906.

Hicks, James E. FRENCH MILITARY WEAPONS 1717–1938. New Milford, CT: A. Flayderman, 1964.

HISTORIQUES DES REGIMENTS DE L'ARMEE FRANCAISE. Paris: J. Dumaine, 1846.

Jablonski, Ludovic. L'ARMEE FRANCAISE A TRAVERS LES AGES. 5 vols. Paris: Charles Lavauzelle, 1890–1894.

Laurent-Chirlonchon, V. HISTOIRE LEGISLATIVE DU CORPS DE L'INTENDANCE MILITAIRE, DEPUIS 1356 JUSQU'A NOS JOURS. Algiers: F. Paysant, 1868.

Léques, L. LES ADMINISTRATIONS MILITAIRES DEPUIS LES TEMPS ANCIENS JUSQU'A NOS JOURS. Tours: Ribaudeau et Chevallier, 1875.

Lyden, Emile. NOS 144 REGIMENTS DE LIGNE. Paris: Librairie illustrée, 1888.

Lynn, John. "The Pattern of French Military Reform, 1750–1795." PROCEEDINGS OF THE CONSORTIUM ON REVOLUTIONARY EUROPE. Gainesville: University of Florida Press, 1978.

Pernot, A. M. APERCU HISTORIQUE SUR LES SERVICE DES TRANSPORTS MILITAIRES. Paris: Henri Charles Lavauzelle, 1894.

Revol, J. HISTOIRE DE L'ARMEE FRANCAISE. Paris: Larousse, 1929.

Romagny, Charles. HISTOIRE GENERALE DE L'ARMEE NATIONALE DEPUIS BOUVINES JUSQU'A NOS JOURS (1214–1892). Paris: Charles Lavauzelle, 1893.

Sicard, François. HISTOIRE DES INSTITUTIONS MILITAIRES DES FRANCAIS. 4 vols. Paris: J. Coréard, jeune, 1834.

Thoumas, Charles A. LES TRANSFORMATIONS DE L'ARMEE FRANCAISE. 2 vols. Paris: Berger-Levrault, 1887. 2 vols.

Thouvein, T.-E. HISTORIQUE GENERAL DU TRAIN DES EQUIPAGES MILITAIRES. Paris: Berger-Levrault, 1900.

Villantte, R. "Le mouvement des idées militaires en France." REVUE D'HISTOIRE MODERNE, 10 new series 4, no. 18 (1935).

Weygand, Maxime. HISTOIRE DE L'ARMEE FRANCAISE. Paris: Larousse, 1938.

Collective Biographies

Ambert, Joachim. GENS DE GUERRE-PORTRAITS. Paris: Chapelot, 1863.

Aumale, duc d'. LES INSTITUTIONS MILITAIRES DE LA FRANCE: LOUVOIS CARNOT SAINT-CYR. Paris: Revue des Deux Mondes, 1867.

Courcelles, J. B. P. DICTIONNAIRE HISTORIQUE ET BIOGRAPHIQUE DES GENERAUX FRANCAIS DEPUIS LE X SIECLE JUSQU'EN 1820. Paris: Chez l'auteur et Arthur Bertrand, 1820–1823.

LeBarrois D'Orgeval, G. LE MARECHALAT DE FRANCE DES ORIGINES A NOS JOURS. 2 vols. Paris: Guitard, 1932.

Michaud, J. F. BIOGRAPHIE UNIVERSELLE. 45 vols. Paris: Ch. Delagrave, 1843.

Nicot. NOS GENERAUX ESQUISSES BIOGRAPHIQUES. 3 vols. Paris: Charles-LaVauzelle, 1881.

Prévost et Roman d'Amat. DICTIONNAIRE DE BIOGRAPHIE FRANCAISE. 12 vols. to date. Paris: Letouzey et Ané, 1933– .

Foreign Armies

Andolenko, Serge, HISTOIRE DE L'ARMEE RUSSE. Paris: Flammarion, 1967.

Barnett, Correlli. BRITAIN AND HER ARMY, 1509–1970. New York: William Morrow, 1970.

Bleckwenn, H. DAS ALTPREUSSISCHE HEER. ERSCHEINUNGS-BILD UND WESSEN, 1713–1807. Osnabruck: Biblio Vertag, 1969.

Busch, Otto. MILITARSYSTEM UND SOZIALLEBEN IM ALTEN PREUSSEN, 1713–1807. Berlin: DeGruyter, 1962.

Buturlin, D. HISTOIRE DES CAMPAGNES DES RUSSES AU 18EME SIECLE. 4 vols. St. Petersburg, 1819–1821.

Clode, Charles. MILITARY FORCES OF THE CROWN. 2 vols. London: John Murray, 1969.

Duffy, Christopher. RUSSIA'S MILITARY WAY TO THE WEST ORIGINS AND NATURE OF RUSSIAN MILITARY POWER 1700–1800. London and Boston: Routledge, 1981.

Fortescue, Sir John. A HISTORY OF THE BRITISH ARMY. 13 vols. London: Macmillan, 1910–1930.

Fuller, J. F. C. BRITISH LIGHT INFANTRY IN THE EIGHTEENTH CENTURY. London: Hutchinson, 1975.

Gieraths, G. DIE KAMPFHANDLUNGEN DER BRANDEN-BUR-GISCH-PREUSSISCHEN ARMEE 1626–1807, EIN QUELLEN-HANDBUCH. Berlin: W. deGruyter, 1946.

HANDBUCH ZUR DEUTSCHEN MILITARGESCHICHTE, 1648–1939. Frankfurt: Bernard u Graefe, 1964.

Haswell, J. THE BRITISH ARMY: A CONCISE HISTORY. London: Thames and Hudson, 1975.

Hellie, Richard. ENSERFMENT AND MILITARY CHANGE IN MUS-COVY. Chicago: University of Chicago Press, 1971.

Houlding J. FIT FOR SERVICE: THE TRAINING OF THE BRITISH ARMY 1715–1795. London: Oxford University Press, 1981.

Jahn, Max. GESCHICHTE DER KRIEGWISSENSCHAFTEN VORNE-HMLICH IN DEUTSCHLAND. 3 vols. Munich and Leipzig: R. Oldenbourg, 1889–1891.

Jany, C. GESCHICHTE DER KONIGLICH-PREUSSICHEN ARMEE. 4 vols. Berlin: K. Sigismund, 1928–1933.

Jeddicka, L., ed. UNSER HEER. 300 JAHRE OSTERREICHISCHES SOLDATENTUM IN KRIEG AND FRIEDLEN. Vienna: Furlinger, 1963.

Kitchen, Martin. A MILITARY HISTORY OF GERMANY FROM THE EIGHTEENTH CENTURY TO THE PRESENT DAY. Bloomington and London: Indiana University Press, 1975.

K. K. Kriegsarchive. OSTERREICHS KRIEGE SEIT 1495. Vienna: Seidel and Sohn, 1878.

Meynert, Hermann. GESCHICHTE DER KK OSTERREICHISCHEN ARMEE. 4 vols. Vienna: C. Gerold und Sohn, 1852–1854.
Regele, O. DER OSTERREICHISCHE HOFKRIEGSRAT. Vienna: Oesterreichische Staatsdruckerei, 1949.
Schels, J. B. KRIEGSGESCHICHTE DER OESTREICHER. Vienna: J. G. Heubner, 1844.
Sheppard, E. W. A SHORT HISTORY OF THE BRITISH ARMY. London: Constable, 1959.
Wrede, A. von. GESCHICHTE DER K. U. K. WEHRMACHT. 5 vols. Vienna: Seidel 7 Sohn, 1898–1903.
Young, Peter. THE BRITISH ARMY. London: William Kimber, 1967.
Young, Peter, and J. P. Lawford. THE HISTORY OF THE BRITISH ARMY. N.p.: Arthur Barker, 1970.

The Service Arms

Infantry 1789–1799

Andlau, G. Comte d'. ORGANISATION ET TACTIQUE DE L'INFANTERIE FRANCAISE DEPUIS SON ORIGINE JUSQU'A L'EPOQUE ACTUELLE. Paris: Dumaine, 1872.
Andolenko, Serge. RECUEIL D'HISTORIQUES DE L'INFANTERIE FRANCAISE. Paris: Eurimprim, 1969.
Bacquet, L. H. L'INFANTERIE AU XVIIIe SIECLE: L'ORGANISATION. Paris: Berger-Levrault, 1907.
Belhomme, Lieutenant-Colonel. HISTOIRE DE L'INFANTERIE EN FRANCE. 5 vols. Paris: Charles Lavauzelle, 1893–1902.
Bottet, Maurice. LA MANUFACTURE D'ARMES DE VERSAILLES. 2 vols. Paris: Leroy, 1903.
————. MONOGRAPHIE DE L'ARME BLANCHE DES ARMEES FRANCAISES DE TERRE ET DE MER, 1789–1870. Paris: Flammarion, 1900.
————. MONOGRAPHIE DE L'ARME A FEU PORTATIVE DES ARMEES FRANCAISES DE TERRE ET DE MER, DE 1718 A NOS JOURS. Paris: Flammarion, 1905.
Capdevielle, Jean-Joseph-Julien. L'ARMEMENT ET LE TIR DE L'INFANTERIE. Paris: Dumaine, 1872.
Chamberet, G. de. PRECIS HISTORIQUE SUR LA GENDARMERIE DEPUIS LES PREMIERS TEMPS DE LA MONARCHIE JUSQU'A NOS JOURS. Paris: J. Dumaine, 1861.
Colin, Jean. L'INFANTERIE AU XVIIIe SIECLE: LA TACTIQUE. Paris: Berger-Levrault, 1907.
Fieffé, Eugène. HISTOIRE DES TROUPES ETRANGERES AU SERVICE DE LA FRANCE DEPUIS LEUR ORIGINE JUSQU'A NOS JOURS, ET DE TOUS LES REGIMENTS LEVES DANS LES PAYS

CONQUIS SOUS LA PREMIERE REPUBLIQUE ET L'EMPIRE. 2 vols. Paris: Dumaine, 1854.

Flocon, Commandant. MILICES ET VOLONTAIRES DU PUY-DE-DOME. ETUDE SUR LE RECRUTEMENT DE L'ARMEE, 1688–1793. Paris, 1911.

Gaudin, M. Historique de la fabrication des armes légères." REVUE HISTORIQUE DE L'ARMEE 12 no. 4 (1956), p. 115–26.

Gérôme, Commandant. ESSAI HISTORIQUE SUR LA TACTIQUE DE L'INFANTERIE DEPUIS L'ORGANISATION DES ARMEES PERMANENTES JUSQU'A NOS JOURS. Paris: Charles-Lavauzelle, 1895.

Larrieu, Général. HISTOIRE DE LA GENDARMERIE, DEPUIS LES ORIGINES DE LA MARECHAUSSEE JUSQU'A NOS JOURS. 2 vols. Paris: Charles Lavauzelle, 1927–1933.

Lasalley. L'ARME BLANCHE SOUS LA REVOLUTION ETUDE HISTORIQUE. Caen: Jouan, 1912.

Lemaitre, Lieutenant-Colonel. HISTORIQUES DE LA GENDARMERIE. Orléans: E. Colas, 1879.

Léques, L. HISTOIRE DE LA GENDARMERIE. Paris: Léautey, 1874.

Lynn, John. "Self-Image and Weaponry: The French Fascination with the Pike 1724–1794." COLLOQUIUM ON MILITARY HISTORY: PROCEEDINGS. Chicago, 1979.

Manceau, Henri. LA MANUFACTURE D'ARMES DE CHARLEVILLE. Charleville: s.n., 1962.

Margerand, J. ARMEMENT ET EQUIPMENT DE L'INFANTERIE FRANCAISE DU XVIe AU XXe SIECLE. Paris: Editions militaires illustrées, 1945.

Pelet, Jean-Jacques-Germain. "De la Division." SPECTATEUR MILITAIRE 2 (1827).

———. "Essai sur les manoeuvres d'un corps d'armée d'infanterie." SPECTATEUR MILITAIRE (1828) and 6 (1828–1829).

Poli, Xavier. HISTOIRE MILITAIRE DES CORSES AU SERVICE DE LA FRANCE (1520–1871). 3 vols. Ajacco and Bastia: Peretti et Ollagnier, 1898–1902.

Quimby, Robert S. THE BACKGROUND OF NAPOLEONIC WARFARE. New York: Columbia University Press, 1957.

Roguet, Commandant. "Etudes sur l'ordre perpendiculaire." SPECTATEUR MILITAIRE 18 (1834–1835).

Ross, Steven. "The Development of the Combat Division in 18th Century French Armies." FRENCH HISTORICAL STUDIES, no. IV (1965), pp. 84–94.

———. "French Revolutionary Infantry Tactics." THE CONSORTIUM ON REVOLUTIONARY EUROPE PROCEEDINGS, 1979, pp. 149–154.

Susane, Louis. HISTOIRE DE L'ANCIENNE INFANTERIE FRAN-
CAISE. 8 vols. Paris: Corréard, 1849–53.
———. HISTOIRE DE L'INFANTERIE FRANCAISE. 5 vols. Paris:
Dumaine, 1876. 5 vols.

Cavalry 1789–1799

Andlau, Gaston. DE LA CAVALERIE DANS LE PASSE ET DANS
L'AVENIR. Paris: Bureau de la revue militaire française, 1869.
Bessières, Albert. CAVALIERS DE FRANCE. Paris: Perrin, 1920.
Desbrière, Edouard, and Maurice Sautai. LA CAVALERIE DE 1740 A
1789. Paris: Berger-Levrault, 1889.
———. LA CAVALERIE PENDANT LA REVOLUTION. 2 vols.
Paris: Berger-Levrault, 1907–1908.
———. LA CAVALERIE SOUS LE DIRECTOIRE. 2 vols. Paris and
Nancy: Berger-Levrault, 1910.
Duputy, J. R. HISTORIQUE DES REGIMENTS DE HUSSARDS
(1689–1892). Paris: Lubois, 1893.
Gérome, A.-C. ESSAI HISTORIQUE SUR LA TACTIQUE DE LA
CAVALERIE. Paris: Charles Lavauzelle, 1900.
Picard, Louis. LA CAVALERIE DANS LES GUERRES DE LA REV-
OLUTION ET DE L'EMPIRE. Samur: Milon, 1895–1896.
Susane, Louis. HISTOIRE DE LA CAVALERIE FRANCAISE. 3 vols.
Paris: Hentzel, 1874.
Unger. L. HISTOIRE CRITIQUE DES EXPLOITS ET VICISSITUDES
DE LA CAVALERIE PENDANT LES GUERRES DE LA REVO-
LUTION ET DE L'EMPIRE. Paris: Corréard, 1848–1849.

Artillery 1789–1799

Allix, J. A. F. SYSTEME D'ARTILLERIE DE CAMPAGNE. Paris:
Anselin et Pochard, 1827.
Apffell, Général. "L'Artillerie lourde de campagne au XVIIIe siècle (de
Vallière à Bonaparte)." REVUE D'ARTILLERIE 115 (1935), p.
485–91.
Bonaparte, Louis N., and Ildephonse Favé. ETUDES SUR LE PASSE
ET L'AVENIR DE L'ARTILLERIE. 6 vols. Paris: Dumaine,
1846–1871.
Boudon, Jacques. "Le service d'artillerie du XVIe siècle à nos jours."
REVUE D'ARTILLERIE 98 (1926).
Brunet, J. HISTOIRE GENERALE DE L'ARTILLERIE. 2 vols. Paris:
Gaultier-Laguionie, 1842. 2 vols.
Buat, Edmond. L'ARTILLERIE DE CAMPAGNE; SON HISTOIRE—
SON EVOLUTION—SON ETAT ACTUEL. Paris: F. Alcan, 1911.

Campana, J. L'ARTILLERIE DE CAMPAGNE 1792–1901. Paris: Berger-Levrault, 1901.

Carrez, J.-P "L'école d'artillerie sous la Convention 20 septembre 1792–26 octobre 1795." REVUE HISTORIQUE DES ARMEES (1975), nos. 1–2, pp. 32–49.

Favé, Idefonse and Reinaud. HISTOIRE DE L'ARTILLERIE. Paris: Dumaine, 1845–1847.

Hennebert, Lieutenant-Colonel. L'ARTILLERIE. Paris: Hachette, 1887.

Hicks, James E., and André Jandot. NOTES ON FRENCH ORDNANCE, 1717 TO 1936. Mt. Vernon, NY, 1938.

Laverma, Matti. L'ARTILLERIE DE CAMPAGNE FRANCAISE PENDANT LES GUERRES DE LA REVOLUTION. Helsinki: Svomalainen Tiedeakatemia, 1956.

Manson, Maréchal de Camp, de. TABLES DES CONSTRUCTIONS DES PRINCIPAUX ATTRAILS DE L'ARTILLERIE, PROPOSEES OU APPROUVEES DEPUIS 1764 JUSQU'EN 1789 PAR M. DE GRIBEAUVAL. 4 vols. Paris: Imprimerie royale, 1792.

Mauny, F. Reviers de. "Etude historique sur le corps de l'artillerie de France." REVUE D' ARTILLERIE 45, 46, 47 (March, April, June, October, November, December, 1895 and January 1896).

Picard, Ernest et L. Jouan. L'ARTILLERIE FRANCAISE AU XVIIIe SIECLE. Paris: Berger-Levrault, 1906.

Rosen, Howard. "Le système Gribeauval et la guerre moderne." REVUE HISTORIQUE DES ARMEES nos. 1–2 (1975), pp. 29–36.

Rouquerol, Gabriel. L'ARTILLERIE AU DEBUT DES GUERRES DE LA REVOLUTION. Paris: Berger-Levrault, 1898.

Susane, Louis. HISTOIRE DE L'ARTILLERIE FRANCAISE. 5 vols. Paris: Hetzel, 1874.

Sutterlin, Louis. "Histoire du comité de l'artillerie (1790–1910)." REVUE HISTORIQUE DES ARMEES, nos. 1–2 (1975), pp. 51–79.

Engineers 1789–1799

Augoyat, Colonel. APERCU HISTORIQUE SUR LES FORTIFICATIONS, LES INGENIEURS ET SUR LE CORPS DU GENIE EN FRANCE. 3 vols. Paris: Dumaine, 1860–1864.

Berthaut, Henri-Marie-Augueste. LES INGENIEURS GEOGRAPHES MILITAIRES 1624–1831. ETUDE HISTORIQUE. 2 vols. Paris: Imprimerie service géographique, 1902.

France. Ministère de la défense nationale et de la guerre. LE SERVICE GEOGRAPHIQUE DE L'ARMEE: SON HISTOIRE, SON ORGANISATION, SES TRAVAUX. Paris: Imprimerie service géographique, 1934.

Lagrange, J. G. ESSAI HISTORIQUE SUR LES MINES MILITAIRES ANCIENNES ET MODERNES. Brussels: Th. Lesigne, 1866.

Legrand-Girade, E. "Etude historique sur le corps du génie." REVUE DE GENIE MILITAIRE (1897–1898).

Lesquen, Colonel de. "Le Génie jusqu'en 1940." REVUE HISTORIQUE DE L'ARMEE (October–December 1955), pp. 67–88.

Prévost, F. ETUDES HISTORIQUES SU LA FORTIFICATION, L'AT-TAQUE ET LA DEFENSE DES PLACES. Paris: J. Dumaine, 1869.

Robert, L., and H. Arnoul. SIEGES MEMORABLES DES FRANCAIS DEPUIS LE XVe SIECLE JUSQU'A NOS JOURS. Paris: J. Dumaine, 1855.

Vauban, Sebastien Le Prestre de. A MANUAL OF SIEGECRAFT AND FORTIFICATION. Trans. George A. Rothrock. Ann Arbor: University of Michigan Press, 1968. (Originally published in London, 1740).

Vauvilliers, L. H. C. RECHERCHES HISTORIQUES SUR LE ROLE ET L'INFLUENCE DE LA FORTIFICATION. Paris: Dumaine, 1845.

Zeller, Gason. L'ORGANISATION DEFENSIVE DES FRONTIERES DU NORD DE L'EST AU XVIIIe SIECLE. Paris: Berger-Levrault, 1928.

Military Schools 1789–1799

Chalmin, Pierre. "L'école du génie de Mézières, 1748–1794." REVUE HISTORIQUE DE L'ARMEE, no. 2 (1961), pp. 141–54.

———. "Les écoles militaires françaises jusqu'en 1914." REVUE HISTORIQUE DE L'ARMEE, no.2 (1954), pp. 129–166.

Chuquet, Arthur. L'ECOLE DE MARS. Paris: Plon, 1899.

Ecole Polytechnique. LE LIVRE DU CENTENAIRE (1794–1894). 3 vols. Paris: Gauthier-Villars, 1894–97.

Fabre de Massaguel, J. L'ECOLE DE SOREZE, DE 1758 AU 19 FRUC-TIDOR AN IV (5 SEPTEMBRE 1796). Toulouse Thesis, 1948.

Pinet, G. HISTOIRE DE L'ECOLE POLYTECHNIQUE. Paris: Baudry et Cie, 1887.

Military Medicine 1789–1799

Ackernect, E. H. MEDICINE AT THE PARIS HOSPTIAL 1794–1848. Baltimore: Johns Hopkins University Press, 1967.

Brice, Leon-Raoul-Marie, and Maurice Bottet. LE CORPS DE SANTE MILITAIRE EN FRANCE, SON EVOLUTION-SES CAMPAGNES, 1708–1882. Paris and Nancy: Berger-Levrault, 1907.

Briot, Docteur. HISTOIRE DE L'ETAT ET DES PROGRES DE LA CHIRURGIE MILITAIRE EN FRANCE PENDANT LES GUERRES DE LA REVOLUTION. Besançon: Gautheir, 1817.

Chomel, C. HISTOIRE DU CORPS DES VETERINAIRES MILI-TAIRES EN FRANCE. Paris: Asselin et Houzeau, 1887.

Corvisier, André. "La mort du soldat depuis la fin du Moyen-Age." RE-
VUE HISTORIQUE, no. 515 (July 1975), pp.3–30.
Guinard, Pierre. ASPECTS DE LA VIE AUX INVALIDES PENDANT
LA REVOLUTION. Paris: Société des amis du musée de l'armée,
1974, no. 78.
Huard, Pierre P. SCIENCES, MEDECINE, PHARMACIE, DE LA
REVOLUTION A L'EMPIRE. Paris: R. Dacosta, 1970.
Knorr, Emil. ENTWICKLUNG UND GESTALTUNG DES HEERES-
SANITATSWESENS DER EUROPAISCHEN STAATEN. Han-
nover: Helwing, 1880. (Issued 1877–1879 in six parts with title UE-
BER ENTWICKLUNG. Each part has special title page).
Lacau, M. R. LE SERVICE PHARMACEUTIQUE AUX ARMEES
DES PYRENEES. Paris: 1946 (thesis).
"Le service de santé militaire des origines à nos jours." REVUE IN-
TERNATIONALE DES SERVICES DE SANTE DES ARMEES DE
TERRE, DE MER, ET DE L'AIR. N.p.: 1951.
Mercier, Raoul. LE MONDE MEDICAL DANS LA GUERRE DE
VENDEE. Tours: Arrault, 1939.
Rieux, J.-B., and Colonel Hassenforder. HISTOIRE DU SERVICE DE
SANTE MILITAIRE ET DU VAL-DE-GRACE. Paris: Charles
Lavauzelle, 1952.
Rouffiandis, E. LES MEDECINS PENDANT LA REVOLUTION
DANS L'ARMEE DES PYRENEES ORIENTALES. N.p., n.d.
Vess, David M. MEDICAL REVOLUTION IN FRANCE 1789–1796.
Gainesville: University Presses of Florida, 1975.
Weiner, Dora. "French Doctors Face War, 1792–1815." FROM THE
ANCIEN REGIME TO THE POPULAR FRONT: ESSAYS IN
HONOR OF SHEPARD B. CLOUGH. Edited by C. K. Warner. New
York: Columbia University Press, 1969.
Woloch, Isser. THE FRENCH VETERAN FROM THE REVOLUTION
TO THE RESTORATION. Chapel Hill: University of North Carolina
Press, 1979.

Uniforms, Flags, and Songs

Barbier, P., and F. Vernillat. HISTOIRE DE FRANCE PAR LES CHAN-
SONS, DES CROISADES A 1920. 7 vols. Paris: Gallimard, 1956–1959.
Brécard, Général. L'ARMEE FRANCAISE A TRAVERS LES AGES.
SES TRADITIONS, SES GLOIRES, SES UNIFORMES. LA CAV-
ALERIE. Paris: Société des éditions militaires, 1931.
Cart, A. UNIFORMS DES REGIMENTS FRANCAIS DE LOUIS XV
A NOS JOURS. Paris: Editions militaires, 1945.
CHANTS, CHANSONS ET CHOEURS DE L'ARMEE FRANCAISE.
Nouveau recueil. Paris: Chiron, 1967.

Dépréaux, Albert. LES UNIFORMES DES TROUPES COLONIALES DE 1666 A 1875. Paris: Vigier et Brunissen, 1931.

Ferron and Jean Brunon. LES DRAPEAUX DES REGIMENTS FRANCAIS DE 1791 A 1794. Marseilles: Musée militaire du souvenir, 1933.

Fonclare, E. L'ARMEE FRANCAISE A TRAVERS LES AGES. SES TRADITIONS, SES GLOIRES, SES UNIFORMES. L'INFANTERIE. Paris: Société des éditions militaires, 1931.

France. Army Uniforms. COSTUMES DE L'ARMEE FRANCAISE DEPUIS LOUIS XIV JUSQU'A CE JOUR. Paris: Aubert, 1849.

———. COSTUMES MILITAIRES; CATALOGUE DES PRINCIPALES SUITES DE COSTUMES MILITAIRES FRANCAISES PARUS TANT EN FRANCE QU'A L'ETRANGER DEPUIS LE REGNE DE LOUIS XIV JUSQU'A NOS JOURS. Paris: H. Vivien, 1900.

Funcken, Liliane and Fred. L'UNIFORME ET LES ARMES DES SOLDATS DE LA GUERRE EN DENTELLE. 2 vols. Paris: Casterman, 1975–1976.

Haythornthwaile, Philip J. UNIFORMS OF THE FRENCH REVOLUTIONARY WARS 1789–1802. Poole, Dorset: Blandford Press, 1981.

Hollander, O. LES DRAPEAUX DES DEMI-BRIGADES D'INFANTERIE DE 1794 A 1804. Paris: Leroy, 1913.

Kastner, G. LES CHANTS DE L'ARMEE FRANCAISE PRECEDES D'UN ESSAI HISTORIQUE SUR LES CHANTS MILITAIRES DES FRANCAIS. Paris: Brandus, 1855.

Lachouque, Henry. DIX SIECLES DE COSTUME MILITAIRE. Paris: Hachette, 1963.

Lienhart, Constant, and R. Humbert. LES UNIFORMES DE L'ARMEE FRANCAISE DEPUIS 1690 A 1904. 5 vols. Leipzig: Ruhl, 1896–1904.

Malibran, Ingénieur. GUIDE A L'USAGE DES ARTISTES ET COSTUMIERS CONTENANT LA DESCRIPTION DES UNIFORMES DE L'ARMEE FRANCAISE DE 1780 A 1848. 2 vols. Paris: Combet, 1907.

Moltzheim, Auguste. L'ARTILLERIE FRANCAISE; COSTUMES UNIFORMES, MATERIELS DEPUIS LE MOYEN AGE JUSQU'A NOS JOURS. Paris: Rothschild, 1870.

Neukomm, Edmond. HISTOIRE DE LA MUSIQUE MILITAIRE. Paris: Chapelot, 1889.

Noirmont, Général, and Général Marbot. COSTUMES MILITAIRES FRANCAIS 1439 A 1814. 3 vols. Paris: Clément, 1846.

Onfroy de Breville, Jacques. TENUES DES TROUPES DE FRANCE; ARMEES DE TERRE ET DE MER A TOUTES LES EPOQUES. 2 vols. Paris: Combat, 1903.

Payard, Colonel. L'ARMEE FRANCAISE A TRAVERS LES AGES. SES TRADITIONS, SES UNIFORMS. LES CHASSEURS A PIED. Paris: Société des éditions militaires, 1930.

Sauzey, Lieutenant-Colonel. ICONOGRAPHIE DES COSTUMES MILITAIRES (REVOLUTION, Ier EMPIRE, IIe REPUBLIQUE, IIe EMPIRE). 3 vols. Paris: Dubois et Chapelot, 1901–1908.

Thorburn, W. A. FRENCH ARMY REGIMENTS AND UNIFORMS FROM THE REVOLUTION TO 1870. Harrisburg, PA: Stackpole Books, 1969.

Titeux, Eugène. HISTORIQUE ET UNIFORMS DES REGIMENTS DE L'ARMEE FRANCAISE, CAVALERIE. Paris: Lévy, 1893.

Vernet, Horace. COLLECTION DES UNIFORMS DES ARMEES FRANCAISES DE 1791 A 1824. 2 vols. Paris: Gide fils, 1822–1825.

Vidal, Général. L'ARMEE FRANCAISE A TRAVERS LES AGES. SES TRADITIONS, SES GLOIRES, SES UNIFORMES. L'ARTILLERIE. Paris: Société des éditions militaires, 1929.

Naval Operations

Bamford, Paul W. FORESTS AND FRENCH SEA POWER, 1660–1789. Toronto: University of Toronto Press, 1956.

Bennett, Geoffrey. NELSON THE COMMANDER. London: B.T. Batsford, 1972.

Boudroit, Jean. LE VAISSEAU DE 74 CANNONS. 3 vols. Grenoble: Editions des quatre seigneurs, 1973.

Brun, V. GUERRES MARITIMES DE LA FRANCE. PORT DE TOULON. Paris: Plon, 1861.

Clowes, William L. THE ROYAL NAVY. A HISTORY FROM THE EARLIEST TIMES TO THE PRESENT. 7 vols. London: S. Low, Marston, 1897–1903.

Douin, Georges. LA CAMPAGNE DE BRUIX EN MEDITERRANEE MARS-AOUT, 1799. Paris: Société d'éditions géographiques, maritimes et coloniales, 1923.

Farrère, Claude. HISTOIRE DE LA MARINE FRANCAISE. Paris: Flammarion, 1934.

Gallois, Napoléon. LES CORSAIRES FRANCAIS SOUS LA REPUBLIQUE ET L'EMPIRE. 2 vols. Le Mans: Julien, Lanier, 1847.

Guérin, Léon. HISTOIRE MARITIME DE FRANCE. 6 vols. Paris: Legrand Pomey et Crouzet, n.d.

Havard, O. HISTOIRE DE LA REVOLUTION DANS LES PORTS DE GUERRE. 2 vols. N.p., 1912.

Hennequin, Joseph F. G. BIOGRAPHIE MARITIME; OU, NOTICES HISTORIQUES SUR LA VIE ET LES CAMPAGNES DES

MARINS CELEBRES FRANCAIS ET ETRANGERS. 3 vols. Paris: Regnault, 1835–1837.

Howarth, David. SOVEREIGN OF THE SEAS: THE STORY OF BRITAIN AND THE SEA. New York: Atheneum, 1974.

James, William. THE NAVAL HISTORY OF GREAT BRITAIN FROM THE DECLARATION OF WAR BY FRANCE IN FEBRUARY 1793 TO THE ACCESSION OF GEORGE IV IN JANUARY 1820. 6 vols. London: Harding Lepard, 1826.

Jenkins, E. H. A HISTORY OF THE FRENCH NAVY. London: Macdonald and Janes, 1973.

Johnson, William B. WOLVES OF THE CHANNEL (1681–1856). London: Wisehart, 1931.

Jouan, René. HISTOIRE DE LA MARINE FRANCAISE. Paris: Payot, 1932.

Kennedy, Paul M. THE RISE AND FALL OF BRITISH NAVAL MASTERY. New York: Charles Scribner's Sons, 1976.

Lewis, Michael. THE HISTORY OF THE BRITISH NAVY. Baltimore: Penguin Books, 1962.

Lewis, Michael A. THE NAVY OF BRITAIN, A HISTORICAL PORTRAIT. London: G. Allen and Unwin, 1948.

Lloyd, Christopher, and Oliver Warner. NELSON AND SEA POWER. London: English Universities Press, 1973.

————. ST. VINCENT AND CAMPERDOWN. London: B. T. Batsford, 1963.

Loir, Maurice. LA MARINE FRANCAISE. Paris: Hachette, 1893.

Mahan, Alfred T. THE INFLUENCE OF SEA POWER UPON THE FRENCH REVOLUTION AND EMPIRE. 11th ed. 2 vols. Boston: Little, Brown, 1902.

Marcus, Geoffrey. THE AGE OF NELSON. London: George Allen and Unwin, 1971.

————. QUIBERON BAY. Barre, MA: Barre Publishing, 1963.

Moulin, Louis H. LES MARINS DE LA REPUBLIQUE. Paris: Charavay frères, 1883.

Padfield, Peter. NELSON'S WAR. London: Hart-Davis, MacGibbon, 1976.

Parkinson, C. Northcote. WAR IN THE EASTERN SEAS, 1793–1815. London: George Allen and Unwin, 1954.

Roncière, Charles de la Clerc. HISTOIRE DE LA MARINE FRANCAISE. 6 vols. Paris: Plon, 1909–1934.

Roncière, Charles de la Clerc, G. Rampal, and Vice-Admiral Lacaze. HISTOIRE DE LA MARINE FRANCAISE. Paris: Larousse, 1934.

Russell of Liverpool, Lord. THE FRENCH CORSAIRS. London: Robert Hale, 1970.

Tramond, J. MANUEL D'HISTOIRE MARITIME DE LA FRANCE DES ORIGINES A 1815. 2nd ed. Paris: Société d'éditions géographiques, maritimes et coloniales, 1927.

Troude, O. BATAILLES NAVALES DE LA FRANCE. 4 vols. Paris: Levot, 1867.

Warner, Oliver. THE BATTLE OF THE NILE. London: Macmillan 1960.

———. FIGHTING SAIL. London: Cassell, 1979.

———. THE GLORIOUS FIRST OF JUNE. New York: Macmillan, 1961.

———. GREAT SEA BATTLES. New York: Macmillan, 1963.

———. NELSON'S BATTLES. New York: Macmillan, 1965.

Wheeler, H. F. B. and A. M. Broadley. NAPOLEON AND THE INVASION OF ENGLAND. 2 vols. London: J. Lane, 1910.

Impact of Revolution

Achorn E. "La Conscription de l'an VII et celle de l'an VII." REVOLUTION FRANCAISE, 77 (1924).

Arches, P. "Aspects sociaux de quelques gardes nationaux au début de la Révolution (1789–1790)." ACTES DU QUATRE-VINGT-UNIEME CONGRES NATIONAL DES SOCIETES SAVANTES. Paris: Rover-Caen, 1956.

Bertaud, Jean-Paul. "Aperçus sur l'insoumission et la désertion à l' époque révolutionnaire: Étude de sources." BULLETIN D'HISTOIRE ECONOMIQUE ET SOCIALE DE LA REVOLUTION FRANCAISE ANNEE 1969. Paris, 1970.

———. "Les armées de l'an II: Administration militaire et combattants." REVUE HISTORIQUE DE L'ARMEE, no. 2. (1969).

———. THE ARMY OF THE FRENCH REVOLUTION. Translated by R. R. Palmer. Princeton: Princeton University Press, 1988.

———. "Notes sur le premier amalgame (février 1793 – janvier 1794)." REVUE D'HISTOIRE MODERNE ET CONTEMPORAINE, 20 (1973).

———. "Notes sur le recrutement et la promotion des officers de 1789 à 1794." REVUE INTERNATIONALE DE L'HISTOIRE MILITAIRE, no. 37 (1977).

———. "Le recrutement et l'avancement des officiers de la Révolution." ANNALES HISTORIQUES DE LA REVOLUTION FRANCAISE, 44 (1972).

———. LA REVOLUTION ARMÉE: LES SOLDATS-CITOYENS ET LA REVOLUTION FRANCAISE. Paris: Robert Laffont, 1979.

Bonnal de Ganges, Edmond. LES REPRESENTANTS DU PEUPLE EN MISSION PRES DES ARMEES; D'APRES LE DEPOT DE LA GUERRE, LES SEANCES DES LA CONVENTION, LES ARCHIVES NATIONALES. Paris: Savaete, 1898–1899.

Bourdeau, Georges. "L'affaire de Nancy—31 août 1790." ANNALES DE L'EST, 12 (1898).

Bricard, Louis Joseph. LA DISCIPLINE AUX ARMEES DE LA PREMIERE REPUBLIQUE. Paris: A. & J. Bricard, 1893.

Cantal, Pierre. ETUDES SUR L'ARMEE REVOLUTIONAIRE. Paris: Charles Lavauzelle, 1907.

Cardenal, de. LE RECRUTEMENT DES ARMEES PENDANT LA PERIODE REVOLUTIONNAIRE EN PERIGORD. Perigueux: Joucla, 1911.

Carnot, Lazare. LES VOLONTAIRES DE LA COTE D'OR; EN CAMPAGNE 1792–1796. Dijon: Les Librairies, 1942.

Cauvin, Christian. LES VOLONTAIRES ET LES REQUISITIONNAIRES DES BASSES-ALPES DE LA LEVEE A L'AMALGAME, 1791–1796. Paris: Chapelot, 1910.

Chalmin, Pierre. "La guerre révolutionnaire sous la Législative et la Convention." REVUE HISTOIRE DE L'ARMEE, no. 3 (1958).

Chamborant de Perissat. L'ARMEE DE LA REVOLUTION: SES GENERAUX ET SES SOLDATS, 1789–1871. Paris: Plon, 1875.

Charnay, Jean Paul. SOCIETE MILITAIRE ET SUFFRAGES POLITIQUES EN FRANCE DEPUIS 1789. Paris: S.E.V.P.E.N., 1964.

Chassin, Charles-Louis. L'ARMEE ET LA REVOLUTION. Paris: Le Chevalier, 1867.

Chassin, Louis, and L. Hennet. LES VOLONTAIRES NATIONAUX PENDANT LA REVOLUTION. 3 vols. Paris: L. Cerf, 1899–1906.

Cobb, Richard. LES ARMEES REVOLUTIONNAIRES: INSTRUMENT DE LA TERREUR DANS LES DEPARTEMENTS, AVRIL 1793. 2 vols. (Floreal an II). Paris: Mouton, 1961–1963.

Colin, Jean. LA TACTIQUE ET LA DISCIPLINE DANS LES ARMEES DE LA REVOLUTION; CORRESPONDANCE DU GENERAL SCHAUENBOURG DU 4 AVRIL AU 2 AOUT, 1793. Paris: R. Chapelot, 1902.

Darquenne, Roger. LA CONSCRIPTION DANS LE DEPARTEMENT DE JAMAPPES, 1798–1813. Mons: Secrétariat du cercle, 1970.

Deprez, Eugène. LES VOLONTAIRES NATIONAUX (1791–1793). ETUDE SUR LA FORMATION ET L'ORGANISATION DES BATTALIONS D'APRES LES ARCHIVES COMMUNALES ET DEPARTMENTALES. Paris: Chapelot, 1908.

D'Hauterive, Ernets. L'ARMEE SOUS LA REVOLUTION (1794–1798). Paris: Ollendorff, 1894.

Ducourneau, Lieutenant. LE POUVOIR LEGISLATIF ET L'ARMEE SOUS LA REVOLUTION. Paris: 1913.

Dufay, Pierre. LES SOCIETES POPULAIRES ET L'ARMEE (1791–1794). Paris: H. Daragon, 1913.

Dufraisse, Roger. "Les populations de la rive gauche du Rhin et le service militaire à la fin de l'ancien Régime et à l'époque révolutionnaire." REVUE HISTOIRE, 1964.

Dulac, Rene. LES LEVEES DEPARTEMENTALES DANS L'ALLIER SOUS LA REVOLUTION, 1791–1796. 2 vols. Paris: Plon Nourrit, 1911.

Dumont, Georges. BATTALIONS DE VOLONTAIRES NATIONAUX. Cadres et historiques. Paris: Lavauzelle, 1914.

Dumont, Georges, and Georges-Eugène. LES VOLONTAIRES NATIONAUX DE LA MARNE (CHALONS, SAINTE MENEHOULD). LEVEE ET RECRUITEMENT, 1791, 1974. Paris: Chapelot, 1910.

Dupuy, Roger. LA GARDE NATIONALE ET LES DEBUTS DE LA REVOLUTION EN ILLE-ET-VILAINE (1789–MARS 1793). Paris: Klinksieck, 1972.

Fabry, G. "Soldats de la Révolution et de l'Empire." REVUE D'HISTOIRE (1910). XXXV.

Follet, André. LES VOLONTAIRES DE LA SAVOIE (1792–1799). Paris: Chapelot, 1887.

Forrest, Allan. SOLDIERS OF THE FRENCH REVOLUTION. Durham, NC: Duke University Press, 1990.

France. Etat-major de l'armée: Section historique. HISTORIQUE DES DIVERSES LOIS SUR LE RECRUTEMENT DE L'ARMEE DEPUIS LA REVOLUTION JUSQU'A NOS JOURS. Paris: Imprimerie nationale, 1902.

———. Etat-major de l'armée: Section historique. NOTICE HISTORIQUE SUR L'AVANCEMENT DANS L'ARMEE DEPUIS LA REVOLUTION JUSQU'A NOS JOURS. Paris: Imprimerie nationale, 1903.

Gallaher, John. "Recruitment in the District of Poitiers: 1793." FRENCH HISTORICAL STUDIES, 4, no. 2 (Fall 1963).

Girard, L. "Réflexions sur la Garde nationale." BULLETIN DE LA SOCIETE D'HISTOIRE MODERNE (May 1955).

Gislain de Bontin, Adrien. LES VOLONTAIRES NATIONAUX ET LE RECRUTEMENT DE L'ARMEE PENDANT LA REVOLUTION DANS LYONNE. Auxerée: A. Galot, 1913.

Godechot, Jacques. "L'Aérostation militaire sous le Directoire." ANNALES HISTORIQUES DE LA REVOLUTION FRANCAISE 8 (1931).

———. LES COMMISSAIRES AUX ARMEES SOUS LE DIRECTOIRE. 2 vols. Paris: Fustier, 1938.

———. FRAGMENTS DES "MEMOIRES" DE C.-A. ALEXANDRE SUR LA MISSION AUX ARMEES DU NORD ET DE SAMBRE-ET-MEUSE. Paris: Presses Universitaires de France, 1941.

Hartmann, Louis. LES OFFICIERS DE L'ARMEE ROYALE ET LA REVOLUTION. Paris: F. Alcan, 1903.

220 • Bibliography

Hennequin, Léon. LA JUSTICE MILITAIRE ET LA DISCIPLINE A L'ARMEE DU RHIN ET A L'ARMEE DE RHIN-ET-MOSELLE (1792–1796). NOTES HISTORIQUES DU CHEF DE BATTALION DU GENIE LEGRAND. Paris: 1909.

Herlaut, General. "Les collaborateurs de Bouchotte." ANNALES HIS-TORIQUES DE LA REVOLUTION FRANCAISE, 4 (1927).

————. "La républicanisation des états-majors et des cadres de l'armée pendant la Révolution." ANNALES HISTORIQUES DE LA REVO-LUTION FRANCAISE, 14 (1937).

HISTORIQUE DES DIVERSES LOIS SUR LE RECRUTEMENT DEPUIS LA REVOLUTION JUSQU'A NOS JOURS. Paris: Im-primerie nationale, 1902.

Houdard, K. "Organisation du service de santé militaire sous la Ière République 1791–1796." REVUE DU SERVICE DE SANTE MILI-TAIRE, no. 5 (May 1938).

Jaurès, Jean. L'ARMEE NOUVELLE. Paris: J. Rouff, 1911.

La Bédollière, Emile Gigault de. HISTOIRE DE LA GARDE NA-TIONALE. Paris: F. Pallier, 1848.

Lachouque, Henry. AUX ARMES, CITOYENS, LES SOLDATS DE LA REVOLUTION. Paris: Perrin, 1969.

Latreille, Albert. L'OEUVRE MILITAIRE DE LA REVOLUTION. Paris: Chapelot, 1914.

Lechartier, Georges. LES SOLDATS DE LA REVOLUTION ET DE L'EMPIRE. Paris: H. Charles-Lavauzelle, 1902.

Lefebvre, Georges. "L'Amalgame et la Convention." LA PENSEE, No. 2 (1944).

Legrand, Robert. LE RECRUTEMENT DES ARMEES ET LES DE-SERTIONS (1791–1815): ASPECTS DE LA REVOLUTION EN PI-CARDIE ABBEVILLE 1957. Abbeville: Société d'émulation et d'histoire d'Abbeville, nd.

Lesseray, André. "Les corps belges et liègeois aux armées de la République." REVUE D'HISTOIRE MODERNE (May 1929).

Leverrier, Jules. LA NAISSANCE DE L'ARMEE NATIONALE 1789–1794. Paris: Editions sociales internationales, 1939.

Levy, Jean Michel. L'ARMEE ET LA CONVENTION, L'OEUVRE SOCIALE DE LA REVOLUTION. Paris: A. Fontemoing, 1901.

————. L'effort de guerre dans le département du Rhône et dans les dé-partements voisins au cours des 10 premières années de la Révolu-tion." CAHIERS D'HISTOIRE (July 1965).

————. LA FORMATION DE LA PREMIERE ARMEE DE LA REV-OLUTION FRANCAISE L'EFFORT MILITAIRE ET LES LEVEES D'HOMMES DANS LE DEPARTEMENT DE L'AIN EN 1791. Paris: Thesis, Paris IV.

Levy-Schneider, Léon. LES SOLDATS DE LA REVOLUTION. Trévoux, 1917.

Lombard, Jean. Un volontaire de 1792. PSYCHOLOGIE REVOLU-TIONNAIRE ET MILITAIRE. Paris: Société d'éditions littéraires et artistiques, 1902.

Lort-Sehrignan, Arthur Comte de. SOLDATS DE LA REVOLUTION ET DE L'EMPIRE; GROGNARDS ET HEROS DE VINGT ANS. Paris: Perrin, 1914.

Lynn, John. THE BAYONETS OF THE REPUBLIC: MOTIVATION AND TACTICS IN THE ARMY OF REVOLUTIONARY FRANCE. Urbana: University of Illinois Press, 1984.

————. "Esquisse sur la tactique de l'infanterie." ANNALES HIS-TORIQUES DE LA REVOLUTION FRANCAISE (Nov.–Dec. 1972).

————. "French Opinion and the Military Resurrection of the Pike, 1792–1794." MILITARY AFFAIRS (February 1977).

Martin, Marc. "Journaux aux armées au temps de la Convention." AN-NALES HISTORIQUES DE LA REVOLUTION FRANCAISE 44 (1972).

————. "Les journaux militaires de Carnot." ANNALES HIS-TORIQUES DE LA REVOLUTION FRANCAISE 49 (1977).

Mege, Francisque. LES BATTALLIONS DE VOLONTAIRES, 1791–1793. Paris: A. Claudin, 1880.

Michelet, Jules. LES SOLDATS DE LA REVOLUTION. Paris: Calman Levy, 1878.

Michon, Georges. "L'armée et la politique intérieure sous la Conven-tion." ANNALES HISTORIQUES DE LA REVOLUTION FRAN-CAISE (1927).

————. "La justice militaire sous la Convention à l'armée des Pyrénées orientales." ANNALES HISTORIQUES DE LA REVOLUTION FRANCAISE 3 (1926).

————. LA JUSTICE MILITAIRE SOUS LA REVOLUTION. Paris: Alcan, 1922.

————. ROBESPIERRE ET LA GUERRE REVOLUTIONNAIRE, 1791–1792. Paris: M. Riveiere, 1937.

Négrier, Francois-Oscar. EDITIONS MILITAIRES. Paris: Delagrave, 1907.

Palmer, R. R. TWELVE WHO RULED. Princeton: Princeton University Press, 1941.

Pétigny, X. de. BEAUREPAIRE ET LE PREMIER DES BATTALIONS DES VOLONTAIRES DE MARNE ET LOIRE A VERDUN, JUIN-SEPTEMBRE, 1792. Angers, 1912.

Picard, Lieutenant-Colonel. AU SERVICE DE LA NATION, 1791–1798. Paris, 1914.

222 • Bibliography

Picq, Capitaine. LA LEGISLATION MILITAIRE DE L'EPOQUE
REVOLUTIONNAIRE. Paris, 1931.
Poisson, Charles. L'ARMEE ET LA GARDE NATIONALE
(1789–1795). 4 vols. Paris: Durand, 1858–1862.
———. LES FOURNISSEURS AUX ARMEES SOUS LA REVOLU-
TION FRANCAISE: LE DIRECTOIRE DES ACHATS (1792–1793).
Paris: Margraff, 1932.
Poulet, Henri. LES VOLONTAIRES DE LA MEURTHE AUX
ARMEES DE LA REVOLUTION (LEVEE DE 1791). Paris: Berger-
Levrault, 1910.
Reinhard, Marcel. L'ARMEE ET LA REVOLUTION PENDANT LA
CONVENTION. Paris: Cours polycopiés au C.D.U., 1957.
———. Nostalgie et service militaire pendant la Révolution." AN-
NALES HISTORIQUES DE LA REVOLUTION FRANCAISE
(1958).
———. "Le rôle révolutionnaire de l'armée dans la Révolution
française." ANNALES HISTORIQUES DE LA REVOLUTION
FRANCAISE, no. 168 (April 1962).
Richard, Antoine. "L'armée des Pyrénées-Orientales et les représentants
en Espagne, 1794–1795." ANNALES HISTORIQUES DE LA REV-
OLUTION FRANCAISE 11 (1934).
Richard, Camille. LE COMITE DE SALUT PUBLIC ET LES FABRI-
CATIONS DE GUERRE. Paris: F. Rieder, 1921.
Rousset, Camille. LES VOLONTAIRES (1791–1794). Paris: Didier,
1882.
Salle, Eugène. "Les volontaires de l'Indre au temps de la Révolution."
REVUE ACADEMIE DU CENTRE (1957).
Sangnier, Georges. LA DESERTION DANS LE PAS-DE-CALAIS DE
1792 A 1802. Blangermont: chez l'auteur, 1965.
Saumade, G. LE CAMP D'INSTRUCTION DE LAUNAC SOUS
MONTPELLIER EN L'AN II. Montpellier: L'Abeille, 1929.
Scott, Samuel. "The French Revolution and the Professionalization of the
French Officer Corps, 1789–1793." ON MILITARY IDEOLOGY.
Rotterdam, 1971.
———. "Gentlemen-Soldiers at the Time of the French Revolution."
MILITARY AFFAIRS 45, no. 3 (October, 1981).
———. "Les officiers de l'infanterie de ligne à la veille de l'amalgame."
ANNALES HISTORIQUES DE LA REVOLUTION FRANCAISE
40 (1968).
———. "Problems of Law and Order During 1790, the 'Peaceful' Year
of the French Revolution." AMERICAN HISTORICAL REVIEW 80
(1975).
———. "The Regeneration of the Line Army During the French Revo-
lution." JOURNAL OF MODERN HISTORY 42 (September 1970).

————. THE RESPONSE OF THE ROYAL ARMY TO THE FRENCH REVOLUTION. THE ROLE AND DEVELOPMENT OF THE LINE ARMY, 1787–1793. London: Oxford University Press, 1978.

————. "Rochambeau's Veterans: A Case Study in the Transformation of the French Army, 1780–1794." THE CONSORTIUM ON REVOLUTIONARY EUROPE PROCEEDINGS (1979).

————. "Les soldats de l'armée de ligne en 1793." ANNALES HISTORIQUES DE LA REVOLUTION FRANCAISE 44 (1972).

Serrant, H. LE SERVICE DU RECRUTEMENT DE 1789 A NOS JOURS. Paris: Charles Lavauzelle, 1935.

Soanen, H. "La Franc-Maçonnerie et l'Armée pendant la Révolution." ANNALES HISTORIQUES DE LA REVOLUTION FRANCAISE (1928).

Soboul, Albert. L'ARMEE NATIONALE SOUS LA REVOLUTION (1789–1794). Paris: Editions France d'abord, 1945.

————. LES SOLDATS DE L'AN II. Paris: Club français du livre, 1959.

————. "Sur la mission de Saint-Just à l'armée du Rhin. Brumaire an II." ANNALES HISTORIQUES DE LA REVOLUTION FRANCAISE (July–December 1954).

Tournes, R. LA GARDE NATIONALE DANS LE DEPARTMENT DE LA MEURTHE PENDANT LA REVOLUTION (1789–1802). Angers: Société Française d'Imprimerie et de Publicité, 1920.

Vallee, Gustave. LA CONSCRIPTION DANS LE DEPARTEMENT DE LA CHARENTE (1789–1807). Paris: Librairie du recueil Sirey, 1937.

Vermale, François. "La désertion dans l'armée des Alpes après Thermidor." ANNALES REVOLUTIONNAIRES (July, 1913).

Vialla, S. L'ARMEE NATION: LES VOLONTAIRES DES BOUCHES-DU-RHONE, 1791–1792. Paris: Chapelot, 1913.

Vidal, Joseph. HISTOIRE ET STATISTIQUE DE L'INSOUMISSION. Paris: M. Girard & E. Brière, 1913.

Vidalenc, Jean. "Le premier battalion de volontaires nationaux du département de la Manche." Cahiers: Leopold Delisle, 1966.

————. "Les volontaires nationaux dans le département de l'Eure (1791–1793)." ANNALES HISTORIQUES DE LA REVOLUTION FRANCAISE (1949).

Vigile, J. LES SOLDATS DE LA REVOLUTION (1789–1793) DANS LE CANTON DE MELE (Orne). N.p.: 1962.

Wagret, P. LES REPRESENTANTS DU PEUPLE EN MISSION ET LA JUSTICE REVOLUTIONNAIRE DANS LES DEPARTEMENTS DE L'AN II (1793–1794). 5 vols. Paris: Hachette, 1889–1890.

Werner, Robert. L'APPROVISIONNEMENT EN PAIN DE LA POPULATION DU BAS-RHIN ET DE L'ARMEE DU RHIN PENDANT LA REVOLUTION (1789–1797). Strasbourg: F. X. Le Roux, 1951.

Campaigns 1792–1799

Austrian General Staff Historical Section. GESCHICHTE DER KAMPFE OESTERREICHS. KREIG GEGEN DIE FRANZOSISCHE REVOLUTION. 2 vols. Vienna: Seidel, 1905.

Bonnal, Edmond. LES ARMEES DE LA REPUBLIQUE, OPERATIONS ET BATAILLES 1792–1800. Paris: Delagrave, 1899.

Bonnal, Henri. L'ESPRIT DE LA GUERRE MODERNE: DE ROSBACH A ULM. Paris: Chapelot, 1903.

Camon, Hubert. LA GUERRE NAPOLEONIENNE. 5 vols. Paris: Chapelot, 1903–1910.

―――. QUAND ET COMMENT NAPOLEON A CONCU SON SYSTEME DE BATAILLE. Paris: Berger-Levrault, 1935.

―――. QUAND ET COMMENT NAPOLEON A CONCU SON SYSTEME DE MANOEUVRE. Paris: Berger-Levrault, 1931.

―――. LE SYSTEME DE GUERRE DE NAPOLEON. Paris: Berger-Levrault, 1923.

Chandler, David G. ATLAS OF MILITARY STRATEGY. New York: Free Press, 1980.

―――. THE CAMPAIGNS OF NAPOLEON. New York: Macmillan, 1966.

―――. DICTIONARY OF THE NAPOLEONIC WARS. New York: Macmillan, 1979.

Chevalier, E. CROQUIS DES OPERATIONS MILITAIRES DE LA FRANCE DE 1789 A NOS JOURS. Paris: P. Dupont, 1883.

Clerget, Charles. TABLEAUX DES ARMEES FRANCAISES PENDANT LES GUERRES DE LA REVOLUTION. Paris: Chapelot, 1905.

COLLECTION DES CARTES D'OPERATIONS ET DES CHAMPS DE BATAILLES EN ITALIE, EN EGYPTE ET EN ALLEMAGNE. Paris: Depôt de la guerre, n.d.

Demoulin M. PRECIS D'HISTOIRE MILITAIRE: REVOLUTION ET L'EMPIRE. 3 vols. Paris: Maison Andriveau-Gujon, 1906.

Desbrière, Edouard. PROJECTS ET TENTATIVE DE DEBARQUEMENT AUX ILES BRITANNIQUES 1793–1805. 4 vols. Paris: Chapelot, 1900–1902.

Dodge, Theodore A. NAPOLEON: A HISTORY OF THE ART OF WAR FROM THE BEGINNING OF THE FRENCH REVOLUTION TO THE END OF THE EIGHTEENTH CENTURY WITH A DETAILED ACCOUNT OF THE WARS OF THE FRENCH REVOLUTION. 4 vols. London: Gay and Bird, 1904–1907.

Dumas, Mathieu. PRECIS DES EVENEMENTS MILITAIRES, OU ESSAI HISTORIQUE SUR LES CAMPAGNES DE 1799 A 1814. 16 vols. Paris: Preuttel, 1816–1821.

Dumolin, Maurice. PRECIS D'HISTOIRE MILITAIRE REVOLU-
TION ET L'EMPIRE. 3 vols. Paris: Maison Andriveau Goujon, 1906.
Dupont, Marcel. NAPOLEON EN CAMPAGNE. 4 vols. Paris: Ha-
chette, 1950–1955.
Duruy, Albert. ETUDES D'HISTOIRE MILITAIRE SOUS LA REVO-
LUTION ET L'EMPIRE. Paris: Calmann-Lévy, 1889.
Esposito, Vincent. A MILITARY HISTORY AND ATLAS OF THE
NAPOLEONIC WARS. London: Faber and Faber, 1964.
Fugier, André. NAPOLEON ET L'ITALIE. Paris: J. B. Janin, 1947.
Goltz, Colmar v.d. VON ROSSBACH BIS JENA. Berlin: E. S. Mittler
und John, 1906.
Guyot, Raymond. LE DIRECTOIRE ET LA PAIX DE L'EUROPE.
Paris: Alcan, 1911.
Hall, R. A. STUDIES IN NAPOLEONIC STRATEGY. London: G.
Allen and Unwin, 1918.
Hayatt, Amj. "The Origins of Napoleonic Warfare: A Survey of Inter-
pretations." MILITARY AFFAIRS 31, no. 1 (1967), pp. 177–185.
HISTOIRE MILITAIRE DES FRANCAIS PAR CAMPAGNES
DEPUIS LE COMMENCEMENT DE LA REVOLUTION JUSQU'A
LA FIN DU REGNE DE NAPOLEON. 8 vols. Paris: A. Dupont,
1826–1829.
HISTOIRE MILITAIRIE. VICTOIRES ET CONQUETES DES ARMEES
FRANCAISES 1792–1801. Paris: Sanard et Derangeon, 1890.
Jomini, Antoine Henri de, Baron. HISTOIRE CRITIQUE ET MILI-
TAIRE DES GUERRES DE LA REVOLUTION. 15 vols. Paris:
Anselin et Pochard, 1820–1824.
Krebs, Léonce, and Henri Moris. CAMPAGNES DANS LES ALPES
PENDANT LA REVOLUTION. 2 vols. Paris: Plon, 1891–1895.
Kriegsgeschichtliche Abteilung des K und K Kriegsarchives. KRIEG
GEGEN DIE FRANZOSISCHE REVOLUTION 1792–1797. 2 vols.
Vienna, 1905.
Lachoque, Henri. NAPOLEON. Paris, 1964.
———. NAPOLEON'S BATTLES: A HISTORY OF HIS CAM-
PAIGNS. Translated by Roy Monkcom. New York: Dutton, 1967.
Mangin, Charles, Franchet d'Esperey, and Gabriel Hanotaux. HIS-
TOIRE MILITAIRE ET NAVALE DE LA CONSTITUANTE A LA
FIN DE LA GUERRE DE 1914–1918. Paris: Plon, 1927.
Marshall Cornwall, James. NAPOLEON AS MILITARY COMMAN-
DER. Princeton: D. Van Nostrand, 1967.
Martin, G., and P. Roussier. SUR L'HISTOIRE DES COLONIES
FRANCAISES PENDANT LA REVOLUTION. Paris: Centre d'E-
tudes de la Révolution Française, Cahier, 1935.
Meynier, Albert. "Quelques précisions nouvelles sur les levées et pertes
militaires en France sous la Révolution et le Premier Empire

(1793–1815)." BULLETIN DE LA SOCIETE D'HISTOIRE MOD-
ERNE, neuvieme serie 6 (Jan. 1938), pp. 3–8.

Musset, Victor. RELATIONS DES PRINCIPAUX SIEGES FAITS OU
SOUTENUS EN EUROPE PAR LES ARMEES FRANCAISES
DEPUIS 1792. Paris: Magimel, 1806.

Nabonne, B. LA DIPLOMATIE DU DIRECTOIRE ET BONAPARTE
D'APRES LES PAPIERS INEDITS DE REUBELL. Paris: 1951.

NAPOLEON'S GREAT ADVERSARIES: ARCHDUKE CHARLES
AND THE AUSTRIAN ARMY, 1792–1814. London: Batsford, 1982.

Nemours, Colonel. HISTOIRE MILITAIRE DE LA GUERRE D'IN-
DEPENDANCE A SAINT-DOMINIQUE. 2 vols. Paris: Berger-Levrault, 1925–1928.

Pelet, Général. ATLAS DES PRINCIPALES BATAILLES DE LA RE-
PUBLIQUE ET DU CONSULAT. Paris: Boulland, 1844.

Phipps, Ramsay. THE ARMIES OF THE FIRST FRENCH REPUBLIC.
5 vols. Oxford: Clarendon Press, 1926–1939.

Poyen, H. de. LES GUERRES DES ANTILLES DE 1793 A 1815. Paris:
1895.

————. HISTOIRE MILITAIRE DE LA REVOLUTION DE SAINT-
DOMINIQUE. Paris, 1900.

Quarre de Verneuil, Capitaine. LA FRANCE MILITAIRE PENDANT
LA REVOLUTION (1789–1798). Paris: Chapelot, 1878.

Reinhard, Marcel. LA FRANCE DU DIRECTOIRE. 2 vols. Paris, 1956.

Romagny, Charles. CAMPAGNES D'UN SIECLE. 26 vols. Paris:
Berger-Levrault, 1895–1902.

Ross, Steven T. QUEST FOR VICTORY: FRENCH MILITARY
STRATEGY 1792–1799. New York: A. S. Barnes; London: Thomas
Yoseloff, 1973.

Rothenberg, Gunther E. THE ART OF WARFARE IN THE AGE OF
NAPOLEON. Bloomington and London: Indiana University Press, 1978.

Rüstow, W. DIE FELDHERRNKUNST DES NEUNZEHNTEN
JAHRHUNDERTS, 1792–1815. Zurich: Schultheiss, 1898.

Sagnac, Philippe. LE RHIN FRANCAIS PENDANT LA REVOLU-
TION ET L'EMPIRE. Paris: F. Alcan, 1917.

Saintoyant, J. LA COLONISATION FRANCAISE PENDANT LA REV-
OLUTION 1789–1799. 2 vols. Paris: Renaissance du Livre, 1930.

Savant, Jean. LES SOLDAT GRECS DE LA REVOLUTION ET DE
L'EMPIRE (1797). Athens: 1940.

Schütz, Général, and Major Schulz. GESCHICHTE DER KRIEGE IN
EUROPA SEIT DEM JAHRE 1792. 2 vols. Leipzig: F. A. Brockhaus,
1827–1830; Berlin: E. S. Mittler, 1833, 1837–1853.

Sciout, Ludovic. LE DIRECTOIRE. 4 vols. Paris: 1895–1897.

Thiry, Commandant. HISTOIRE DE LA TACTIQUE DE L'INFAN-
TERIE FRANCAISE DE 1791 A 1905. Paris: Chapelot, 1905.

Thoumas, Charles A. AUTOUR DU DRAPEAU TRICOLORE 1789–1889. CAMPAGNES DE L'ARMEE FRANCAISE DEPUIS CENT ANS. Paris: A. Levasseur, 1889.

Vachée, Colonel. NAPOLEON EN CAMPAGNE. Paris: Berger-Levrault, 1913.

Vallaux, Camille. LES CAMPAGNES DES ARMEES FRANCAISES 1792–1815. Paris: Alcan, 1899.

VICTOIRES ET CONQUETES, DESASTRES, REVERS ET GUERRES CIVILES DES FRANCAIS DE 1791 A 1815 PAR UNE SOCIETE DE MILITAIRES ET DE GENS DE LETTRES. 27 vols. Paris: Panchoucke, 1817–1822.

Viennet, J. P. G., M. and B. Saintine, A. F. Guesdon, M. Saint-Maurice, M. Beauvais, M. Martonval. HISTOIRE MILITAIRE DES FRANCAIS PAR CAMPAGNES, DEPUIS LE COMMENCEMENT DE LA REVOLUTION JUSQU'A LA FIN DU REGNE DE NAPOLEON. 6 vols. Paris: Ambroise Dupont, 1826.

Wohlfeil, R. VOM STEHENDEN HEER DES ABSOLUTISMUS ZUR ALLGEMEINEN WEHRPFLICHT (1789–1814). Frankfurt: Bernard and Graefe, 1964.

York von Wartenburg, Maximilian. NAPOLEON AS A GENERAL. 2 vols. London: Gilbert and Rivington, 1902.

Campaigns 1792–1797

Anon. "Le rôle de Pichegru à Mannheim (Septembre 1795)." REVUE D'HISTOIRE no. 103 (July 1909), pp. 1–96.

Barreau, J. "La Campagne de 1795." BULLETIN OF THE SOCIETY OF HISTORIC GUADELOUPE, no. 28 (1977).

Becays-Ferrand, J. H. PRECIS DE LA DEFENSE DE VALENCIENNES. . . . Paris: Bidault, 1805.

Bertaud, Jean-Paul. VALMY: LA DEMOCRATIE EN ARMEES. Paris: Jillard, 1970.

Biro, Sydney S. THE GERMAN POLICY OF REVOLUTIONARY FRANCE. 2 vols. Cambridge, MA: Harvard University Press, 1957.

Bonnal, E. LA GUERRE DE HOLLANDE ET L'AFFAIRE DU TEXEL (1793–1795). Paris: Chapelot, 1886.

Bourdeau, H. LES ARMEES DU RHIN AU DEBUT DU DIRECTOIRE (SAMBRE-ET-MEUSE, RHIN-ET-MOSELLE). Paris: C. Lavauzelle, 1909.

Boyer, Gaston. "L'Armée des Pyrénées Orientales pendant la Ière République." BULLETIN DU CENTRE (1961).

Brace, R. M. "General Dumouriez and the Girondins." AMERICAN HISTORICAL REVIEW 56 (1951), pp. 493–509.

Caron, Pierre. LA DEFENSE NATIONALE DE 1792 A 1795. Paris: Hachette, 1912.

Chaudelot, Gabriel. LE SIEGE DE LUXEMBOURG EN 1795. Luxembourg: Les amis de l'histoire, 1792.

Chuquet, Arthur. L'ARMEE DE SAMBRE-ET-MEUSE EN 1796. Paris: Académie des Sciences Morales et Politiques, 1910.

———. LA CAMPAGNE DE L'ARGONNE 1792. Paris: Leopolk Cerf, 1886.

———. HOCHE ET LA LUTTE POUR L'ALSACE (1793–1794). Paris: Plon-Nourrit, 1893.

———. HONDSCHOOTE. Paris: L. Chailley, 1896.

———. JEMAPPES ET LA CONQUETE DE LA BELGIQUE (1792–1793). Paris: L. Cerf, 1888.

———. LA LEGION GERMANIQUE 1792–1793. Paris: R. Chapelot, 1904.

———. MAYENCE (1792–1793). Paris: Plon-Nourrit, 1892.

———. LA PREMIERE INVASION PRUSSIENNE (11 AOUT–2 SEPTEMBRE 1792). Paris: Plon-Nourrit, 1886.

———. QUATRE GENERAUX DE LA REVOLUTION: HOCHE ET DESAIX, KLEBER ET MARCEAU. Paris: Fontemoing, 1911.

———. LA RETRAITE DE BRUNSWICK. Paris: Plon-Nourrit, 1914.

———. LA TRAHISON DE DUMOURIEZ. Paris: E. Plon-Nourrit, 1891.

———. VALENCIENNES (1793). Paris: Plon-Nourrit, 1896.

———. VALMY. Paris: L. Cerf, 1887.

———. WEISSEMBOURG (1793). Paris: L. Chailley, 1893.

Clapham, J. H. THE CAUSES OF THE WAR OF 1792. Cambridge: Cambridge University Press; New York: Octagon Books, 1969.

Colin, Jean. CAMPAGNE DE 1793 EN ALSACE ET DANS LE PALATINAT. Paris: Chapelot, 1902.

Cottin, Paul. TOULON ET LES ANGLAIS EN 1793. Paris: P. Ollendorff, 1898.

Coutanceau, H., and C. de la Jonquière. LA CAMPAGNE DE 1794 A L'ARMEE DU NORD. 5 vols. Paris: Chapelot, 1903–1908.

Cruplants, Eugène. DUMOURIEZ DANS LE CI-DEVANT PAYS-BAS AUTRICHIEN. JEMAPPES NEERWINDEN, LA DEFECTION. 2 vols. Brussels: A. de Boeck, 1912.

Dedon, François. PRECIS HISTORIQUE DES CAMPAGNES DE L'ARMEE DE RHIN ET MOSELLE PENDANT L'AN IV ET L'AN V. Paris: Magimel, 1798.

Derode, Victor. LE SIEGE DE LILLE EN 1792. Lille: L. Danel, 1842.

Despres, Claude. L'ARMEE DE SAMBRE-ET-MEUSE. Paris: J. Dumaine, 1856.

————. LES ARMEES DE SAMBRE-ET-MEUSE ET DU RHIN (1793–1797). Paris: Chapelot, 1884.

Desprez, Jean. KLEBER ET MARCEAU. Paris: Baudoin, 1892.

Ducéré, Edouard. L'ARMEE DES PYRENEES OCCIDENTALES AVEC ECLAIRCISSEMENTS HISTORIQUES SUR LES CAMPAGNES DE 1793, 1794, 1795. Bayonne: H. Horquet, 1881.

Dupuis, V. LA CAMPAGNE DE 1793 DE L'ARMEE DU NORD ET DES ARDENNES. 2 vols. Paris: Chapelot, 1906, 1909.

————. LES OPERATIONS MILITAIRES SUR LA SAMBRE EN 1794: BATAILLE DE FLEURS. Paris: Chapelot, 1907.

Dutell, Joseph Baron. L'ECOLE D'ARTILLERIE D'AUXONNE ET LE SIEGE DE TOULON. Paris: A. Picard, 1897.

Fabry, Gabriel. HISTOIRE DE LA CAMPAGNE DE 1794 EN ITALIE. 2 vols. Paris: Chapelot, 1905.

Fervel, N. N. CAMPAGNES DE LA REVOLUTION FRANCAISE DANS LES PYRENEES-ORIENTALES. 2 vols. Paris: Dumaine, 1861.

Foucart, Paul, and Jules Finot. LA DEFENSE NATIONALE DANS LE NORD. 2 vols. Lille: Lefebvre-Ducrocq, 1890–1893.

Friedrich, Wilhelm III. DOCUMENTS RELATIFS AUX CAMPAGNES EN FRANCE ET SUR LE RHIN PENDANT LES ANNEES 1792 ET 1793 TIRES DES PAPIERS MILITAIRES DE S.M. LE FEU ROI DE PRUSSE FREDERIC GUILLAUME III. Paris: Corréard, 1848.

Ganniers, Arthur. "La dernière campagne du Maréchal Rochambeau (1792)." REVUE DES QUESTIONS HISTORIQUES 26 (1901), pp. 74–132, 438–470.

————. "Le maréchal Luekner et la première campagne de Belgique en 1792." REVUE DES QUESTIONS HISTORIQUES, 19 (1898). pp. 437–508.

Gasmann, E. LA BATAILLE D'HONDSCHOOTE, EPISODE DES GUERRES DE LA REVOLUTION EN FLANDRE. Hazebrouck: L. Guermonprez, 1857.

Gay de Vernon, Baron. MEMOIRE SUR LES OPERATIONS MILITAIRES DES GENERAUX-EN CHEF CUSTINE ET HOUCHARD (1792–1793). Paris: Firmin-Didot, 1844.

Glagau, H. DIE FRANZOSISCHE LEGISLATIVE UND DER URSPRUNG DER REVOLUTIONS KRIEGE. Berlin: 1896.

Glover, Richard. "The Battle of Valmy: A Reconsideration." ARMY QUARTERLY 34 (1937), pp. 337–48.

Goetz-Bernstein, H. A. LA DIPLOMATIQUE DE LA GIRONDE; JACQUES PIERRE BRISSOT. Paris: Hachette, 1912.

Grimoard, Philippe Henri, and Joseph Servan. TABLEAU HISTORIQUE DE LA GUERRE DE LA REVOLUTION DE FRANCE

DEPUIS SON COMMENCEMENT EN 1792 JUSQU'A LA FIN DE 1794. 3 vols. Paris: Treuttel, 1808.

Hardy, E. LA BATAILLE DE FLEURS. Paris: Chapelot, 1876.

Heckmann, Paul. FELIX DE WIMPFFEN ET LE SIEGE DE THIONVILLE EN 1792; UN EPISODE DES GUERRES DE LA REVOLUTION. Paris: Perrin, 1926.

Hennequin, Léon. LA CAMPAGNE DE 1794 ENTRE RHIN ET MOSELLE. Paris: Chapelot, 1909.

Hennet, Léon. LE GENERAL ALEXIS DUBOIS: LA CAVALERIE AUX ARMEES DU NORD ET DE SAMBRE-ET MEUSE PENDANT LES CAMPAGNES DE 1794 ET 1795. Paris: L. Baudoin, 1897.

Herdrich, Kurt. PREUSSEN IN KAMPFE GEGEN DIE FRANZOSIS-CHE REVOLUTION BIS ZUR ZWEITEN TEILUNG POLENS. Berlin: Cotta. 1908.

Joinville, A. CAMPAGNE DE 1792 EN FRANCE. Paris: Imprimerie de Bourgogne, 1841.

Jones, E. H. S. AN INVASION THAT FAILED. Oxford: Blackwell, 1950.

—————. THE LAST INVASION OF BRITAIN. Cardiff: University of Wales Press, 1950.

Jonquière, Clément de la. LA BATAILLE DE JEMAPPES. Paris: Chapelot, 1902.

Juyan, Lois. LA CAMPAGNE DE 1794 DANS LES PAYS BAS. Paris: Fournier, 1915.

—————. LA CONQUETE DE LA BELGIQUE MAI-JUILLET 1794. Paris: L. Fournier, 1914.

Libermann, H. LA MISSION DE CL. MARIE CARNOT AUX ARMEES DE LA MOSELLE ET DU RHIN, 1792. Paris, 1920.

Longy, Louis. LA CAMPAGNE DE 1797 SUR LE RHIN. Paris: Chapelot, 1909.

Lort-Sérignan, Arthur, Maximilien Timoléon, Comte de. LA PRE-MIERE INVASION DE LA BELGIQUE (1792). Paris: Perrin, 1903.

Lufft, August von. DER FELDZUG AM MITTELRHEIN VON MITTE AUGUST BIS ENDE DEZEMBER 1793. Freiburg: J.C.B. Mohr, 1881.

Marcillac, Pierre Louis. HISTOIRE DE LA GUERRE ENTRE LA FRANCE ET L'ESPAGNE PENDANT LES ANNEES DE LA REV-OLUTION FRANCAISE 1793, 1794 ET PARTIE DE 1795. Paris: Chez Migimel, 1808.

Marmottan, Paul. LE GENERAL FROMENTIN ET L'ARMEE DU NORD (1792–1794). Paris: Dubois, 1891.

Mathiez, Albert. LA VICTOIRE EN L'AN II, ESQUISSES HIS-TORIQUES SUR LA DEFENSE NATIONALE. Paris: F. Alcan, 1916.

Mautouchet, P. LE GOUVERNEMENT REVOLUTIONNAIRE. Paris: 1912.

Mérat, Paul. VERDUN EN 1792. Verdun: Lallemant, 1849.
Nabonne, Bernard. LA DIPLOMATIE DU DIRECTOIRE ET BONA-PARTE. Paris: Nouvelle Edition, 1951.
Navez, Louis. LES CHAMPS DE BATAILLE HISTORIQUES DE LA BELGIQUE. 2 vols. Brussels: Lebegue, 1902–1903.
Pallain, G. LE MINISTERE DE TALLEYRAND SOUS LE DIREC-TOIRE. Paris: 1891.
Picard, Louis. HUIT JOURS TRAGIQUES A L'ARMEE DU RHIN EN 1793. Saumur: Girouard & Richou, 1933.
Piérart, Z. J. LA GRANDE EPOPEE DE L'AN II. SOUVENIRS, RAP-PROCHEMENTS, RECTIFICATIONS ET FAITS INEDITS RE-LATIFS AUX BATAILLES DE WATTINGNIES, DE FLEURS ET AUX PASSAGES DE LA SAMBRE EN 1793 ET 1794. Paris: Ferround, 1887.
Pingaud, Léonce. L'INVASION AUSTRO-PRUSSIENNE, 1792–1794. Paris: Picard, 1895.
Pionnier, E. HISTOIRE DE LA REVOLUTION A VERDUN. Paris, 1906.
Porth, Wenzel. DIE SCHLACHT BEI NEERWINDEN DEN 18 MARZ 1793. Vienna: R. V. Waldheim, 1877.
Rambaud, Alfred. LES FRANCAIS SUR LE RHIN (1792–1804). Paris: Didier, 1883.
Recouly, Raymond. L'AURORE DE NAPOLEON: BONAPARTE A TOULON. Paris: Editions de France, 1929.
Rose, J. Holland. LORD HOOD AND THE DEFENSE OF TOULON. Cambridge: Cambridge University Press, 1922.
Sorel, Albert. BONAPARTE ET HOCHE EN 1797. Paris: Plon, 1896.
Vivenot, Alfred. RITTER VON THUGUT CLERFAYT UND WURM-SER. ORIGINAL DOCUMENTE AUS DEM K. K. HAUSHOF—UND STAATS ARCHIV UND DEM K. K. KRIEGS-ARCHIVIM WIEN VON JULI 1794 BIS FEBRUARY 1797. Vienna: K. K. Hauptmann, 1869.
Zelle, L. J. DIE BLOCKADE DER FESTUNG LUXEMBURG DURCH DIE TRUPPEN DER FRANZOSISCHEN REPUBLIK 1794–1795. Publications de la Société Historique d'Institut du g-d. de Luxembourg, vol. 42. N.p.: 1892.

Counterrevolution

Barreau, Colonel Jean. "Généraux et Représentants du peuple en Vendée, Mars-Octubre 1793." REVUE HISTORIQUE DES ARMEES 2 (1980), pp. 63–93.
———. "Quiberon 1795." REVUE HISTORIQUE DES ARMEES, no. 1 (1979), pp. 94–122.

Barrvol, J. La Contré. REVOLUTION EN PROVENCE. N.p.: Cavarillon, 1928.

Berk, Paul-Henri. THE FRENCH REVOLUTION SEEN FROM THE RIGHT, LOCAL THEORIES IN MOTION, 1789–1799. Philadelphia: Transactions of the American Philosophical Society, Vol. 46, Part 1, 1956.

Bittard des Portes, René. CHARETTE ET LA GUERRE DE VENDEE. Paris: Emile-Paul, 1902.

————. CONTRE LA TERREUR: L' INSURRECTION DE LYON EN 1793. Paris: Emile-Paul, 1906.

————. LES GUERRES DE VENDEE: GRANDE GUERRE POUR LOUIS XVII. Paris: Hachette, 1960.

Blanc, Louis. LA CONTRE-REVOLUTION: PARTISANS, VENDEENS, EMIGRES 1794–1800. Paris: Hachette, 1961.

————. HISTOIRE DE L'ARMEE DE CONDE. Paris: Dentu, 1896.

Bordonove, Georges. LA GUERRE DE VENDEE. Paris: R. Juillard, 1964.

————. LA VIE QUOTIDIENNE EN VENDEE PENDANT LA REVOLUTION. Paris: Hachette, 1976.

Carré, Adrien. "Des milices de la monarchie à l'insurrection de 1793: Bretons et Vendéens et la défense du royaume." REVUE HISTORIQUE DES ARMEES 4, no. 4 (1977), pp. 34–65.

Caudrillier, Gustaaf. LA TRAHISON DE PICHEGRU ET LES INTRIGUES ROYALISTES DANS L'EST AVANT FRUCTIDOR. Paris: F. Alcan, 1908.

Chassin, Charles-Louis. ETUDES DOCUMENTAIRES SUR LA REVOLUTION FRANCAISE: LES GUERRES DE VENDEE ET LA CHOUANNERIE. 10 vols. Nantes: Bellanger, 1873.

————. LE GENERAL HOCHE A QUIBERON. Paris: Dupont, 1907.

————. LES PACIFICATIONS DE L'QUEST 1794–1800. 3 vols. Paris: Dupont, 1896–1900.

————. LA PREPARATION DE LA GUERRE DE VENDEE (1789–1793). 3 vols. Paris: P. Dupont, 1892.

————. LA VENDEE PATRIOTE 1793–1800. 4 vols. Paris: Felix Joven, 1893–1895.

Chaudeurge, Alfred. LES CHOUANS DE NORMANDIE. Netherlands: Normand, 1975.

Cottin, Paul. TOULON ET LES ANGLAIS EN 1793. Paris: Ollendorff, 1898.

Crétineau-Joly, Jacques. HISTOIRE DE LA VENDEE MILITAIRE. Paris: Maison de la Bonne Presse, 1896–1897. 5 vols.

Daudet, Ernest. LA CONJURATION DE PICHEGRU ET LES COMPLOTS ROYALISTES DU MIDI ET DE L'EST, 1795–1797 D'APRES DES DOCUMENTS INEDITS. Paris: Plon-Nourrit, 1901.

————. LES EMIGRES ET LA SECONDE COALITION. Paris: 1886.

————. HISTOIRE DE L'EMIGRATION PENDANT LA REVOLU-
TION FRANCAISE. 3 vols. Paris: Hachette, 1905–1907.

————. HISTOIRE DES CONSPIRATIONS ROYALISTES DU MIDI
SOUS LA REVOLUTION (1790–1793). Paris: Hachette, 1881.

Dubreyil, Léon. HISTOIRE DES INSURRECTIONS DE L'OUEST.
Paris: Rieder, 1929.

Facheux, Marcel. L'INSURRECTION VENDEENNE DE 1793: AS-
PECTS ECONOMIQUES ET SOCIAUX. Paris: Imprimerie Nationale, 1864.

Forneron, Henri. HISTOIRE GENERALE DES EMIGRES PENDANT
LA REVOLUTION FRANCAISE. 3 vols. Paris: E. Plon-Nourrit,
1884–1890.

Gabory, E. L'ANGLETERRE ET LA VENDEE. 2 vols. Paris:
1930–1931.

Gabory, Emile. LES GRANDES HEURES DE LA VENDEE: LES
CONVULSIONS DE L'OUEST. Paris: Club du Meilleur Livre, 1961.

————. LA REVOLUTION ET LA VENDEE D'APRES DES DOCU-
MENTS INEDITS. 3 vols. Paris: Perrin, 1941.

Godechot, Jacques. LA CONTRE-REVOLUTION; DOCTRINE ET
ACTION 1789–1804. Paris: Presses Universitaires de France, 1961.

La Rochejaquelein, Henri du Vergier. HENRI DE LA ROCHEJAQUE-
LEIN ET LA GUERRE DE LA VENDEE. Paris: Champion, 1890.

La Sicotire, Pierre-François Leon Duchesne de. LOUIS DE FROTTE ET
L'INSURRECTION NORMANDE (1793–1832). 3 vols. Paris: Plon,
1889.

Lavigne, Bertrand. HISTOIRE DE L'INSURRECTION ROYALISTE
DE L'AN VII. Paris: 1887.

Le Goffie, Charles H. LA COUANNERIE, BLANCS CONTRE BLEUS
1790–1800. Paris: Hachette, 1930.

Le Menuet de la Jugannière. LE CHOUAN CARLOS LOURDAT ET
SON PERE, L'AGENT ROYAL. Paris: Fermen-Didot, 1932.

Lenotre, G. LE MARQUIS DE LA ROUAIRIE, PSEUDONYME ET
LA CONJURATION BRETONNE 1790–1793. Paris, 1910.

Lindove, Marcel. LES VENDEENS DE 93. Paris: Editions du Sevil, 1971.

Madelin, Louis. LA CONTRE-REVOLUTION SOUS LA REVOLU-
TION. Paris: Plon, 1935.

Mitchell, Harvey. THE UNDERGROUND WAR AGAINST REVOLU-
TIONARY FRANCE: THE MISSIONS OF WILLIAM WICKHAM
1794–1800. Oxford: Clarendon Press, 1965.

Montagnon, André. LES GUERRES DE VENDEE 1793–1832. Paris:
Perrin, 1974.

Morvan, Jean. LES CHOUANS DE LA MAYENNE 1792–1796. Paris:
Calmann-Lévy, 1901.

Muraise, E. "L'insurrection royaliste de l'Ouest (1791–1800)." REVUE MILITAIRE GENERALE (May 1966).

Orts, A. LA GUERRE DES PAYSANS (1789–1799). Brussels, 1863.

Paret, Peter. INTERNAL WAR AND PACIFICATION, THE VENDEE 1789–1796. Princeton: Princeton Center for International Studies, 1961.

Petitfrere, C. "Les grandes composantes sociales des armées Vendéennes d'Anjoyu." ANNALES HISTORIQUES DE LA REVOLUTION FRANCAISE (1973).

Pinasseau, Jean. L'EMIGRATION MILITAIRE. Paris: Picard, 1974.

———. L'EMIGRATION MILITAIRE, 1792, ARMEE ROYALE (COMPOSITION, ORDERES DE BATAILLES). 2 vols. Paris: Picard, 1964.

Riffaterre, C. "LE MOUVEMENT ANTI-JACOBIN ET ANTI-PARISIEN A LYON ET DANS LE RHONE-ET-LOIRE EN 1793." ANNALES DE LA FACULTE DES LETTRES DE LYON, 1912 AND 1928. 2 vols.

Robuchon, Jean. LES CHEFS VENDEENS DE 93. Fontenay: Impr. Lussaud, 1974.

Roincé, J. de. HISTOIRES DES CHOUANS. Paris: F. Lanore, 1978.

Ross, Michael. BANNERS OF THE KING: THE WAR OF THE VENDEE 1793–1794. New York: Hippocrene Books, 1975.

Roussel, Philippe. DE CADOUDAL A FROTTE: LA CHOUANNERIE DE 1792 A 1800. Paris: Editions de La Seula France, 1962.

Sherwig, John M. GUINEAS AND GUNPOWDER BRITISH FOREIGN AID IN THE WARS WITH FRANCE, 1793–1815. Cambridge: Harvard University Press, 1969.

Tilly, Charles. "Civil Constitution and Counter-Revolution in Southern Anjou." FRENCH HISTORICAL STUDIES (1959), p. 172–199.

———. "Local Conflicts in the Vendée Before the Rebellion of 1793." FRENCH HISTORICAL STUDIES (1959), p. 209–31.

———. "Some Problems in the History of the Vendée." AMERICAN HISTORICAL REVIEW, LXVII (1961), p. 19–33.

———. THE VENDEE: A SOCIOLOGICAL ANALYSIS OF THE COUNTERREVOLUTION OF 1793. Cambridge: Harvard University Press, 1964.

Vidalenc, Jean. LES EMIGRES FRANCAIS 1789–1825. Caen: Associations des Publications de la Faculté des Lettres et Science Humaines de l'Université de Caen, 1963.

Vingtrinier, Emmanuel. HISTOIRE DE LA CONTRE-REVOLUTION. 2 vols. Paris: Emile Paul Frères, 1924–1925.

Walter, Gérard. LA GUERRE DE VENDEE. Paris: Plon, 1935.

Weiner, M. THE FRENCH EXILES, 1789–1815. London, 1960.

Italy 1796–1797

Adlow, Elijah. NAPOLEON IN ITALY 1796–1797. Boston: W. J. Rochfort, 1948.

Andreossy, Antoine. OPERATIONS DES PONTONNIERS FRAN-CAIS EN ITALIE PENDANT LES CAMPAGNES DE 1795 A 1797. Paris: J. Corréard, 1843.

Béchu, Marcel. NAPOLEON EN CAMPAGNE. 3 vols. Paris: Hachette, 1950–1955.

Bouvier, Félix. BONAPARTE EN ITALIE, 1796. Paris: Librairie Leopold Cerf, 1899.

Burton, Reginald G. NAPOLEON'S CAMPAIGNS IN ITALY, 1796–1797 AND 1800. London: G. Allen, 1912.

Camon, Hubert. LA PREMIERE MANOEUVRE DE NAPOLEON: MANOEUVRE DE TURIN 12–28 AVRIL 1796. Paris: Berger-Levrault.

Cheland, Raoul. LES ARMEES FRANCAISES JUGEES PAR LES HABITANTS DE L'AUTRICHE 1797–1800–1809 D'APRES DES RAPPORTS DE L'EPOQUE. Paris: Librarie Plon, E. Plon, Nourrit, 1893.

Chodzko, Léonard. HISTOIRE DES LEGIONS POLONAISES EN ITALIE SOUS LE COMMANDEMENT DU GENERAL DOM-BROWSKI. 2 vols. Paris: Barbezat, 1829.

Clausewitz, Carl. LA CAMPAGNE DE 1796 EN ITALIE (TRADUIT DE L'ALLEMAND PAR J. COLIN). Paris: Baudouin, 1899.

Colin, Jean. ETUDES SUR LA CAMPAGNE DE 1796. Paris: Baudouin, 1898.

Derrécagaix, Victor. NOS CAMPAGNES AU TYROL, 1797–1799–1805–1809. Paris: Chapelot, 1910.

Fabry, Gabriel. HISTOIRE DE L'ARMEE D'ITALIE 1796–1797. 3 vols. Paris: Champion, 1900–1901.

————. MEMOIRE SU LA CAMPAGNE DE 1796 EN ITALIE. Paris: Chapelot, 1905.

————, ed. RAPPORTS HISTORIQUES DES REGIMENTS DE L'ARMEE D'ITALIE PENDANT LA CAMPAGNE DE 1796–1797. Paris: Chapelot, 1905.

Ferrero, Guglielmo. AVENTURE: BONAPARTE EN ITALIE (1796–1797). Paris: Plon, 1936.

Gachot, E. HISTOIRE MILITAIRE DE MASSENA: LA PREMIERE CAMPAGNE D'ITALIE 1796–1798. Paris: Perrin, 1901.

Godechot, J. "L'Armée d'Italie 1796–1799." CAHIER DE LA REVO-LUTION, no. 4 (1936), pp. 9–32.

Grazioli, Général. "Les Enseignements de Rivoli." REVUE HISTORIQUE DE L'ARMÉE, no. 3 (1969), pp. 60–77.

Grazioli, Francisco. LA BATALIA DI RIVOLI 14–15 GENNAIO 1797. Florence: Le Monnier, 1925.

Heriot, Angus. THE FRENCH IN ITALY. London: Chatto and Windus, 1957.

Hortig, Viktor. BONAPARTE VOR MANTUA ENDE JULI 1796. Rostock: University of Rostock, 1903.

Jackson, William. ATTACK IN THE WEST: NAPOLEON'S FIRST CAMPAIGN RE-READ TODAY. London: Eyre & Spottiswoode, 1953.

Juin, Alphonse. LA CAMPAGNE D'ITALIE. Paris: G. Victor, 1962.

Kircheisen, Friedrich Max. NAPOLEONS FELDZUG IN ITALIEN UND OSTERRICH 1796–1797. Munich: G. Muller, 1913.

Lehr, Henry. SITUATION DE L'ARTILLERIE AU LENDEMAIN DU 18 BRUMAIRE. 4 vols. Carnet de la Sabretache, 4th series, 1934.

Richard, Jules. L'ARMEE FRANCAISE EN ITALIE, SES OFFICERS SES GENERAUX, SES REGIMENTS. Paris: E. Denu, 1859.

Rustow, W. DIE ERSTEN FELDZÜGE. NAPOLEON BONAPARTE'S IN ITALIEN UND DEUTSCHLAND 1796 UND 1797. Zurich: Fried. Schulthess, 1867.

Scherer, Général. PRECIS DES OPERATIONS MILITAIRES D'ITALIE, DEPUIS LE 21 VENTOSE JUSQU'AU 7 FLOREAL DE L'AN VII. Paris: Dentu, 1799.

Schwarz, Georg. DIE VORGESCHICHTE DES FELDZUGES VON 1796 IN ITALIEN UND DIE GEFECHTE VOM 10–15 APRIL. Bonn: Seb. Foppen, 1910.

Sorel, Albert. BONAPARTE EN ITALIE. Paris: Flammarion, 1933.

Teil, Joseph du Rome. NAPLES ET LE DIRECTOIRE, ARMISTICES ET TRAITES 1796–1797. Paris: Plon-Nourrit, 1902.

Thiry, Baron. BONAPARTE EN ITALIE 1796–1797. Paris: Berger Levrault, 1973.

Wilkinson, Spencer. THE RISE OF GENERAL BONAPARTE. Oxford: Clarendon Press, 1930.

Egypt and Syria

Bainville, Jacques. BONAPARTE EN EGYPTE. Paris: Flammarion, 1936.

Benoist-Méchin, Jacques. BONAPARTE EN EGYPTE. OU LE REVE INASSOUVI. Lausanne: Clairfontaine, 1966.

Boulay de la Meurthe, Alfred. LE DIRECTOIRE ET L'EXPEDITION D'EGYPTE. Paris: 1885.

Burgogne, Sir John Montagu. A SHORT HISTORY OF THE NAVAL AND MILITARY OPERATIONS IN EGYPT FROM 1798–1802. London: S. Low, Marston, Searle, and Rivington, 1885.

Charles-Roux, François. L'ANGLETERRE ET L'EXPEDITION FRANCAISE EN EGYPTE. Cairo: Imprimerie de l'Institut Français d'Archéologie Orientale Pour La Société Royale de Géographie d'Egypte, 1925.

———. BONAPARTE, GOUVERNEUR D'EGYPTE. Paris: Plon, 1936.

———. LES ORIGINES DE L'EXPEDITION FRANCAISE EN EGYPTE. Paris: Plon-Nourrit, 1910.

Constantini, Pierre. BONAPARTE EN PALESTINE. Paris: d'Halluin, 1967.

———. LA GRANDE PENSEE DE BONAPARTE DE SAINT-JEAN-D'ACRE AU 18 BRUMAIRE. Paris: Baudinière, 1940.

Desenettes, René. HISTOIRE MEDICALE DE L'ARMEE D'ORIENT. Paris: F. Bidot Frères, 1830.

Douin, Georges. LA FLOTTE DE BONAPARTE SUR LES COTES D'EGYPTE. Paris: Imprimerie de l'Institut Français d'Archéologie Orientale pour la Société Royale de Géographie d'Egypte, 1922.

———. LA PREMIERE GUERRE DE SYRIE. 2 vols. Cairo: Société Royale de Géographie d'Egypte, 1931.

Dufriche-Desgenottes, R. N. HISTOIRE MEDICALE DE L'ARMEE D'ORIENT. 2 vols. Paris: 1802.

Elgood, Percival. BONAPARTE'S ADVENTURE IN EGYPT. London: Oxford University Press, 1931.

Fahmy-Bey, Jeanne. BONAPARTE ET L'EGYPTE. Paris: A. Lemerre, 1914.

Gichon, M. "Acre 28th March 1799. Napoleon's First Assault." ARMY QUARTERLY 89 (1964), pp. 100–108.

Goodspeed, D. J. NAPOLEON'S EIGHTY DAYS. Boston: Houghton Mifflin, 1965.

Guitry, Paul. L'ARMEE DE BONAPARTE EN EGYPTE 1798–1799. Paris: Flammarion, 1898.

Hentry, George. AT ABOUKIR AND ACRE: A STORY OF NAPOLEON'S INVASION OF EGYPT. New York: C. Scribner's Sons, 1898.

Herold, J. Christopher. BONAPARTE IN EGYPT. New York: Harper and Row, 1962.

Jonquière, Clément. L'EXPEDITION D'EGYPTE (1798–1801). 5 vols. Paris: Charles Lavauzella, 1899–1907.

Lacroix, Désiré. BONAPARTE EN EGYPTE (1798–1799). Paris: Garnier, 1899.

Lloyd, Christopher. "The Defense of Acre, 1799." HISTORY TODAY (August, 1978), pp. 500–506.

NAPOLEON I. CAMPAGNES D'ITALIE, D'EGYPTE ET DE SYRIE. 3 vols. Paris: Hachette, 1872.

Pastre, Jules. BONAPARTE EN EGYPTE. Paris: Editions des Portigues, 1932.

Peyre, Roger. L'EXPEDITION D'EGYPTE. Paris: Firmin-Didot, 1890.

Reybaud, Louis. HISTOIRE SCIENTIFIQUE ET MILITAIRE DE L'EXPEDITION FRANCAISE D'EGYPTE. 10 vols. Paris: A. J. Denain, 1830–1836.

Richardot, Lieutenant-Colonel. RELATION DE LA CAMPAGNE DE SYRIE. SPECIALEMENT DES SIEGES DE JAFFA ET DE SAINT-JEAN-D'ACRE. Paris: J. Corréard, 1839.

Rigault, Georges. LE GENERAL ABADALLAH MENOU ET LA DERNIERE PHASE DE L'EXPEDITION D'EGYPTE. (1799–1801). Paris: Plon-Nourrit, 1911.

Rose, J. Holland. "The Political Reactions of Bonaparte's Eastern Expedition." ENGLISH HISTORICAL REVIEW (1923).

Rousseau, François. KLEBER ET MENOU EN EGYPTE DEPUIS LE DEPART DE BONAPARTE (AOUT 1799–SEPTEMBRE 1801). Paris: Picard, 1900.

Silvera, Alain. "The Origins of the French Expedition to Egypt in 1798." ISLAMIC QUARTERLY (1977), pp. 21–30.

Thibaudeau, Antoine Comte. HISTOIRE DE LA CAMPAGNE D'EGYPTE SOUS LE REGNE DE NAPOLEON. Paris, Mme. Huzard, 1839.

Thiry, Jean. BONAPARTE EN EGYPTE. Paris: 1973.

Vertray, M. L'ARMEE FRANCAISE EN EGYPTE. Paris: G. Charpentier, 1883.

Winograd, Lee. STRATEGICAL CONSIDERATIONS CONCERNING THE BATTLE OF ACRE. Tel Aviv: Jabotinsky Institute, 1973.

Campaigns 1798–1799

Bonnamy, Général. COUP D'OEIL RAPIDE SUR LES OPERATIONS DE LA CAMPAGNE DE NAPLES. Paris: Dentu, 1799.

Bourke, F. S. "The French Invasion of 1798: A Forgotten Eyewitness." IRISH SWORD (1955), pp. 288–294.

Clausewitz, Carl von. LA CAMPAGNE DE 1799 EN ITALIE ET EN SUISSE. TRADUIT DE L'ALLEMAND PAR A. NIESSEL. Paris: Chapelot, 1906.

Dedon, François. RELATION DETAILLEE DU PASSAGE DE LA LIMAT, EFFECTUE 3 VENDEMIAIRE AN VII. Paris: Didot, 1801.

Dickson, Charles. "The Battle of Vinegar Hill 1798." IRISH SWORD (1954), pp. 293–95.

———. REVOLT IN THE NORTH ANTRIM AND DOWN IN 1798. Dublin, 1960.

———. THE WEXFORD RISING IN 1798: ITS CAUSES AND ITS COURSE. Tralee, 1955.

Escande, Georges. HOCHE EN IRLANDE 1795–1798. Paris: F. Alcan, 1888.

Fontaine, Octave. NOTICE HISTORIQUE DE LA DESCENTE DES FRANCAIS EN IRLANDE AU MOIS DE THERMIDOR AN IV SOUS LES ORDES DU GENERAL HUMERT. Paris: Montardier, 1799.

Froude, J. A. THE ENGLISH IN IRELAND IN THE EIGHTEENTH CENTURY. 3 vols. London: Longmans, Green, 1874.

Gachot, Edouard. LES CAMPAGNES DE 1799, JOURDAN EN ALLE-MAGNE ET BRUNE EN HOLLANDE. Paris: Perrin, n.d.

———. HISTOIRE MILITAIRE DE MASSENA: LA CAMPAGNE D'HELVETIE, 1799. Paris: Perrin, 1904.

———. SOUVAROW EN ITALIE. Paris: Perrin, 1903.

Godechot, Jacques. HISTOIRE DE MALTE. Paris: Presses Universitaires de France, 1951.

———. "Les insurrections militaires sous le Directoire." ANNALES HISTORIQUES DE LA REVOLUTION FRANCAISE, pp. 129–152, 194–221.

Guillon, E. LA FRANCE ET L'IRLANDE PENDANT LA REVOLUTION. Paris: A. Colin, 1888.

Hardman, William. A HISTORY OF MALTA. London: Longmans, Green, 1909.

Hartmann, Otto. DER ANTEIL DER RUSSEN AM FELDZUG VON 1799 IN DER SCHWEIZ. Zurich: A. Munk, 1892.

Hayes-McCoy, Gerard Anthony. IRISH BATTLES. Harlow: Longmans, c. 1969.

Hennequin, Léon. ZURICH: MASSENA EN SUISSE (1799). Paris: Berger-Levrault, 1911.

Heuffer, Herman. "La campagne de 1799: L'armée russe en Suisse." REVUE HISTORIQUE 72 (1900), pp. 324–33.

———. "Fin de la République Napolitaine." REVUE HISTORIQUE, 73/74 (1903–1904).

———. DER KRIEG DES JAHRES 1799 UND DIE ZWEITE KOALITION. 2 vols. Gotha: F. A. Perthes, 1904–1905.

Karl, Archduke of Austria. GESCHICHTE DES FELDZUGES VON 1799 IN DEUTSCHLAND UND IN DER SCHWEITZ MIT KARTEN UND PLANEN. 2 vols. Vienna: A. Strauss, 1819.

Lecky, W. E. H. A HISTORY OF IRELAND IN THE EIGHTEENTH CENTURY. 5 vols. New York: 1893.

Mackesy, Piers. THE STRATEGY OF OVERTHROW 1798–1799. London: Longman, 1974.

Madden, Richard R. THE UNITED IRISHMEN: THEIR LIVES AND TIMES. 4 vols. Dublin, 1857–1860.

Mahon, Patrice. ETUDES SUR LES ARMEES DU DIRECTOIRE JOUBERT A L'ARMEE D'ITALIE, CHAMPIONNET A L'ARMEE DE ROME OCTOBRE 1798—JANVIER 1799. 3 vols. Paris: Chapelot, 1905.

Mangourit, M. A. B. DEFENSE D'ANCONE ET DES DEPARTEMENTS ROMAINS, LE TRONTO, LE MUSONE ET LE METAURO PAR LE GENERAL MONNIER AUX ANNEES VII ET VIII. 2 vols. Paris: C. Pougens, 1802.

Mares, Officer du Génie. PRECIS HISTORIQUE DE LA CAMPAGNE DU GENERAL MASSENA DANS LES GRISSONE ET EN HELVETIE DEPUIS LE PASSAGE DU RHIN JUSQU'A LA PRISE DE POSITION SUR L'ALBIS. Paris: Vatar Jouannet, 1799.

McDowell, R. B. IRELAND IN THE AGE OF IMPERIALISM AND REVOLUTION 1760–1801. New York: Clarendon Press, 1977.

Miliutin, Colonel. GESCHICHTE DES KRIEGS RUSSLANDS MIT FRANKREICH UNTER DER REGIERUNG KAISER PAUL'S I IM JAHRE 1799. Translated by C. Schmitt. 5 vols. Munich: Lindauer, 1856–1858.

Pakenham, Thomas. "Humbert's Raid on Ireland, 1799." HISTORY TODAY (October 1969), p. 688–95.

———. THE YEAR OF LIBERTY: THE STORY OF THE GREAT IRISH REBELLION OF 1798. Englewood Cliffs, NJ: Prentice-Hall, 1970.

Piechowiak, A. B. "The Anglo-Russian Expedition to Holland in 1799." SLAVONIC AND EAST EUROPEAN REVIEW (1962–1963), pp. 182–95.

Rodger, A. B. THE WAR OF THE SECOND COALITION 1798–1801: A STRATEGIC COMMENTARY. Oxford: Clarendon Press, 1964.

Rose, J. H., and Broadley, A. M. DUMOURIEZ AND THE DEFENSE OF ENGLAND AGAINST NAPOLEON. New York: J. Lane, 1909.

Sarrazin, General John. "An Officer's Account of the French Campaign in Ireland in 1798." IRISH SWORD (1955), pp. 110–18.

Shadwell, Lawrence. MOUNTAIN WARFARE ILLUSTRATED BY THE CAMPAIGN OF 1799 IN SWITZERLAND. London: H. S. King, 1875.

Teeling, Charles Hamilton. HISTORY OF THE IRISH REBELLION OF 1798; AND SEQUEL TO THE HISTORY OF THE IRISH REBELLION OF 1798. Shannon: Irish University Press, 1972.

Vingtrineir, E. "UNE INSURRECTION MILITAIRE A ROME." LA REVOLUTION FRANCAISE (1899), pp. 236–45.

Vivenot, Alfred von. KORSSAKOF UND DIE BETEILIGUNG DER RUSSEN AN DER SCHLACHT BEI ZURICH 25 UN 26 SEPTEMBER 1799. Vienna: W. Braumüller, 1869.

Weller, Jac. WELLINGTON IN INDIA. London: Longmans, 1972.
Wertheimer, Eduard, "Erzherzog Carl und die Zweite Coalition bis zum Frieden von Luneville 1798–1801." ARCHIV FUER OESTER-RISCHE GESCHICHTE 67 (1882), 193–52.
Wheeler, H. F. B., and Broadly, A. M. NAPOLEON AND THE INVASION OF ENGLAND. 2 vols. London, New York: J. Lane, 1809.
Wrede, Alphons, von. GESCHICHTE DER K.U.K. WEHRMACHT. 5 vols. Vienna: Seidel, 1898–1905.

Biographies

Amic, Auguste. HISTOIRE DE MASSENA. Paris: Dentu, 1864.
Angeli, Moriz von. ERZHERZOG KARL ALS FELDHEER UND HEERESORGANISATOR. 5 vols. Vienna and Leipzig: Braumüller, 1896–98.
Angers, D., ed. MEMOIRES DE LAREVELLIERE LEPAUX. 3 vols. Paris, 1895.
Anne, T. LE GENERAL OUDINOT, DUC DE REGGIO. Paris: L. Tinterlin, 1863.
Atteridge, Andrew. THE BRAVEST OF THE BRAVE: MICHEL NEY, MARSHAL OF FRANCE, DUKE OF ELCHINGEN, PRINCE OF MOSKOWA 1769–1815. London: Methuen, 1912.
Aubrey, Octave. NAPOLEON. Paris: 1936.
Aubry, Paul. MONGE LE SAVANAT AMI DE NAPOLEON BONA-PARTE 1748–1818. Paris: Gauthier Villars, 1954.
Augustin-Thierry, A. MASSENA. Paris: Albin Michel, 1947.
Austria-Hungary Kriegsarchiv. BIOGRAPHEN K. K. HEERFUEHRER UND GENERALE. 2 vols. Vienna: K. K. Kriegsarchiv, 1888.
Babie, F., and L. Beaumont. GALERIE MILITAIRE OU NOTICE HISTORIQUE SUR LES GENERAUX EN CHEF, GENERAUX DE DIVISION, ETC.; VICE-AMIRAUX, CONTRE-AMIRAUX ETC, QUI ONT COMMANDE LES ARMEES FRANCAISES DEPUIS LE COMMENCEMENT DE LA REVOLUTION JUSQU'A L'AN XIII. 5 vols. Paris: Barba, 1805.
Bainville, Jacques. NAPOLEON. Paris, 1931.
Barault-Roulon, C. H. LE MARECHAL SUCHET, DUC D'AL-BUFERA. Paris: J. Corréard, 1854.
Barrucand, Victor. LA VIE VERITABLE DU CITOYEN JEAN ROSSIGNOL, VAINQUER DE LA BASTILLE ET GENERAL EN CHEF DES ARMEES DE LA REPUBLIQUE DANS LA GUERRE DE VENDEE (1759–1802). Paris: Plon-Nourrit, 1896.
Bartel, Paul. LA JEUNESSE INEDITE DE NAPOLEON. 1954.
———. LA JEUNESSE INEDITE DE NAPOLEON, D'APRES DE NOMBREUX DOCUMENTS. Paris: Amiot-Dumont, 1954.

Barton, Sir Dunbar Plunket. THE AMAZING CAREER OF BERNADOTTE (1763–1844). Boston: Houghton, 1930.

————. BERNADOTTE AND NAPOLEON 1763–1810. London: J. Murray, 1921.

Barton, Dunbar. BERNADOTTE: THE FIRST PHASE 1763–1799. London: J. Murray, 1914.

Beauchamp, Alphonse de. VIE POLITIQUE, MILITAIRE ET PRIVEE DU GENERAL MOREAU. Paris: Le Prieur, 1814.

Béchu, Marcel. MURAT: CAVALIER, MARECHAL DE FRANCE, PRINCE ET ROI. Paris: Hachette, 1934.

Bédoyère, Georges J. L. M. LE MARECHAL NEY. Paris: Calmann-Lévy, 1902.

Begue, S. "Un autre bicentenaire Celii du Marechal Lannes," REVUE HISTORIQUE DE L'ARMÉE, no. 3 (1969), p. 127–34.

Besancenet, Alfred de. UN OFFICIER ROYALISTE AU SERVICE DE LA REPUBLIQUE D'APRES LES LETTERS INEDITES DU GENERAL DE DOMMARTIN 1786 A 1799. Paris: Librairie général, 1876.

Bessières, Albert. LE BOYARD DE LA GRANDE ARMEE. LE MARECHAL BESSIERES, DUC D'ISTRIE (1768–1813). Paris: Charles-Lavauzelle, 1941.

Biron, Armand Louis de Gontaut. UN DUC ET PAIR AU SERVICE DE LA REVOLUTION. LE DUC DE LAUZUNC, GENERAL BIRON (1791–1792). CORRESPONDANCE INTIME. Paris: Perrin, 1906.

Blácam, Aodh. THE LIFE STORY OF WOLFE TONE. Dublin: Talbot Press, 1935.

Blease, W. L. SUVOROF. London: Constable, 1920.

Bleibtreau, Karl. MARSCHALL SOULT. NAPOLEONS GROSSTER SCHULER. Berlin: A. Schall, 1902.

Blocqueville, Marquis de. LE MARECHAL DAVOUT. 4 vols. Paris: Didier, 1879–1880.

Blythe, Legette. MARSHAL NEY: A DUAL LIFE. New York: Stackpole, 1937.

Boguslawski, A. DAS LEBEN DES GENERALS DUMOURIEZ. Berlin: F. Luckhardt, 1879.

Bompar, Victor. LE GENERAL FOY (1775–1825). Paris: Editions de la Plume d'oie, 1925.

Bonnal de Ganges, Edmond. CARNOT D'APRES LES ARCHIVES NATIONALES, LE DEPOT DE LA GUERRE ET LES SEANCES DE LA CONVENTION. Paris: Dentus, 1888.

————. HISTOIRE DE DESAIX: ARMEE DU RHIN, EXPEDITION D'ORIENT, MARENGO. Paris: Denue, Dumaine, 1881.

————. LA VIE MILITAIRE DU MARECHAL NEY. 2 vols. Paris: Chapelot, 1910–1911.

Bonnechose, François. LAZARE HOCHE, GENERAL-EN-CHEF DES ARMEES DE LA MOSELLE, D'ITALIE, DES COTES DE CHERBOURG, DE BREST ET DE L'OCEAN, DE SAMBRE-ET-MEUSE ET DU RHIN, SOUS LA CONVENTION ET LE DIRECTOIRE, 1793–1797. Paris: Hachette, 1880.

Botidoux, M. de. ESQUISSE DE LA CARRIERE MILITAIRE DE FRANCOIS-CHRISTOPHE DE KELLERMANN, DUC DE VALMY, PAIR ET MARECHAL DE FRANCE. Paris: J.-M. Ebhart, 1817.

Bouchard, Georges. UN ORGANISATEUR DE LA VICTOIRE: PRIEUR DE LA COTE-D'OR MEMBRE DU COMITE DE SALUT PUBLIC. Paris: Claureu, 1946.

Browning, Oscar. THE BOYHOOD AND YOUTH OF NAPOLEON. London and New York: John Lane, 1906.

Burne, Alfred H. THE NOBLE DUKE OF YORK; THE MILITARY LIFE OF FREDERICK DUKE OF YORK AND ALBANY. London and New York: Staples Press, 1949.

Butterfield, Herbert. NAPOLEON. London: Gerald Duckworth, 1939.

Calohar, F. NOTICE HISTORIQUE SUR LA TOUR-D'AUVERGRE CORRET, PREMIER GRENADIER DE FRANCE. Paris: Gaultier-Laguionie, 1841.

Carré, Henri. LE GRAND CARNOT, 1753–1823. Paris: La Table Ronde, 1947.

Carro, Antoine. SANTERRE, GENERAL DE LA REPUBLIQUE FRANCAISE: SA VIE POLITIQUE ET PRIVEE. N.p., n.d.

Castelot, André. BONAPARTE. 2 vols. Paris: Perrin, 1967–1968.

Charavay, Etienne. LE GENERAL LAFAYETTE 1757–1834. Paris: Au siège de la société, 1898.

Charavay, Jacques. LES GENERAUX MORTS POUR LA PATRIE, 1792–1871. Paris: Société de l'histoire de la Révolution Française, 1893.

Chardigny, Louis. LES MARECHAUX DE NAPOLEON. Paris: Flammarion, 1946.

Châteauneuf, A. H. LE GENERAL LAFAYETTE. Paris: Dumont, 1831.

———. HISTOIRE DES GENERAUX FRANCAIS DEPUIS 1792 JUSQU'A NOS JOURS. 4 vols. Paris: P. Didot l'âiné, 1810–1812.

———. HISTOIRE DES GRANDS CAPITAINES DE LA FRANCE PENDANT LA GUERRE DE LA LIBERTE (DE 1792 A 1802). 2 vols. Paris: Abel Lance, 1820.

———. HISTOIRE DU GENERAL CHAMPIONNET, PREMIER CONQUERANT DE NAPLES. Paris: Chez l'éditeur, 1808.

———. HISTOIRE DU GENERAL MOREAU. Paris: L.-G. Michaud, 1814.

Chavanon, Jules. JOACHIM MURAT (1767–1815). Paris: Hachette, 1905.

244 • Bibliography

Chénier, Louis. HISTOIRE DE LA VIE POLITIQUE, MILITAIRE ET ADMINISTRATIVE DU MARECHAL DAVOUT, DUC D'AUER-STAEDT, PRINCE D'ECKMUHL. 2 vols. Paris: Casse, Marchal, 1866.

Chénier, L.-J.-G. ELOGE HISTORIQUE DE MARECHAL MONCEY, DUC DE CONEGLIANO. Paris: J. Dumaine, 1848.

Choppin, H. LE GENERAL DE DIVISION KELLERMANN ANS VII–XI. Paris: Berger Levrault, 1898.

Chuquet, Arthur. DUGOMMIER, 1738–1794. Paris: Fontemoing, 1904.

———. DUMOURIEZ. Paris: Hachette, 1914.

———. LE GENERAL DAGOBERT (1736–1794). L'ARMEE SOUS L'ANCIEN REGIME ET SOUS LA REVOLUTION. Paris: A. Fontemoing, 1913.

———. LA JEUNESSE DE NAPOLEON. 3 vols. Paris: Colin, 1897–1899.

Colin, Jean. L'EDUCATION MILITAIRE DE NAPOLEON. Paris: R. Chapelot, 1900.

Conegliano, Charles. LE MARECHAL MONCEY, DUC DE CONEG-LIANO 1754–1842. Paris: Calmann-Levy, 1902.

Criste, Oskar. ERZHERZOG CARL VON OESTERREICH. 3 vols. Vienna and Leipzig: Braumüller, 1912.

Cronin, Vincent. NAPOLEON BONAPARTE: AN INTIMATE BIOG-RAPHY. New York: William Morrow, 1972.

Cuneo d'Ornano, Ernest. HOCHE. 2 vols. Paris: Baudouin, 1892.

Curits, Eugene Newton. SAINT-JUST, COLLEAGUE OF ROBES-PIERRE. New York: Columbia University Press, 1935.

Dard, Emile. LE COMTE DE NARBONNE. Paris: Plon, 1943.

———. UN CONFIDENT DE L'EMPEREUR; LE COMTE DE NAR-BONNE. Paris: Plon, 1943.

Debidour, Antonin. LE GENERAL FABVIER: SA VIE MILITAIRE ET POLITIQUE. Paris: Plon-Nourrit, 1904.

Delderfield, R. F. NAPOLEON'S MARSHALS. Philadelphia: Chilton Books, 1966.

Deroul de, Paul. LE PREMIER GRENADIER DE FRANCE: LA TOUR D'AUVERGNE. Paris: Hurtrel, 1886.

Derrecagaix, Victor. LE MARECHAL BERTHIER, PRINCE DE WA-GRAM ET DE NEUCHATEL. Paris: Chapelot, 1904.

Despreaux, Frignet. JULES CHARLES, LE MARECHAL MORTIER, DUC DE TREVISE. 3 vols. Paris: Berger-Levrault, 1913–1920.

———. LE MARECHAL MORTIER, DUC DE TREVISE. Paris: Berger-Levrault, 1913–1914.

Desprez, Claude. DESAIX. Paris: L. Baudouin, 1884.

———. LAZARE HOCHE. Paris: Chapelot, 1887.

Dible, J. Henry. NAPOLEON'S SURGEON. London: 1970.

Donntenville, J. LE GENERAL MOREAU. Paris: Delagrave, 1899.

Dourille, Henri. HISTOIRE DE CHAMPIONNET. Valence: H. Dourille, 1838.

Driault, E. LA VRAIE FIGURE DE NAPOLEON. Paris: 1928.

Dubouloz-Dupas, F., and A. Folliet. LE GENERAL DUPAS ITALIE-EGYPTE-GRANDE-ARMEE (1792–1813). Paris: Chapelot, 1899.

Du Casse, A. LE GENERAL VANDAMME. 2 vols. Paris: Didier, 1870.

Duchesne de Gillevoisin, C. A. G. LE MARECHAL MONCEY (1754–1842). Paris: Calmann Lévy, 1902.

Du Motey, Henry Renault. UN HEROS DE LA GRANDE ARMEE: JEAN GASPARD HULOT DE COLLART, OFFICER D'ARTILLERIE (1780–1854). Paris: A. Picard, 1911.

Dunn-Pattison, R. P. NAPOLEON'S MARSHALS. Boston: Little, Brown & Co., 1909.

Dupre, Huntley. LAZARE CARNOT, REPUBLICAN PATRIOT. Oxford, OH: Mississippi Valley Press, 1940.

Duteil, Joseph. NAPOLEON BONAPARTE, L'ECOLE D'ARTILLERIE D'AUXONNE ET LE SIEGE DE TOULON. Paris: Picard, 1897.

——. UNE FAMILLE MILITAIRE AU XVIIIe SIECLE. Paris: Picard, 1896.

Dutemple, Edmond. VIE DU GENERAL HOCHE. Paris: Abyle, 1888.

Ellery, E. BRISSOT DE WARVILLE. Boston, 1905.

Ernouf, Alfred. LE GENERAL KLEBER: MAYENCE ET VENDEE, ALLEMAGNE, EXPEDITION D'EGYPTE. Paris: Didier, 1870.

——. MARET DUC DE BASSANO. Paris, 1884.

Fabre, Marc. HOCHE, L'ENFANT DE LA VICTOIRE 1768–1797. Paris: Hachette, 1947.

Fage, René. LE GENERAL SOUHAM. Paris: Picard, 1897.

Fazi du Bayet, Comte de. LES GENERAUX AUBERT DU BAYET, CARRA SAINT-CYR, ET CHARPENTIER: CORRESPONDANCES ET NOTICES BIOGRAPHIQUES, 1757–1834. Paris: Champion, 1902.

Fisher, Herbert Albert Laurens. NAPOLEON. New York: Henry Holt, 1913.

Forrest, Denys. TIGER OF MYSORE: THE LIFE AND DEATH OF TIPU SULTAN. London: Chatto & Windus, 1970.

Fortescue, Sir John William. WELLINGTON. London: Williams and Norgate, 1925.

Foster, John. NAPOLEON'S MARSHALS: THE LIFE OF MARSHAL NEY. New York: W. Morrow, 1968.

Fournier, Auguste. NAPOLEON I: EINE BIOGRAPHIE. 3 vols. Vienna: 1904–1906.

Friant, Comte. VIE MILITAIRE DU LIEUTENANT-GENERAL, COMTE FRIANT. Paris: Dentu, 1857.

Furber, Holden. HENRY DUNDAS, FIRST VISCOUNT MELVILLE. Oxford: 1931.

Gaffarel, Paul. PRIEUR DE LA COTE-D'OR. DIJON. Noury: 1900.

Gallaher, John. THE IRON MARSHAL: A BIOGRAPHY OF LOUIS N. DAVOUT. Carbondale: Southern Illinois University Press, 1976.

Garnier, Jean Paul. NEY, LE BRAVE DES BRAVES. Paris: Amiot Dumont, 1955.

Gautherot, Gustave. UN GENTILHOMME DE GRAND CHEMIN, LE MARECHAL DE BOURMONT (1733–1846) D'APRES SES PAPIERS INEDITS. Paris: Presses Universitaires de France, 1926.

Gay de Vernon, Jean. VIE DU MARECHAL GOUVION SAINT-CYR. Paris: Firmin-Didot, 1856.

Gershoy, Leo. BERTRAND BARERE: A RELUCTANT TERRORIST. Princeton: Princeton University Press, 1962.

Girod de l'Ain, Maurice. BERNADOTTE, CHEF DE GUERRE ET CHEF D'ETAT. Paris: Perrin, 1968.

————. LE GENERAL DROUOT (1774–1847). Paris: Berger-Levrault, 1890.

————. GRANDS ARTILLEURS: DROUOT, SENARMONT, EBLE. Paris: Berger-Levrault, 1895.

————. VIE MILITAIRE DU GENERAL FOY. Paris: Plon-Nourrit, 1900.

Glover, Michael. WELLINGTON AS MILITARY COMMANDER. London: Batsford, 1968.

Goepp, Edovard. LES GRANDS HOMMES DE LA FRANCE. HOMMES DE GUERRE. QUATRIEME SERIE . . . LA TOUR D'AUVERGNE. Paris: P. Duerocq, 1884.

Gosselin, Louis. MONSIEUR DE CHARETTE LE ROI DE VENDEE. Paris: Hachette, 1924.

Graux, Lucien. LE MARECHAL DE BEURNONVILLE. Paris: Champion, 1929.

Griffiths, Arthur. FRENCH REVOLUTIONARY GENERALS. London: Chapman and Hall, 1891.

Gross-Hoffinger, A.-J. Erzherzog. CARL VON OESTERREICH UND DIE KRIEG VON 1792–1815. Leipzig: C.-B. Lorck, 1847.

Guillon, E. LES GENERAUX DE LA REPUBLIQUE. Paris: Librairie des Publications Populaires, 1884.

Hauterive, Ernest d'. LE GENERAL DUMAS, UN SOLDAT DE LA REVOLUTION (1762–1807). Paris: Ollendorff, 1897.

Haye, Alexandre de. DESAIX: ETUDE POLITIQUE ET MILITAIRE. SA CARRIERE—SES PREMIERS ARMES—NOS GUERRES SUR LE RHIN AVANT LA REVOLUTION. Paris: J. Leroy, 1909.

Headley, Joël. NAPOLEON AND HIS MARSHALS. 2 vols. New York: Scribner, 1855.

Heim, Maurice. LE NESTOR DES ARMEES FRANCAISES, KELLERMANN, DUC DE VALMY. Paris: Nouvelle-Edition, 1949.

Heitz, Louis. LE GENERAL SALME 1766–1811; ETUDE HISTORIQUE. Paris: Charles-Lavauzelle, 1895.

Hennet, Léon. LE MARECHAL DAVOUT, DUC D'AUERSTAEDT, PRINCE D'ECKMUHL. Paris: Baudouin, 1885.

Henry, René. UN GRAND TOURANGEAX, LE BARON NICOLAS HEURTELOUP, CHIRURGIEN EN CHEF DES ARMEES DE LA REVOLUTION ET DE L'EMPIRE. Paris: Centre Medical d'études et de Recherches, 1957.

Herlaut, Auguste. LE COLONEL BOUCHETTE, MINISTRE DE LA GUERRE EN L'AN II. 2 vols. Paris: C. Poisson, 1946.

Höjer, Torwald. BERNADOTTE, MARECHAL DE FRANCE, TRADUIT DU SUEDOIS PAR LUCIEN MAURY. Paris: Plon, 1943.

Homan, G. D. "Jean Frances Reubell." FRENCH HISTORICAL STUDIES I, 1960. pp. 416–435.

Hourtoulle, F. G. DAVOUT LE TERRIBLE. Paris: Maloine S. A. Editeur, 1975.

———. LE GENERAL, COMTE CHARLES LASALLE, 1775–1809. Paris: 1970.

Jackson, Stuart W. LA FAYETTE, A BIBLIOGRAPHY. New York: W. E. Rudge, 1930.

Jacoby, J. SOUVAROV 1730–1800. Paris: 1935.

Joly, Charles. LE MARECHAL DAVOUT, PRINCE D'ECKMÜHL. Auxerre: Gustave Perriquet, 1864.

Jomini, Henri. LIFE OF NAPOLEON. 4 vols. New York: Nostrand, 1854. 4 vols.

———, ed. VIE POLITIQUE ET MILITAIRE DE NAPOLEON, RACONTEE PAR LUI-MEME. 4 vols. Paris: Anselin, 1827.

Jung, Théodore. L'ARMEE ET LA REVOLUTION, DUBOIS-CRANCE (EDMOND-ALEXIS-LOUIS) MOUSQUETAIRE, CONSTITUTANT, CONVENTIONNEL, GENERAL DE DIVISION, MINISTRE DE LA GUERRE 1747–1814. 2 vols. Paris: Charpentier, 1884.

Khan, Mohibbul Hasan. HISTORY OF TIPU SULTAN. Calcutta, 1951.

Kircheisen, Friedrich Max. NAPOLEON I SEIN LEBEN UND SEINE ZEIT. 9 vols. Munich, 1911–1934.

Klippel, G. H. DAS LEBEN DES GENERALS VON SCHARNHORST. Leipzig, 3 vols. 1869–1871.

La Barre de Raillicourt, Dominique. GENERAUX ET AMIRAUX DE LA REVOLUTION ET DE L'EMPIRE. Paris: Chez l'Auteur, 1966.

La Bédoyère, Georges Comte de. LE MARECHAL NEY. Paris: Calmann-Lévy, 1902.

Lacroix, Désiré. LES MARECHAUX DE NAPOLEON. Paris: Garnier, 1896.

Lannes, Charles. LE MARECHAL LANNES, DUC DE MONTE-BELLO, PRINCE, SOUVERAIN DE SIEVERS EN POLOGNE. RESUME DE SA VIE. Tours: A. Mame, 1900.

Launay, Louis de. MONGE, FONDATEUR DE L'ECOLE POLYTECHNIQUE. Paris: 1933.

Laverne, P. de. HISTOIRE DU FELD-MARECHAL SOUVAROF LIEE A CELLE DE SON TEMPS. Paris: Desenne, 1809.

Le Barbier, Louis. LE GENERAL DE LA HORIE 1760–1812. Paris: Dujarric, 1904.

Le Claire, Théodore. MEMOIRE DU GENERAL LECLAIRE. Paris: Chaelot, 1904.

Le Corbeiller, Armand. CHARLES SEPHER, SUISSE DE SAINT-EUSTACHE ET GENERAL DE DIVISION. Paris: Firmin-Didot, 1930.

Lecourbe, Claude. LE GENERAL LECOURBE D'APRES SES ARCHIVES, SA CORRESPONDANCE ET AUTRES DOCUMENTS. Paris: Charles-Lavauzelle, 1895.

Lefebvre, G. "Sur Danton." ANNALES HISTORIQUES DE LA REVOLUTION FRANCAISE 9 (1932), pp. 385–424, 484–500.

Lehmann, M. SCHARNHORST. 2 vols. Leipzig: 1886–1887.

Leproux, Marc. UN GRAND FRANCAIS: LE GENERAL DUPONT 1765–1840. Paris: Berger-Levrault, 1934.

Lloyd, Ernest Marsh. VAUBAN, MONTALEMBERT, CARNOT: ENGINEER STUDIES. London: Chapman and Hall, 1887.

Longford, Elizabeth. WELLINGTON THE YEARS OF THE SWORD. New York: Harper and Row, 1969.

Longworth, Philip. THE ART OF VICTORY: THE LIFE AND ACHIEVEMENTS OF FIELD-MARSHAL SUVOROV 1729–1800. New York: Henry Holt, 1966.

Lort de Sérignan, Arthur. NAPOLEON ET LES GRANDS GENERAUX DE LA REVOLUTION ET DE L'EMPIRE. Paris, 1914.

Loth, David. THE PEOPLE'S GENERAL: THE PERSONAL STORY OF LAFAYETTE. New York: Scribner, 1951.

Lottin, Anatole. UN CHEF D'ETAT-MAJOR SOUS LA REVOLUTION: LE GENERAL BILLY, D'APRES SA CORRESPONDANCE ET SES PAPIERS. Paris: Berger-Levrault, 1901.

Lucas-Dubreton, Jean. JEAN MURAT. Paris: Fayard, 1944.

———. KLEBER 1753–1800. Paris: P. Hartmann, 1937.

———. LE MARECHAL NEY 1769–1815. Paris: Fayard, 1941.

MacDermot, Frank. THEOBOLD WOLFE TONE: A BIOGRAPHICAL STUDY. London: Macmillan, 1939.

Macdonell, Archibald. NAPOLEON AND HIS MARSHALS. New York: Macmillan, 1934.

Madden, Richard. THE UNITED IRISHMEN, THEIR LIVES AND TIMES. 4 vols. Dublin, 1857–1860.

Margerand, J. LES AIDES DE CAMP DE BONAPARTE 1793–1804. Paris: P. Boussuet, 1831.

Marion, Général. MEMOIRE SUR LE LIEUTENANT-GENERAL D'ARTILLERIE ALEXANDRE DE SENARMONT. Paris: J. Correard, 1846.

Markham, Felix. NAPOLEON. New York: New American Library, 1963.

Marmottan, Paul. LE GENERAL FROMENTNET L'ARMEE DU NORD (1792–1794). Paris: E. Dubois, 1891.

Marshall-Cornwall, James. MARSHAL MASSENA. London and New York: Oxford University Press, 1965.

Martel, Tandréde. UN GALLANT CHEVALIER, LE GENERAL LASALLE (1775–1809). Paris: A. Lemerre, 1929.

Martha-Beker, Felix. LE GENERAL DESAIX ETUDE HISTORIQUE. Paris: Didier, 1852.

Martha-Beker, F., and Comte de Mons. ETUDES HISTORIQUES SUR LE GENERAL DESAIX. Clermont-Ferrand: Perol, 1852.

Martin de Condé, Henry. UNE SILHOUETTE MILITAIRE DE L'EPOQUE REVOLUTIONNAIRE: L'ADJUTANT-GENERAL JEAN-JACQUES LANDRIEUX. Bilancourt: Mercier, 1906.

Masson, Frédéric. NAPOLEON DANS SA JEUNESSE, 1769–1793. Paris: A. Michel, 1922.

———. NAPOLEON ET SA FAMILLE. 13 vols. Paris, 1897–1919.

Masson, F., and G. Biagi. NAPOLEON INCONNU. Paris, 1895.

Mathiez, Albert. AUTEUR DE DANTON. Paris, 1926.

———. DANTON ET LA PAIX. Paris, 1919.

Mathiot, Charles. POUR VAINCRE; VIE, OPINIONS ET PENSEES DE LAZARE CARNOT, L'ORGANISATEUR DE LA VICTOIRE, SUIVIES DE QUELQUES ANECDOTES. Paris: Flammarion, 1916.

Mathrey, Albert. "Danton; L'histoire et la légende." ANNALES HISTORIQUE DE LA REVOLUTION FRANCAISE 4 (1927), pp. 417–61.

Maze, H. LES GENERAUX DE LA REPUBLIQUE. Paris: Libraire des publications populaires, 1887.

Maze, Hippolyte. LE GENERAL F. MARCEAU, SA VIE, SA CORRESPONDANCE D'APRES DES DOCUMENTS INEDITS. Paris: H. E. Martin, 1889.

Mendels, P. H. W. DAENDELS 1762–1807. The Hague, 1890.

Michaux, M. "La gloire de Hoche." REVUE HISTORIQUE DE L'ARMEE, no. 2 (1968), pp. 85–92.

Mignard, Thomas. BIOGRAPHIE DU GENERAL BARON TESTOT-FERRY, VETERAN DES ARMEES REPUBLICANES ET IMPERI-ALES ET EXPOSE DES EVENEMENTS MILITAIRES DE 1792 A 1815. Paris: Aubry, 1859.

Mirhl, Marcel. NAPOLEON D'AJACCIO 1947. Paris: Editions Siboney, 1947.

Monchanin, Adolphe. DUMOURIEZ 1739–1823. Paris: Ollendorff, n.d.

Montégut, E. LE MARECHAL DAVOUT, SON CARACTERE ET SON GENIE. Paris: A. Quantin, 1882.

Montier, Armand. ROBERT LINDET . . . MEMBRE DU COMITE DE SALUT PUBLIC . . . Paris: Alcan, 1889.

Moreel, Léon. LE MARECHAL MORTIER, DUC DE TREVISE, 1768–1835. Paris: Editions internationales, 1957.

Morton, John B. MARSHAL NEY. London: A. Barker, 1958.

Nabonne, Bernard. BERNADOTTE. Paris: A. Michel, 1964.

Nollet-Fabert, Jules. LE GENERAL RICHEPANSE. Nancy: 1853.

————. HISTOIRE DE NICOLAS CHARLES OUDINOT, MARECHAL DE L'EMPIRE ET DUC DE REGGIO BAR-LE-DUC. Rolinil, 1850.

NOUVELLE BIOGRAPHIE GENERALE DEPUIS LE TEMPS LES PLUS RECULES JUSQU'A NOS JOURS AVEC LES RENSEIGNEMENTS BIBLIOGRAPHIQUES ET L'INDICATION DES SOURCES A CONSULTER. 46 vols. Paris: Firmin-Didot, 1855–1866.

Ollivier, Albert. SAINT-JUST ET LA FORCE DES CHOSES. Paris: Gallimard, 1954.

Osipov, K. ALEXANDER SUVOROV. New York: Hutchinson, 1941.

Pajol, Général le Comte, Charles. KLEBER, SA VIE ET SA CORRESPONDANCE. Paris: Firmin-Didot, 1877.

————. PAJOL, GENERAL EN CHEF. 3 vols. Paris: Firmin-Didot, 1874.

Paoli, F. A. "Le Général Desaix." REVUE HISTORIQUE DE L'ARMÉE no. 2 (1968), pp. 75–83.

Paret, Peter. YORK AND THE ERA OF PRUSSIAN REFORM 1807–1815. Princeton: Princeton University Press, 1966.

Parfait, Noël. LE GENERAL MARCEAU. Paris: Lévy, 1892.

Pertz, G. H., and H. Delbrück. DAS LEBEN DES FELD-MARSCHALLS GRAFEN NEITHARDT VON GNEISENAEU. 5 vols. Berlin: 1864–1880.

Petitfrère, Claude. LE GENERAL DUPUY ET SA CORRESPONDANCE (1792–1798). Paris: Bibliothèque d'histoire révolutionnaire, 1962.

Philebert, Général. LE GENERAL LECOURBE. Paris: Lavauzelle, 1895.

Picard, Ernest. BONAPARTE ET MOREAU L'ENTENTE INITIALE, LES PREMIERS DISSENTIMENTS, LA RUPTURE. Paris: Plon-Nourrit, 1905.

Picaud, A. Carnot. L'ORGANISATEUR DE LA VICTOIRE 1792–1815. Paris: Charavay Frères 1885.

Pionsot, Edmond. LE MARECHAL NEY D'APRES LES DOCUMENTS AUTHENTIQUES. Paris: A. Le Chevalier, 1869.

Pouget de Saint-André, H. LE GENERAL DUMOURIEZ (1739–1823) D'APRES DES DOCUMENTS INEDITS. Paris: Perrin, 1914.

Pratt, Fletcher. THE ROAD TO EMPIRE: THE LIFE AND TIMES OF BONAPARTE, THE GENERAL 1795–1799. New York: Doubleday, Doran, 1939.

Rabel, André. LE MARECHAL BESSIERS, DUC D'ISTRIE. Paris: Calmann-Lévy, 1903.

Reichel, Daniel. DAVOUT ET L'ART DE LA GUERRE. Neuchatel and Paris: Delachaux et Niestlé, 1975.

————. LE MARECHAL DAVOUT, DUC DE AUERSTAEDT, PRINCE D'ECKMUHL (1770–1823). Neuchatel and Paris: Delachout et Niestlé, 1975.

Reinhard, Marcel. LE GRAND CARNOT. 2 vols. Paris: Hachette, 1950.

Rivollet, Georges. GENERAL DE BATAILLE CHARLES ANTOINE LOUIS MORAND, COMTE DE L'EMPIRE (1771–1835). GENERAUX FRIANT ET GUDIN DU 3e CORPS DE LA GRANDE ARMEE. Paris: J. Peyronnet, 1963.

Rose, John Holland. LIFE OF NAPOLEON I. 2 vols. London: Macmillan, 1901–1902.

————. LIFE OF WILLIAM PITT. London: Bell, 1923.

————. A SHORT LIFE OF WILLIAM PITT. London: Bell, 1925.

Rousseau, François. LA CARRIERE DU MARECHAL SUCHET, DUC D'ALBUFERA. DOCUMENTS INÉDITS. Paris: Firmin-Didot, 1898.

Rousselin, A. VIE DE LAZARE HOCHE, GENERAL DES ARMEES DE LA REPUBLIQUE FRANCAISE. 2 vols. Paris: F. Buisson, 1798.

Rousselin, D. DE SAINT ALBIN CHAMPIONNET, GENERAL DES ARMEES DE LA REPUBLIQUE FRANCAISE. Paris: Poulet Malassis et de Broise, 1860.

Saint-Albin, Alexandre, Comte de. CHAMPIONNET, GENERAL DES ARMEES DE LA REPUBLIQUE FRANCAISE, OU LES CAMPAGNES DE HOLLANDE, DE ROME ET DE NAPLES. Paris: Poulet-Malaissis and De Broise, 1860.

————. VIE DE LAZARE HOCHE, GENERAL DES ARMEES DE LA REPUBLIQUE FRANCAISE, COMMANDANT EN CHEF DE CELLES DE LA MOSELLE ET DU RHIN, DES COTES DE CHERBOURG, DE BREST, DE L'OCEAN, D'IRLANDE, DE SAMBRE ET MEUSE ET DU RHIN REUNIES. Paris: Brisson, 1800.

Sainte-Chapelle, de. LES MINISTRES DE LA GUERRE PENDANT LA REVOLUTION FRANCAISE. Paris: Anselin, 1837.

Saint-Marc, Pierre. LE MARECHAL MARMONT, DUC DE RAGUSE 1774–1852. Paris: Fayard, 1957.

Sauzet, Armand. DESAIX LE "SULTANT JUSTE." Paris: Hachette, 1954.

Savant, Jean. NAPOLEON A AUXONNE. Paris: Nouvelles éditions latines, 1946.

Scheidawind, F. J. A. CARL ERZHERZOG VON OESTERREICH UND DIE OESTERREICHISCHE ARMEE UNTER IHM. 2 vols. Bamberg: Litterarisch-artistisches Institut, 1840.

Sedgwick, Henry D. LAFAYETTE. Indianapolis: Bobbs-Merrill, 1928.

Six, Georges. DICTIONAIRE BIOGRAPHIQUE DES GENERAUX ET ADMIRAUX FRANCAIS DE LA REVOLUTION ET DE L'EMPIRE (1792–1814). 2 vols. Paris: Librairie historique et nobiliaire Georges Saffroy, éditeur, 1937.

————. LES GENERAUX DE LA REVOLUTION ET DE L'EMPIRE. Paris: Bordas, 1947.

Smitt, F. VON SUWOROWS LEBEN UND HEERESZUGE. Leipzig, 1833.

Soubiran, André. LE BARON LARREY, CHIRURGIEN DE NAPOLEON. Paris: Fayard, 1966.

Southey, Robert. THE BRITISH ADMIRALS. 5 vols. London: Longman, 1833–48.

Tarlé, A. MURAT. Paris: Chapelot, 1914.

Thompson, J. M. NAPOLEON BONAPARTE, HIS RISE AND FALL. London: Oxford University Press, 1952.

Thoumas, Charles. LE GENERAL CURELY: ITINERAIRE D'UN CAVALIER LEGER DE LA GRANDE ARMEE (1793–1815). Paris: Berger-Levrault, 1887.

————. LE GENERAL, LE MARECHAL LANNES. Paris: Calmann-Lévy, 1891.

————. LES GRANDS CAVALIERS DU PREMIER EMPIRE: NOTICES BIOGRAPHIQUES. 2 vols. Paris: Berger-Levrault, 1890–1892.

Tierso, J. ROUGET DE L'ISLE. SON OEUVRE. Paris: Delagrave, 1892.

Titeux, Eugène. LE GENERAL DUPONT; UNE ERREUR HISTORIQUE. 3 vols. Puteaux-sur-seine: Prieur et Dubois, 1903.

Tonselli, Jean. NOTICE BIOGRAPHIQUE SUR MASSENA. Nice: Gautheir, 1869.

Tourly, Victor. HISTOIRE DES HEROS ET MARTYRS DE LA LIBERTE. 5 vols. Paris: 1849.

Triaire, Paul. DOMINIQUE LARREY ET LES CAMPAGNES DE LA REVOLUTION ET DE L'EMPIRE 1786–1842. Tours: Mame, 1902.

Tuetey, Louis. SERURIER (1742–1819). Paris: Berger-Levrault, 1899.

Vachée, Commandant. ETUDE DU CARACTERE MILITAIRE DU MARECHAL DAVOUT. Paris: Berger-Levrault, 1907.

Valentine, René. LE MARECHAL JOURDAN (1762–1833). Paris: Charles-Lavauzelle, 1957.

————. LE MARECHAL MASSENA (1758–1817). Paris: Charles-Lavauzelle, 1960.

Vermeil de Conchard, Paul. ETUDES HISTORIQUES SUR LE MARECHAL BRUNE D'APRES DES DOCUMENTS ANCIENS, NOUVEAUX ET INEDITS. Paris: Boussus, 1918.

Victor, François. VICTOR (CLAUDE-VICTOR PERRIN), DUC DE BELLUNE. Paris: Dumaine, 1847.

Vigier, Joseph. DAVOUT: MARECHAL D'EMPIRE, DUC D'AUER-STAEDT, PRINCE D'ECKMUHL. 2 vols. Paris: Paul Ollendorff, 1898.

Villard, Marius. NOUVELLE ETUDE CRITIQUE SUR CHAMPI-ONNET. Valence: Jules Céas, 1904.

Vox, Maximilien. NAPOLEON. Paris, 1959.

Walter, G. ROBESPIERRE. 2 vols. Paris, 1936–1938.

Warshauer, R. STUDIEN ZUR ENTWICKLUNG DER GEDANKEN LAZARE CARNOTS UBER KRIEGSFUHRUNG. Berlin: Historische Abhandlungen No. 7, 1937.

Watson, S. J. BY COMMAND OF THE EMPEROR: A LIFE OF MARSHAL BERTHIER. London: Bodley Head, 1957.

————. CARNOT. London: Bodley Head, 1954.

Welschinger, H. LE MARECHAL NEY. Paris: Plon, 1893.

Wencker, Friedrich. BERNADOTTE, A BIOGRAPHY. Translated by K. Kirkness. London: Jarrolds, 1936.

Whitlock Brand. LAFAYETTE. 2 vols. New York: Dodd Mead, 1899.

Wickwire, Franklin and Mary. CORNWALLIS: THE IMPERIAL YEARS. Chapel Hill: University of North Carolina Press, 1980.

Wilson, P. WILLIAM PITT THE YOUNGER. New York, 1934.

Wirth, Joseph. LE MARECHAL LEFEBVRE, DUC DE DANTZIG. Paris: Perrin, 1904.

Young, P. NAPOLEON'S MARSHALS. New York: Hippocrene Books, 1973.

Zurlinden, Emile. NAPOLEON ET SES MARECHAUX. 2 vols. Paris: Hachette, 1910.

Regulations, Manuals, Memoirs and Treatises

L'ART DU MILITAIRE OU TRAITE COMPLET DE L'EXERCICE DE L'INFANTERIE, CAVALERIE, DU CANON, DE LA BOMBE ET DES PIQUES. Paris: Fr. Dutart, 1793.

Aulard, F. A., ed. RECUEIL DES ACTES DU COMITE DE SALUT PUBLIC AVEC LA CORRESPONDANCE OFFICIELLE DE REPRESENTANTS EN MISSION ET LE REGISTRE DU CONSEIL EXECUTIF PROVISOIRE. 25 vols. Paris: Imprimerie nationale, 1889–1918.

Avril, J. B. AVANTAGES D'UNE BONNE DISCIPLINE. Paris: Migne, 1824.

Bardin, Général. MEMORIAL DE L'OFFICIER D'INFANTERIE. Paris: Magimel, 1813.

Bardin, Major. MANUEL D'INFANTERIE OU RESUME DE TOUS LES REGLEMENTS, DECRETS, USAGES, RENSEIGNEMENTS CONCERNANT L'INFANTERIE. Paris: Magimel, 1807.

Belair, A. P. J. Chef de brigade. ELEMENTS DE FORTIFICATION. Paris: F. Didot, 1792.

————. INSTRUCTION ADRESSEE AUX OFFICIERS D'INFAN-TERIE POUR TRACER ET CONSTRUIRE TOUTES SORTES D'OUVRAGES DE CAMPAGNE. Paris: Magimel, 1793.

Bordesoulle, Comte de. MANUEL DE CAVALERIE. Paris: Didot, 1817.

Bottée, Jean Joseph, and Jean-René-Denis Riffault. TRAITE DE L'ART DE FABRIQUER LA POUDRE A CANON, CONTENANT L'EX-TRACTION . . . LA FABRICATION . . . L'EXPURATION . . . LES AMELIORATIONS . . . LES DIVERS MOYENS . . . LA DESCRIP-TION DES ATELIERS, MACHINES ET UTENSILES EMPLOYES A CES DIFFERENTS GENRES DE TRAVAUX, PRECEDE D'UN EX-POSE HISTORIQUE SUR L'ETABLISSEMENT DU SERVICE DES POUDRES ET SALPETRES EN FRANCE . . . Paris: Leblanc, 1811.

Bousmard, Ingénieur. ESSAI GENERAL DE FORTIFICATION. 4 vols. Paris: Magimel, 1814.

Buchez, P. J. B., and P. C. Roux. HISTOIRE PARLEMENTAIRE DE LA REVOLUTION FRANCAISE; OU JOURNAL DES ASSEMBLEES NATIONALES DEPUIS 1789 JUSQU'EN 1815. 40 vols. Paris: Paulin, 1834–1838.

Caron, Pierre, ed. LES PAPIERS DES COMITES MILITAIRES DE LA CONSTITUANTE, DE LA LEGISLATIVE ET DE LA CONVEN-TION (1789—AN IV). Paris: Au siége de la Société, 1912.

Debidour, A., ed. RECUEIL DES ACTES DU DIRECTOIRE EXECU-TIF. 4 vols. Paris: Imprimerie nationale, 1910–1917.

d'Harembure, Maréchal de camp. ELEMENTS DE CAVALERIE. Paris: Magimel, 1795.

Duhesme, Guillaume-Philibert. ESSAIS SUR L'INFANTERIE LEG-ERE, OU TRAITE DES PETITES OPERATIONS DE LA GUERRE A L'USAGE DES JEUNES OFFICERS. Paris: L. G. Michaud, 1814.

Duvergier, J. B. COLLECTION COMPLETE DES LOIS, DECRETS, ORDONNANCES REGLEMENTS, ETC., DE 1788 A 1824. 24 vols. Paris: 1824–1828.

ETAT MILITAIRE DE LA GARDE NATIONALE DE FRANCE POUR L'ANNEE 1790. 2 vols. Paris: Le Tellier et Garnery, 1790.

France. Artillery. AIDE-MEMOIRE A L'USAGE DES OFFICERS D'ARTILLERIE DE FRANCE. Paris: Magimel, 1798.

————. Berriat, H. LEGISLATION MILITAIRE OU RECUEIL METHODIQUE ET RAISONNE DE LOIS, DECRETS, ARRETES, REGLEMENTS ET INSTRUCTIONS ACTUELLEMENT EN VIGEUR SUR TOUTES LES BRANCHES DE L'ETAT MILITAIRE. 7 vols. Perpignan: Tastu, 1812–1817.

————. COLLECTION DE TOUS LES DECRETS LOIS, PROCLAMATIONS ETC., RELATIFS AU MILITAIRE 1789–1795. 20 vols. Metz: Collignon, 1795.

————. CONSTITUTION DE L'ARMEE FRANCAISE DECRETEE PAR LES ASSEMBLEES NATIONALE, CONSTITUANTE, LEGISLATIVE ET CONVENTIONNELLE. 5 vols. Paris: Prault, 1793.

————. MANUEL DU CANONNIER, OU INSTRUCTION GENERALE SUR LE SERVICE DE TOUTES LES BOUCHES A FEU EN USAGE DANS L'ARTILLERIE . . . Paris: Lepetit, 1792.

France, Army. CODE MILITAIRE. 3 vols. Paris: Prault, 1793.

————. CODE MILITAIRE. Paris: 5 vols. Devaux, 1791–1792.

————. ETAT MILITAIRE DE FRANCE POUR L'ANNEE 1793. Paris: Siège de la Société, 1903.

————. ETAT MILITAIRE DE LA REPUBLIQUE FRANCAISE DE L'AN VIII A L'AN XIII. 6 vols. Paris: Onfroy et Leblanc, 1800–1805.

————. EMPLACEMENT DES TROUPES, 1788–1789, ANS VIII, IX, X, XI, XII, XIII, XIV, 1806 A 1817, 1823, 1824–1836, 1858 A 1871, 1873–1874, 1881–1882. 86 vols. Paris: Imprimerie royale impériale et de la République, 1799–1882.

————. ETAT MILITAIRE DE FRANCE (1758–1793). 37 vols. Paris: Chez Guillyn, 1758–1776; Chez Onfroy, 1777–1793.

France, Ministère de la guerre. EXTRAIT POUR LES MAIRES DE L'INSTRUCTION GENERALE SUR LA CONSCRIPTION. 2 vols. Paris: Firmin-Didot, 1811. 2 vols.

————. RAPPORT FAIT PAR LE MINISTRE DE LA GUERRE SUR L'ADMINISTRATION DE SON DEPARTEMENT AN IV A AN VII. 6 vols. Paris: Imprimerie de la République an V et VIII.

————. Army Artillerie. AIDE-MEMOIRE A L'USAGE DES OFFICERS D'ARTILLERIE DE FRANCE. Paris: Magimel, 1795.

————. Infantry. REGLEMENT POURTANT INSTRUCTION AUX COMMANDANTS DES BATAILLONS D'INFANTERIE LEGERE . . . DU 1er AVRIL 1791. Paris: Imprimerie royale, 1791.

————. Cavalry. REGLEMENT SUR LA FORMATION, LES APPOINTMENTS ET LA SOLDE DE LA CAVALERIE. Paris: Imprimerie royale, 1791.

————. LOIS RELATIVES A LA COMPOSITION DE L'ARMEE DONNEE A PARIS LE 21 OCTOBRE 1791. Paris: Imprimerie royale, 1791.

————. Uniforms. COLLECTION DES TYPES DE TOUS LES CORPS ET DES UNIFORMS MILITAIRES DE LA REPUBLIQUE ET DE L'EMPIRE. Paris: J. J. Dubochet, 1844.

————. Infantry. INSTRUCTION PROVISOIRE POUR LES OFFICIERS GENERAUX CHARGES DE L'INSPECTION DES TROUPES D'INFANTERIE DU 15 NOVEMBRE 1791. Paris: Imprimerie royale, 1791.

————. Army National Guard. LOI RELATIVE A L'ORGANISATION DE LA GARDE NATIONALE DONNEE A PARIS LE 14 OCTOBRE, 1791. Angers: de l'Imprimerie du Département de Mayenne-et-Loire, 1791.

————. INSTRUCTION POUR LES GARDES NATIONALES ARRETEE PAR LE COMITE MILITAIRE . . . DU 1er JANVIER 1791. Paris: Imprimerie nationale, 1791.

————. Army. INSTRUCTION PROVISOIRE SUR L'HABILLEMENT DES TROUPES DU 1er AVRIL 1791. Paris: Imprimerie royale, 1792.

————. INSTRUCTION POUR LES GARDES NATIONALES. Paris: Imprimerie nationale, 1791.

————. CODES DES GARDES NATIONALES. Paris: Prault, 1793.

————. DECRET SUR LA FORMATION DE L'ECOLE DE MARS. Paris: Imprimerie nationale, 1794.

————. Cavalerie. INSTRUCTION DE DETAIL BASEE SUR L'ORDONNANCE DE 1788 . . . 2 vols. Versailles: Jacob, 1801.

France. Ministère de la guerre. REGLEMENT CONCERNANT LE SERVICE INTERIEUR, LA POLICE ET LA DISCIPLINE DE L'INFANTERIE DU 24 JUIN 1792. Paris: Magimel, 1795 and 1813.

————. REGLEMENT CONCERNANT L'EXERCICE ET LES MANOEUVRES DE L'INFANTERIE DU PREMIER AOUT 1791. Paris: Chez Maginel, 1812.

————. REGLEMENT CONCERNANT LE SERVICE INTERIEUR, LA POLICE ET LA DISCIPLINE DE L'INFANTERIE DU 24 JUIN 1792. Paris: Magimel, 1913.

————. MANUEL DE LA CAVALERIE CONCERNANT L'EXERCICE ET LES MANOEUVRES DES TROUPES A CHEVAL AU SERVICE DE LA REPUBLIQUE. 2 vols. Paris: Le Petit, 1793.

————. INSTRUCTION PROVISOIRE SUR LE CHAMPEMENT DES TROUPES A CHEVAL. REGLEMENT PROVISOIRE SUR LEUR SERVICE EN CAMPAGNE. CODE MILITAIRE. Valenciennes: H. J. Prignet, 1793.

France, Cavalerie. INSTRUCTION CONCERNANT L'EXERCICE ET LES MANOEUVRES DES TROUPES A CHEVAL. Paris: Maginel, an VII.

————. Artillerie. PETIT MANUEL DU CANONNIER OU IN-STRUCTION GENERALE SUR LE SERVICE DE TOUTES LES BOUCHES A FEU. Paris: Maginel, 1793.

————. INSTRUCTION GENERALE SUR LE SERVICE DE TOUTES LES BOUCHES A FEU EN USAGE DANS L'AR-TILLERIE. Paris: Firmin-Didot, 1791.

————. RAPPORT DU COMITE MILITAIRE SUR L'ARTILLERIE ET LE GENIE FAIT A L'ASSEMBLEE NATIONALE LE 9 SEP-TEMBRE 1790. Paris: Imprimerie nationale, 1790.

France, Administration. INSTRUCTION SUR LA SOLDE ET LES TRAITEMENTS MILITAIRES. Paris: Imprimerie de la République, 1798.

France, Medecine Militaire. REGLEMENT CONCERNANT L'OR-GANISATION, L'ADMINISTRATION ET LA POLICE DES HOPITAUX MILITAIRES. Paris: Imprimerie de la République, 1798.

Gassendi, Jean-Jacques. AIDE-MEMOIRE A L'USAGE DES OF-FICIERS DU CORPS ROYAL DE L'ARTILLERIE DE FRANCE ATTACHES AU SERVICE DE TERRE. Paris: Magimel, 1798.

Goupy, J.B. DE LA LEGISLATION CRIMINELLE DE L'ARMEE FRANCAISE CONSIDEREE DANS TOUS SES RAPPORTS. Paris: Prault Saint-Martin, 1792.

Hennet, Léon, ed. ETAT MILITAIRE DE FRANCE POUR L'ANNEE 1793. Paris: Au siège de la Société, 1903.

La Martillière, Jean. REFLEXIONS SUR LA FABRICATION EN GENERAL DES BOUCHES A FEU ET OBSERVATIONS SUR LES EPREUVES EXTRAORDINAIRES ET COMPARATIVES DE DIF-FERENTES ESPECES DE BOUCHES A FEU QUI ONT EU LIEU A DOUAI EN 1786. Paris: Magimel, 1796.

Le Dran, Henri François. TRAITES OUT REFLEXIONS TIREES DE LA PRATIQUE SUR LES PLAIES D'ARMES A FEU. Paris: Théophile Barrois, 1793.

Lespinasse, Augustin. ESSAI SUR L'ORGANISATION DE L'ARMEE DE L'ARTILLERIE. Paris: Magimel, 1800.

MANUEL DU CITOYEN ARMEE DE PIQUES. Paris: F. Buisson, 1792.

Meunier, Claude Victor. EVOLUTIONS PAR BRIGADES. Paris: Magimel, 1814.

Michaud, Citoyen. DES FORTIFICATIONS ET LES RELATIONS GENERALES DE LA GUERRE DE SIEGE. Paris: Magimel, 1793.

Monge, Gaspard. DESCRIPTION DE L'ART DE FABRIQUER LES CANONS FAITE EN EXECUTION DE L'ARRETE DU COMITE DE SALUT PUBLIC DU 18 PLUVIOSE DE L'AN 2 DE LA REPUBLIQUE FRANCAISE, UN ET INDIVISIBLE. Paris: Imprimerie par ordre du Comité de Salut Public, 1794.

Noizet, Saint-Paul Gaspard. TRAITE COMPLET DE FORTIFICATION. Paris: Barrois l'aîné, 1799.

Picq, Antoine. LA LEGISLATION MILITAIRE DE L'EPOQUE REVOLUTIONNAIRE: INTRODUCTION A L'ETUDE DE LA LEGISLATION MILITAIRE ACTUELLE. Paris: 1931.

Quillet, P. N. ETAT ACTUEL DE LA LEGISLATION SUR L'ADMINISTRATION DES TROUPES. 3 vols. Paris: Magimel, 1811.

Schauenburg, Général. INSTRUCTION CONCERNANT LES MANOEUVRES DE L'INFANTERIE. Maestricht: Nypels, An VIII.

Urtubie, Theodore. MANUEL DE L'ARTILLEUR CONTENANT TOUS LES OBJETS DONT LA CONNAISSANCE EST NECESSAIRE AUX OFFICIERS ET SOUS-OFFICIERS DE L'ARTILLERIE, SUIVANT L'APPROBATION DE M. GRIBEAUVAL. Paris: Didot, 1791.

Memoirs

Alexandre, Charles. FRAGMENTS DES MEMOIRES DE CHARLES ALEXIS ALEXANDRE SUR SA MISSION AUX ARMEES DU NORD ET DE SAMBRE ET MEUSE. Paris: Presses Universitaires de France, 1941.

Barras, Paul Francois. MEMOIRES DE BARRAS. 4 vols. Paris: Hachette 1895–1896.

Beatson, Alexander. A VIEW OF THE ORIGIN AND CONDUCT OF THE WAR WITH TIPPOO SULTAN. London: G. and W. Nicol, 1800.

Belot, Denis. JOURNAL D'UN VOLONTAIRE DE 1791. Paris: Perrin, 1888.

Berthier, Louis. MEMOIRES DU MARECHAL BERTHIER, PRINCE DE NEUCHATEL ET DE WAGRAM, MAJOR-GENERAL DES ARMEES FRANCAISES. CAMPAGNE D'EGYPTE. Paris: Baudouin, n.d.

————. RELATIONS DE L'EXPEDITION DE SYRIE DE LA BATAILLE D'ABOUKIR ET DE LA REPRISE DU FORT DE CE NOM. Paris: J. Gratiot, 1800.

Besenval, Pierre Baron de. MEMOIRES DU BARON BESENVAL. 2 vols. Paris: Baudouin, 1821.

Bigot, Charles Jules. GLOIRES ET SOUVENIRS MILITAIRES D'APRES LES MEMOIRES DU CANONNIER BRICARD, DU MARECHAL BUGEAUD, DU CAPITAINE COIGNET. Paris: Hachette, 1900.

Blocqueville, Marquis de, and A. L. d'Eckmühl. LE MARECHAL DAVOUT PRINCE D'ECHMUHL RACONTE PAR LES SIENS ET PAR LUI-MEME. 4 vols. Paris: Didier, 1879–1880.

Boulart, Baron. MEMOIRES MILITAIRES DU GENERAL VON BOULART SUR LES GUERRES DE LA REPUBLIQUE ET DE L'EMPIRE. Paris: Librairie Illustrée, 1892.

Bouloiseau, M., G. Lefevre, and A. Soboul. OEUVRES DE MAXIMILIEN ROBESPIERRE. 9 vols. Paris: 1953.

Bourgogne, Sergent. MEMOIRES. Paris: Hachette, 1935.

Boutoue, Jules Alexandre Léger. LETTRES D'UN CHEF DE BRIGADE 33e DE LIGNE, 65e ET 68e DEMI-BRIGADES, 56e DE LIGNE. Paris: Baudouin, 1891.

Bricard, Louis Joseph. JOURNAL DU CANONNIER BRICARD 1792–1802. Paris: Charles Delagrave, 1891.

Brissot, J. P. MEMOIRES DE BRISSOT PUBLIES PAR SON FILS. 4 vols. Paris, 1832.

Bunbury, Henry Edward. NARRATIVES OF SOME PASSAGES IN THE GREAT WAR WITH FRANCE FROM 1799 TO 1810. London: R. Bentley, 1854.

Busquet, Raoul, Robert Bruno, and A. J. Pares. MEMOIRES DE LOUIS RICHARD SUR LA REVOLTE DE TOULON ET L'EMIGRATION. Paris: Rieder, 1930.

Carnot, H., and Angers, D. d'. MEMOIRES DE B. BARERE. 4 vols. Paris: 1842–1844.

Carnot, Lazare. MEMOIRES HISTORIQUES ET MILITAIRES SUR CARNOT. Paris: Baudouin, 1824.

Castelnau, Louis, Aimable de Joseph, and Baron de Richard. LETTRES DU BARON DE CASTELNAU, OFFICIER DE CARABINIERS, 1728–1793. Paris: H. Champion, 1911.

Championnet, Jean. SOUVENIRS DU GENERAL CHAMPIONNET. Paris: Flammarion, 1904.

Charavay, Etienne. CORRESPONDANCE GENERALE DE CARNOT (1792–1795). 4 vols. Paris: Imprimerie nationale, 1892–1907.

Chuquet, Arthur, ed. LETTRES DE 1792. Paris: Champion, 1911.

———. LETTRES DE 1793. Paris: Champion, 1911.

———. UN JOURNAL DE VOYAGE DU GENERAL DESAIX, SUSSE ET ITALIE (1797). Paris: Plon-Nourrit, 1907.

Cloney, Thomas. A PERSONAL NARRATIVE OF THOSE TRANSACTIONS IN THE COUNTY, WEXFORD, IN WHICH THE

AUTHOR WAS ENGAGED DURING THE AWFUL PERIOD OF 1798. Dublin: For the author by J. McMullen, 1832.

Cognet, Abbé. SOUVENIRS MILITAIRES D'UN JEUNE ABBE, SOLDAT DE LA REPUBLIQUE (1793–1801). Paris: Didier, 1881.

Coignet, Jean. LES CAHIERS DU CAPITAINE COIGNET (1799–1815). Paris: Hachette, 1909.

Colbert-Chabanais, Auguste Marquis de. TRADITIONS ET SOUVENIRS, OU MEMOIRES TOUCHANT LE TEMPS ET LA VIE DU GENERAL AUGUSTE COLBERT 1793–1809. 5 vols. Paris: Firmin-Didot, 1863–1873.

Comeau de Charry, Sebastien Joseph. SOUVENIRS DES GUERRES D'ALLEMAGNE PENDANT LA REVOLUTION ET L'EMPIRE. Paris: Plon-Nourrit, 1900.

Crossard, Jean, Baron de. MEMOIRES MILITAIRES ET HISTORIQUES POUR SERVIR A L'HISTOIRE DE LA GUERRE DEPUIS 1792 JUSQU'EN 1815. 6 vols. Paris: Migneret, 1829.

Croy, Emmanuel Duc de. JOURNAL INEDIT. Edited by Comte de Grouchy and Paul Cottin. 4 vols. Paris: E. Flammarion, 1906–1907.

Custine, Adam, Comte de. MEMOIRES DU GENERAL CUSTINE SUR LES GUERRES DE LA REPUBLIQUE PRECEDES D'UNE NOTICE SUR LE GENERAL DUMOURIEZ. Paris: Philippe, 1831.

Decaen, Charles. MEMOIRES ET JOURNAUX DU GENERAL DECAEN. 2 vols. Paris: Plon-Nourrit, 1910–1911.

Dellard, Jean Pierre, Baron. MEMOIRES MILITAIRES DU GENERAL DELLARD SUR LES GUERRES DE LA REPUBLIQUE ET L'EMPIRE. Paris: Librairie illustrée, 1892.

Desachy, Paul. LES CAHIERS DU COLONEL GIRARD 1766–1846. Paris: Plon, 1951.

Desaix, Louis Charles-Antoine. JOURNAL. Paris: Plon, 1907.

Desgenettes. SOUVENIRS D'UN MEDECIN DE L'ARMEE D'EGYPTE. 1892.

Doguereau, Jean Pierre. JOURNAL DE L'EXPEDITION D'EGYPTE. Paris: Perrin, 1904.

Dumonceau, François. MEMOIRES DE GENERAL COMTE FRANCOIS DUMONCEAU. 3 vols. Brussels: Brepols, 1958–1963.

Dumouriez, Charles. LA VIE ET LES MEMOIRES DU GENERAL DUMOURIEZ. 4 vols. Paris: Baudouin, 1822–1823.

Dupuy, Victor. SOUVENIRS MILITAIRES DE VICTOR DUPUY, CHEF D'ESCADRONS DE HUSSARDS 1794–1816. Paris: Calmann-Lévy, 1892.

DuPuy-Lauron. MARECHAL DE CAMPS: TACTIQUE FRANCAISE. Paris: Firmin-Didot, 1792.

Duruy, G., ed. MEMOIRES DE BARRAS. 4 vols. Paris: 1896.

Favier, Gilbert. DEUX VOLONTAIRES DE 1791; LES FRERES FAVIER DE MONTLUCON. Montlucon: A. Herbin, 1909.

Galli, H., ed. JOURNAL D'UN OFFICIER DE L'ARMEE D'EGYPTE. Paris, 1883.

Gervais, Capitaine. A LA CONQUETE DE L'EUROPE; SOUVENIRS D'UN SOLDAT DE LA REVOLUTION ET DE L'EMPIRE. Paris: Calmann-Lévy, 1939.

Girard, Etienne. LES CAHIERS DU COLONEL GIRARD 1766–1846. Paris: Plon, 1951.

Godart, Roch, Baron. MEMOIRES DU GENERAL BARON ROCH GODART (1792–1815). Paris: Flammarion, 1895.

Goethe, Johann Wolfgang von. "Campagne in Frankreich." GOETHES SAMTLICHE WERKE, JUBILAUMS AUSGABE, vol. 28. Stuttgart, 1903.

Gonneville, Aymar Olivier. SOUVENIRS MILITAIRES DU COLONEL DE GONNEVILLE. Paris: Didier, 1876.

Gridel, E., and Capitaine Richard. CAHIERS DE VIEUX SOLDATS DE LA REPUBLIQUE ET DE L'EMPIRE. Paris: Chapelot, 1903.

Grobert, Jacques. DIVERS MEMOIRES SUR L'ARTILLERIE. Paris: Journal de Paris, 1795.

Grouchy, Emmanuel, Marquis de. MEMOIRES DU MARECHAL DE GROUCHY. 5 vols. Paris: Dentu, 1973–1974.

Hardy, Jean. MEMOIRES MILITAIRES DU GENERAL JEAN HARDY. Paris: Chapelot, 1891.

Hauterive, M. A. d'. LETTRES D'UN CHEF DE BRIGADE. Paris: Chapelot, 1891.

Hautpoul, Alphonse. MEMOIRES DU GENERAL MARQUIS ALPHONSE D'HAUTPOUL, PAIR DE FRANCE 1789–1865. Paris: Perrin, 1906.

Jacquin, François-Joseph. CARNET DE ROUTE D'UN GROGNARD DE LA REVOLUTION ET DE L'EMPIRE. Paris: Claurevil, 1960.

Joliclerc, François-Xavier. JOLICLERC, VOLONTAIRE AUX ARMEES DE LA REVOLUTION, SES LETTRES (1793–1796). Paris: Perrin, 1905.

Jourdon, Jean Baptiste. MEMOIRES POUR SERVIR A L'HISTOIRE DE LA CAMPAGNE DE 1796, CONTENANT LES OPERATIONS DE L'ARMEE DE SAMBRE ET MEUSE, SOUS LES ORDRES DU GENERAL EN CHEF JOURDAN. Paris: Magimel Angelin et Pochard, 1818.

————. PRECIS DES OPERATIONS DE L'ARMEE DU DANUBE. Paris: Charles, 1800.

Lafayette, Marie Joseph Paul, Marquis de. THE MEMOIRS CORRESPONDENCE AND MANUSCRIPTS OF MARQUIS DE LAFAYETTE. 3 vols. London: Saunders and Otley, 1837.

Lahure, Louis Joseph, Baron. SOUVENIRS DE LA VIE MILITAIRE DU LIEUTENANT-GENERAL BARON L. J. LAHURE 1787–1815. Paris: Lahure, 1895.

Lamarque, Jean M. MEMOIRES ET SOUVENIRS DU GENERAL MAXMILIEN LAMARQUE, PUBLIES PAR SA FAMILLE. 3 vols. Paris: H. Fournier, 1835–1836.

Larehey, Lorédan. JOURNAL DE MARCHE D'UN VOLONTAIRE DE 1792 (FRICASSE, SERGENT A LA 127e DEMI-BRIGADE) 1792–1802. Paris: Hachette, 1882.

Larrey, D. J. CLINIQUE CHIRURGICALE EXERCEE PARTICULIEREMENT DANS LES CAMPS ET LES HOPITAUX MILITAIRES DEPUIS 1792 JUSQU'EN 1829. 5 vols. Paris: Baillière, 1832–1836.

————. MEMOIRES DE CHIRURGIE MILITAIRE ET CAMPAGNES DE D. J. LARREY. 4 vols. Paris: J. Smith, 1812–1817.

Laus de Boissy, M. A. BONAPARTE AU CAIRE OU MEMOIRES SUR L'EXPEDITION DE CE GENERAL EN EGYPTE. Paris: Prault, 1799.

Leclaire, Général. MEMOIRES ET CORRESPONDENCE (1793). Paris: Chapelot, 1904.

Lejeune, Louis François. MEMOIRS OF BARON LEJEUNE, AIDE-DE-CAMP TO MARSHALS BERTHEIR, DAVOUT, AND OUDINOT. Translated by Mrs. Arthur Bell. 2 vols. London: Longmans, Green, 1897.

LeRoy, Claude. SOUVENIRS DE C. F. M. LEROY, MAJOR D'INFANTERIE, VETERAN DES ARMEES DE LA REPUBLIQUE ET DE L'EMPIRE, 1767–1851. Dijon: P. Berthier, 1914.

Loir, Maurice. AU DRAPEAU. RECITS MILITAIRES EXTRAITS DES MEMOIRES DE G. BUSSIERE (ET AL). Paris: Hachette, 1905.

Lorencez, Guillaume. SOUVENIRS MILITAIRES DU GENERAL CTE DE LORENCEZ. Paris: Emile-Paul, 1902.

Macdonald, Etienne. SOUVENIRS DU MARECHAL MACDONALD DUC DE TARENTE. Paris: Plon-Nourrit, 1892.

Malus, Etienne. L'AGENDA DE MALUS; SOUVENIRS DE L'EXPEDITION D'EGYPTE 1798–1801. Paris: Champion, 1892.

Mangourit, M. A. B. DEFENSE D'ANCONE ET DES DEPARTEMENTS ROMAINS LE TORONTO, LE MUSONE ET LE METAINO PAR LE GENERAL MONNIER AUX ARMEES. VII et VIII. 2 vols. Paris: 1802.

Marbot, Jean Baptiste, Baron de. MEMOIRES DU GENERAL BARON DE MARBOT. 3 vols. Paris: Nourrit, 1891.

Marcassus, Casimir J.-P. Translated by Dr. Rowley. LE CONSERVATEUR DE LA SANTE DES DEFENSEURS DE LA PATRIE. Toulouse: Noel-Etienne Sens, 1793.

Marmont, Auguste. MEMOIRES DU MARECHAL MARMONT, DUC DE RAGUSE DE 1792 A 1841. 9 vols. Paris: Perrotin, 1857.

Masséna, André, Prince d'Essling. MEMOIRES D'ANDRE MASSENA, DUC DE RIVOLI, PRINCE D'ESSLING, MARECHAL D'EMPIRE, REDIGES D'APRES LES DOCUMENTS QU'IL A LAISSES ET SUR CEUX DU DEPOT DE LA GUERRE ET DU DEPOT DES FORTIFICATIONS. RECUEILLIS PAR LE GENERAL KOCH. 7 vols. Paris: J. de Bonnot, 1966–1967.

Masson, F., and G. Biagi. NAPOLEON: MANUSCRITS INEDITS 1786–1791. Paris, 1912.

Masson, Frédérick. AVENTURES DE GUERRE, 1792–1809. SOUVENIRS ET RECITS DE SOLDATS, RECUEILLIS ET PUBLIES. Paris: Boussod, Valadon, 1894.

MEMOIRES SUR LA DERNIERE GUERRE ENTRE LA FRANCE ET L'ESPAGNE DANS LES PYRENEES OCCIDENTALES. Paris: Trevtiel et Wurtz, 1801.

Mérat, Paul. "Souvenirs de la Campagne de 1792." JOURNAL DES SCIENCES MILITAIRES 9 (January 1849), pp. 107–27.

Michon, G., ed. CORRESPONDANCE DE MAXIMILIEN ET AUGUSTIN ROBESPIERRE. 2 vols. Paris, 1946.

Miot, J. MEMOIRES POUR SERVIR A L'HISTOIRE DES EXPEDITIONS EN EGYPTE ET EN SYRIE. Paris: Demonville, 1804.

Monnet, Robert. AVEC LES VOLONTAIRES DU 1er BATAILLON DE LA HAUTE-SAONE DIT BATAILLON DE GRAY 1791–1815. Gray: Presse de Gray, 1974.

Murat, Joachim, Prince. CORRESPONDANCE DE JOACHIM MURAT, CHASSEUR A CHEVAL, GENERAL, MARECHAL D'EMPIRE, GRAND-DUC DE CLEVES ET DE BERG (JUILLET 1791–JUILLET 1808). Turin: Roux Frassati, 1899.

———. LETTRES ET DOCUMENTS POUR SERVIR A L'HISTOIRE DE JOACHIM MURAT 1767–1815. 8 vols. Paris: Plon-Nourrit, 1908–1914.

Napoleon I. CORRESPONDENCE DE NAPOLEON Ier. 32 vols. Paris: Imprimerie impériale, 1858–1869.

———. CORRESPONDENCE MILITAIRE DE NAPOLEON Ier EXTRAITS DE LA CORRESPONDANCE GENERALE ET PUBLIEE PAR ORDRE DU MINISTRE DE LA GUERRE. 10 vols. Paris: Plon-Nourrit 1876–1897.

———. UNPUBLISHED CORRESPONDENCE OF NAPOLEON I PRESERVED IN THE WAR ARCHIVES PUBLISHED BY E. PICARD AND L. TUETEY. Translated by Louise Seymour. 3 vols. New York: Duffield, 1913.

Ney, Michel. MEMOIRS OF MARSHAL NEY PUBLISHED BY HIS FAMILY. 2 vols. Philadelphia: Carey, 1834.

Noel, Jean Nicolas Auguste, Colonel. SOUVENIRS MILITAIRES D'UN OFFICER DU PREMIER EMPIRE (1795–1832). Paris, 1895.

Noel, Joseph. AU TEMPS DES VOLONTAIRES 1792; LETTRES D'UN VOLONTAIRE DE 1792. Paris: Plon-Nourrit, 1912.

Orson, Louis François. MEMOIRES DU PORTE-DRAPEAU LOUIS FRANCOIS ORSON (1789–1799). Paris: J. Tallendier, n.d.

Orson, Sergent-Major. "Histoire du Sergent-Major Orson de la 109e Demi-Brigade." CARNET DE LA SABRETACHE, 2nd series, 12 vols. (1903), pp. 353–76.

Oudinot, Nicolas Charles, Duc de Reggio. MEMOIRS OF MARSHAL OUDINOT DUC DE REGGIO. COMPILED FROM THE HITHERTO UNPUBLISHED SOUVENIRS OF THE DUCHESSE DE REGGIO. Edited by Gaston Stiegler. Translated by Alexander Teixeira de Mattos. London: H. Henry, 1896.

Pelleport, Pierre. SOUVENIRS MILITAIRES ET INTIMES DU GENERAL VICOMTE DE PELLEPORT DE 1793 A 1853. 2 vols. Paris: Didier, 1857.

Percy, Chirurgien-Major. MANUEL DU CHIRURGIEN D'ARMEE. Paris: M. Quignon l'ainé, 1794.

Percy, Pierre Baron. JOURNAL DES CAMPAGNES DU BARON PERCY, CHIRURGIEN EN CHEF DE LA GRANDE ARMEE (1754–1825). Paris: Plon-Nourrit, 1904.

Perrin, Claude-Victor. EXTRAITS D'UNE HISTOIRE INEDITE DES GUERRES DE LA REPUBLIQUE ET DE L'EMPIRE. Paris: Dondey-Dupré, 1853.

Picard, E., and A. Tuetey. CORRESPONDANCE INEDITE DE NAPOLEON Ier CONSERVEE ANX ARCHIVES DE LA GUERRE. 4 vols. Paris: 1912–1913.

Pion des Loches, Colonel. D'ARTILLERIE DES CAMPAGNES (1792–1815). Paris, 1889.

Poiger, A. "Lettres de Pierre Cohin, Volontaire a l'armée du nord et de membres de sa famille." ANNALES HISTORIQUES DE LA RÉVOLUTION FRANÇAISE (1955), pp. 124–42.

Reinhard, Marcel R. AVEC BONAPARTE EN ITALIE, D'APRES LETTRES INEDITES DE SON AIDE DE CAMP, JOSEPH SULKOWSKI. Paris: Hachette, 1946.

Reynier, Jean Louis. DE L'EGYPTE D'APRES LA BATAILLE D'HELIOPOLIS ET CONSIDERATIONS GENERALES SUR L'ORGANISATION PHYSIQUE ET POLITIQUE DE CE PAYS. Paris: C. Pougens, 1802.

―――. MEMOIRES DU COMTE REYNIER, GENERAL DE DIVISION. CAMPAGNE D'EGYPTE, PARTIE II. Paris: Baudouin, 1827.

Richardot, M. NOUVEAUX. MEMOIRES SUR L'ARMEE FRANCAISE EN EGYPTE ET EN SYRIE. Paris: Chapelot, 1848.

Rouget, François, Comte. MEMOIRES MILITAIRES DU LIEU-TENANT-GENERAL, COMTE ROUGET (FRANCOIS). 4 vols. Paris: J. Dumaine, 1862–1865.

Routier, Léon. RECITS D'UN SOLDAT DE LA REPUBLIQUE ET DE L'EMPIRE 1792–1830. Paris: Vermot, 1899.

Saint-Cyr, Gouvion. MEMOIRES POUR SERVIR A L'HISTOIRE MILITAIRE SOUS LE DIRECTOIRE, LE CONSULAT ET L'EM-PIRE. 4 vols. Paris: Angelin, 1934.

————. MEMOIRES SUR LES CAMPAGNES DES ARMEES DU RHIN ET DE RHIN-ET-MOSELLE DE 1792 JUSQU'A LA PAIX DE CAMP-FORMIO. 2 vols. Paris: Anselin, 1829.

Savary, A.-J.-M.-R. MEMOIRES OF THE DUKE OF ROVIGO (M. SA-VANY). 4 vols. London: H. Colburn, 1828.

Séruzier, Théodore, Baron. MEMOIRES MILITAIRES DU BARON SERUZIER, COLONEL D'ARTILLERIE LEGERE. Paris: Anselin et Pochard, 1823.

Simon, Claude. CORRESPONDANCE DE CLAUDE SIMON LIEU-TENANT DE GRENADIERS DU REGIMENT DE WALSH (NO 92) AUX ARMEES DU NORD, DES ARDENNES ET DE SAMBRE-ET-MEUSE 1792–1793. Grenoble: Allier, 1899.

Soult, Nicholas, Maréchal. MEMOIRES. Paris: Hachette, 1955.

————. MEMOIRES DU MARECHAL-GENERAL SOULT. 3 vols. Paris: Librairie d'Amoyt, 1854.

Stock, Joseph A. NARRATIVE OF WHAT PASSED AT KILLALA (IN THE COUNTY OF MAYO, AND THE PARTS ADJACENT), DUR-ING THE FRENCH INVASION IN THE SUMMER OF 1798–1800. Dublin: Printed by and for R. E. Mercier & Co.; and for John Jones. London, Printed for J. Stockdale (etc.), n.d.

Thiébault, Paul Charles. MEMOIRES DU GENERAL BARON THIEBAULT. 5 vols. Paris: Plon-Nourrit, 1895–1897.

Tourtier, Chantal, Baron de, and Simone de Saint-Exupéry. LES ARCHIVES DU MARECHAL NEY ET DE SA FAMILLE CON-SERVEES AUX ARCHIVES NATIONALES. Paris: Imprimerie Na-tionale, 1962.

Turreau de Linières Louis, Baron. MEMOIRES POUR SERVIR A L'HIS-TOIRE DE LA GUERRE DE LA VENDEE. Paris: Baudouin, 1824.

Vallée, G. and G. Pariset. CARNET D'ETAPES DU DRAGON MAR-QUANT DEMARCHES ET ACTIONS DE L'ARMEE DU CENTRE PENDANT LA CAMPAGNE DE 1792. Paris: Berger-Levrault, 1898.

Vauban, Jacques, Comte de. MEMOIRES POUR SERVIR A L'HIS-TOIRE DE LA GUERRE DE LA VENDEE. Paris: Maison de Com-mission en librairie, 1806.

Vaxelaire, J. C. MEMOIRES D'UN VETERAN DE L'ANCIENNE ARMEE (1791–1800). Paris: Ch. Delagrave, 1899.

Vellay, Charles, ed. OEUVRES COMPLETES DE SAINT-JUST. 2 vols. Paris: 1908.

Vermale, François. "Lettres à un Soldat de l'An II." ANNALES HISTORIQUES DE LA RÉVOLUTION FRANCAISE (1931), pp. 125–39.

Vernère, Jean F. CAHIERS D'UN VOLONTAIRE DE '91. Paris: Fayard, 1910.

Victor, Claude-Victor Perrin. MEMOIRES. Paris: J. Dumaine, 1846.

About the Author

Professor Steven Ross holds a Ph.D. from Princeton. He has taught at the Naval War College since 1973, and has served as a political-military analyst for the Defense Intelligence Agency and the Central Intelligence Agency. He has published many books, including *European Diplomatic History 1789–1815; Quest for Victory; French Military Strategy 1779–1799; From Flintlock to Rifle: Infantry Tactics, 1740–1866; American War Plans 1919–1941;* and *American War Plans, 1945–1950.* He has just completed a study of U.S. war plans during World War II, entitled *American War Plans 1941–1945.* Currently, he is writing a history of the wars of the First French Republic. Among his scholarly presentations have been the Harmon Memorial Lecture at the Air Force Academy and the Biggs Lecture at Virginia Military Institute.